W9-AYE-113

MY SiDEWALKS ON
SCOTT FORESMAN
READING STREET
Teacher's Guide

**Level B
Volume 1**

PEARSON
Scott Foresman

Editorial Offices: Glenview, Illinois • Parsippany, New Jersey • New York, New York
Sales Offices: Boston, Massachusetts • Duluth, Georgia • Glenview, Illinois
Coppell, Texas • Sacramento, California • Mesa, Arizona

ISBN: 0-328-21388-8

4 5 6 7 8 9 10 V064 15 14 13 12 11 10 09 08 07
CC1

MY SIDEWALKS ON
SCOTT FORESMAN
READING STREET
Intensive Reading Intervention

A Safe Place to Learn

MY SIDEWALKS ON
SCOTT FORESMAN
READING STREET
Intensive Reading Intervention

What can you do when a core reading program with small group instruction isn't enough for your struggling students? You can give them someplace safe where they can learn. Someplace where you can focus your instruction on their specific needs. Someplace where your students feel comfortable and confident as they accelerate and progress to on-level reading. Someplace like *My Sidewalks*.

My Sidewalks is a research-based, intensive reading intervention program that follows the Response to Intervention model. It works side-by-side with *Scott Foresman Reading Street* or any core reading program. It is designed to provide the most effective intervention for students who are struggling to read, with special consideration for English Language Learners. With daily instruction written specifically for Tier III students, you can help struggling readers steadily take steps to become proficient and confident readers.

3-TIER MODEL

TIER I
Core Program

TIER II
Core Plus
Strategic Intervention

TIER III
Intensive
Intervention ←— *My Sidewalks*

Three Steps Toward Creating a Safe Place to Learn

1 SUSTAINED INSTRUCTION

My Sidewalks contains lesson plans for 30 full weeks. Every day, for 30–45 minutes, you can put your struggling readers—monolingual and English Language Learners— on solid footing. With instruction that is systematic and explicit, *My Sidewalks* helps you create a learning environment that is both consistent and predictable so your students can sustain progress every day. Your students will make strides with:

• Increased time on task
• Explicit teacher modeling
• Multiple response opportunities
• Tasks broken down into smaller steps

2 INTENSIVE LANGUAGE AND CONCEPT DEVELOPMENT

Research shows that a child's vocabulary entering first grade is a strong predictor of comprehension at eleventh grade. This is a critical area where Tier III students are deficient. *My Sidewalks* helps build a foundation for future comprehension success with daily, intensive language and concept development:

• Unit themes organized around science and social studies concepts
• Five to seven new vocabulary words tied directly to the week's theme
• Four weekly selections that build on the unit concept
• Concepts that connect from week to week

3 CRITICAL COMPREHENSION SKILLS

Along with daily vocabulary instruction, *My Sidewalks* provides explicit and systematic instruction on the comprehension skills and strategies researchers have identified as being the most critical for developing reading success:

• Drawing Conclusions
• Compare/Contrast
• Sequence
• Main Idea and Supporting Details

Components

Student Readers

My Sidewalks takes high-interest reading selections and puts them in an engaging magazine format. Every week, your Tier III students read four different selections that work together to develop a science or social studies concept. Week in and week out, these fiction and nonfiction selections help your students get a better understanding of the overall unit theme (the same themes and concepts found in *Scott Foresman Reading Street!*). *30 lessons, organized into 6 units. (5 units at Level A)*

Teacher's Guides

My Sidewalks keeps your intervention instruction running smoothly. The Teacher's Guides contain everything you need for Tier III instruction. Complete lesson plans focus on high priority skills and provide daily routines with suggested time frames to help you keep your instruction focused and on time.
2 Volumes per level

Practice Books

Finally, a practice book written specifically for Tier III students. These consumable workbooks/ blackline masters give your students additional practice in phonics, comprehension, vocabulary, and writing. Books are available for each level and have multiple practice selections for every lesson. Plus, each page contains a Home Activity to strengthen the school-home connection. *A Teacher's Manual with answer key is also available.*

Benchmark Readers

What's working for your students? Which students need more targeted instruction? Accurately assess your Tier III students' progress with these unit readers. Each 8-page book contains examples of all the skills targeted in the unit so you can find out instantly whether a student is ready to transition out of *My Sidewalks* or still needs additional intervention.

Alphabet Cards

Help your Tier III students practice letter names and sounds with these colorful cards. *(Level A)*

Assessment Book

All your assessment needs, all in one book. Along with assessment instruction, you'll find progress-monitoring forms, placement tests, unit assessments in individual and group formats, and guidelines for students to exit *My Sidewalks*.

Finger Tracing Cards

Hands-on Tracing Cards allow students to connect sounds to letters while they learn their letter shapes. *(Level A)*

Manipulative Letter Tiles

Sturdy, plastic, manipulative tiles are easy for little fingers to practice word building. *(Levels A–B)*

AudioText CD

Recordings of the Student Readers read at a fluent pace give Tier III students complete access to every selection.

Sing with Me Big Book

Large, illustrated Big Books develop oral vocabulary and build background. Pages inspire small-group discussions using vocabulary words and include songs that demonstrate the words in context. *(Levels A–B)*

Sing with Me Audio CD

Song recordings accompany each Sing with Me Big Book. *(Levels A–B)*

Sound-Spelling Cards

Colorful cards with instructional routines introduce each sound-spelling in the intervention lesson. *(Levels A–C)*

Sound-Spelling Wall Charts

Large-size formats of the Sound-Spelling Cards are ideal for use in small-group instruction. *(Levels A–C)*

Tested Vocabulary Cards

Flash cards build important vocabulary knowledge and provide additional practice.

Welcome to *My Sidewalks*

This handy guide shows you how to provide effective instruction, manage your time, and help students catch up.

Write-On/Wipe-Off Cards

These cards have a write-on/wipe-off surface and writing lines for practicing letter forms, letter-sounds, spelling, and writing.

Level	Grade
A	1
B	2
C	3
D	4
E	5

MY SIDEWALKS ON
SCOTT FORESMAN
READING STREET
Intensive Reading Intervention

Authors

My Sidewalks was created by the leading researchers in the area of reading intervention instruction. Their work has helped struggling readers and is the basis for the 3-Tier model of instruction.

"Research shows that for students to make significant progress, they need systematic and intensive instruction that is tailored to their current instructional level."

Sharon Vaughn

Connie Juel, Ph.D.
Professor of Education
School of Education
Stanford University

Jeanne R. Paratore, Ed.D.
Associate Professor of Education
Department of Literacy and
Language Development
Boston University

Deborah Simmons, Ph.D.
Professor
College of Education and
Human Development
Texas A&M University

Sharon Vaughn, Ph.D.
H.E. Hartfelder/Southland
Corporation Regents
Professor
University of Texas

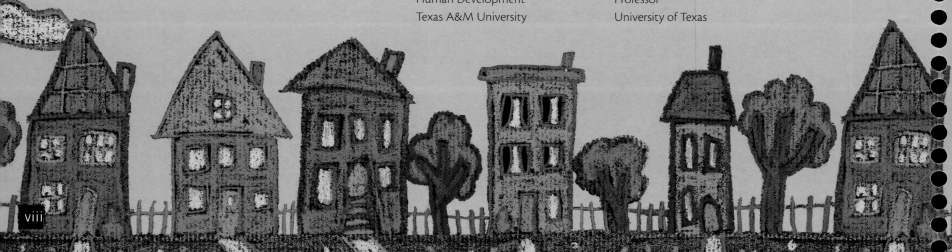

Contents

Unit 1   Exploration

Unit 2 Working Together

Unit 3   Creative Ideas

Resources

Distinctions Between Levels

Understanding the Levels of *My Sidewalks*

The goal of the *My Sidewalks* program is to enable struggling readers to succeed with the reading material used in their regular classrooms. To achieve this, *My Sidewalks* focuses on accelerating students' acquisition of priority skills. Each level of *My Sidewalks* is designed to provide a year and a half of reading growth. Consequently there is an overlap of skills between one *My Sidewalks* level and the next.

These pages describe the skills students should have to successfully begin each level of *My Sidewalks* and what they will learn in that level. Use the Placement Tests to help you determine the correct level at which to enter each student.

To begin this level a child should know:	**In this level**, the instructional focus is on:
Early Reading Intervention (Grade K)	
	• Phonological and phonemic awareness • Letter names and sounds • Blending regular short-vowel words • Sentence reading
Level A (Grade 1)	
• Some phonological awareness	• Phonemic awareness • Letter names • Consonants: Individual letter-sounds, blends, and digraphs • Vowels: Short, long (CVCe), and *r*-controlled • Blending words and fluent word reading • High-frequency words • Oral vocabulary and concept development • Building fluency (40–60 WCPM) • Passage reading and retelling

To begin this level a student should know:	**In this level**, the instructional focus is on:
• Letter names • Individual consonant letter-sounds • Some basic high-frequency words • And be able to read Benchmark Reader A2 with accuracy and comprehension	• Phonemic awareness • Letter names and sounds • Blending words and fluent word reading • High-frequency words • Oral vocabulary and concept development • Building fluency (70–90 WCPM) • Passage reading and retelling
• Consonants: Individual letter-sounds, blends, and digraphs • Vowels: Short and long (CVCe) and be able to distinguish between them • A wider range of high-frequency words • And be able to read Benchmark Reader B2 with accuracy and comprehension	• Blending words and fluent word reading • Decoding multisyllabic words, including words with one or more affixes • Phonics: Vowels • Concept vocabulary • Building fluency (100–120 WCPM) • Passage reading and summarizing
Level D (Grade 4)	
• Consonants: Individual letter-sounds, blends, and digraphs • Vowels: Short and long (CVCe) and be able to distinguish between them • How to decode regular VC/CV words with short and long (CVCe) vowels • Many high-frequency words • And be able to read Benchmark Reader C1 with accuracy and comprehension	• Decoding multisyllabic words, including words with one or more affixes • Phonics: Less frequent vowel patterns, such as vowel diphthongs • Concept vocabulary • Building fluency (110–130 WCPM) • Passage reading and summarizing
Level E (Grade 5)	
• Consonants: Individual letter-sounds, blends, and digraphs • Vowels: Short and long (CVCe) and be able to distinguish between them • How to decode regular VC/CV words with short and long (CVCe) vowels • Many high-frequency words • And be able to read Benchmark Reader D1 with accuracy and comprehension	• Decoding multisyllabic words, including words with one or more affixes • Phonics: Less frequent vowel patterns, such as vowel diphthongs • Concept vocabulary • Building fluency (120–140 WCPM) • Passage reading and summarizing

Differentiating Instruction

The charts on these pages show instruction during a week in *My Sidewalks*. The charts can also be used as guides for **reteaching** or **accelerating** through parts of the lessons. In addition, the ***If... then...*** directions will help you identify how to customize instruction for your students.

Reteaching To meet the needs of the lowest performing readers, it may be necessary to modify the pacing and intensity of instruction. Activities shown in gray boxes on the charts may be repeated for these students.

Accelerating A child who shows mastery of skills following initial instruction may be ready for instruction at a faster pace with fewer repetitions. Activities shown in green boxes might be omitted for these students.

Levels A–B

	PHONEMIC AWARENESS	PHONICS	HIGH-FREQUENCY WORDS	CONCEPTS/ ORAL VOCABULARY	PASSAGE READING	FLUENCY	WRITING
Day 1	Phonemic Awareness	Blending Strategy	High-Frequency Words	Concepts/ Oral Vocabulary	Read a Passage	Reread for Fluency	
Day 2	Phonemic Awareness	Blending Strategy	High-Frequency Words		Read a Passage	Reread for Fluency	Write
Day 3	Phonemic Awareness	Blending Strategy	High-Frequency Words	Concepts/ Oral Vocabulary	Read a Passage	Reread for Fluency	
Day 4		Fluent Word Reading		Concepts/ Oral Vocabulary	Read Together	Reread for Fluency	Write
Day 5		Assess Word Reading	Assess Word/ Sentence Reading	Check Oral Vocabulary	Assess Passage Reading/ Reread		Write

■ **Reteach**   ■ **Omit for acceleration**

If... a child is struggling with word reading,
then... reteach Word Work activities and include More Practice extensions.

If... a child lacks oral language,
then... elicit extended language from the child, provide ample opportunities for the child to respond when building concepts, and expand the structured picture walks before reading each selection.

If... a child's reading is so slow that it hinders comprehension,
then... provide additional models of fluent reading, give more corrective feedback during fluency practice, and include More Practice extensions when rereading for fluency.

If... an English learner struggles with sounds,
then... repeat appropriate practice activities.

Levels C–E

	VOCABULARY	COMPREHENSION	PASSAGE READING	PHONICS	FLUENCY	WRITING
Day 1	Vocabulary		Read a Passage	Blending Strategy (Level C)	Reread for Fluency	Write (Levels D–E)
Day 2	Vocabulary	Comprehension Skill	Read a Passage	Phonics	Reread for Fluency	Write (Levels D–E)
Day 3	Vocabulary	Comprehension Skill Assess (Levels D–E)	Read a Passage	Phonics	Reread for Fluency	Write
Day 4	Vocabulary	Comprehension Skill/Strategy Assess (Levels D–E)	Read Together (Level C) Read a Passage (Levels D–E)	Phonics Review (Level C)	Reread for Fluency	Write
Day 5	Vocabulary	Assess Comprehension	Read Together (Levels D–E) Reread (Level C)	Assess Sentence Reading (Level C)	Assess Fluency	Write

If... a student is struggling with word reading, **then...** reteach Vocabulary and Phonics activities and include More Practice extensions.

If... a student lacks oral language, **then...** elicit extended language from the student, provide ample opportunities for the student to respond when building concepts, and expand the After Reading discussion for each selection.

If... a student's reading is so disfluent that it hinders comprehension, **then...** provide additional models of fluent reading, give more corrective feedback during fluency practice, and include More Practice extensions for fluency.

If... a student lacks comprehension and is unable to retell or summarize, **then...** reteach comprehension skills and strategies, provide additional modeling of retelling and summarizing, and give more corrective feedback during practice.

If... an English learner lacks English vocabulary for known concepts, **then...** say the unknown English word, have the student repeat it, and ask questions that will allow the student to use the word in a meaningful context.

Meeting ELL Needs

My Sidewalks was developed to provide intensive reading intervention for Tier III students struggling to read and write. The program has been designed to reflect current research on literacy instruction for English language learners (ELLs)—not as additional notes, but integral to all elements of instruction. From its original conception, instruction to meet the needs of both native English speakers and English learners (who have some basic English conversational skills) has been integrated into the curriculum, teaching practices, and learning activities. Since English language learners acquire literacy skills in much the same way as their English-speaking peers, both will benefit from the same good instructional practices.

Research Says "**ELLs at risk for reading problems profit considerably in their literacy skills from systematic and explicit interventions that address the core reading skills of beginning reading: phonemic awareness, phonics, fluency, vocabulary, and comprehension. . . . Our work with ELLs suggests that postponing interventions to wait for language to become more proficient is not necessary, and supporting literacy acquisition in the language of instruction provided by the school for students at risk is beneficial.**" Vaughn, S., Linan-Thompson, S., *et al.* 2005. "Interventions for 1st Grade English Language Learners with Reading Difficulties." *Perspectives,* 31 (2), p. 31–35.

English language learners need. . .	*My Sidewalks* provides. . .
Phonemic Awareness	
• to develop familiarity with the sounds of English • to practice identifying, segmenting, and blending sounds in English words • to learn the sounds of English within words, in isolation and in meaningful contexts	• explicit and systematic modeling of sounds in words • scaffolded instruction that evokes active responses by children • ample practice identifying, counting, segmenting, blending, adding, and deleting sounds in words • clear lessons that tie phonemic awareness to phonics
Phonics	
• to learn the letters and letter-sound correspondences of English • to master identifying, segmenting, and blending the variety of sounds that letters represent in English words • to understand how to complete phonics activities • to use the phonics they learn—seeing, saying, reading, and writing words—with growing proficiency • to learn the sounds and spellings of written English words in meaningful contexts	• explicit phonics instruction with regular practice • routines for practicing the core English phonics elements • clear, step-by-step blending strategies understandable to students learning English as they learn to read • active learning—hearing, speaking, reading, and writing—that ties phonics to decodable text (Levels A–C) and to decoding of multisyllabic words in text (Levels D–E) • practice decoding and reading words related to concepts explored in oral language and texts

English language learners need. . .	My Sidewalks provides. . .

Vocabulary

<ul><li>to develop oral vocabulary in English, including words already familiar to English-speaking children</li><li>to learn functional English vocabulary, including high-frequency words</li><li>to encounter new words in meaningful oral and written contexts</li><li>to hear, see, and use new words repeatedly</li><li>to learn academic English vocabulary</li></ul>	<ul><li>multiple exposures to each vocabulary word</li><li>a routine for learning high-frequency words (at Levels A and B)</li><li>a routine for learning oral vocabulary (at Levels A and B)</li><li>a focus on words related to science and social studies concepts</li><li>multiple opportunities to practice using and producing oral and written vocabulary, including academic English</li><li>development of deep meaning for key concepts and words</li></ul>

Comprehension

<ul><li>to continually improve their comprehension of oral English</li><li>to read comprehensible texts and develop abilities to interpret more complex written language</li><li>to use their prior knowledge in order to comprehend texts</li><li>to acquire understanding of sentence structures and text organizations of academic English</li><li>to learn about cultural concepts embodied in the readings</li></ul>	<ul><li>an emphasis on oral language and concept development, to improve students' English proficiency and comprehension</li><li>an abundance of comprehensible reading materials focused on science and social studies concepts</li><li>modeling, instruction, and practice of priority comprehension skills and reading strategies, including prereading routines</li><li>explicit instructional routines that model new skills, build on students' prior knowledge, use visual elements to clarify ideas, and incorporate ample practice and review</li><li>exposure to the structures of English, text organization, and cultural concepts of the readings and lessons</li></ul>

Fluency

<ul><li>to hear models of fluent reading of instructional-level texts</li><li>corrective feedback on their reading</li><li>to practice and improve their fluent reading</li></ul>	<ul><li>teacher modeling to familiarize students with expressive, meaningful reading of instructional-level academic texts</li><li>engaging practice opportunities that include choral reading, paired reading, and reading with AudioText, which provide many models for building fluency</li><li>instruction in reading rate, accuracy, expression, and intonation</li><li>repeated readings and corrective feedback, to help students see words in context and pronounce them</li><li>progress monitoring and assessments to aid in fluency growth</li></ul>

Writing

<ul><li>to develop their English proficiency by writing as well as reading</li><li>to write about ideas related to reading topics</li><li>to practice communicating their ideas in English through manageable, interesting writing activities</li></ul>	<ul><li>opportunities to respond to literature about themes</li><li>scaffolded writing instruction including sentence frames for young children, manageable writing prompts for all students, and self-checking activities</li><li>feedback for writers from teacher and fellow students</li></ul>

Unit 1
Skills Overview

Why These Skills? *My Sidewalks* focuses on the priority skills children need in order to succeed at learning to read. **Priority skills** are the critical elements of early reading—phonemic awareness, phonics, fluency, vocabulary, and text comprehension. Scientifically based research has shown that these skills are the foundations of early reading and must be taught in a systematic sequence.

		WEEK 1 4–25 **Neighborhoods**	**WEEK 2** 26–51 **Outer Space**
Phonemic Awareness		Blend Sounds	Blend Sounds
Phonics	Blending Strategy	Short *a*; Final *ck* REVIEW Consonants	Short *i*; Final *ng*, *nk* REVIEW Double Consonants; Consonant Letter Sounds *ck*, *ng*, *nk*
	Spelling	Words with Short *a*	Words with Short *i*
	High-Frequency Words	*always, laugh, only, told*	*afraid, so, surprise, worry*
Vocabulary	Concept	What might we discover in a new neighborhood?	Why would anyone want to explore space?
	Oral Vocabulary	*avenue, investigate, rural, suburb, urban*	*ascend, descend, journey, orbit, universe*
Comprehension	Skill	Sequence	Main Idea
	Strategies	Preview, Ask Questions, Use Story Structure, Summarize	Preview, Ask Questions, Use Story Structure, Summarize
	Writing	Response to Literature	Response to Literature
Fluency		Reread for Fluency Practice	Reread for Fluency Practice

WEEK 3	WEEK 4	WEEK 5
52–71	72–95	96–127
Out in the Woods	**Sand All Around**	**Who Can We Ask?**
Blend Sounds Add Initial or Final Sounds	Segment Words into Sounds Add Ending Sounds	Segment and Count Sounds
Short *o*; Consonant Blends REVIEW Short *a, i, o*	Short *e*; Ending *-s* REVIEW Consonant Blends	Short *u*; Digraphs *sh, th* REVIEW Short *a, e, i, o, u*
Words with Short *o*	Words with Short *e*	Words with Short *u*
answer, different, ever, learn	*draw, eye, picture, read* /red/	*also, among, early, today*
What can we discover by exploring nature?	**What can we learn by exploring the desert?**	**When we are searching for answers, who can we ask?**
camouflage, galaxy, mammal, tranquil, wildlife	*arid, cactus, dune, landform, precipitation*	*curious, delicate, information, inquire, sturdy*
Main Idea	Main Idea	Draw Conclusions
Preview, Ask Questions, Use Story Structure, Summarize	Preview, Ask Questions, Use Story Structure, Summarize	Preview, Ask Questions, Use Story Structure, Summarize
Response to Literature	Response to Literature	Response to Literature
Reread for Fluency Practice	Reread for Fluency Practice	Reread for Fluency Practice

Unit 2
Skills Overview

Why These Skills? *My Sidewalks* focuses on the priority skills children need in order to succeed at learning to read. **Priority skills** are the critical elements of early reading—phonemic awareness, phonics, fluency, vocabulary, and text comprehension. Scientifically based research has shown that these skills are the foundations of early reading and must be taught in a systematic sequence.

	WEEK 1 4–25 **Danger!**	**WEEK 2** 26–47 **Team Spirit**
Phonemic Awareness	Segment and Count Sounds Delete Ending Sounds	Add Ending Sounds
Phonics — Blending Strategy	Consonant Digraphs *ch, tch, wh*; Ending *-ing* **REVIEW** Consonant Digraphs *ch, sh, th, wh, tch*	Ending *-ed*; Inflected Endings **REVIEW** Endings *-s, -ed, -ing*
Spelling	Words with *ch, tch, wh*	Words with *-ed*
High-Frequency Words	*around, eight, enough, nothing*	*build, carry, heavy, water*
Vocabulary — Concept	What can we do in a dangerous situation?	What makes a team?
Oral Vocabulary	*courageous, hazard, prevent, rescue, wildfire*	*ability, compete, contribute, recreation, victory*
Comprehension — Skill	Sequence	Sequence
Strategies	Preview, Ask Questions, Use Story Structure, Summarize	Preview, Ask Questions, Use Story Structure, Summarize
Writing	Response to Literature	Response to Literature
Fluency	Reread for Fluency Practice	Reread for Fluency Practice

WEEK 3	WEEK 4	WEEK 5	
48–71 **Sharing**	72–99 **Side by Side**	100–127 **Let's Celebrate**	
Segment and Count Sounds Segment and Blend Sounds	Segment and Count Sounds Add Final Sounds	Segment and Count Sounds Add Phonemes	
Long *a* (CVC*e*); *c*/s/, *g*/j/ **REVIEW** Short and Long *a*	Long *i* (CVC*e*); Inflected Endings **REVIEW** Short and Long *i*	Long *o*: (CVC*e*); Possessives **REVIEW** Short and Long *o*	
Words with Long *a:* CVC*e*	Words with Long *i:* CVC*e*	Words with Long *o:* CVC*e*	
another, enjoy, few, toward	*across, instead, moon, through*	*father, mother, remember, touch*	
When does sharing make sense?	When should we work together? When should we work alone?	How can we contribute to a celebration?	
conflict, greedy, inhabit, portion, resolve	*companion, independent, partnership, solution, survival*	*decorate, dine, float* (n.), *holiday, participate*	
Sequence	Main Idea	Draw Conclusions	
Preview, Ask Questions, Use Story Structure, Summarize	Preview, Ask Questions, Use Story Structure, Summarize	Preview, Ask Questions, Use Story Structure, Summarize	
Response to Literature	Response to Literature	Response to Literature	
Reread for Fluency Practice	Reread for Fluency Practice	Reread for Fluency Practice	

Unit 3
Skills Overview

Why These Skills? *My Sidewalks* focuses on the priority skills children need in order to succeed at learning to read. **Priority skills** are the critical elements of early reading—phonemic awareness, phonics, fluency, vocabulary, and text comprehension. Scientifically based research has shown that these skills are the foundations of early reading and must be taught in a systematic sequence.

	WEEK 1 4–27 **Ideas Become Inventions**	**WEEK 2** 28–53 **Ways to Communicate**
Phonemic Awareness	Segment and Count Sounds Blend Sounds	Segment and Blend Sounds Add Phonemes
Phonics — Blending Strategy	Long *u* and Long *e* (CVC*e*); Contractions *'s, n't* **REVIEW** Short and Long *u, e*	Vowel Sounds of *y*; Ending *-es* **REVIEW** Base Words and Endings
Spelling	Words with Long *u* and Long *e*	Words with Vowel Sounds of *y*
High-Frequency Words	*house, idea, machine, sign*	*against, found, stood, wild*
Vocabulary — Concept	How do inventors turn ideas into inventions?	How many ways can we communicate?
Oral Vocabulary	*construct, contraption, project, sidekick, unique*	*conversation, correspond, postage, reply, transport*
Comprehension — Skill	Draw Conclusions	Draw Conclusions
Strategies	Preview, Ask Questions, Use Story Structure, Summarize	Preview, Ask Questions, Use Story Structure, Summarize
Writing	Response to Literature	Response to Literature
Fluency	Reread for Fluency Practice	Reread for Fluency Practice

WEEK 3	WEEK 4	WEEK 5
54–83	84–113	114–143
What a Smart Idea!	**Figure It Out**	**Where Ideas Come From**
Add Initial Phonemes	Segment Words into Syllables, Syllables into Sounds	Blend Sounds Add Initial Phonemes
r-Controlled *ar*; *r*-Controlled *or, ore* REVIEW Long Vowels (CVC*e*)	Syllables VC/CV REVIEW Possessives	Contractions *'ll, 'm*; *r*-Controlled *er, ir, ur*; Syllable *er* REVIEW *r*-Controlled Vowels
Words with *r*-controlled *ar*	Words with Syllables VC/CV	Words with Contractions *'ll, 'm*
become, even, front, thought	*easy, follow, knew, usual*	*along, both, color, guess*
When are creative ideas good? When are they bad?	When can creative ideas solve problems?	Where do creative ideas come from?
brainstorm, brilliant, consume, prey, shrewd	*abundant, assist, baffle, generous, struggle*	*accomplish, excel, inspiration, process, research*
Main Idea	Sequence	Sequence
Preview, Ask Questions, Use Story Structure, Summarize	Preview, Ask Questions, Use Story Structure, Summarize	Preview, Ask Questions, Use Story Structure, Summarize
Response to Literature	Response to Literature	Response to Literature
Reread for Fluency Practice	Reread for Fluency Practice	Reread for Fluency Practice

Concept Development
to Foster Reading Comprehension

Theme Question: What can we learn from exploring new places and things?

Concept: Exploration

EXPAND THE CONCEPT

Week 1	Week 2	Week 3	Week 4	Week 5
Lesson Focus What might we discover in a new neighborhood?	**Lesson Focus** Why would anyone want to explore space?	**Lesson Focus** What can we discover by exploring nature?	**Lesson Focus** What can we learn by exploring the desert?	**Lesson Focus** When we are searching for answers, who can we ask?

DEVELOP LANGUAGE

Oral Vocabulary avenue investigate rural suburb urban	**Oral Vocabulary** ascend descend journey orbit universe	**Oral Vocabulary** camouflage galaxy mammal tranquil wildlife	**Oral Vocabulary** arid cactus dune landform precipitation	**Oral Vocabulary** curious delicate information inquire sturdy
Background Reading "Let's Find Out: Neighborhoods"	**Background Reading** "Let's Find Out: Outer Space"	**Background Reading** "Let's Find Out: Out in the Woods"	**Background Reading** "Let's Find Out: Sand All Around"	**Background Reading** "Let's Find Out: Who Can We Ask?"

READ THE LITERATURE

Narrative Nonfiction "A Pack of Colors"	**Biography** "Franklin Chang-Diaz, Astronaut"	**Expository Nonfiction** "Can You See Them?"	**Narrative Nonfiction** "A Report About the Desert"	**Narrative Nonfiction** "A Bird Trick"
Animal Fantasy "Blue Jack"	**Realistic Fiction** "It Fell from Space"	**Animal Fantasy** "Lost in the Woods"	**Realistic Fiction** "Sand Blast!"	**Realistic Fiction** "The Just Facts Club"
Poetry "City Song" and "Hayloft"	**Diagram** "What Would You Wear in Outer Space?"	**Recipe** "Let's Make Trail Mix"	**Expository Article** "Did You Know?"	**Diagram** "A Visit to the Library"

TEACH CONTENT

Time for SOCIAL STUDIES	TIME FOR Science	TIME FOR Science	TIME FOR Science	Time for SOCIAL STUDIES
• Geography: Urban, Suburban, Rural • Exploration	• Space Exploration • Careers in Science • Solar System	• Living/Nonliving • Habitats • Day/Night Sky	• The Desert • Geography • Climate	• Locating Information • Libraries

 Unit 1 develops the same concepts, vocabulary, and content-area knowledge as in Scott Foresman's *Reading Street*, Grade 2, Unit 1.

Concept Development
to Foster Reading Comprehension

Theme Question: How can we work together?

Concept: Working Together

EXPAND THE CONCEPT

Week 1	Week 2	Week 3	Week 4	Week 5
Lesson Focus What can we do in a dangerous situation?	**Lesson Focus** What makes a team?	**Lesson Focus** When does sharing make sense?	**Lesson Focus** When should we work together? When should we work alone?	**Lesson Focus** How can we contribute to a celebration?

DEVELOP LANGUAGE

Oral Vocabulary courageous hazard prevent rescue wildfire	**Oral Vocabulary** ability compete contribute recreation victory	**Oral Vocabulary** conflict greedy inhabit portion resolve	**Oral Vocabulary** companion independent partnership solution survival	**Oral Vocabulary** decorate dine float (n.) holiday participate
Background Reading "Let's Find Out: Danger!"	**Background Reading** "Let's Find Out: Team Spirit"	**Background Reading** "Let's Find Out: Sharing"	**Background Reading** "Let's Find Out: Side by Side"	**Background Reading** "Let's Find Out: Let's Celebrate"

READ THE LITERATURE

Narrative Nonfiction "Danger on the Job"	**Narrative Nonfiction** "The Red Fins"	**Expository Nonfiction** "Who Can Share a Tree?"	**Expository Nonfiction** "Animals Together, Animals Alone"	**Narrative Nonfiction** "Big, Big Balloon"
Realistic Fiction "Fire on the Hill"	**Realistic Fiction** "Jon and Jen"	**Realistic Fiction** "A Snack for Grace"	**Realistic Fiction** "Sliding Boxes"	**Fantasy** "The Balloon Ride"
Poster "Fire Safety at Home"	**Cartoon** "Be a Good Sport!"	**Cartoon** "Share with a Brother"	**Song** "All Work Together"	**Directions** "Make a Greeting Card"

TEACH CONTENT

Time for SOCIAL STUDIES	*Time for* SOCIAL STUDIES	TIME FOR Science	TIME FOR Science	*Time for* SOCIAL STUDIES
• Heroes • Community Services • Safety	• Cooperation • Self-Direction • Teamwork	• Physical Environment • Habitat • Cooperation	• Interdependence • Survival • Cooperation	• National Celebrations • Patriotism • Traditions

Unit 2 develops the same concepts, vocabulary, and content-area knowledge as in Scott Foresman's *Reading Street*, Grade 2, Unit 2.

Concept Development
to Foster Reading Comprehension

Theme Question: What does it mean to be creative?

Concept: Creative Ideas

EXPAND THE CONCEPT

Week 1	Week 2	Week 3	Week 4	Week 5
Lesson Focus How do inventors turn ideas into inventions?	**Lesson Focus** How many ways can we communicate?	**Lesson Focus** When are creative ideas good? When are they bad?	**Lesson Focus** When can creative ideas solve problems?	**Lesson Focus** Where do creative ideas come from?

DEVELOP LANGUAGE

Oral Vocabulary construct contraption project sidekick unique	**Oral Vocabulary** conversation correspond postage reply transport	**Oral Vocabulary** brainstorm brilliant consume prey shrewd	**Oral Vocabulary** abundant assist baffle generous struggle	**Oral Vocabulary** accomplish excel inspiration process research
Background Reading "Let's Find Out: Ideas Become Inventions"	**Background Reading** "Let's Find Out: Ways to Communicate"	**Background Reading** "Let's Find Out: What a Smart Idea!"	**Background Reading** "Let's Find Out: Figure It Out"	**Background Reading** "Let's Find Out: Where Ideas Come From"

READ THE LITERATURE

Biography "In-Line Skates" **Fantasy** "Zute" **Time Line** "A Time Line of Fun!"	**Biography** "Dots and Dashes" **Realistic Fiction** "Gramps Learns New Things" **Reference Sources** "A to Z in Sign Language"	**Narrative Nonfiction** "A Nutty Story" **Realistic Fiction** "Think Smart!" **Poem** "I Built a Fabulous Machine"	**Biography** "Justin's Bikes for Kids" **Folk Tale** "The Huge Turnip" **Puzzle** "Pet Puzzle"	**Expository Nonfiction** "Beautiful Ideas" **Fantasy** "Yelp! Help!" **Biographical Sketch** "Meet Scott Gustafson"

TEACH CONTENT

TIME FOR Science	Time for SOCIAL STUDIES	TIME FOR Science	Time for SOCIAL STUDIES	TIME FOR Science
• Inventions • Tools and Machines • Experiments	• Communication • Signs and Symbols • Technology	• Nature • Animals • Birds	• Family • Teamwork • Social Responsibility	• Research and Development • Fine Arts

 Unit 3 develops the same concepts, vocabulary, and content-area knowledge as in Scott Foresman's *Reading Street*, Grade 2, Unit 3.

Unit 1 Week 1 *Neighborhoods*

What might we discover in a new neighborhood?

Objectives *This week students will...*

Phonemic Awareness
- blend sounds in words

Phonics
- blend and read words with short *a* and final *ck*
- apply knowledge of letter-sounds to decode unknown words when reading
- recognize high-frequency words *always, laugh, only, told*

Fluency
- practice fluency with oral rereading

Vocabulary
- build concepts and oral vocabulary: *avenue, investigate, rural, suburb, urban*

Text Comprehension
- read connected text
- identify sequence to improve comprehension
- write in response to literature

Word Work *This week's phonics focus is . . .*

Short *a*   Final *ck*

High-Frequency Words *Tested Vocabulary*

The first appearance of each word in the Student Reader is noted below.

always	If you do something **always,** you do it all the time or every time. (p. 8)
laugh	When you **laugh,** you make sounds that show you are happy. (p. 9)
only	He is an **only** child. (p. 6) This is the **only** path to school.
told	If you **told** something, you put it into words or said it. (p. 7)

Amazing Words *Oral Vocabulary*

The week's vocabulary is related to the concept of what we might encounter in a new neighborhood.

avenue	another name for a street
investigate	to try to find out all about something
rural	an area with farms and lots of open spaces
suburb	a town just outside or near a city
urban	a place with many neighborhoods and tall buildings

Student Reader Unit 1 *This week students will read the following selections.*

Daily Lesson Plan

	ACTIVITIES	MATERIALS
Day 1	**Word Work** Phonemic Awareness: Blend Sounds Phonics: Blend Words with Short *a* High-Frequency Words *always, laugh, only, told* **Build Concepts** *investigate, rural, urban* **Read a Passage** "Neighborhoods," pp. 6–9 Comprehension: Use Strategies Reread for Fluency	Student White Boards Sound-Spelling Card 1 Tested Vocabulary Cards *Sing with Me Big Book* and Audio CD Student Reader: Unit 1 Routine Cards 1, 2, 3, 4, 6, 7 AudioText Practice Book, p. 1, Short *a*
Day 2	**Reread for Fluency** **Word Work** Phonemic Awareness: Blend Sounds Phonics: Blend Words with Final *ck* High-Frequency Words *always, laugh, only, told* **Read a Passage** "A Pack of Colors," pp. 10–15 Comprehension: Use Strategies **Write** Response to Literature: Shared Writing	Student Reader: Unit 1 Student White Boards Sound-Spelling Card 6 Tested Vocabulary Cards Routine Cards 1, 2, 3, 4, 6, 7 AudioText Practice Book, p. 2, Final *ck*
Day 3	**Reread for Fluency** **Word Work** Phonemic Awareness: Blend Sounds Phonics: Fluent Word Reading High-Frequency Words *always, laugh, only, told* **Build Concepts** *avenue, suburb* **Read a Passage** "Blue Jack," pp. 16–23 Comprehension: Sequence	Student Reader: Unit 1 Student White Boards Tested Vocabulary Cards Routine Cards 1, 2, 3, 4, 6 AudioText Practice Book, p. 3, Sequence
Day 4	**Reread for Fluency** **Word Work** Phonics: Spiral Review Phonological and Phonemic Awareness Activities, pp. 280–283 **Read Together** "City Song" and "Hayloft," p. 24 Comprehension: Listening **Build Concepts** *avenue, investigate, rural, suburb, urban* **Write** Response to Literature: Interactive Writing	Student Reader: Unit 1 Routine Cards 1, 4 AudioText Letter Tiles *a, c, l, m, n, p, r, t* Practice Book, p. 4, High-Frequency Words
Day 5	**Assessment Options** Fluency, Comprehension Sentence Reading; Passage Reading Phonological and Phonemic Awareness Activities, pp. 280–283 **Use Concepts** *avenue, investigate, rural, suburb, urban* **Read to Connect** "Neighborhoods," pp. 6–9 Comprehension: Sequence **Write** Response to Literature: Independent Writing	Reproducible p. 247 Sentence Reading Chart, p. 252 Student White Boards Fluency Progress Chart, p. 245 Student Reader: Unit 1 Routine Card 5 Practice Book, p. 5, Writing

See pp. xvi–xvii for how *My Sidewalks* integrates instructional practices for ELL.

Phonemic Awareness Blend Sounds

To Do	To Say	*2 minutes*
Scaffold instruction. Distribute white boards. Write *at*.	**Model** Listen as I say these sounds: /aaa/, /t/. Now listen as I say them slowly and then blend them quickly to say the word: /aaa/, /t/, *at*. Repeat. This time have children write the letters *a, t* as you write them. Now you say the sounds slowly as you point to the letters. Then blend them quickly. What is the word? (/a/ /t/, *at*)	
Write *bat.* Lead children in blending sounds.	**Teach and Practice** Say the sounds /b/ /a/ /t/ as you point to the letters. Have children blend the sounds to make a word: *bat.* Continue with these words: an sad bag mad	

Blending Strategy Short *a*

To Do	To Say	*5–10 minutes*
Use the blending routine. Write the letter *a*.	**1 Connect** This is the letter *a*. Is it a vowel or a consonant? (vowel) Now let's look more at the letter *a* and the short *a* vowel sound.	*Routine*
Display Sound-Spelling Card 1.	**2 Use Sound-Spelling Card** This is an astronaut. What sound do you hear at the beginning of *astronaut?* (/a/) Say it with me: /a/. The letter *a* at the beginning of *astronaut* stands for the short *a* sound.	
	3 Listen and Write Write the letter *a* for /a/. As you write, say the sound to yourself: /a/. Now say the sound aloud.	
Scaffold instruction. Write *man.*	**4 Model** The letter *a* stands for /a/. This is how I blend this word: /m/ /a/ /n/, *man.* Now you try: /m/ /a/ /n/, *man.* When *a* is the only vowel at the beginning or in the middle of a word, it usually stands for its short sound, /a/. $$\underset{\longrightarrow}{m} \ \underset{\longrightarrow}{a} \ \underset{\longrightarrow}{n}$$	
CORRECTIVE FEEDBACK Write each practice word. Monitor student practice.	**5 Group Practice** Let's try the same thing with these words. Give feedback, using the *if . . . then* statements on Routine Card 1.* an hat van* nap has jazz*	
	6 Individual Practice Write the words; have each child blend two of them. as pan cab* bad rat pass	
Check understanding of practice words.	*Children need to make sense of words that they segment and blend. If needed, help children with meanings. A *van* is a covered truck used for carrying people or things. (Point to the van in the picture on p. 6.) *Jazz* is a kind of music with a strong beat. A *cab* is a car with a driver who you pay to take you somewhere. (Point to the cab on p. 6.)	
MORE PRACTICE Model spelling short *a* words.	**Spell and Write** What sounds do you hear in *man?* (/m/ /a/ /n/) What is the letter for /m/? Let's all write *m.* What is the letter for /a/? Write *a.* What is the letter for /n/? Write *n.* Continue practice as time allows. Have children confirm their spelling by comparing it to what you've written. tan jam fat wag ran cap	

* Routine Cards are located in the back of this book.

High-Frequency Words *always, laugh, only, told*

To Do	To Say	

3 minutes

Teach high-frequency words.

Display *always.*

1 Say, Spell, Write Use the Tested Vocabulary Cards. Display *always.* Here are some words that we won't sound out. We'll spell them. This word is *always: a, l, w, a, y, s* (point to each letter), *always.* What is this word? What are the letters in the word? Now you write *always.*

Point to the *l* and *w* in *always.*

2 Identify Letter-Sounds Let's look at the sounds in *always* that you do know. What is this letter? What is the sound for this letter? (/l/) Continue with *w* (/w/).

3 Demonstrate Meaning Tell me a sentence using *always.* Model a sentence if children need help.

Display *laugh, only,* and *told.*

Repeat the Routine with *laugh, only,* and *told.* Children can identify these letter-sounds: *laugh* (/l/), *only* (/n/, /l/), *told* (/t/, /l/, /d/). Have children write the words in their word banks. Add the words to the Word Wall.

ACTIVITY **2** Build Concepts

Oral Vocabulary *investigate, rural, urban*

To Do	To Say

5–10 minutes

Introduce oral vocabulary.

Scaffold instruction.

Display p. 1 of *Sing with Me Big Book.* Play audio CD.

This week you will learn about neighborhoods. Listen for the Amazing Words *investigate, rural,* and *urban* as I sing this song. Play or sing the song. Then have children sing it with you.

Follow the Routine to teach *investigate, rural,* and *urban.*

1 Introduce, Demonstrate, and Apply

investigate The song is called "Let's Go Investigate!" When you *investigate* something, you try to find out all about it. Have children say the word. You could *investigate* a new neighborhood by walking through it and looking carefully at the people, places, and things you find there. What is the first place you would *investigate* in a new neighborhood?

rural The first part of the song describes a *rural* place. The country is a *rural* place. Have children say the word. A *rural* place has farms and lots of open spaces. What other kinds of things would you find in a *rural* area?

urban The second verse of the song describes an *urban* place. The city is an *urban* place. Have children say the word. An *urban* place has many neighborhoods to walk through and lots of tall buildings. What other kinds of things would you find in an *urban* area?

Display the words on the Amazing Words board.

2 Display the Words Have children say each word as they look at it. You can find sounds you know in big words. Read *rur/al* as you run your hand under the syllables. What consonant letter and sound is at the beginning and in the middle of *rural*? (/r/) For *investigate* and *urban*, children can identify these letter-sounds: *investigate* (/v/, /g/), *urban* (/b/).

Monitor understanding.

3 Use the Words Ask children to use each word in a sentence. Model a sentence if children need help.

MORE PRACTICE

Use oral vocabulary to discuss the song. What places in the song could you *investigate*? Which place does the song say is peaceful, an *urban* place or a *rural* place? Which place is noisy?

Read a Passage

Build Background "Neighborhoods," pp. 6–9

	To Do	To Say	
			10 minutes

Develop language and concepts.

See Routine Card 7. Read aloud pp. 1–5 of the student book.

Preview the Book Read aloud the title on p. 1. The selections in this book are about exploring different places. Use p. 2 to preview the weeks in this unit and pp. 4–5 to preview the selections in this week. Ask children what they think each selection will be about.

Scaffold instruction.

See Routine Card 6. Display pp. 6–9.

Ask questions and elaborate on answers to develop language.

Key concepts: *jams, chat, city, urban, farm, barn, shed, country, rural*

Before Reading Read the title aloud. Do a structured picture walk with children.

pp. 6–7 What do you see in the street? (cars) Point to and name the van, cab, and bus. Who is running fast? (kids) What are some of the other people doing? (playing music, shopping, talking, skateboarding, and so on) Point to the band. The band jams, or plays music. Other people chat, or talk in a friendly way, with each other. Is this neighborhood in the city or in the country? (the city) The city is an urban place with many cars and people.

pp. 8–9 What animals do you see? (pigs, chickens, cats, fish) Point to each kind of animal. Where do these animals live? (on a farm) What buildings do you see? (a barn and a shed) Farm animals live in a barn. People store things in a shed. What are the people in the pictures doing? (playing baseball, fixing a shed) Is this neighborhood in the city or in the country? (the country) The country is a rural place with farms and open spaces. Let's read to find out more about the city and the country.

Guide comprehension.

Read pp. 6–9.

Model strategic reading. Use Routine Card 2.

During Reading Ask children to read along with you. As we read, ask yourself: What did I learn about each neighborhood? What is this mainly about? Read pp. 6–9 aloud with the group. Stop on each page to model asking questions. For example, for p. 8: After I read, I ask myself: What did I learn about this neighborhood? The author talks about the animals and plants in the country. I learned that plants, fish, pigs, cats, and hens live in neighborhoods with lots of land.

Monitor independent reading.

Use Routine Card 3.

Reread Have children read the selection aloud together without you. Then have them read it on their own in a whisper. Listen in on each child. Monitor reading, using Routine Card 3.

Summarize.

Use oral vocabulary to develop the concept.

After Reading What kinds of neighborhoods did the author *investigate?* What did you learn about an *urban* neighborhood? What did you learn about a *rural* neighborhood?

Reread for Fluency "Neighborhoods," pp. 6–7

	To Do	To Say	
			5–10 minutes

CORRECTIVE FEEDBACK

Monitor oral reading.

Read pp. 6–7 aloud. Read them three or four times so your reading gets better each time. Give feedback on children's oral reading and use of the blending strategy. See Routine Cards 1 and 4.

MORE PRACTICE

Instead of rereading just pp. 6–7, have children reread the entire selection three or four times. You may want to have children read along with the AudioText.

Homework Practice Book, p. 1, Phonics: Short *a*

ACTIVITY 1 Reread for Fluency

Paired Reading "Neighborhoods," pp. 8–9

	To Do	To Say	*5–10 minutes*
CORRECTIVE FEEDBACK	Pair children. Monitor paired reading.	Children read pp. 8–9 orally, switching readers at the end of the first page. Have partners reread; now the other partner begins. For optimal fluency, children should reread three or four times. Give feedback on children's oral reading and use of the blending strategy. See Routine Cards 1 and 4.	
MORE PRACTICE		Instead of rereading just pp. 8–9, have children reread the entire selection three or four times. You may want to have children read along with the AudioText.	

ACTIVITY 2 Word Work

Phonemic Awareness Blend Sounds

	To Do	To Say	*2 minutes*
Scaffold instruction.	Distribute white boards. Write *sack.*	**Model** Listen as I say these sounds: /sss/ /aaa/ /k/. Now listen as I say them slowly and then blend them quickly to say the word: /sss/ /aaa/ /k/, *sack.* Repeat. This time have children write the letters as you write them. Now you say the sounds slowly as you point to the letters. Then blend them quickly. What is the word? *(sack)* A *sack* is a bag.	
	Write *back.* Lead children in blending sounds.	**Teach and Practice** Have children blend sounds for *b, a, ck.* (/b/ /a/ /k/) What is the word? *(back)* Continue the activity with these words: Zack pack sick lick duck	

Blending Strategy Final *ck*

	To Do	**To Say**	
			5–10 minutes

Routine

Use the blending routine.

Write *cap* and *kid*.

1 Connect You already can read words like these. What are the words? What sound do they both start with? (/k/) What letter stands for this sound in *cap*? (c) In *kid*? (k) Today we are learning how the letters *ck* together stand for one sound, /k/, at the end of a word.

Scaffold instruction.

Display Sound-Spelling Card 6.

2 Use Sound-Spelling Card This is a computer. What sound do you hear at the beginning of *computer*? (/k/) Say it with me: /k/. The two letters *ck* stand for one sound, /k/, when they are together.

3 Listen and Write Write the two letters that together stand for the sound /k/. As you write, say the sound to yourself: /k/. Now say the sound aloud.

Write *pack*.

4 Model The two letters *ck* at the end of this word stand for /k/. This is how I blend this word: /p/ /a/ /k/, *pack*. Now you try it: /p/ /a/ /k/, *pack*.

Point out that *ck* can come at the end of a word *(pack)* or in the middle of a word *(packing)*, but not at the beginning of a word.

p a c k

CORRECTIVE FEEDBACK

Write each practice word. Monitor student practice.

5 Group Practice Let's try the same thing with these words. Give feedback, using the *if . . . then* statements on Routine Card 1.

lock   sock   check   clock   truck   chick*

6 Individual Practice Write the words; have each child blend two of them.

tack*   kick   quack   luck   black   thick

Check understanding of practice words.

*Children need to make sense of words as they segment and blend. If needed, help children with meanings. **A *chick* is a young chicken. A *tack* is a kind of short pin.** (Show children a tack and demonstrate how to use it to post a piece of paper on a corkboard.)

MORE PRACTICE

Model spelling *ck* words.

Spell and Write What sounds do you hear in *back*? (/b/ /a/ /k/) What is the letter for /b/? Let's all write *b*. What is the letter for /a/? Write *a*. What are the letters for /k/ at the end? Write *ck*. Continue practice as time allows. Have children confirm their spelling by comparing it to what you've written.

sack   pick   duck   tack   deck   rock

High-Frequency Words *always, laugh, only, told*

	To Do	**To Say**	
			3 minutes

Teach high-frequency words.

Display *always, laugh, only,* and *told*.

Use the Tested Vocabulary Cards. Point to a word. Say and spell it. Have children say and spell the word. Ask children to identify familiar letter-sounds. Have them take turns reading the words.

ACTIVITY 3 | Read a Passage

Reading "A Pack of Colors," pp. 10–15

| To Do | To Say | *10–15 minutes* |

Develop language and concepts.

See Routine Cards 6 and 7. Display pp. 10–15.

Scaffold instruction.

Ask questions and elaborate on answers to develop language.

Key concepts: *sidewalk, pals, chalk, city, farm, country, rural*

Before Reading Have children recall what they learned about the city and the country. Read the title. Do a structured picture walk with children.

pp. 10–11 Where are the two boys standing? (in front of a brick wall) The two boys in front of the wall are pals, or friends. What is inside the tan sack? (a pack of chalk) Chalk is used for writing or drawing. What are the boys doing with the chalk? (drawing a picture on the sidewalk) Yes, they are drawing a picture of a cow on the sidewalk.

pp. 12–13 Point to the drawing of the duck on p. 12. What animal did the boys draw? (a duck)

pp. 14–15 What other things did they draw? (pig, barn) The boys drew animals on a farm. What kind of neighborhood has farms? (the country) Rural places, like the country, have farms.

Guide comprehension.

See Routine Card 2. Read pp. 10–15.

During Reading Ask children to read along with you. As we read, ask yourself: Who are Zack and Rick? What do the boys do in this selection? Read pp. 10–11 aloud with the group. Then ask: What did you learn about Zack and Rick? (They are best pals.) Yes, we learned that Zack and Rick are best pals who are glad to help each other.

Read pp. 12–15 aloud with the group. Then ask: What happens in this part of the selection? (Zack and Rick draw pictures on the sidewalk.) Yes, Zack and Rick worked together to draw pictures of a farm.

Monitor independent reading.

Use Routine Card 3.

Reread Have children read the selection aloud together without you. Then have them read it on their own in a whisper. Listen in on each child. Monitor reading, using Routine Card 3.

Model summarizing.

Think aloud.

After Reading What did you learn about things kids can do in a neighborhood? What is the selection mainly about? Model how to summarize. The first two pages tell how Zack and Rick like to help each other. They get out chalk to draw on the sidewalk. The next pages tell how they use the chalk to draw pictures of a farm. I put that all together and pick the most important ideas. The selection is mainly about how Zack and Rick worked together to draw pictures of a farm. They had fun helping each other.

MORE PRACTICE

Develop oral vocabulary.

How can you *investigate* the boys' drawings to find out about a *rural* place? How is a *rural* place different from an *urban* place?

ACTIVITY 4 | Write

Response to Literature Shared Writing

| To Do | To Say | *5 minutes* |

Guide shared writing.

Write sentence frames. Read the questions.

What was in the tan sack? The tan sack had a thick _____.
What did Zack and Rick draw? Zack and Rick drew _____.

Invite children to suggest answers. Discuss and record answers to complete the sentence frames. While writing, model connecting sounds to letters and forming letters (see pp. 257–259). Have children read answers aloud as you track print.

Homework

Practice Book, p. 2, Phonics: Final *ck*

ACTIVITY 1 | Reread for Fluency

Oral Reading "A Pack of Colors," pp. 12–15

5–10 minutes

	To Do	To Say
CORRECTIVE FEEDBACK	Monitor oral reading.	**Read pp. 12–15 aloud. Read them three or four times so your reading gets better each time.** Give feedback on children's oral reading and use of the blending strategy. See Routine Cards 1 and 4.
MORE PRACTICE		Instead of rereading just pp. 12–15, have children reread the entire selection three or four times. You may want to have children read along with the AudioText.

ACTIVITY 2 | Word Work

Phonemic Awareness Blend Sounds

2 minutes

	To Do	To Say
Scaffold instruction.	Distribute white boards. Write *jam*.	**Model** Listen as I say these sounds. Stretch the sounds /j/ /aaa/ /mmm/ as you write *j, a, m*. Now listen as I say them slowly and then blend them to say a word. Repeat. This time have children write the letters as you write. Now you say the sounds slowly as you point to the letters, then blend them quickly. What is the word? *(jam)*
	Write *Jack*. Lead children in blending sounds.	**Teach and Practice** Have children blend sounds for *J, a, ck.* (/j/ /a/ /k/) What is the word? *(Jack)* Continue with these words:
		cat Dad back rack

Fluent Word Reading Short *a*, Final *ck*

5–10 minutes

Routine

	To Do	To Say
Use the word-reading routine.	Write *had*.	**1 Connect** You can read this word because you know that *a* can stand for /a/. What sound does *a* in this word stand for? *(/a/)* What's the word? *(had)*
	Write *can* and *sick*.	**2 Model** When you come to a new word, look at all the letters in the word and think about its vowel sound. Say the sounds in the word to yourself, and then read the word. Model reading *can* and *sick* in this way. When you come to a new word, what are you going to do?
Scaffold instruction.	Write each practice word.	**3 Group Practice** Let's read these words. Look at all the letters, think about the vowel sound, and say the sounds to yourself. We will read words with short *a* and *ck*. When I point to the word, let's read it together. Allow 2–3 seconds previewing time for each word.
		mat sock nap neck bag lock duck sat block
CORRECTIVE FEEDBACK	**MONITOR PROGRESS**	*If . . .* children have difficulty previewing and reading whole words, *then . . .* have them use sound-by-sound blending.
		If . . . children can't read the words fluently at a rate of 1–2 seconds per word, *then . . .* continue practicing the list.

| MORE PRACTICE | Model reading words in sentences. | When I read a sentence, I read each word without stopping between the words. If I come to a word I don't know, I blend it. Then I read the sentence again. Model reading this sentence, stopping to blend *black: The cat is black.* |
| | Write practice sentences. | Have each child read a sentence.

Jack has that sock.
I am mad at Nick.
Rick had a tan sack. |

High-Frequency Words *always, laugh, only, told*

3 minutes

	To Do	**To Say**
Review high-frequency words.	Display *always*, *laugh*, *only*, and *told*.	Use the Tested Vocabulary Cards. Point to a word. Say and spell it. Have children say and spell the word. Ask children to identify familiar letter-sounds. Have them take turns reading the words.

ACTIVITY 3 Build Concepts

Oral Vocabulary *avenue, suburb*

5–10 minutes

	To Do	**To Say**
Teach oral vocabulary.	Display p. 16 of the student book. Follow the Routine to teach *avenue* and *suburb*.	Today you will read about the things a rabbit named Jack and his dad do when they visit an *avenue* in a *suburb*. **1 Introduce, Demonstrate, and Apply** **avenue** This story is about what happens on a visit to an *avenue*. An *avenue* is a street. Have children say the word. You can go to different shops on an *avenue*. Have you ever walked along an *avenue*? What places did you visit there? **suburb** This story takes place in a *suburb*. A *suburb* is a town just outside or near a city. Have children say the word. There is usually more room between homes in a *suburb* than there is in a city. Do you live in a *suburb*? Have you ever visited a *suburb*?
	Display the words on the Amazing	**2 Display the Words** Have children say each word as they look at it. You can find sounds you know in big words. What letter do you see at the beginning of ___? What sound does it make? (/a/) Read *sub/urb* as you run your hand ___ syllables. Children can identify *sub* and /b/. **___ Words** Ask children to use each word in a sentence. Model a sentence ___ need help.
MORE PRACTICE		___ cabulary to discuss neighborhoods. What kinds of places might you find ___ ue? What kinds of things might you see in a *suburb*? Are there many tall ___ a *suburb*? Why or why not? Are there many farms in a *suburb*? Why or

Handwritten note:

Read – A Pack of Colors
　　　multiple times
White Boards – Blend sounds
　　short ă __ck pg 10
HFW – point and spell
OV – avenue, suburb pg 11
Reread Pack of Colors

3

ACTIVITY 4 Read a Passage

Reading "Blue Jack," pp. 16–23

	To Do	To Say
		10 minutes
Teach sequence. **Scaffold instruction.**	Introduce the skill. Model the skill. Apply the skill.	Today you are going to learn how to keep track of the order in which things happen in a story. When you put events in order, you tell what happened first, next, and last. For example, I can tell you what I did at home this morning in order from first to last. First, I woke up. Next, I got dressed. Last, I ate breakfast. Think about what we have done in class today. **What did we do first?** (Possible answer: Take attendance.) **What did we do next?** (Possible answer: Had a math lesson.) **What did we do last?** (Possible answer: Went to art class.)
Develop language and concepts.	See Routine Card 6. Display pp. 16–23. Model using key words and concepts. Key concepts: *rabbits, hop, shop, snacks, melt, drip, chat, raccoon, grin, laugh* Monitor children's use of vocabulary.	**Before Reading** Read the title. Do a structured picture walk. **pp. 16–19** The rabbits hop to a food shop. **How do rabbits hop?** Have children demonstrate hopping. They buy milk and jam. **Where do you shop for things like milk and jam?** **pp. 20–21** The rabbits buy snacks. The cold snacks are starting to melt and drip. Point to the snack that drips. When it is hot outside, a cold snack will melt. **p. 22** The rabbits chat with the raccoon. Point to the raccoon. **What is he holding?** **p. 23** The rabbit grins and laughs. To grin is to smile. Point to his grin. **Do you grin when you laugh?** Now turn to your partner and talk about the pictures, using the same words I did.
Guide comprehension.	Read pp. 16–23. Use Routine Card 2.	**During Reading** Ask children to read along with you. **As we read, ask yourself: What happens first, next, and last?** Read pp. 16–19 aloud with the group. Then ask: **Where do Jack and Dad go first? What do they do there?** (The food shop; they buy milk and jam.) Read pp. 20–21 aloud with the group. Then ask: **Where is the next place Jack and Dad go? What do they do there?** (The snack shop; they buy snacks to eat.) Read pp. 22–23 aloud with the group. Then ask: **What is the last thing that Jack and Dad do in the story?** (They stop to chat with Mack.)
Monitor independent reading.	Use Routine Card 3.	**Reread** Have children read the selection aloud together without you. Then have them read it on their own in a whisper. Listen in on each child. Monitor reading, using Routine Card 3.
Guide retelling.	Prompt children as they retell the story.	**After Reading** Have one child retell the story while the others assist. **What did Jack and Dad do first, next, and last on their visit to the avenue?** (First, they bought milk and jam. Next, they bought and ate snacks. Last, they stopped to chat with Mack.) See Monitor Retelling, p. 246.
	Homework	Practice Book, p. 3, Sequence

ACTIVITY **1** Reread for Fluency

Paired Reading "Blue Jack," pp. 20–21

To Do	To Say	*5–10 minutes*

CORRECTIVE FEEDBACK

Pair children. Monitor paired reading.

Children read pp. 20–21 orally, switching readers at the end of the first page. Have partners reread; now the other partner begins. For optimal fluency, children should reread three or four times. Give feedback on children's oral reading and use of the blending strategy. See Routine Cards 1 and 4.

MORE PRACTICE

Instead of rereading just pp. 20–21, have children reread the entire selection three or four times. You may want to have children read along with the AudioText.

ACTIVITY **2** Word Work

Spiral Review Consonant Letter-Sounds

To Do	To Say	*5 minutes*

Review consonant letter-sounds.

Write *nap.*

Look at this word. You can read this word because you know how to blend the sounds of the letters *n, a,* and *p.* What sound does *n* make? (/n/) What sound does *a* make? (/a/) What sound does *p* make? (/p/) Now let's blend the sounds to say the word: /n/ /a/ /p/, *nap.*

Scaffold instruction.

Provide letter tiles *a, c, l, m, n, p, r,* and *t.*

Build Words Write *mat.* Can you blend this word? (*mat*) Spell *mat* with letter tiles. Now change the *m* in *mat* to *p.* What is the new word? (*pat*)

- Change the *t* in *pat* to *l.* What is the new word? (*pal*)
- Change the *l* in *pal* to *n.* What is the new word? (*pan*)
- Change the *p* in *pan* to *r.* What is the new word? (*ran*)
- Change the *n* in *ran* to *p.* What is the new word? (*rap*)
- Change the *r* in *rap* to *c.* What is the new word? (*cap*)

CORRECTIVE FEEDBACK

MONITOR PROGRESS

If . . . children have difficulty reading the new words,
then . . . have them use sound-by-sound blending.

MORE PRACTICE

Model reading words in sentences.

When I read a sentence, I read each word without stopping between the words. If I come to a word I don't know, I blend it. Then I read the sentence again. Model reading this sentence, stopping to blend *gab: Dan and Jan like to gab.*

Write practice sentences.

Have each child read a sentence.

Dad has a big tan van.
Pam got a yellow cab.
The fat cat sat on my lap.

Phonological and Phonemic Awareness

Optional practice activities, pp. 280–283

Read Together

Choral Reading "City Song" and "Hayloft," p. 24

	To Do	To Say	*10 minutes*
Develop language and concepts.	Display p. 24.	**Before Reading** The girl is jumping in hay. What do you know about hay? (Allow children to share what they know.) Where might you find a lot of hay? (on a farm) Share information about hay. Hay is grass that is cut and dried. Horses and cows on a farm eat hay. A hayloft is a place where a farmer keeps large piles of hay.	
Model fluent reading.	Model prosody.	Read the titles of the poems. Ask children to predict what each poem is about. Look at the end of each poem. The first poem ends with an exclamation mark. I'll read that part with excitement. The second poem ends with a period. I'll read that part with less excitement. Listen as I read these poems. Read each poem, adjusting your expression to match the end punctuation. Then read each poem a second time, having children point to each word.	
	Build fluency through choral reading.	**Choral Reading** Now read the poems aloud with me. Pay attention to end marks as we read. Reread each poem several times with children.	
Develop concepts.	Monitor listening comprehension.	**After Reading** Which poem describes an *urban* place? What are some of the many things you see and hear in a city? Which poem describes a *rural* place? What is the girl doing in the country?	

Build Concepts

Oral Vocabulary *avenue, investigate, rural, suburb, urban*

	To Do	To Say	*5–10 minutes*
Review oral vocabulary.	Read the words on the Amazing Words board.	**Focus on Letter-Sounds** Remember, you can find sounds you know in big words. • What word begins with *r?* What word begins with *a?* • What word starts with *in?* • Which word has the most letters? How many letters does it have?	
	Encourage discussion.	**Provide Multiple Contexts** Review the meanings of the words. Then ask questions to place the words in diverse contexts. • Name a place you would like to *investigate.* Is it a *rural* place, an *urban* place, or a *suburb?* What things might you find there? • What things could you *investigate* in this classroom? How might you use your eyes, ears, and hands when you *investigate?* • Is there an *avenue* close to where you live? What kinds of shops are on the *avenue* near you?	
MORE PRACTICE	Apply oral vocabulary to new situations.	• I will describe things you might find when you *investigate* an *urban* or a *rural* place. For each description, say "urban" or "rural": many cars, trucks, and buses (urban), a farm (rural), lots of grass, trees, and land (rural), a large apartment building (urban), cabs honking (urban), cows mooing (rural). • If anything I say could be found on an *avenue,* clap and say "avenue." If not, do nothing: food shops (avenue), farms (not), people walking (avenue), cows and sheep (not), sidewalks (avenue).	

ACTIVITY **5** | Write

Response to Literature Interactive Writing

| To Do | To Say | 5–10 minutes |

Generate ideas.

Share the pen.

Review the story "Blue Jack."

Have children participate in writing a list of things they might shop for on an avenue.

What kinds of places did Jack and Dad visit on the avenue? What did they do at each place? Discuss the different places they visited in the story.

Write *I could shop for _____.* Have children read the words you wrote. Then have them supply endings for the sentence. Invite individuals to write familiar letter-sounds, word parts, and high-frequency words. Have them find the spelling of high-frequency words on the Word Wall. Ask questions such as:

- **What is the first sound in** *jam?* (/j/) **What is the letter for /j/?** *(j)*
- **What is the vowel sound in** *jam?* (/a/) **What is the letter for /a/?** *(a)*
- **What is the last sound in** *jam?* (/m/) **What is the letter for /m/?** *(m)*

Writing elements: conventions

Frequently reread what has been written while tracking the print. Point out that each sentence starts with a capital letter and ends with a period. Point out the extra space between words.

Read the completed list aloud, having children read with you. (For example, *I could shop for jam. I could shop for milk. I could shop for snacks.*)

MORE PRACTICE

Prompt independent writing.

Journal Writing Tell about where you like to shop.

Homework

Practice Book, p. 4, High-Frequency Words

5

ACTIVITY 1 — Assessment Options

Sentence Reading

	To Do	To Say	*5 minutes*
Assess sentence reading.	Use reproducible p. 247.	Have each child read the sentences. Record scores on the Sentence Reading Chart, p. 252. Work with one child as others complete Write Sentences below. I always laugh with my pals. We told Jack to pack a bag. He can only pick one rock.	
CORRECTIVE FEEDBACK	**MONITOR PROGRESS**	*If . . .* children have trouble reading words with *a/a/* or *ck,* *then . . .* reteach the blending strategy lessons on pp. 4 and 8. *If . . .* children cannot read a high-frequency word, *then . . .* mark the missed word or words on a high-frequency word list and send the list home for additional practice or have them practice with a fluent reader. *If . . .* children misread a word, *then . . .* correct the error and have them reread the word and then the sentence.	
Practice sentence writing.	Provide white boards.	**Write Sentences** Have children copy the sentences from reproducible p. 247 on white boards. Have them confirm spellings by comparing the words they wrote to the words in the sentences.	
	Phonological and Phonemic Awareness	Optional practice activities, pp. 280–283	

Passage Reading

	To Do	To Say	*5–10 minutes*
Assess fluency and comprehension.	Determine which children to assess this week.	Choose from these options: monitoring fluency (see pp. 244–245) and/or monitoring retelling (see p. 246). Have children reread "Blue Jack." Be sure each child is assessed every other week.	
		If you have time, assess every child.	

ACTIVITY 2 — Use Concepts

Oral Vocabulary *avenue, investigate, rural, suburb, urban*

	To Do	To Say	*5 minutes*
Check understanding of oral vocabulary.	Use the Amazing Words to wrap up the week's concept. Monitor understanding of oral vocabulary, using Routine Card 5.	As time allows, ask questions such as these. • Tell me about the pictures on pp. 6–9 using some of the week's Amazing Words. • Do people walk on sidewalks or on grass when they visit an *avenue?* • Where do you see tall buildings and bright lights, in a *rural* place or an *urban* place? Will you see mountains and lakes in an *urban* place? • How is a *suburb* different from a city? How is it different from the country? • Name some things you might *investigate* during a walk in the woods. (trees and other plants, rocks, insects and other animals, and so on)	

<table>
<tr><td>Preview next week's concept.</td><td>To Do</td><td>To Say
Next week you will read about exploring outer space.</td></tr>
</table>

ACTIVITY 3 Read to Connect

Reread "Neighborhoods," pp. 6–9

10 minutes

	To Do	**To Say**
Monitor comprehension: sequence.	Have children reread "Neighborhoods" silently.	As you read, think about the order in which the neighborhoods are described. After rereading, ask: • What neighborhood is described first? What can you find in that neighborhood? • What neighborhood is described last? What can you find in that neighborhood? Record children's ideas in two lists on the board. (For example: in the city—many vans, cabs, buses, and busy people; in the country—farms with pigs and hens, ponds, lots of grass and open spaces) Children will use these lists for Activity 4.
Make connections.	Have children make connections across texts.	We also read "A Pack of Colors." Find that. What happened first in that selection? What happened next? What happened last? Record children's ideas in an ordered list. We also read "Blue Jack," about a visit to an avenue. Did Jack and Dad visit the food shop first or last? (first) What did they do next? (They bought a snack.) When did they chat with Mack, first or last? (last) Have children help you make a list of the correct sequence of events. Where did the selections we read this week take place? (in the city, in the country, in the suburbs) Are all neighborhoods the same? Why or why not? (No; because we find different things in the city, country, or suburbs.)

ACTIVITY 4 Write

Response to Literature Independent Writing

5–10 minutes

	To Do	**To Say**
Assign descriptive writing.		Today you will write about how the country is different from the city. Describe the different things you see and hear in rural and urban places. Encourage children to use words you wrote on the board for Activity 3 as they write.
Guide sentence correction.	Writing elements: conventions, support	Have children check their writing by asking themselves these questions. • Did I begin each sentence with a capital letter? • Did I end each sentence with a period? • Did I use describing words?
MORE PRACTICE		Have children share their sentences with the group. Write their sentences on the board and have children practice reading and writing each other's sentences.
Homework		Practice Book, p. 5, Writing

Unit 1 Week 2 *Outer Space*

Why would anyone want to explore space?

Objectives *This week students will...*

Phonemic Awareness
- blend sounds in words

Phonics
- blend and read words with short *i*, *ng*/ng/, and *nk*/ngk/
- apply knowledge of letter-sounds to decode unknown words when reading
- recognize high-frequency words *afraid, so, surprise, worry*

Fluency
- practice fluency with oral rereading

Vocabulary
- build concepts and oral vocabulary: *ascend, descend, journey, orbit, universe*

Text Comprehension
- read connected text
- identify main idea to improve comprehension
- write in response to literature

Word Work *This week's phonics focus is . . .*

Short *i*   Final *ng, nk*

High-Frequency Words *Tested Vocabulary*

The first appearance of each word in the Student Reader is noted below.

afraid	When you are **afraid,** you feel scared about something. (p. 30)
so	Don't eat **so** fast. (p. 31) The wind felt cold, **so** he went inside.
surprise	A **surprise** is something that happens that you did not plan. (p. 31)
worry	When you **worry,** you feel upset about something. (p. 30)

Amazing Words *Oral Vocabulary*

The week's vocabulary is related to the concept of space exploration.

ascend	to go up
descend	to go down
journey	a long trip
orbit	to go around a planet or something else in space
universe	everything there is

Student Reader Unit 1 *This week students will read the following selections.*

Daily Lesson Plan

	ACTIVITIES	MATERIALS
Day 1	**Word Work** Phonemic Awareness: Blend Sounds Phonics: Blend Words with Short *i* High-Frequency Words *afraid, so, surprise, worry* **Build Concepts** *ascend, descend, orbit* **Read a Passage** "Outer Space," pp. 28–33 Comprehension: Use Strategies Reread for Fluency	Student White Boards Sound-Spelling Card 15 Tested Vocabulary Cards *Sing with Me Big Book* and Audio CD Student Reader: Unit 1 Routine Cards 1, 2, 3, 4, 6 AudioText Practice Book, p. 6, Short *i*
Day 2	**Reread for Fluency** **Word Work** Phonemic Awareness: Blend Sounds Phonics: Blend Words with *ng*/ng/, *nk*/ngk/ High-Frequency Words *afraid, so, surprise, worry* **Read a Passage** "Franklin Chang-Diaz, Astronaut," pp. 34–41 Comprehension: Use Strategies **Write** Response to Literature: Shared Writing	Student Reader: Unit 1 Student White Boards Sound-Spelling Cards 21 and 22 Tested Vocabulary Cards Routine Cards 1, 2, 3, 4, 6, 7 AudioText Practice Book, p. 7, *ng*/ng/, *nk*/ngk/
Day 3	**Reread for Fluency** **Word Work** Phonemic Awareness: Blend Sounds Phonics: Fluent Word Reading High-Frequency Words *afraid, so, surprise, worry* **Build Concepts** *journey, universe* **Read a Passage** "It Fell from Space," pp. 42–49 Comprehension: Main Idea	Student Reader: Unit 1 Student White Boards Tested Vocabulary Cards Routine Cards 1, 2, 3, 4, 6 AudioText Practice Book, p. 8, Main Idea
Day 4	**Reread for Fluency** **Word Work** Phonics: Spiral Review Phonological and Phonemic Awareness Activities, pp. 280–283 **Read Together** "What Would You Wear in Outer Space?" p. 50 Comprehension: Listening **Build Concepts** *ascend, descend, journey, orbit, universe* **Write** Response to Literature: Interactive Writing	Student Reader: Unit 1 Routine Cards 1, 4 AudioText Letter Tiles *a, c, i, g, k, l, l, n, s, w* Practice Book, p. 9, High-Frequency Words
Day 5	**Assessment Options** Fluency, Comprehension Sentence Reading; Passage Reading Phonological and Phonemic Awareness Activities, pp. 280–283 **Use Concepts** *ascend, descend, journey, orbit, universe* **Read to Connect** "Outer Space," pp. 28–33 Comprehension: Main Idea **Write** Response to Literature: Independent Writing	Reproducible p. 247 Sentence Reading Chart, p. 252 Student White Boards Fluency Progress Chart, p. 245 Student Reader: Unit 1 Routine Card 5 Practice Book, p. 10, Writing

See pp. xvi–xvii for how *My Sidewalks* integrates instructional practices for ELL.

ACTIVITY 1 Word Work

Phonemic Awareness Blend Sounds

To Do	To Say	*2 minutes*

Scaffold instruction.

Distribute white boards.
Write *in*.

Write *win*.
Lead children in blending sounds.

Model The sound for *i* is /i/ and the sound for *n* is /n/. Listen as I blend the sounds for *i* and *n*. Stretch the sounds /iii/ /nnn/ as you write *i, n*. Repeat. This time have children write the letters as you write. **What is the word?** *(in)*

Teach and Practice Have children blend sounds for *w, i, n*. (/w/ /i/ /n/) **What is the word?** *(win)* Continue with these words:

it   rip   fit   dig

Blending Strategy Short *i*

To Do	To Say	*5–10 minutes*

Use the blending routine.

Write *if*.

Routine

1 Connect You already can read this word. What is the first letter? *(i)* Is this letter a vowel or a consonant? (vowel) The last letter is a consonant. What is the last letter? *(f)* What is the word? *(if)* What is the beginning sound in *if?* (/i/) What is the end sound? (/f/) Now let's look more at the letter *i* and the sound it can make, /i/.

Display Sound-Spelling Card 15.

2 Use Sound-Spelling Card These are insects. What sound do you hear at the beginning of *insects?* (/i/) Say it with me: /i/. The letter *i* stands for the sound /i/ at the beginning of *insects.*

3 Listen and Write Write the letter *i* for /i/. As you write, say the sound to yourself: /i/. Now say the sound aloud.

Scaffold instruction.

Write *big*.

4 Model The letter *i* stands for /i/. This is how I blend this word: /b/ /i/ /g/, *big.* Now you try: /b/ /i/ /g/, *big.*

Point out that when *i* is the only vowel at the beginning or in the middle of a word, it usually stands for its short sound, /i/.

$$\underset{\rightarrow}{b} \; \underset{\rightarrow}{i} \; \underset{\rightarrow}{g}$$

CORRECTIVE FEEDBACK

Write each practice word.
Monitor student practice.

5 Group Practice Let's try the same thing with these words. Give feedback, using the *if . . . then* statements on Routine Card 1.

kid   lit*   kick   his   pin   thick*

6 Individual Practice Write the words; have each child blend two of them.

sit   lick   did   tick*   mix   hill

Check understanding of practice words.

*Children need to make sense of words that they segment and blend. If needed, help children with meanings. **When something is *lit,* it lights up.** (Demonstrate by turning off a classroom light and then turning it on again.) **A thing that is big from one side to the other is *thick*.** (Show a thick book.) **A *tick* is the sound a clock makes.** (Demonstrate with an analog clock.)

MORE PRACTICE

Model spelling short *i* words.

Spell and Write What sounds do you hear in *hit?* (/h/ /i/ /t/) What is the letter for /h/? Let's all write *h*. What is the letter for /i/? Write *i*. What is the letter for /t/? Write *t*. Continue practice as time allows. Have children confirm their spelling by comparing it to what you've written.

him   bit   sick   pig   lip   pick

High-Frequency Words *afraid, so, surprise, worry*

To Do	To Say	
		3 minutes

Teach high-frequency words.

Display *afraid*.

1 Say, Spell, Write Use the Tested Vocabulary Cards. Display *afraid*. Here are some words that we won't sound out. We'll spell them. This word is *afraid*: *a, f, r, a, i, d* (point to each letter), *afraid*. What is this word? What are the letters in the word? Now you write *afraid*.

Point to the *f, r,* and the *d* in *afraid*.

2 Identify Letter-Sounds Let's look at the sounds in *afraid* that you do know. What is this letter? *(f)* What is the sound for this letter? *(/f/)* Continue with *r* and *d*. *(r/r/, d/d/)*

3 Demonstrate Meaning Tell me a sentence using *afraid*. Model a sentence if children need help.

Display *so, surprise,* and *worry*.

Repeat the Routine with *so, surprise,* and *worry*. Children can identify these letter-sounds: *so (s/s/), surprise (s/s/, p/p/, r/r/), worry (w/w/, r/r/)*. Have children write the words in their word banks. Add the words to the Word Wall.

Routine

ACTIVITY **2** Build Concepts

Oral Vocabulary *ascend, descend, orbit*

To Do	To Say	
		5–10 minutes

Introduce oral vocabulary.

Scaffold instruction.

Display p. 2 of *Sing with Me Big Book.* Play audio CD.

This week you will learn about outer space. Listen for the Amazing Words *ascend, descend,* and *orbit* as I sing this song. Play or sing the song. Then have children sing it with you.

Routine

Follow the Routine to teach *ascend, descend,* and *orbit*.

1 Introduce, Demonstrate, and Apply

ascend The astronauts *ascend* to outer space in their spaceship. *Ascend* means to go up. Have children say the word. You *ascend* to the next floor when you walk upstairs. Show me how you *ascend* stairs. (Children can use two fingers to act out walking up stairs, raising their hands as they "walk.")

descend When they are finished exploring outer space, the astronauts *descend* back to Earth in their spaceship. *Descend* means to go down. Have children say the word. You *descend* when you walk down stairs. Show me how you *descend* stairs.

orbit When the astronauts are in outer space, they *orbit* Earth. *Orbit* means to go around a planet or something else in space. Have children say the word. Earth and other planets *orbit*, or go around, the Sun. Spaceships *orbit* Earth. Imagine that you are in a spaceship and your desk is Earth. Show me how you *orbit* Earth.

Display the words on the Amazing Words board.

2 Display the Words Have children say each word as they look at it. You can find sounds you know in big words. Read *as/cend* as you run your hand under the syllables. Can you find the *d?* What sound does the *d* make? For *orbit* and *descend*, children can identify these letter-sounds and word parts: *orbit* (high-frequency word *or, bit*), *descend (d/d/)*.

Monitor understanding.

3 Use the Words Ask children to use each word in a sentence. Model a sentence if children need help.

MORE PRACTICE

Use oral vocabulary to discuss the song. How does Earth look to the astronauts after they *ascend* to outer space? What do the astronauts do while in *orbit?* How do the astronauts feel when they *descend* back to Earth?

Build Background "Outer Space," pp. 28–33

To Do	To Say	

10 minutes

Develop language and concepts.

Scaffold instruction.

Read aloud p. 27 of the student book.

See Routine Card 6. Display pp. 28–33.

Ask questions and elaborate on answers to develop language.

Key concepts: *moon, craters, dust, blast, space, ascend, descend, astronauts, disks, print*

Preview the Week Use pp. 26–27 to preview the selections in this week. The selections this week are about outer space. Read aloud the titles and descriptions on p. 27. Ask children what they think each selection will be about.

Before Reading Read the title aloud. Do a structured picture walk.

pp. 28–29 What does the first picture show? (the moon) The dark spots on the moon are deep pits called craters. The light parts show the thick dust that covers the moon. Point to dark and light areas. What is happening in this second picture? Yes, the spaceship is starting to blast off into space, the area around Earth. The ship will ascend, or go up, to outer space.

pp. 30–31 Who do you think is inside the spaceship? (astronauts) Yes, astronauts are people trained to fly spaceships. Where has this spaceship landed? (the moon) Flat, round disks help the ship sit on the moon's thick dust. Point to the disks. What is the print in the dust? (a shoe print) Yes, the print shows where an astronaut stepped on the moon.

pp. 32–33 What does the first picture show? (Earth) The astronauts descend, or go down, to Earth after exploring the moon. What is this girl dressed as? (an astronaut) Yes, this girl is at space camp. Let's read to find out about outer space.

Teach story words.

Write *astronaut* and *space.*

Guide comprehension.

Read pp. 28–33.

Model strategic reading. Use Routine Card 2.

You will read these words in the selection. They are *astronaut* and *space.* Have children say the words and spell them. Review their meanings.

During Reading Ask children to read along with you. As we read, ask yourself: What did I learn? What is this mainly about? Read pp. 28–33 aloud with the group. Stop on each page to model asking questions. For example, for p. 28: After I read, I ask myself: What is this mainly about? The author talks about a place the astronauts go that has big rocks, sand, and thick dust. I think this page is mainly about the moon.

Monitor independent reading.

Use Routine Card 3.

Reread Have children read the selection aloud together without you. Then have them read it on their own in a whisper. Listen in on each child. Monitor reading, using Routine Card 3.

Summarize.

Use oral vocabulary to develop the concept.

After Reading How do the astronauts feel when they *ascend* to outer space? What do the astronauts see from their ship as they *orbit* around the moon? What will the astronauts do after they *descend* to Earth?

Reread for Fluency "Outer Space," pp. 28–30

To Do	To Say	

5–10 minutes

CORRECTIVE FEEDBACK

Monitor oral reading.

Read pp. 28–30 aloud. Read them three or four times so your reading gets better each time. Give feedback on children's oral reading and use of the blending strategy. See Routine Cards 1 and 4.

MORE PRACTICE

Instead of rereading just pp. 28–30, have children reread the entire selection three or four times. You may want to have children read along with the AudioText.

Homework

Practice Book, p. 6, Phonics: Short *i*

ACTIVITY 1 Reread for Fluency

Paired Reading "Outer Space," pp. 31–33

To Do	To Say	*5–10 minutes*

CORRECTIVE FEEDBACK

Pair children. Monitor paired reading.

Children read pp. 31–33 orally, switching readers at the end of the first page. Have partners reread; now the other partner begins. For optimal fluency, children should reread three or four times. Give feedback on children's oral reading and use of the blending strategy. See Routine Cards 1 and 4.

MORE PRACTICE

Instead of rereading just pp. 31–33, have children reread the entire selection three or four times. You may want to have children read along with the AudioText.

ACTIVITY 2 Word Work

Phonemic Awareness Blend Sounds

To Do	To Say	*2 minutes*

Scaffold instruction.

Distribute white boards.
Write *ink.*

Model The sound for *i* is /i/ and the sound for *nk* is /ngk/. Listen as I blend the sounds for these letters. Stretch the sounds /iii/ /ngk/ as you write *i, nk.* Repeat. This time have children write the letters as you write. **What is the word?** *(ink)* **Ink is used for writing. A pen is filled with ink.**

Write *sang.*
Lead children in blending sounds.

Teach and Practice Have children blend sounds for *s, a, ng.* (/s/ /a/ /ng/) **What is the word?** *(sang)* Continue with these words:

sink   rang   wing   bank

Blending Strategy Final *ng*/ng/, *nk*/ngk/

	To Do	To Say	
Use the blending routine.	Write *back* and *sick*.	**1 Connect** You already can read words like these. What are the words? What sound do they end with? (/k/) What letters stand for the sound? *(ck)* Today we are learning about two other sounds that come at the end of words and are spelled with two letters.	*Routine*

5–10 minutes

Scaffold instruction. — Display Sound-Spelling Cards 21 and 22.

2 Use Sound-Spelling Cards This is a swing and this is a skunk. What sound do you hear at the end of *swing*? (/ng/) Say it with me: /ng/. The two letters *ng* stand for the sound /ng/ when they are together. What sound do you hear at the end of *skunk*? (/ngk/) Say it with me: /ngk/. The two letters *nk* stand for the sound /ngk/ when they are together.

3 Listen and Write Write the letters *ng* for /ng/ and *nk* for /ngk/. As you write, say each sound to yourself: /ng/, /ngk/. Now say each sound aloud.

Write *ring*.

4 Model The two letters *ng* at the end of this word stand for /ng/. This is how I blend this word: /r/ /i/ /ng/, *ring*. Now you try it: /r/ /i/ /ng/, *ring*.

Write *sank*.

Repeat with *sank*. Point out that *nk* and *ng* will never come at the beginning of a word and will always follow a vowel.

r i n g   s a n k

CORRECTIVE FEEDBACK — Write each practice word. Monitor student practice.

5 Group Practice Let's try the same thing with these words. Give feedback, using the *if . . . then* statements on Routine Card 1.

bang   mink*   hang   tank*   sing   junk

6 Individual Practice Write the words; have each child blend two of them.

wink*   rang   think   rink*   thing   lung*

Check understanding of practice words.

*Children need to make sense of words as they segment and blend. If needed, help children with meanings. A *mink* is a small, furry animal. A *tank* can hold water or gas. When you *wink*, you close and open one eye. (Demonstrate.) A *rink* is the ice that ice skaters use. Your *lung* is the part of your body that holds the air you breathe. (Breathe in and out deeply.)

MORE PRACTICE — Model spelling *ng* and *nk* words.

Spell and Write What sounds do you hear in *bank*? (/b/ /a/ /ngk/) What is the letter for /b/? Let's all write *b*. What is the letter for /a/? Write *a*. What are the letters for /ngk/? Write *nk*. Continue practice as time allows. Have children confirm their spelling by comparing it to what you've written.

pink   sang   king   sunk   thank   wing

High-Frequency Words *afraid, so, surprise, worry*

3 minutes

	To Do	To Say
Teach high-frequency words.	Display *afraid, so, surprise,* and *worry*.	Use the Tested Vocabulary Cards. Point to a word. Say and spell it. Have children say and spell the word. Ask children to identify familiar letter-sounds. Have them take turns reading the words.
Lead cumulative review.		Use the Tested Vocabulary Cards to review high-frequency words from previous weeks.

ACTIVITY 3 Read a Passage

Reading "Franklin Chang-Diaz, Astronaut," pp. 34–41

10–15 minutes

	To Do	**To Say**
Develop language and concepts. **Scaffold instruction.**	See Routine Cards 6 and 7. Display pp. 34–41. Ask questions and elaborate on answers to develop language. Key concepts: *uniform, space, astronaut*	**Before Reading** Have children recall what they learned about space travel. Read the title. Do a structured picture walk with children. **pp. 34–37** What is the man in the first picture wearing? (a spacesuit) **A spacesuit is a uniform that a person wears in space. What is the man's job?** (an astronaut) **What is the boy doing in the other pictures?** (sitting in a box; working in school) **Yes, this boy is pretending to go up in space in a box.** **pp. 38–41** Here are pictures of the same boy and man. Where do you think the man is? (in a spaceship) **What do you think he does there?** (Possible answer: flies the ship; fixes things, just like the boy is fixing a bike) **Yes, astronauts can fly spaceships and fix things on the ship.**
Teach story words.	Write *astronaut* and *space.*	You will read the words *astronaut* and *space* in the selection. Have children say the words and spell them. Review their meanings.
Guide comprehension.	Read pp. 34–41. See Routine Card 2.	**During Reading** Ask children to read along with you. As we read, ask yourself: What am I learning? What is this mainly about? Read pp. 34–37 aloud with the group. Then ask: What is this mainly about so far? (Franklin Chang-Diaz wanted to be an astronaut.) Yes, he had a big wish. Read pp. 38–41 aloud with the group. Then ask: What more did you learn about Franklin Chang-Diaz? (He became an astronaut.) Yes, he got his wish. He learned to fix things. Now he fixes things in space.
Monitor independent reading.	Use Routine Card 3.	**Reread** Have children read the selection aloud together without you. Then have them read it on their own in a whisper. Listen in on each child. Monitor reading, using Routine Card 3.
Model summarizing.	Think aloud.	**After Reading** What did you learn? What was the selection mainly about? Model how to summarize. The first four pages were about how Franklin Chang-Diaz had a wish to become an astronaut. The next pages told how he learned to fix things and became an astronaut. I put that all together and pick the most important ideas. The selection is mainly about how Franklin Chang-Diaz became an astronaut.
MORE PRACTICE	Develop oral vocabulary.	Where does a spaceship go when it *ascends?* when it *descends?* What might astronauts do while their ship *orbits* Earth?

ACTIVITY 4 Write

Response to Literature Shared Writing

5 minutes

	To Do	**To Say**
Guide shared writing.	Write sentence frames. Read the questions.	What was Franklin Chang-Diaz's wish? He wanted to _____. What should you do if you want to be an astronaut? You should _____. Invite children to suggest answers. Discuss and record answers to complete the sentence frames. While writing, model connecting sounds to letters and forming letters (see pp. 257–259). Have children read answers aloud as you track print.
Homework		Practice Book, p. 7, Phonics: *ng*/ng/, *nk*/ngk/

3

ACTIVITY 1 Reread for Fluency

Oral Reading "Franklin Chang-Diaz, Astronaut," pp. 38–39

5–10 minutes

	To Do	To Say
CORRECTIVE FEEDBACK	Monitor oral reading.	Read pp. 38–39 aloud. Read the pages three or four times so your reading gets better each time. Give feedback on children's oral reading and use of the blending strategy. See Routine Cards 1 and 4.
MORE PRACTICE		Instead of rereading just pp. 38–39, have children reread the entire selection three or four times. You may want to have children read along with the AudioText.

ACTIVITY 2 Word Work

Phonemic Awareness Blend Sounds

2 minutes

	To Do	To Say
Scaffold instruction.	Distribute white boards. Write *is*.	**Model** For this word, the sound for *i* is /i/ and the sound for *s* is /z/. Listen as I blend the sounds together. Stretch the sounds /iii/ /zzz/ as you write *i, s*. Repeat. This time have children write the letters as you write. What is the word? *(is)*
	Write *pink*. Lead children in blending sounds.	**Teach and Practice** Have children blend sounds for *p, i, nk*. (/p/ /i/ /ngk/) What is the word? *(pink)* Continue with these words:
		it fix sink sing

Fluent Word Reading Short *i, ng*/ng/, *nk*/ngk/

5–10 minutes

	To Do	To Say
Use the word-reading routine. **Scaffold instruction.**	Write *fig*.	**1 Connect** You can read this word because you know that *i* can stand for /i/. What sound does *i* stand for in this word? (/i/) What's the word? *(fig)* A *fig* is a small, sweet fruit.
	Write *pick, bang,* and *sink*.	**2 Model** When you come to a new word, look at all the letters in the word and think about its vowel sound. Say the sounds in the word to yourself, and then read the word. Model reading *pick, bang,* and *sink* in this way. When you come to a new word, what are you going to do?
	Write each practice word.	**3 Group Practice** Let's read these words. Look at all the letters, think about the vowel sound, and say the letter-sounds to yourself. We will read words with short *i, ng,* and *nk*. When I point to the word, let's read it together. Allow 2–3 seconds previewing time for each word.
		pit lick gang bank pig Rick sank hang think
CORRECTIVE FEEDBACK	**MONITOR PROGRESS**	*If . . .* children have difficulty previewing and reading whole words, *then . . .* have them use sound-by-sound blending.
		If . . . children can't read the words fluently at a rate of 1–2 seconds per word, *then . . .* continue practicing the list.

Routine

| **MORE PRACTICE** | Model reading words in sentences. | When I read a sentence, I read each word without stopping between the words. If I come to a word I don't know, I blend it. Then I read the sentence again. Model reading this sentence, stopping to blend *bank: It is a big bank.* |
| | Write practice sentences. | Have each child read a sentence.

Rick sang a song.
I have a pink wig.
I think that is Frank. |

High-Frequency Words *afraid, so, surprise, worry*

To Do   **To Say**   *3 minutes*

| **Review high-frequency words.** | Display *afraid, so, surprise,* and *worry.* | Use the Tested Vocabulary Cards. Point to a word. Say and spell it. Have children say and spell the word. Ask children to identify familiar letter-sounds. Have them take turns reading the words. |

ACTIVITY 3 Build Concepts

Oral Vocabulary *journey, universe*

To Do   **To Say**   *5–10 minutes*

Teach oral vocabulary.	Display p. 42 of the student book.	Today you will read about how some children found a space rock that took a *journey* to Earth from another part of the *universe.*	*Routine*
	Follow the Routine to teach *journey* and *universe.*	**1 Introduce, Demonstrate, and Apply**	
		journey In this story, children find a rock that took a *journey* through space. A *journey* is a long trip. Have children say the word. When a family drives for several days to go somewhere, they go on a *journey.* Have you ever gone on a *journey* with your family? Where did you go?	
		universe The space rock in the story is part of the *universe.* The *universe* is made up of everything there is. Have children say the word. The *universe* includes Earth, the Sun, the moon, and all the other planets and stars in the sky. Are trees and grass part of the *universe?* What else makes up the *universe?*	
	Display the words on the Amazing Words board.	**2 Display the Words** Have children say each word as they look at it. You can find sounds you know in big words. What letter do you see at the beginning of *journey? (j)* What sound does it make? (/j/) Point to the *n* in *journey.* What sound does *n* make? (/n/) Read *u/ni/verse* as you run your hand under the syllables. Children can identify /n/, /v/, and /s/.	
	Monitor understanding.	**3 Use the Words** Ask children to use each word in a sentence. Model a sentence if children need help.	
MORE PRACTICE		Use oral vocabulary to discuss outer space. Who takes a *journey* to outer space in a spaceship? What might an astronaut explore in the *universe?*	

ACTIVITY 4 Read a Passage

Reading "It Fell from Space," pp. 42–49

	To Do	To Say	10 minutes

Teach main idea.

Scaffold instruction.

Introduce the skill.

Model the skill. Display p. 16 of the student book.

Apply the skill.

Today you are going to learn how to find the main idea of a story. The main idea is the most important idea. As you read, ask yourself what the whole story is all about. For example, I can find the main idea of the story "Blue Jack" that we read last week. I think about what happened in the story and decide on the most important idea. Jack and Dad bought food and ate a snack. They talked to Mack. What is the story all about? It is about Jack and Dad doing different things together as they visited shops.

Listen to this short story. What is it all about? A family moves in to a new home. The family has a mom and two children. They paint the house blue. What is the main idea of this story? (A family moves.)

Develop language and concepts.

See Routine Card 6. Display pp. 42–49.

Model using key words and concepts.

Key concepts: *twins, chunk, crust, surprise, space*

Monitor children's use of vocabulary.

Before Reading Read the title. Do a structured picture walk.

pp. 42–25 On p. 42, a dad is talking to his sons. What do you notice about his sons? They look alike because they are twins. Twins are brothers or sisters born at the same time.

pp. 46–47 What did the children find? (a rock) Yes, they found a chunk of rock, a big piece from an even bigger rock. What is the rock like? It has a black crust. A crust is a hard outside covering.

pp. 48–49 The twins show the rock to their dad. Look at their faces. They look surprised. Why? (The rock is from space.) I would be surprised to find a space rock too!

Now turn to your partner and talk about the pictures, using the same words I did.

Teach story words.

Write *space.*

You will read this word in the story. It is *space.* Have children say the word and spell it. Review its meaning.

Guide comprehension.

Read pp. 42–49. Use Routine Card 2.

During Reading Ask children to read along with you. As we read, ask yourself: What is the story all about? Read pp. 42–45 aloud with the group. Then ask: What is the most important idea of these pages? (Mick and Rick and their friends find a rock in a pit while they pick up sticks and twigs.)

Read pp. 46–47 aloud with the group. Then ask: What did the children do with the rock? (They ran to ask Dad about it.)

Read pp. 48–49 aloud with the group. Then ask: Where did the big rock come from? (outer space) What is the story all about? (Mick, Rick, and their friends find a space rock.)

Monitor independent reading.

Use Routine Card 3.

Reread Have children read the selection aloud together without you. Then have them read it on their own in a whisper. Listen in on each child. Monitor reading, using Routine Card 3.

Guide retelling.

Prompt children as they retell the story.

After Reading Have one child retell the story while the others assist. What did the children go to pick up? (sticks and twigs) What surprising thing happened instead? (They found a space rock.) See Monitor Retelling, p. 246.

Homework Practice Book, p. 8, Main Idea

ACTIVITY **1** Reread for Fluency

Paired Reading "It Fell from Space," pp. 44–45

5–10 minutes

	To Do	To Say
CORRECTIVE FEEDBACK	Pair children. Monitor paired reading.	Children read pp. 44–45 orally, switching readers at the end of the first page. Have partners reread; now the other partner begins. For optimal fluency, children should reread three or four times. Give feedback on children's oral reading and use of the blending strategy. See Routine Cards 1 and 4.
MORE PRACTICE		Instead of rereading just pp. 44–45, have children reread the entire selection three or four times. You may want to have children read along with the AudioText.

ACTIVITY **2** Word Work

Spiral Review Consonant Letter-Sounds

5–10 minutes

	To Do	To Say
Review consonant letter-sounds. **Scaffold instruction.**	Write *pass.*	You can read this word because you know how to read words that end with two letters that are the same. What sound do the two *s*'s stand for? (/s/) Now blend *p, a, ss.* What is the word? *(pass)*
	Write *pick, king,* and *sink.*	You can read these words because you know how to read words that end with *ck, ng,* and *nk.* Each pair of letters stands for one sound. What sound does *ck* stand for? (/k/) What sound does *ng* stand for? (/ng/) What sound does *nk* stand for? (/ngk/) Now say the sounds in each word to yourself and read the words. Have children read each word aloud as you point to it.
	Provide letter tiles *a, c, i, g, k, l, l, n, s,* and *w.*	**Build Words** Write *will.* Can you blend this word? (/w/ /i/ /l/, *will*) Spell *will* with letter tiles. Now change the *ll* in *will* to *nk.* What is the new word? *(wink)* • Change the *k* in *wink* to *g.* What is the new word? *(wing)* • Change the *w* in *wing* to *s.* What is the new word? *(sing)* • Change the *i* in *sing* to *a.* What is the new word? *(sang)* • Change the *ng* in *sang* to *ck.* What is the new word? *(sack)*
CORRECTIVE FEEDBACK	**MONITOR PROGRESS**	**If . . .** children have difficulty reading the new words, **then . . .** have them use sound-by-sound blending.
MORE PRACTICE	Model reading words in sentences.	When I read a sentence, I read each word without stopping between the words. If I come to a word I don't know, I blend it. Then I read the sentence again. Model reading this sentence, stopping to blend *Hank* and *sang: Nick and Hank sang on the hill.*
	Write practice sentences.	Have each child read a sentence. Give a pill to the sick pig. Rick and Jill thank the king. I will win the pink ring.
Phonological and Phonemic Awareness		Optional practice activities, pp. 280–283.

4

ACTIVITY 3 Read Together

Choral Reading "What Would You Wear in Outer Space?" p. 50

	To Do	**To Say**	*10 minutes*
Develop language and concepts.	Display p. 50.	**Before Reading** This astronaut is standing on the moon. What have you learned about astronauts exploring outer space? (Allow children to share what they know.) Why must astronauts wear spacesuits on the moon? Share information about astronauts and spacesuits. An astronaut needs a special spacesuit to breathe and walk on the moon.	
Model fluent reading.		Read the title of the selection. Ask children to predict what it is about. Listen as I read the sentences in this box. Point out the question marks. Notice how my voice changes when I ask a question. Read the questions, raising your voice at the end of each sentence. Read them a second time, having children point to each word. These other words name the parts of the spacesuit. Point to each word as you say it. Have children repeat each word.	
	Build fluency through choral reading.	**Choral Reading** Now read the questions aloud with me. Try to make your voice sound like mine as we read. Reread the questions several times with children.	
Develop concepts.	Monitor listening comprehension.	**After Reading** What are the different parts of a spacesuit? Why do you think an astronaut needs a helmet and a visor? Why does he or she need boots? What could be in the MMU?	

ACTIVITY 4 Build Concepts

Oral Vocabulary *ascend, descend, journey, orbit, universe*

	To Do	**To Say**	*5–10 minutes*
Review oral vocabulary.	Read the words on the Amazing Words board.	**Focus on Letter-Sounds** Remember, you can find sounds you know in big words. • Which word begins with *d?* Which word begins with *j?* • Which word ends with *t?* • Which words have the letters *scend* in them?	
	Encourage discussion.	**Provide One Context for All the Words** Review the meanings of the words. Then ask questions to show relationships between words by placing them in a single context. • What would an astronaut ride in to *ascend* to space? • How does a spaceship travel when it *orbits* the moon? To what other places in the *universe* might an astronaut take a *journey?* • How might an astronaut feel when the spaceship begins to *descend* back to Earth? How do you think you might feel?	
MORE PRACTICE	Apply oral vocabulary to new situations.	• If you climb up a ladder, do you *ascend, descend,* or *orbit* the ladder? (ascend) If you slide down a slide, do you *ascend, descend,* or *orbit* the slide? (descend) • If you take a train ride to visit a city, do you take a *journey* or a *universe?* (journey) If you look up at the sky at night, do you see parts of a *journey* or the *universe?* (universe)	

ACTIVITY 5 | Write

Response to Literature Interactive Writing

| To Do | To Say | *5–10 minutes* |

Generate ideas.

Share the pen.

To Do	To Say
Review the story "It Fell from Space."	**What did the children find? What did it look like? Where did it come from?** Discuss characteristics of the rock the children found.
Have children participate in writing questions about the rock and some answers they learned from the story.	Write a word or words to begin each question, such as *Where* and *What color.* Have children read the words you wrote and supply endings to complete the questions. Then write words to begin each answer, and have children suggest the endings. Invite individuals to write familiar letter-sounds, word parts, and high-frequency words. Have them find the spelling of high-frequency words on the Word Wall. Ask questions such as: • **What is the first sound in** *rock?* (/r/) **What is the letter for /r/?** *(r)* • **What is the vowel sound in** *rock?* (/o/) **What is the letter for /o/?** *(o)* • **What is the last sound in** *rock?* (/k/) **What two letters stand for /k/?** *(ck)*
Writing elements: conventions	Frequently reread what has been written while tracking the print. Point out that each question ends with a question mark. The answers end with a period. Point out the extra space between words. Read the completed list of questions and answers aloud, having children read with you. (For example, *Where did the rock come from? It came from space. What color was the rock? The rock was black.*)

MORE PRACTICE

| Prompt independent writing. | **Journal Writing** Tell about other things you think can be found in space. |

Homework   Practice Book, p. 9, High-Frequency Words

ACTIVITY 1 — Assessment Options

Sentence Reading

To Do	To Say

5 minutes

Assess sentence reading.

Use reproducible p. 247.

Have each child read the sentences. Record scores on the Sentence Reading Chart, p. 252. Work with one child as others complete Write Sentences below.

Ling is afraid Tim will worry.
That fish tank is so big!
I think the bang was a surprise.

CORRECTIVE FEEDBACK

MONITOR PROGRESS

If . . . children have trouble reading words with *i*/i/, *ng*/ng/, or *nk*/ngk/,
then . . . reteach the blending strategy lessons on pp. 20 and 24.

If . . . children cannot read a high-frequency word,
then . . . mark the missed word or words on a high-frequency word list and send the list home for additional practice or have them practice with a fluent reader.

If . . . children misread a word in the sentence,
then . . . correct the error and have them reread the word and then the sentence.

Practice sentence writing.

Provide white boards.

Write Sentences Have children copy the sentences from reproducible p. 247 on white boards. Have them confirm spellings by comparing the words they wrote to the words in the sentences.

Phonological and Phonemic Awareness

Optional practice activities, pp. 280–283

Passage Reading

To Do	To Say

5–10 minutes

Assess fluency and comprehension.

Determine which children to assess this week.

Choose from these options: monitoring fluency (see pp. 244–245) and/or monitoring retelling (see p. 246). Have children reread "It Fell from Space." Be sure each child is assessed every other week.

If you have time, assess every child.

ACTIVITY 2 — Use Concepts

Oral Vocabulary *ascend, descend, journey, orbit, universe*

To Do	To Say

5 minutes

Check understanding of oral vocabulary.

Use the Amazing Words to wrap up the week's concept.

Monitor understanding of oral vocabulary, using Routine Card 5.

As time allows, ask questions such as these.

- Describe the pictures on pp. 28–33 using some of the week's Amazing Words.
- Describe one way to *ascend* to the top floor of a very tall building. How might you *descend* from the top of a mountain?
- What other things besides Earth *orbit* the Sun?
- If you could go on a *journey* to another country, where would you go? Why?
- Are people part of the *universe?* Are animals? What about stars and planets?

Preview next week's concept.

Next week you will read about things you may discover in the woods.

ACTIVITY 3 Read to Connect

Reread "Outer Space," pp. 28–33

To Do	To Say	*10 minutes*

Monitor comprehension: main idea.

Have children reread "Outer Space" silently.

A topic is what a selection is all about. The title may help you find the topic. As you read, think about the topic of the selection and the most important idea about this topic. After rereading, ask:

- In a word or two, what is the topic of this selection? What is this all about?
- What is the most important idea, or main idea, about outer space?
- What are some things astronauts do and find on the moon?

Record children's answers to the last question on the board. (For example: astronauts walk on the moon, they find rocks, they find thick dust.) Children will use the list for Activity 4.

Make connections.

Have children make connections across texts.

We also read "Franklin Chang-Diaz, Astronaut." Find that. What did you learn about how someone becomes an astronaut? Write "an astronaut's job" in the center of a word web and record children's responses.

We also read "It Fell from Space." How did the characters feel when they found a space rock on Earth? How would it feel to find a rock on the moon?

What did all the selections we read this week show us about outer space? What is the big idea? (Exploring outer space can be exciting and surprising.)

ACTIVITY 4 Write

Response to Literature Independent Writing

To Do	To Say	*5–10 minutes*

Assign personal narrative.

Today you will imagine that you are an astronaut going to the moon. Write about the things you would find and do on your trip. Encourage children to use words you wrote on the board for Activity 3 as they write. Suggest they make the first sentence tell the main idea, using this sentence frame: *A trip to the moon is _____.*

Guide sentence correction.

Writing elements: conventions, focus

Have children check their writing by asking themselves these questions.

- Did I put an extra space between words?
- Did I begin each sentence with a capital letter and end each sentence with a period?
- Are all my sentences about going to the moon?

MORE PRACTICE

Have children share their sentences with the group. Write their sentences on the board and have children practice reading and writing each other's sentences.

Homework   Practice Book, p. 10, Writing

Unit 1 Week 3 *Out in the Woods*

What can we discover by exploring nature?

Objectives *This week students will...*

Phonemic Awareness
- blend sounds in words
- add initial or final sound

Phonics
- blend and read words with short *o* and consonant blends
- apply knowledge of letter-sounds to decode unknown words when reading
- recognize high-frequency words *answer, different, ever, learn*

Fluency
- practice fluency with oral rereading

Vocabulary
- build concepts and oral vocabulary: *camouflage, galaxy, mammal, tranquil, wildlife*

Text Comprehension
- read connected text
- identify main idea to improve comprehension
- write in response to literature

Word Work *This week's phonics focus is . . .*

Short *o*   Consonant Blends

High-Frequency Words *Tested Vocabulary*

The first appearance of each word in the Student Reader is noted below.

answer	An **answer** is what is said when a question is asked. (p. 55)
different	When two things are **different,** they are not alike. (p. 56)
ever	Is he **ever** at home? (p. 57)
learn	If you **learn** something, you find out about it. (p. 57)

Amazing Words *Oral Vocabulary*

The week's vocabulary is related to the concept of exploring nature.

camouflage	the shapes, colors, and patterns that help animals blend in with things around them
galaxy	a very large group of stars
mammal	an animal with a backbone and fur or hair; baby mammals drink milk from their mother's body
tranquil	calm, peaceful, and quiet
wildlife	wild animals and plants

Student Reader Unit 1 *This week students will read the following selections.*

Daily Lesson Plan

	ACTIVITIES	MATERIALS
Day 1	**Word Work** Phonemic Awareness: Blend Sounds Phonics: Blend Words with Short *o* High-Frequency Words *answer, different, ever, learn* **Build Concepts** *galaxy, tranquil, wildlife* **Read a Passage** "Out in the Woods," pp. 54–57 Comprehension: Use Strategies Reread for Fluency	Student White Boards Sound-Spelling Card 23 Tested Vocabulary Cards *Sing with Me Big Book* and Audio CD Student Reader: Unit 1 Routine Cards 1, 2, 3, 4, 6, 7 AudioText Practice Book, p. 11, Short *o*
Day 2	**Reread for Fluency** **Word Work** Phonemic Awareness: Add Initial or Final Sound Phonics: Blend Words with Consonant Blends High-Frequency Words *answer, different, ever, learn* **Read a Passage** "Can You See Them?" pp. 58–61 Comprehension: Use Strategies **Write** Response to Literature: Shared Writing	Student Reader: Unit 1 AudioText Student White Boards Tested Vocabulary Cards Routine Cards 1, 2, 3, 4, 6, 7 Practice Book, p. 12, Consonant Blends
Day 3	**Reread for Fluency** **Word Work** Phonemic Awareness: Blend Sounds Phonics: Fluent Word Reading High-Frequency Words *answer, different, ever, learn* **Build Concepts** *camouflage, mammal* **Read a Passage** "Lost in the Woods," pp. 62–69 Comprehension: Main Idea	Student Reader: Unit 1 AudioText Student White Boards Tested Vocabulary Cards Routine Cards 1, 2, 3, 4, 6 Practice Book, p. 13, Main Idea and Supporting Details
Day 4	**Reread for Fluency** **Word Work** Phonics: Spiral Review Phonological and Phonemic Awareness Activities, pp. 280–283 **Read Together** "Let's Make Trail Mix," p. 70 Comprehension: Listening **Build Concepts** *camouflage, galaxy, mammal, tranquil, wildlife* **Write** Response to Literature: Interactive Writing	Student Reader: Unit 1 AudioText Routine Cards 1, 4 Student White Boards Practice Book, p. 14, High-Frequency Words
Day 5	**Assessment Options** Fluency, Comprehension Sentence Reading; Mid-Unit Passage Reading Phonological and Phonemic Awareness Activities, pp. 280–283 **Use Concepts** *camouflage, galaxy, mammal, tranquil, wildlife* **Read to Connect** "Out in the Woods," pp. 54–57 Comprehension: Main Idea **Write** Response to Literature: Independent Writing	Reproducible p. 247 Sentence Reading Chart, p. 252 Student White Boards Assessment Book, p. 79 Fluency Progress Chart, p. 245 Student Reader: Unit 1 Routine Card 5 Practice Book, p. 15, Writing

See pp. xvi–xvii for how *My Sidewalks* integrates instructional practices for ELL.

ACTIVITY **1** Word Work

Phonemic Awareness Blend Sounds

To Do	To Say	

2 minutes

Scaffold instruction.

Distribute white boards.
Write *log*.

Write *fox*.
Lead children in blending sounds as they write.

Model Listen as I blend the sounds for *l, o, g.* Stretch the sounds /lll/ /ooo/ /g/ as you write *l, o, g.* Repeat. This time have children write the letters as you write. **What is the word?** *(log)*

Teach and Practice Have children blend the sounds for *f, o, x* as you point to the letters. (/f/ /o/ /x/) **What is the word?** *(fox)* Continue blending sounds to form these words:

pot   top   not   hop   doll   rock

Blending Strategy Short *o*

To Do	To Say	

5–10 minutes

Routine

Use the blending routine.

Write *cat* and *hat*.

1 Connect You already can read words like these. **What are the words? What is the vowel sound in** *cat?* (/a/) **in** *hat?* (/a/) Now let's look at another vowel sound.

Display Sound-Spelling Card 23.

2 Use Sound-Spelling Card This is an octopus. **What sound do you hear at the beginning of** *octopus?* (/o/) Say it with me: /o/. In *octopus,* the first letter *o* stands for the sound /o/.

3 Listen and Write Write the letter *o* for /o/. As you write, say the sound to yourself: /o/. Now say the sound aloud.

Scaffold instruction.

Write *hot*.

4 Model The letter *o* stands for /o/. This is how I blend this word: /h/ /o/ /t/, *hot.* Now you try: /h/ /o/ /t/, *hot.*

Point out that when *o* is the only vowel at the beginning or in the middle of a word, it usually stands for its short sound, /o/.

$$\underset{\longrightarrow}{h} \ \underset{\longrightarrow}{o} \ \underset{\longrightarrow}{t}$$

CORRECTIVE FEEDBACK

Write each practice word.
Monitor student practice.

5 Group Practice Let's try the same thing with these words. Give feedback, using the *if . . . then* statements on Routine Card 1.

mom   box   job   mop   nod*   lock

6 Individual Practice Write the words; have each child blend two of them.

got   rob*   cot*   Bob   sock   dock*

Check understanding of practice words.

*Children need to make sense of words that they segment and blend. If needed, help children with meanings. When you *nod,* you move your head up and down a little bit. (Demonstrate.) When people *rob,* they take things that don't belong to them. A *cot* is a bed that folds up. A *dock* is a place near the water where you can sit or stand. (Point to the dock on p. 55.)

MORE PRACTICE

Model spelling short *o* words.

Spell and Write What sounds do you hear in *hot?* (/h/ /o/ /t/) What is the letter for /h/? Let's all write *h.* What is the letter for /o/? Write *o.* What is the letter for /t/? Write *t.* Continue practice as time allows. Have children confirm their spelling by comparing it to what you've written.

dot   pop   sob   fog   ox   rock

High-Frequency Words *answer, different, ever, learn*

	To Do	To Say
Teach high-frequency words.	Display *answer*.	**1 Say, Spell, Write** Use the Tested Vocabulary Cards. Display *answer*. Here are some words that we won't sound out. We'll spell them. This word is *answer: a, n, s, w, e, r* (point to each letter), *answer.* What is this word? What are the letters in the word? Now you write *answer.*
	Point to the first three letters in *answer*.	**2 Identify Letter-Sounds** Let's look at the sounds in *answer* that you do know. What are these letters? (*a, n, s*) Now let's blend the letters together. *(ans)*
		3 Demonstrate Meaning Tell me a sentence using *answer.* Model a sentence if children need help.
	Display *different, ever,* and *learn*.	Repeat the Routine with *different, ever,* and *learn.* Children can identify these letter-sounds and word parts: *different* (dif, ent), *ever* (ev), *learn* (/l/, /n/). Have children write the words in their word banks. Add the words to the Word Wall.

Routine

ACTIVITY **2** Build Concepts

Oral Vocabulary *galaxy, tranquil, wildlife*

	To Do	To Say
Introduce oral vocabulary. **Scaffold instruction.**	Display p. 3 of *Sing with Me Big Book.* Play audio CD.	This week you will learn about exploring nature. Listen for the Amazing Words *galaxy, tranquil,* and *wildlife* as I sing this song. Play or sing the song. Then have children sing it with you.
	Follow the Routine to teach *galaxy, tranquil,* and *wildlife.*	**1 Introduce, Demonstrate, and Apply**
		galaxy In the song, the campers look at a *galaxy.* A *galaxy* is a very large group of stars. Have children say the word. You need a spaceship to travel across a *galaxy.* Would it be better to study a *galaxy* during the day or at night? Why?
		tranquil The nights are *tranquil. Tranquil* means calm, peaceful, and quiet. Have children say the word. Places can be *tranquil* and so can people. I am *tranquil* when I sit on a log in the woods. I am *tranquil* when I see a beautiful sunset. What makes you *tranquil?*
		wildlife The campers hope to see deer and other kinds of *wildlife.* Wild animals and plants are *wildlife.* There are many kinds of *wildlife.* Fish, squirrels, lions, bushes, and trees are all examples of *wildlife.* Have children say the word. Animals that are *wildlife* are not tame animals, like pets. You can see *wildlife* in the woods or at the zoo. You can even find *wildlife* in your own neighborhood. What kinds of *wildlife* live or grow near your home?
	Display the words on the Amazing Words board.	**2 Display the Words** Have children say each word as they look at it. You can find sounds you know in big words. Read *tran/quil* as you run your hand under the syllables. Can you find the *a?* What sound does the *a* make? (/a/) For *galaxy* and *wildlife,* children can identify these letter-sounds and word parts: *galaxy* (gal), *wildlife* (w/w/, ld/ld/, f/f/).
	Monitor understanding.	**3 Use the Words** Ask children to use each word in a sentence. Model a sentence if children need help.

Routine

MORE PRACTICE

Use oral vocabulary to discuss the song. How can you tell that the night described in the song is *tranquil?* Can you count all the stars in a *galaxy?* What kind of *wildlife* do the campers in the song hope to see?

ACTIVITY 3 Read a Passage

Build Background "Out in the Woods," pp. 54–57

	To Do	**To Say**	10 minutes

Develop language and concepts.

See Routine Card 7. Read aloud p. 53 of the student book.

Preview the Week Read aloud the titles and descriptions on p. 53. **The selections this week are all about the woods and what you can find there.** Use pp. 52–53 to preview the selections. Ask children what they think each selection will be about.

Scaffold instruction.

See Routine Card 6. Display pp. 54–57.

Ask questions and elaborate on answers to develop language.

Key concepts: *logs, campfire, ducks, wildlife, frogs, fish, pond, bugs, foxes*

Before Reading Read the title aloud. Do a structured picture walk with children.

pp. 54–55 Where are the children on p. 54? (in the woods) What are they doing? (cooking over a fire) Yes, when you go camping, you burn logs to make a campfire. You can cook food over a campfire. What do you see in the top picture on p. 55? (ducks) Yes, big and little ducks are kinds of wildlife you can see at a pond in the woods. Frogs and fish live in ponds. What else might the children see at the pond? (trees, water, dock)

pp. 56–57 What animals do you see in the pictures? (bugs, a fox) Yes, bugs and foxes can make their homes in logs. When do you think the picture on p. 57 was taken? (at night) Yes, it was taken at night because it shows stars. It is easier to see stars at night in the woods away from city lights. Let's read to find out more about what is in the woods.

Guide comprehension.

Read pp. 54–57.

Model strategic reading. Use Routine Card 2.

During Reading Ask children to read along with you. **As we read, ask yourself: What did I learn about the woods? What is this mainly about?** Read pp. 54–57 aloud with the group. Stop on each page to model asking questions. For example, for p. 55: After I read, I ask myself: What is this mainly about? The author says, "Lots of frogs, fish, and ducks swim in this pond." I think this page is mainly about animals that live in a pond.

Monitor independent reading.

Use Routine Card 3.

Reread Have children read the selection aloud together without you. Then have them read it on their own in a whisper. Listen in on each child. Monitor reading, using Routine Card 3.

Summarize.

Use oral vocabulary to develop the concept.

After Reading What did you learn about the *wildlife* that live or grow in the woods? What can people see and do when they camp in the woods? Would you feel *tranquil* watching *wildlife* near a pond or looking at a *galaxy* of stars? Why?

Reread for Fluency "Out in the Woods," pp. 54–55

	To Do	**To Say**	5–10 minutes

CORRECTIVE FEEDBACK

Monitor oral reading.

Read pp. 54–55 aloud. Read them three or four times so your reading gets better each time. Give feedback on children's oral reading and use of the blending strategy. See Routine Cards 1 and 4.

MORE PRACTICE

Instead of rereading just pp. 54–55, have children reread the entire selection three or four times. You may want to have children read along with the AudioText.

Homework

Practice Book, p. 11, Phonics: Short *o*

ACTIVITY 1 Reread for Fluency

Paired Reading "Out in the Woods," pp. 56–57

To Do	To Say	5–10 minutes

CORRECTIVE FEEDBACK

To Do: Pair children. Monitor paired reading.

To Say: Children read pp. 56–57 orally, switching readers at the end of the first page. Have partners reread; now the other partner begins. For optimal fluency, children should reread three or four times. Give feedback on children's oral reading and use of the blending strategy. See Routine Cards 1 and 4.

MORE PRACTICE

Instead of rereading just pp. 56–57, have children reread the entire selection three or four times. You may want to have children read along with the AudioText.

ACTIVITY 2 Word Work

Phonemic Awareness Add Initial or Final Sound

To Do	To Say	2 minutes

Scaffold instruction.

To Do: Distribute white boards. Write *top*. Add *s* to form *stop*.

Model Listen as I blend the sounds for *t, o, p.* Stretch the sounds /t/ /ooo/ /p/ as you write *t, o, p.* Repeat. This time have children write the letters as you write. **What is the word?** *(top)* Now I'll add /s/ to the beginning of *top*. Write *s* to form *stop*, and stretch the sounds /sss/ /t/ /ooo/ /p/ as you point to each letter. Repeat. This time have children add *s* to *top* along with you. **What is the new word we just made?** *(stop)*

To Do: Write *win*. Add *d* to form *wind*. Lead children in adding sounds to form new words.

Teach and Practice Blend the sounds for *w, i, n.* (/w/ /i/ /n/) **What is the word?** *(win)* Now let's add the letter for /d/ to the end of *win*. Blend the sounds for *w, i, n, d.* (/w/ /i/ /n/ /d/) **What is the new word?** *(wind)* Continue the activity with these words:

pot/spot   ram/ramp   lip/flip   rag/drag   lit/slit   tan/stand

Blending Strategy Consonant Blends

	To Do	To Say	
			5–10 minutes

Routine

Use the blending routine.

Write *cap* and *lap*.

1 Connect You can read words like these already. What are the words? (*cap, lap*) What consonant is at the beginning of *cap*? (*c*) at the beginning of *lap*? (*l*) Today we are learning about consonants whose sounds are blended together in words.

Scaffold instruction.

Write *clap*.

2 Model This word begins with two consonants, *c* and *l*. We blend these two consonant sounds together to read the word. Listen as I blend the sounds for *c, l, a, p*: /k/ /l/ /a/ /p/, *clap*. Now you try it: /k/ /l/ /a/ /p/, *clap*.

Write *camp*.

Repeat with *camp*. Point out that consonant blends can come at the beginning or end of a word.

Write *scrap*.

Repeat with *scrap*. Point out that some words have three consonants blended together. Also point out that children can blend words by saying the sounds before the vowel together, saying the sounds of all the rest of the letters together, and then blending the two chunks.

c l a p   c a m p   s c r a p

3 Listen and Write What sounds do you hear at the beginning of the word *clap*? (/k/ /l/). Blend these two sounds with me: /kl/. Write the letters for /kl/. (*cl*) As you write, say the blended sounds to yourself: /kl/. Now say the sounds aloud.

CORRECTIVE FEEDBACK

Write each practice word. Monitor student practice.

4 Group Practice Let's blend consonant sounds to read the words. Give feedback, using the *if . . . then* statements on Routine Card 1.

twig*   fast   swim   pond   string   stomp*

5 Individual Practice Write the words; have each child blend two of them.

frog   mask*   grass   stick   drink   spring   splash*   plant

Check understanding of practice words.

*Children need to make sense of words as they segment and blend. If needed, help children with meanings. A *twig* is a very small tree branch. When you *stomp*, you bring your foot down hard. (Demonstrate.) A *mask* hides or protects your face. When you *splash*, you make water or another liquid fly in the air.

MORE PRACTICE

Model spelling words with consonant blends.

Spell and Write What sounds do you hear in *band*? (/b/ /a/ /n/ d/) What is the letter for /b/? Let's all write *b*. What is the letter for /a/? Write *a*. What are the letters for /nd/? Write *nd*. Continue practice as time allows. Have children confirm their spelling by comparing it to what you've written.

land   twin   lost   grab   clock   strip   stamp

High-Frequency Words *answer, different, ever, learn*

	To Do	To Say	
			3 minutes

Teach high-frequency words.

Display *answer, different, ever,* and *learn*.

Use the Tested Vocabulary Cards. Point to a word. Say and spell it. Have children say and spell the word. Ask children to identify familiar letter-sounds. Have them take turns reading the words.

Lead cumulative review.

Use the Tested Vocabulary Cards to review high-frequency words from previous weeks.

ACTIVITY 3 Read a Passage

Reading "Can You See Them?" pp. 58–61

	To Do	**To Say**	*10–15 minutes*

Develop language and concepts.

See Routine Cards 6 and 7. Display pp. 58–61.

Ask questions and elaborate on answers to develop language.

Scaffold instruction.

Key concepts: *wildlife, blend, big cat, fox, prey*

Before Reading Have children recall what they learned about wildlife in the woods. Read the title. Do a structured picture walk with children.

pp. 58–59 What kinds of wildlife do you see? (bug, frog) Why are the animals hard to see? (They blend in.) Right, the bug looks like the twig it rests on. The frog is covered with mud. The animals' shapes and colors help them blend in with the things around them.

pp. 60–61 Why is the big cat hard to see? (It is hiding in grass.) Yes, the big cat's color is like the grass so it blends in with it. Would a red fox be easy or hard to see in the snow? Why? (It would be easy because red fur does not blend in with white snow.) Why might animals try to hide? (They're scared.) Yes, a scared animal might hide so others can't see it. Big cats might hide to help them hunt prey.

Guide comprehension.

Read pp. 58–61. See Routine Card 2.

During Reading Ask children to read along with you. As we read, ask yourself: What am I learning about wildlife? What is this selection mainly about? Read pp. 58–59 aloud with the group. Then ask: What is this mainly about so far? (A bug and a frog hide.) Yes, they hide by blending in. Let's read to find more animals that blend in.

Read pp. 60–61 aloud with the group. Then ask: What makes these animals blend in? (They look like the things near them.) Yes, their shapes and colors help them blend in with their surroundings.

Monitor independent reading.

Use Routine Card 3.

Reread Have children read the selection aloud together without you. Then have them read it on their own in a whisper. Listen in on each child. Monitor reading, using Routine Card 3.

Model summarizing.

Think aloud.

After Reading What did you learn about how wildlife hides? What was the selection mainly about? Model how to summarize. The first two pages showed animals using their shapes and colors to hide. The next pages showed other animals that blend in. I put that all together. The selection is mainly about how animals' shapes and colors help them blend in with things around them.

MORE PRACTICE

Develop oral vocabulary.

How can *wildlife* hide? If a plane flew across a *galaxy* of stars, would you see it better if it had red or white lights? Would you be *tranquil* if a stick bug suddenly moved on a twig you were holding?

ACTIVITY 4 Write

Response to Literature Shared Writing

	To Do	**To Say**	*5 minutes*

Guide shared writing.

Write sentence frames.

Read the questions.

Where can a frog hide? A frog can hide in _____. Why are the animals hard to see? The animals are hard to see because they _____. Invite children to suggest answers. Discuss and record answers to complete the sentence frames. While writing, model connecting sounds to letters and forming letters (see pp. 257–259). Have children read answers aloud as you track print.

Homework Practice Book, p. 12, Phonics: Consonant Blends

ACTIVITY 1 Reread for Fluency

Oral Reading "Can You See Them?" pp. 58–59

	To Do	**To Say**	
			5–10 minutes
CORRECTIVE FEEDBACK	Monitor oral reading.	Read pp. 58–59 aloud. Read them three or four times so your reading gets better each time. Give feedback on children's oral reading and use of the blending strategy. See Routine Cards 1 and 4.	
MORE PRACTICE		Instead of rereading just pp. 58–59, have children reread the entire selection three or four times. You may want to have children read along with the AudioText.	

ACTIVITY 2 Word Work

Phonemic Awareness Blend Sounds

	To Do	**To Say**	
			2 minutes
Scaffold instruction.	Distribute white boards. Write *mop*.	**Model** Listen as I blend the sounds for *m, o, p*. Stretch the sounds /mmm/ /ooo/ /p/ as you write *m, o, p*. Repeat. This time have children write the letters as you write. What is the word? *(mop)*	
	Lead children in blending sounds as they write.	**Teach and Practice** Blend the sounds for *s, p, o, t* together. (/s/ /p/ /o/ /t/) What is the word? *(spot)* Continue the activity with these words:	
		hop shop lots pond lost block	

Fluent Word Reading Short *o*, Consonant Blends

	To Do	**To Say**	
			5–10 minutes
Use the blending routine.	Write *drop*.	**1 Connect** You can read this word because you know that short *o* stands for /o/. What consonant blend is at the beginning of this word? (/dr/) What is the word? *(drop)*	*Routine*
Scaffold instruction.	Write *cost, plop,* and *stomp*.	**2 Model** When you come to a new word, look at all the letters in the word and think about its vowel sound. Say the sounds in the word to yourself and then read the word. Model reading *cost, plop,* and *stomp* in this way. When you come to a new word, what are you going to do?	
	Write each practice word.	**3 Group Practice** Let's read these words. Look at all the letters, think about the vowel sound, and say the sounds to yourself. We will read words with short *o* and consonant blends. Allow 2–3 seconds previewing time for each word.	
		frog hand flop brick trot strap flock snack print	
CORRECTIVE FEEDBACK	**MONITOR PROGRESS**	**If . . .** children have difficulty previewing and reading whole words, **then . . .** have them use sound-by-sound blending.	
		If . . . children can't read the words fluently at a rate of 1–2 seconds per word, **then . . .** continue practicing the list.	

MORE PRACTICE

Model reading words in sentences.	When I read a sentence, I read each word without stopping between the words. If I come to a word I don't know, I blend it. Then I read the sentence again. Model reading this sentence, stopping to blend *tromp: Bob and Tom tromp up and down the hill*.
Write practice sentences.	Have each child read a sentence.
	This clock is not the best one in the shop. Two frogs hop in the grass. The pond has rocks and green plants.

High-Frequency Words *answer, different, ever, learn*

To Do	To Say	3 minutes

Review high-frequency words.

Display *answer, different, ever,* and *learn*.	Use the Tested Vocabulary Cards. Point to a word. Say and spell it. Have children say and spell the word. Ask children to identify familiar letter-sounds. Have them take turns reading the words.

ACTIVITY **3** Build Concepts

Oral Vocabulary *camouflage, mammal*

To Do	To Say	5–10 minutes

Teach oral vocabulary.

Display p. 58 of the student book.

Yesterday you read about animals using *camouflage* to hide. Some of the animals you learned about were *mammals.* Today we'll read a make-believe story about two mammals that get lost in the woods.

Routine

Follow the Routine to teach *camouflage* and *mammal*.

1 Introduce, Demonstrate, and Apply

camouflage "Can You See Them?" was about animal *camouflage. Camouflage* is the shapes, colors, and patterns that help animals blend in with things around them. Have children say the word. In the woods, animals' *camouflage* makes them hard to see. What kind of *camouflage* did the animals in "Can You See Them?" have?

mammal The big cat and the fox in "Can You See Them?" are *mammals. Mammals* have fur or hair. They have backbones. Mother *mammals* feed their babies with milk from their bodies. Have children say the word. Some *mammals,* like elephants, are big. Some, like mice, are small. People are *mammals.* What are some other *mammals?*

Display the words on the Amazing Words board.

2 Display the Words Have children say each word as they look at it. You can find sounds you know in big words. What letters do you see at the beginning of *camouflage? (c, a, m)* How do you read this word part? *(cam)* What consonant blend is in the middle of *camouflage? (fl)* Read *mam/mal* as you run your hand under the syllables. Children can identify *mam,* /l/.

Monitor understanding.

3 Use the Words Ask children to use each word in a sentence. Model a sentence if children need help.

MORE PRACTICE

Use oral vocabulary to discuss animals found in woods. What kinds of *camouflage* do animals have? How does their *camouflage* help them? You learned that *mammals* have fur. Is a frog a *mammal?* Are squirrels *mammals?*

ACTIVITY 4 Read a Passage

Reading "Lost in the Woods," pp. 62–69

	To Do	**To Say**	*10 minutes*

Teach main idea.

Scaffold instruction.

Introduce the skill.

Model the skill. Display p. 54.

Apply the skill. Display p. 58.

Today you are going to find the topic and the main idea in a story. The topic is what the selection is about. The main idea is the most important idea about the topic. For example, the topic of "Out in the Woods" is camping. The most important idea is that kids can see and learn a lot of things when they camp.

What is the topic of "Can You See Them?" Think of one or two words that tell about it. (animal camouflage) What is the main idea? Think of a sentence that tells the most important idea about animal camouflage. (An animal's camouflage helps it hide.)

Develop language and concepts.

See Routine Card 6. Display pp. 62–69.

Model using key words and concepts.

Key concepts: *nuts, path, drop, snack, lost, plan, back*

Monitor children's use of vocabulary.

Before Reading Read the title. Do a structured picture walk.

pp. 62–63 One beaver is putting nuts in a basket. Then they both walk on a path. (Point to path.) Have you ever followed a path? Are these beavers like real beavers? (No, real beavers don't wear clothes. They don't smile.)

pp. 64–65 What does one beaver drop on the path? (nuts) The beavers are eating a snack. What is your favorite snack?

pp. 66–67 One beaver looks worried. Maybe they are lost. What would you do if you got lost in the woods?

pp. 68–69 The beavers are looking at the nuts one of them dropped on the path. What is their plan to get back?

Now turn to your partner and talk about the pictures, using the same words I did.

Guide comprehension.

Read pp. 62–69. Use Routine Card 2.

During Reading Ask children to read along with you. As we read, ask yourself: What is the topic? What is the main idea about the topic? Read pp. 62–65 aloud with the group. Then ask: What is the topic? (beavers in the woods) What is the most important idea so far? (Dot has a plan so they won't get lost.)

Read pp. 66–67 aloud with the group. Then ask: What is the main idea of these pages? (The beavers are lost.)

Read pp. 68–69 aloud with the group. Then ask: What is the main idea of the whole story? (Dot's plan helps the lost beavers get back.)

Monitor independent reading.

Use Routine Card 3.

Reread Have children read the story aloud together without you. Then have them read it on their own in a whisper. Listen in on each child. Monitor reading, using Routine Card 3.

Guide retelling.

Prompt children as they retell the story.

After Reading Have one child retell the story while the others assist. Who are the characters? (Dot and Tom) What happens at the beginning? Then what happens? See Monitoring Retelling Chart, p. 246.

Homework Practice Book, p. 13, Main Idea and Supporting Details

ACTIVITY **1** # Reread for Fluency

Paired Reading "Lost in the Woods," pp. 62–63

To Do	To Say	

5–10 minutes

CORRECTIVE FEEDBACK

Pair children. Monitor paired reading.

Children read pp. 62–63 orally, switching readers at the end of the first page. Have partners reread; now the other partner begins. For optimal fluency, children should reread three or four times. Give feedback on children's oral reading and use of the blending strategy. See Routine Cards 1 and 4.

MORE PRACTICE

Instead of rereading just pp. 62–63, have children reread the entire selection three or four times. You may want to have children read along with the AudioText.

ACTIVITY **2** # Word Work

Spiral Review Short Vowels *a, i, o*

To Do	To Say	

5–10 minutes

Review Short Vowels *a, i, o.*

Write *odd*.

You can read this word because you know that *o* can stand for /o/. What sound does *o* in this word stand for? (/o/) What's the word? *(odd)* Remember, when there is only one vowel at the beginning or in the middle of a word, it usually stands for its short sound.

Scaffold instruction.

Write *hat, pit,* and *Dot*.

You can read these words because you know the short vowel sounds /a/, /i/, and /o/. Say the sounds in each word to yourself, and then read the word. Model reading *hat, pit,* and *Dot* in this way. When you come to a new word, what are you going to do?

Distribute white boards.

Write *bag, sit, dock, spot, fish* and *back*.

Sort Words Let's read these words. Look at all the letters, think about the vowel sound, and say the sounds to yourself. When I point to the word, let's read it together: *bag, sit, dock, spot, fish, back.* Write the column headings Short *a*, Short *i*, and Short *o* on the board. Now copy the chart headings and write each word in the column with its short vowel.

Short *a*	Short *i*	Short *o*
bag	sit	dock
back	fish	spot

CORRECTIVE FEEDBACK

MONITOR PROGRESS

If . . . children cannot identify the vowel sounds,
then . . . say the words, emphasizing each sound. Have them echo you.

MORE PRACTICE

Model reading words in sentences.

When I read a sentence, I read each word without stopping between the words. If I come to a word I don't know, I blend it. Then I read the sentence again. Model reading this sentence, stopping to blend *splash: Kids can splash in the pond.*

Write practice sentences.

Have each child read a sentence.

Grab a snack and then sit down.
A fox ran fast on the rock path.
Bob and Tim sing and clap.

Phonological and Phonemic Awareness

Optional practice activities, pp. 280–283.

ACTIVITY 3 | Read Together

Choral Reading "Let's Make Trail Mix," p. 70

	To Do	To Say	10 minutes

Develop language and concepts.

Display p. 70.

Before Reading This is a recipe for trail mix. What do you know about recipes? (Allow children to share what they know.) What ingredients, or foods, are in this trail mix? (nuts, raisins, pretzels, cereal) Share information about trail mix. **Raisins are a kind of dried fruit. They are dried grapes.**

Model fluent reading.

Model reading directions in correct sequence using an appropriate rate. Listen as I read the recipe. When I read directions, I read the steps in order. I read more slowly and pause after each step to make sure I understand it. Read it a second time, having children point to each word.

Build fluency through choral reading.

Choral Reading Now read the recipe aloud with me. Let's read the steps in order, speaking clearly and carefully. Reread the recipe several times with children.

Develop concepts.

Monitor listening comprehension.

After Reading What do you do with the trail mix ingredients? (put them in a plastic bag and shake them) Why do you shake the bag? (to mix up the ingredients) Why is trail mix a good snack for a walk in the woods?

ACTIVITY 4 | Build Concepts

Oral Vocabulary *camouflage, galaxy, mammal, tranquil, wildlife*

	To Do	To Say	5–10 minutes

Review oral vocabulary.

Read the words on the Amazing Words board.

Focus on Letter-Sounds Remember, you can find sounds you know in big words.

- What words have the sound /a/? What word has the sound /i/?
- Which word begins with a consonant blend?

Encourage discussion.

Provide Personal Contexts Review the meanings of the words. Then ask questions to place the words in personal contexts.

- When are you *tranquil?* When are you not *tranquil?*
- Have you ever looked at a *galaxy* in the sky? Why did you look at it?
- What kinds of *wildlife* have you seen? Where did you see it?
- What animal *camouflage* have you seen? Have you ever seen a person wearing *camouflage?*
- Which *mammals* do you know the most about?

MORE PRACTICE

Apply oral vocabulary to new situations.

- Smile and say "tranquil" after each thing that makes people *tranquil:* sunset (tranquil), **tornado** (no), **soft music** (tranquil).
- Raise your hand and say "mammal" after each kind of *wildlife* that is a *mammal:* snake (no), bird (no), rabbit (mammal).
- Put your hands in front of your face and say "camouflage" after each example of animal *camouflage:* a red bug on a red flower (camouflage), a red bug on a white flower (no), a red bug on a pink-and-blue flower (no).
- Stand and say "star" when you hear a word that has to do with stars: *wildlife* (no), *tranquil* (no), *galaxy* (star), *mammal* (no).

ACTIVITY **5** | Write

Response to Literature Interactive Writing

| To Do | To Say | 5–10 minutes |

Generate ideas. | Review the story "Lost in the Woods." | **How does Dot's plan help the beavers when they get lost?** Discuss the trail of nuts that Dot drops on the path as the beavers walk in the woods.

Share the pen. | Have children participate in describing the beavers' adventure. | Write *Dot and Tom saw _____.* Have children read the words you wrote. Then have them supply endings for the sentence. Invite individuals to write familiar letter-sounds, word parts, and high-frequency words. Have them find the spelling of high-frequency words on the Word Wall. Ask questions such as:

• **What is the first sound in** *rock?* (/r/) **What is the letter for /r/?** *(r)*

• **What is the vowel sound in** *rock?* /o/ **What is the letter for /o/?** *(o)*

• **What is the last sound in** *rock?* /k/ **What are the letters for /k/?** *(ck)*

Writing elements: conventions | Frequently reread what has been written while tracking the print. Point out that each sentence and character name starts with a capital letter. Point out the extra space between words and the periods at the ends of sentences.

Read the completed sentences aloud, having children read with you. (For example, *Dot and Tom saw a rock. Dot and Tom saw a path. Dot and Tom saw a fox. Dot and Tom saw a pond.*)

MORE PRACTICE | Prompt independent writing. | **Journal Writing** Describe an animal you might see on a walk in the woods.

Homework | Practice Book, p. 14, High-Frequency Words

5

ACTIVITY 1 Assessment Options

Sentence Reading

To Do	To Say	*5 minutes*

Assess sentence reading.

To Do: Use reproducible p. 247.

To Say: Have each child read the sentences. Record scores on the Sentence Reading Chart, p. 252. Work with one child as others complete Write Sentences below.

Tom will learn lots of different tricks at camp.
Did Brent ever get his socks?
I put my hand up before I said the answer.

CORRECTIVE FEEDBACK

MONITOR PROGRESS

If . . . children have trouble reading words with short *o* or consonant blends,
then . . . reteach the blending strategy lessons on pp. 36 and 40.

If . . . children cannot read a high-frequency word,
then . . . mark the missed word or words on a high-frequency word list and send the list home for additional practice or have them practice with a fluent reader.

If . . . children misread a word in the sentence,
then . . . correct the error and have them reread the word and then the sentence.

Practice sentence writing.

To Do: Provide white boards.

Write Sentences Have children copy the sentences from reproducible p. 247 on white boards. Have them confirm their spelling by comparing it to the sentences.

Phonological and Phonemic Awareness   Optional practice activities, pp. 280–283

Mid-Unit Passage Reading

To Do	To Say	*5–10 minutes*

Assess fluency and comprehension.

To Do: Determine which children to assess. Use Assessment Book, p. 79.

To Say: Chose from these options: monitoring fluency (see pp. 244–245) and/or monitoring retelling (see p. 246). Have children read the Unit 1 Mid-Unit Fluency Passage in the Assessment Book. Be sure each child is assessed every other week.

ACTIVITY 2 Use Concepts

Oral Vocabulary *camouflage, galaxy, mammal, tranquil, wildlife*

To Do	To Say	*5 minutes*

Check understanding of oral vocabulary.

To Do: Use the Amazing Words to wrap up the week's concept.

Monitor understanding of oral vocabulary, using Routine Card 5.

To Say: As time allows, ask questions such as these.

- Tell me about the pictures on pp. 54–57 using some of the week's Amazing Words.
- What would *tranquil* woods look like? sound like?
- What do you see when you look at a *galaxy?* Would you rather explore a *galaxy* far away or study *wildlife* living in the woods?
- How is *wildlife* different from pets? What kinds of *wildlife* live in the woods? What kinds of *wildlife* live in a pond?
- What surprised you about animal *camouflage?* What kind of *camouflage* would you wear to hide in the woods? in the snow?
- Which *mammals* did you learn about this week? What are some ways that all *mammals* are alike?

Preview next week's concept.

Next week you will read about life in the desert.

ACTIVITY 3 Read to Connect

Reread "Out in the Woods," pp. 54–57

10 minutes

To Do	To Say

Monitor comprehension: main idea.

Have children reread "Out in the Woods" silently.

As you read, think about the selection's topic, one or two words that tell what it is about. Then think about the selection's main idea, the most important idea about the topic. After rereading, ask:

- What is the topic of "Out in the Woods"?
- What is the main idea of "Out in the Woods"?

Make connections.

Have children make connections across texts.

We also read "Can You See Them?" about animals that hide. Find that. What did you learn about animal camouflage? Record children's ideas in a list on the board. (For example: Their color helps them blend in; their shape helps them blend in; their pattern helps them blend in.) Children will use the list for Activity 4.

We also read "Lost in the Woods," about two beavers walking in the woods. Are the woods in this story like the woods you read about in the other selections? What happens to the beavers when they explore the woods? Record ideas on a chart.

What did all the selections we read this week show us about exploring the woods? (There are many kinds of wildlife in the woods.)

ACTIVITY 4 Write

Response to Literature Independent Writing

5–10 minutes

To Do	To Say

Assign expository writing.

Today you will write about some things you learned about wildlife in the woods. Encourage children to use words you wrote on the board for Activity 3 as they write.

Guide sentence correction.

Writing elements: conventions, support

Have children check their writing by asking themselves these questions.

- Did I begin each sentence with a capital letter?
- Did I end each sentence with a period?
- Did I check my spelling of words?
- Did I give details about the wildlife?

MORE PRACTICE

Have children share their sentences with the group. Write their sentences on the board and have children practice reading and writing each other's sentences.

Homework

Practice Book, p. 15, Writing

Unit 1 Week 4 *Sand All Around*

What can we learn by exploring the desert?

Objectives *This week students will...*

Phonemic Awareness
- segment words into sounds
- add ending sounds

Phonics
- blend and read words with short *e*, inflected ending *-s*, and plural *-s*
- apply knowledge of letter-sounds to decode unknown words when reading
- recognize high-frequency words *draw, eye, picture, read* /red/

Fluency
- practice fluency with oral rereading

Vocabulary
- build concepts and oral vocabulary: *arid, cactus, dune, landform, precipitation*

Text Comprehension
- read connected text
- identify main idea to improve comprehension
- write in response to literature

Word Work *This week's phonics focus is . . .*

Short *e*   Ending *-s*

High-Frequency Words *Tested Vocabulary*

The first appearance of each word in the Student Reader is noted below.

draw	When you **draw** something, you make a picture of it with pen, pencil, or crayon. (p. 81)
eye	Your **eye** is the part of your body you use to see. (p. 77)
picture	A **picture** is a drawing, photograph, or painting of someone or something. (p. 81)
read	Have you **read** that book yet? (p. 81)

Amazing Words *Oral Vocabulary*

The week's vocabulary is related to the concept of exploring the desert.

arid	very dry
cactus	a plant with a thick, fleshy stem that usually has spines but no leaves
dune	hill of sand
landform	a shape formed on the land
precipitation	rain or snow

Student Reader Unit 1 *This week students will read the following selections.*

Daily Lesson Plan

	ACTIVITIES	MATERIALS
Day 1	**Word Work** Phonemic Awareness: Segment Words into Sounds Phonics: Blend Words with Short *e* High-Frequency Words *draw, eye, picture, read* /red/ **Build Concepts** *arid, landform, precipitation* **Read a Passage** "Sand All Around," pp. 74–81 Comprehension: Use Strategies Reread for Fluency	Student White Boards Sound-Spelling Card 9 Tested Vocabulary Cards *Sing with Me Big Book* and Audio CD Student Reader: Unit 1 Routine Cards 1, 2, 3, 4, 6, 7 AudioText Practice Book, p. 16, Short *e*
Day 2	**Reread for Fluency** **Word Work** Phonemic Awareness: Add Ending Sounds /s/, /z/ Phonics: Blend Words with Inflected Ending *-s* and Plural *-s* High-Frequency Words *draw, eye, picture, read* /red/ **Read a Passage** "A Report About the Desert," pp. 82–85 Comprehension: Use Strategies **Write** Response to Literature: Shared Writing	Student Reader: Unit 1 Student White Boards Tested Vocabulary Cards Routine Cards 1, 2, 3, 4, 6, 7 AudioText Practice Book, p. 17, Ending *-s*, Plural *-s*
Day 3	**Reread for Fluency** **Word Work** Phonemic Awareness: Segment Words into Sounds Phonics: Fluent Word Reading High-Frequency Words *draw, eye, picture, read* /red/ **Build Concepts** *cactus, dune* **Read a Passage** "Sand Blast!" pp. 86–93 Comprehension: Main Idea	Student Reader: Unit 1 Student White Boards Tested Vocabulary Cards Routine Cards 1, 2, 3, 4, 6 AudioText Practice Book, p. 18, Main Idea and Supporting Details
Day 4	**Reread for Fluency** **Word Work** Phonics: Spiral Review Phonological and Phonemic Awareness Activities, pp. 280–283 **Read Together** "Did You Know?" p. 94 Comprehension: Listening **Build Concepts** *arid, cactus, dune, landform, precipitation* **Write** Response to Literature: Interactive Writing	Student Reader: Unit 1 Routine Cards 1, 4 AudioText Practice Book, p. 19, High-Frequency Words
Day 5	**Assessment Options** Fluency, Comprehension Sentence Reading; Passage Reading Phonological and Phonemic Awareness Activities, pp. 280–283 **Use Concepts** *arid, cactus, dune, landform, precipitation* **Read to Connect** "Sand All Around," pp. 74–81 Comprehension: Main Idea **Write** Response to Literature: Independent Writing	Reproducible p. 248 Sentence Reading Chart, p. 252 Student White Boards Fluency Progress Chart, p. 245 Student Reader: Unit 1 Routine Card 5 Practice Book, p. 20, Writing

See pp. xvi–xvii for how *My Sidewalks* integrates instructional practices for ELL.

Phonemic Awareness Segment Words into Sounds

2 minutes

	To Do	To Say
Scaffold instruction.	Distribute white boards. Write *leg.* Write *nest.* Lead children in segmenting sounds.	**Model** Listen to the sounds in *leg.* Stretch the sounds /lll/ /eee/ /g/ as you write *l, e, g.* Repeat. This time have children write the letters as you write. Now let's say the sounds as I point to the letters: /l/ /e/ /g/. **Teach and Practice** What are the sounds in *nest?* Have children say the sounds with you as you point to the letters. (/n/ /e/ /s/ /t/) Continue the activity with these words: wet yes fell neck sled desk

Blending Strategy Short *e*

5–10 minutes

	To Do	To Say
Use the blending routine.	Write *pat, pit,* and *pot.*	**1 Connect** You already can read words like these. What are the words? What is the vowel sound in *pat?* (/a/) What is the vowel sound in *pit?* (/i/) What is the vowel sound in *pot?* (/o/) Now let's look at another short vowel sound.
	Display Sound-Spelling Card 9.	**2 Use Sound-Spelling Card** This is an elephant. What sound do you hear at the beginning of *elephant?* (/e/) Say it with me: /e/. The letter *e* can stand for /e/.
		3 Listen and Write Write the letter *e* for /e/. As you write, say the sound to yourself: /e/. Now say the sound aloud.
Scaffold instruction.	Write *pet.*	**4 Model** In this word, the letter *e* stands for /e/. This is how I blend this word: /p/ /e/ /t/, *pet.* Now you try: /p/ /e/ /t/, *pet.*

Remind children that when there is only one vowel at the beginning or in the middle of a word, it usually stands for its short sound.

p e t

	To Do	To Say
CORRECTIVE FEEDBACK	Write each practice word. Monitor student practice.	**5 Group Practice** Let's try the same thing with these words. Give feedback, using the *if . . . then* statements on Routine Card 1. egg jet* den* mess spell tent
		6 Individual Practice Write the words; have each child blend two of them. web bed men bell stem* rest* dress smell

*Children need to make sense of words they segment and blend. If needed, help students with meanings. A *jet* is a big airplane. A *den* is a wild animal's home. It can also be a room in a house. A *stem* is the main part of a plant that grows above the ground. When you *rest,* you are still and quiet or even asleep.

	To Do	To Say
MORE PRACTICE	Model spelling short *e* words.	**Spell and Write** What sounds do you hear in *pet?* (/p/ /e/ /t/) What is the letter for /p/? Let's all write *p.* What is the letter for /e/? Write *e.* What is the letter for /t/? Write *t.* Continue practice as time allows. Have children confirm their spelling by comparing it to what you've written. let hen red get tell help step belt

High-Frequency Words *draw, eye, picture, read /red/*

Teach high-frequency words.

To Do	To Say

Display *draw.*

1 Say, Spell, Write Use the Tested Vocabulary Cards. Display *draw.* Here are some words that we won't sound out. We'll spell them. This word is *draw:* *d, r, a, w* (point to each letter), *draw.* What is this word? What are the letters in the word? Now you write *draw.*

Point to the first and second letters in *draw.*

2 Identify Letter-Sounds Let's look at the sounds in *draw* that you do know. What is this letter? *(d)* What is the sound for this letter? (/d/) What is this letter? *(r)* What is the sound for this letter? (/r/) What is the sound of *d* and *r* blended together? (/dr/) Point to the word *eye.* The word *eye* is said just like the word *I,* (/ī/).

Display *eye* and *I.*

3 Demonstrate Meaning Tell me a sentence using *draw.* Model a sentence if children need help.

Display *picture* and *read /red/.*

Repeat the Routine with *picture* and *read.* Children can identify these letter-sounds and word parts: *picture (pic), read (r/r/, d/d/).* Have children write the words in their word banks. Add the words to the Word Wall.

ACTIVITY 2 Build Concepts

Oral Vocabulary *arid, landform, precipitation*

Introduce oral vocabulary.

Scaffold instruction.

To Do	To Say

Display p. 4 of *Sing with Me Big Book.* Play audio CD.

This week you will learn about the desert. Listen for the Amazing Words *arid, landform,* and *precipitation* as I sing this song. Play or sing the song. Then have children sing it with you.

Follow the Routine to teach *arid, landform,* and *precipitation.*

1 Introduce, Demonstrate, and Apply

arid The sandy desert in the song is *arid.* An *arid* place is very dry. Have children say the word. The desert is *arid* because not much rain falls there. Not many kinds of animals and plants can live in hot *arid* deserts. Can you name any?

landform The song tells us that the desert is a *landform.* A *landform* is a shape formed on the land. Have children say the word. Hills, mountains, and plains are kinds of *landforms.* What *landforms* have you seen?

precipitation The song says the desert is without *precipitation. Precipitation* is rain or snow. *Precipitation* falls from clouds in the sky. Have children say the word. Dry places like deserts have very little *precipitation.* Wet places like rain forests have a lot of *precipitation.*

Display the words on the Amazing Words board.

2 Display the Words Have children say each word as they look at it. You can find sounds you know in big words. Read *ar/id* as you run your hand under the syllables. Can you find the *i*? What sound does the *i* make? (/i/) Can you find the *d*? What sound does the *d* make? (/d/) For *landform* and *precipitation,* children can identify these letter-sounds and word parts: *landform (land, f/f/, m/m/), precipitation (pr/pr/, c/s/, ip, it, n/n/).*

Monitor understanding.

3 Use the Words Ask children to use each word in a sentence. Model a sentence if children need help.

MORE PRACTICE

Use oral vocabulary to discuss the song. What is the *arid* desert like? What makes the desert *landform* special? Does the desert have a lot of or a little *precipitation*?

Read a Passage

Build Background "Sand All Around," pp. 74–81

	To Do	To Say	
			10 minutes

Develop language and concepts.

See Routine Card 7. Read aloud p. 73 of the student book.

See Routine Card 6. Display pp. 74–81.

Ask questions to develop language.

Key concepts: *desert, cactus, stems, bird, owl, sand, rain, fox, rat, camel, arid*

Preview the Week Use pp. 72–73 to preview the selections in this week. The selections this week are about the desert. Read aloud the titles and descriptions on p. 73. Ask children what they think each selection will be about.

Before Reading Read the title aloud. Do a structured picture walk.

pp. 74–77 Do you see plants in the desert? Yes, this desert plant is a cactus. They have thick stems with sharp pinlike parts. Why should you be careful near a cactus? Do you see an animal? Yes, this bird is a kind of owl. Where does the owl live? (in the cactus) Look at all the sand! Deserts are very dry. Not much rain falls on the ground.

pp. 78–81 Do you know what these animals are called? Point to and name kit fox, pack rat, and camel. Where do these animals live? (in the desert) I wonder how these animals make their homes in such a hot, arid place! Would you like to live in a desert?

Guide comprehension.

Read pp. 74–81.

Model strategic reading. Use Routine Card 2.

During Reading Ask children to read along with you. As we read, ask yourself: What did I learn about the desert? What is this mainly about? Read pp. 74–81 aloud with the group. Stop on each page to model asking questions. For example, for p. 77: After I read, I ask myself: What is this mainly about? The author writes about a plant with a bird inside it. I think this page is mainly about a desert plant in which a bird makes its nest.

Teach story words.

Write *bird, desert,* and *rain.*

You will read these words in the selection. They are *bird, desert,* and *rain.* Have children say each word and spell it. Review their meanings.

Monitor independent reading.

Use Routine Card 3.

Reread Have children read the selection aloud together without you. Then have them read it on their own in a whisper. Listen in on each child. Monitor reading, using Routine Card 3.

Summarize.

Use oral vocabulary to develop the concept.

After Reading What did you learn about the desert and the plants and animals that live there? Is the desert a *landform* that gets lots of *precipitation* or is it *arid*? How do you know?

Reread for Fluency "Sand All Around," pp. 74–77

	To Do	To Say	
			5–10 minutes

CORRECTIVE FEEDBACK

Monitor oral reading.

Read pp. 74–77 aloud. Read them three or four times so your reading gets better each time. Give feedback on children's oral reading and use of the blending strategy. See Routine Cards 1 and 4.

MORE PRACTICE

Instead of rereading just pp. 74–77, have children reread the entire selection three or four times. You may want to have children read along with the AudioText.

Homework

Practice Book, p. 16, Phonics: Short *e*

ACTIVITY 1　Reread for Fluency

Paired Reading "Sand All Around," pp. 78–81

To Do	To Say	5–10 minutes

CORRECTIVE FEEDBACK

Pair children. Monitor paired reading.

Children read pp. 78–81 orally, switching readers at the end of the first page. Have partners reread; now the other partner begins. For optimal fluency, children should reread three or four times. Give feedback on children's oral reading and use of the blending strategy. See Routine Cards 1 and 4.

MORE PRACTICE

Instead of rereading just pp. 78–81, have children reread the entire selection three or four times. You may want to have children read along with the AudioText.

ACTIVITY 2　Word Work

Phonemic Awareness Add Ending Sounds /s/, /z/

To Do	To Say	2 minutes

Scaffold instruction.

Distribute white boards.
Write *map.* Add *-s* to form *maps.*

Write *sell.* Add *-s* to form *sells.*
Lead children in adding /s/ or /z/ as they write.

Model Listen to the sounds in *map.* Stretch the sounds /mmm/ /aaa/ /p/ as you write *m, a, p.* Repeat. This time have children write the letters as you write. Then add *-s* to the end of *map* as you say /mmm/ /aaa/ /p/ /sss/. **The sound at the end of *maps* is /sss/.** Repeat, having children say the sound as they add *s* to *map.*

Teach and Practice Listen to the sounds in *sell.* Have children say the sounds with you as you point to the letters. (/s/ /e/ /l/) Add *-s* to the end of *sell* as you say /s/ /e/ /l/ /z/. **What sound is at the end of *sells*? (/z/) The letter *s* at the end of a word can stand for /s/ or /z/.** Let's add /s/ or /z/ to some other words. Continue the activity.

pot　　rip　　pick　　bed　　ring　　tell

Blending Strategy Inflected Ending -s, Plural -s

To Do	To Say	5–10 minutes

Use the blending routine.

Scaffold instruction.

Write *sit* and *sand*.

1 Connect You already can read words like these. What are these words? What sound do they start with? (/s/) What letter stands for /s/? (s) Today we are learning about the letter *s* at the end of words.

Write *hits*.

2 Model Look at the word. It tells about an action. If I cover up the -s ending, I see a word I know: /h/ /i/ /t/, *hit*. Then I uncover and read the ending, /s/. Finally I blend the two parts together: *hits*. Now you try it: /h/ /i/ /t/ /s/, *hits*.

Write *eggs*.

Look at this word. I see the word *egg* at the beginning. The letter *s* at the end tells me there is more than one egg. First, I read the word I know: *egg*. Next, I read the ending, /z/. Finally, I blend the two parts together: /e/ /g/ /z/, *eggs*. Now you try it: /e/ /g/ /z/, *eggs*.

Remind children that the letter *s* can stand for /s/ or /z/. Point out that when *s* comes after letters such as *t, p,* or *k,* it usually stands for /s/. When *s* comes after letters such as *g, l, n, b,* or *d,* it usually stands for /z/.

h i t s   e g g s

3 Listen and Write Write the word *help.* Write *s* after it. Say the base word to yourself. Then say the ending to yourself. Finally blend the parts and say the word aloud.

CORRECTIVE FEEDBACK

Write each practice word. Monitor student practice.

4 Group Practice Let's blend these words the same way. Give feedback, using the *if . . . then* statements on Routine Card 1.

bags   sips   mats   spins*   yells   crops*

6 Individual Practice Write the words; have each child blend two of them.

rats   legs   sobs*   pets   picks   smells

Check understanding of practice words.

*Children need to make sense of words as they segment and blend. If needed, help children with meanings. A person *spins* wool on a machine to make rugs. *Crops* are plants like corn or wheat that are grown for food. When a baby *sobs,* it cries hard. (Demonstrate.)

MORE PRACTICE

Model building words with inflected ending -s and plural -s.

Build Words Write verbs and nouns to which the ending -s can be added without a spelling change. Have children copy the words on their white boards. With the first word, model adding -s to the word and then blending the two parts to read the new word. Have children continue the activity. They can circle the new words ending with /s/ and put zigzag lines under words ending with /z/.

pet   tap   nod   hill   ask   belt   sing   drink

High-Frequency Words *draw, eye, picture, read /red/*

To Do	To Say	3 minutes

Teach high-frequency words.

Lead cumulative review.

Display *draw, eye, picture,* and *read.*

Use the Tested Vocabulary Cards. Point to a word. Say and spell it. Have children say and spell the word. Ask children to identify familiar letter-sounds. Have them take turns reading the words.

Use the Tested Vocabulary Cards to review high-frequency words from previous weeks.

ACTIVITY 3 Read a Passage

Reading "A Report About the Desert," pp. 82–85

To Do	To Say

10–15 minutes

Develop language and concepts.

Scaffold instruction.

See Routine Cards 6 and 7. Display pp. 82–85.

Ask questions and elaborate on answers to develop language.

Key concepts: *desert, cloth, hut, set up, crafts, tools*

Before Reading Have children recall what they learned about the desert. Read the title. Do a structured picture walk with children.

pp. 82–83 What are these kids doing? (drawing pictures and writing) Yes, they are writing a report about the desert. What did they draw? (a picture of a man wearing blue cloth) This man is called a "Blue Man of the Desert."

pp. 84–85 What did the kids draw here? (a person and a camel) Many people in the desert set up camp, live in that spot for a while, then pack up and move to a new spot. The man on this page is making jewelry.

Teach story words.

Write *desert*.

You will read this word in the selection. It is *desert.* Have children say the word and spell it. Review its meaning.

Guide comprehension.

Read pp. 82–85. See Routine Card 2.

During Reading Ask children to read along with you. As we read, ask yourself: What am I learning about the desert? What is this mainly about? Read pp. 82–83 aloud with the group. Then ask: What is this mainly about so far? (Peg and Matt write a report. The first part of the report is about the clothing a man wears in the desert.) His clothing protects him from the sand and hot sun. Let's read to find out more.

Read pp. 84–85 aloud with the group. Then ask: What else did you learn about desert people? (Some move often; some make jewelry.) Right, this man makes crafts. He makes jewelry to sell. What crafts have you made?

Monitor independent reading.

Use Routine Card 3.

Reread Have children read the selection aloud together without you. Then have them read it on their own in a whisper. Listen in on each child. Monitor reading, using Routine Card 3.

Model summarizing.

Think aloud.

After Reading What did you learn? What is the selection mainly about? Model how to summarize. The first two pages tell about desert people's clothing, homes, and work. The next pages tell about their crafts. I put that all together and pick the most important ideas. The selection is mainly about how desert people live.

MORE PRACTICE

Develop oral vocabulary.

Is the place where these people live wet or *arid?* What is the *landform* called? How much *precipitation* falls there?

ACTIVITY 4 Write

Response to Literature Shared Writing

To Do	To Say

5 minutes

Guide shared writing.

Write sentence frames. Read the questions.

What do desert people plant? Desert people plant _____.
What do desert people make? Desert people make _____.

Invite children to suggest answers. Discuss and record answers to complete the sentence frames. While writing, model connecting sounds to letters and forming letters (see pp. 257–259). Have children read answers aloud as you track print.

Homework Practice Book, p. 17, Phonics: Ending *-s*, Plural *-s*

3

ACTIVITY 1 Reread for Fluency

Oral Reading "A Report About the Desert," pp. 82–83

	To Do	**To Say**	*5–10 minutes*
CORRECTIVE FEEDBACK	Monitor oral reading.	**Read pp. 82–83 aloud. Read them three or four times so your reading gets better each time.** Give feedback on children's oral reading and use of the blending strategy. See Routine Cards 1 and 4.	
MORE PRACTICE		Instead of rereading just pp. 82–83, have children reread the entire selection three or four times. You may want to have children read along with the AudioText.	

ACTIVITY 2 Word Work

Phonemic Awareness Segment Words into Sounds

	To Do	**To Say**	*2 minutes*
Scaffold instruction.	Distribute white boards. Write *bet*.	**Model** Listen to the sounds in *bet*. Stretch the sounds /b/ /eee/ /t/ as you write *bet*. Repeat. This time have children write the letters as you write. Now let's say the sounds as I point to the letters: /b/ /e/ /t/.	
	Write *yells*. Lead children in segmenting sounds as they write.	**Teach and Practice** What are the sounds in *yells?* Have children say the sounds with you as you point to the letters. (/y/ /e/ /l/ /z/) Continue the activity with these words:	
		set well tent neck webs nets tells pecks	

Fluent Word Reading Short *e*, Inflected Ending *-s*, Plural *-s*

	To Do	**To Say**	*5–10 minutes*
Use the word-reading routine.	Write *beds*.	**1 Connect** You can read this word because you know that *e* can stand for /e/ and that the ending *-s* can stand for /s/ or /z/. What sound does *e* stand for in this word? (/e/) What sound does the ending *-s* make in this word? (/z/) What is the word? *(beds)*	*Routine*
Scaffold instruction.	Write *next, stems,* and *picks*.	**2 Model** When you come to a new word, look at all the letters in the word and think about its vowel sound. Say the letter-sounds in the word to yourself, and then read the word. Model reading *next, stems,* and *picks* in this way. Remind children that when they see a word that ends in *-s*, they should look for a base word, say the base word and the ending, and then blend the two parts together. When you come to a new word, what are you going to do?	
	Write each practice word.	**3 Group Practice** Let's read these words. Look at all the letters, think about the vowel sound, and say the letter-sounds to yourself. We will read words with short *e* and *-s* endings. When I point to the word, let's read it together. Allow 2–3 seconds previewing time for each word.	
		beg test steps bells melts grabs packs fills stops	
CORRECTIVE FEEDBACK	**MONITOR PROGRESS**	*If . . .* children have difficulty previewing and reading whole words, *then . . .* have them use sound-by-sound blending.	
		If . . . children can't read the words fluently at a rate of 1–2 seconds per word, *then . . .* continue practicing the list.	

| MORE PRACTICE | Model reading words in sentences. | When I read a sentence, I read each word without stopping between the words. If I come to a word I don't know, I blend it. Then I read the sentence again. Model reading this sentence, stopping to blend *bends: Greg bends his left leg and claps his hands.* |
| | Write practice sentences. | Have each child read a sentence.

Ten hens rest on eggs.
The pack rats slept in dens.
Deb helps Ted set up the tents and beds. |

High-Frequency Words *draw, eye, picture, read* /red/

3 minutes

| Review high-frequency words. | **To Do** Display *draw, eye, picture,* and *read.* | **To Say** Use the Tested Vocabulary Cards. Point to a word. Say and spell it. Have children say and spell the word. Ask children to identify familiar letter-sounds. Have them take turns reading the words. |

ACTIVITY **3** Build Concepts

Oral Vocabulary *cactus, dune*

5–10 minutes

Teach oral vocabulary.	**To Do** Display pp. 86–93 of the student book.	**To Say** Today you will read about a trip to a place with *cactuses* and *dunes.*
	Follow the Routine to teach *cactus* and *dune.*	**1 Introduce, Demonstrate, and Apply** ***cactus*** This story is about a trip to the desert. One plant you can see in many deserts is a *cactus.* Point to the cactus on p. 88. *Cactuses* don't need much rain to grow. That's why they can live in the desert. Have children say the word. Be careful when you touch a *cactus!* Does anyone know why? ***dune*** In many deserts you can see *dunes.* Point to the dunes on pp. 86–87. *Dunes* are hills of sand. The wind blows sand to make these hills. *Dunes* may have plants growing on them or no plants at all. Are there any *dunes* close to where we live?
	Display the words on the Amazing Words board.	**2 Display the Words** Have children say each word as they look at it. You can find sounds you know in big words. Which letter is in *cactus* twice? (c) What sound does it make? (/k/) What letter is at the end? (s) What sound does it make? (/s/) Read *dune* as you run your hand under the letters. Children can identify *d*/d/ and *n*/n/.
	Monitor understanding.	**3 Use the Words** Ask children to use each word in a sentence. Model a sentence if children need help.
MORE PRACTICE		Use oral vocabulary to discuss deserts. Do *cactuses* only grow in deserts? Have you ever seen a small *cactus* growing in a pot? All *dunes* are made of sand, but not all *dunes* are in the desert. Some *dunes* are on beaches too. What would it feel like to climb a *dune?*

ACTIVITY 4 Read a Passage

Reading "Sand Blast!" pp. 86–93

	To Do	**To Say**	*10 minutes*
Teach main idea and details.	Introduce the skill. Model the skill.	Today you are going to learn more about finding the main idea. Remember, the main idea is the most important idea about the story's topic. Small pieces of information that tell more about the main idea are called *details.* In a story about a girl's vacation, details might describe where the girl stayed and what she did.	
Scaffold instruction.	Apply the skill.	Suppose I read a story about a party someone gave to celebrate a birthday. The topic would be a birthday party and the main idea might be that everyone had fun at the birthday party. What might be some details? (food, presents, games, music)	
Develop language and concepts.	See Routine Card 6. Display pp. 86–93. Model using key words and concepts. Key concepts: *desert, sand, dunes, cactus, bird, bucks, wind, sand blast* Monitor children's use of vocabulary.	**Before Reading** Read the title. Do a structured picture walk. **pp. 86–87** These children are on a class trip. Look through the bus windows. Where are the children? (in the desert) Yes, deserts have hills of sand called dunes and prickly cactuses with thick stems. **pp. 88–90** What animals do the children see? The bird is near the cactus. The animals racing by are bucks. Bucks are male deer. What other animals could you see on a trip to the desert? **p. 91** What does the wind do? (It blows the sand.) Strong winds are called blasts. This picture shows a sand blast. **pp. 92–93** What do the pictures above the children's heads show? (cactuses, bucks, sand blast) They show what each child remembers most about the desert trip. What part would you remember most? Now turn to your partner and talk about the pictures, using the same words I did.	
Teach story words.	Write *bird* and *desert.*	You will read these words in the story. Read each word aloud. Have children say the words and spell them. Review their meanings.	
Guide comprehension.	Read pp. 86–93. Use Routine Card 2.	**During Reading** Ask children to read along with you. As we read, ask yourself: What is the main idea? What details tell more about the main idea? Read pp. 86–87 aloud with the group. Then ask: What are these pages mostly about? (a class trip to the desert) What details tell more about the class trip? (bus, rocks, sand, and plants) Read pp. 88–90 aloud with the group. Then ask: What are some details on these pages? (the animals and plants in the desert) Read pp. 91–93 aloud with the group. Then ask: Which of these sentences tells the main idea of the whole story? a) Children see plants, animals, and blowing sand on a trip to the desert. b) Deb gets sand on her cap and neck. (Sentence a)	
Monitor independent reading.	Use Routine Card 3.	**Reread** Have children read the story aloud together without you. Then have them read it on their own in a whisper. Listen in on each child. Monitor reading, using Routine Card 3.	
Guide retelling.	Prompt children as they retell the story.	**After Reading** Have one child retell the story while the others assist. Who are the characters in the story? What happened at the beginning? in the middle? at the end? See Monitoring Retelling Chart, p. 246.	
Homework		Practice Book, p. 18, Main Idea and Supporting Details	

ACTIVITY 1 Reread for Fluency

Paired Reading "Sand Blast!" pp. 86–89

To Do	To Say	5–10 minutes

CORRECTIVE FEEDBACK

Pair children. Monitor paired reading.

Children read pp. 86–89 orally, switching readers at the end of the first page. Have partners reread; now the other partner begins. For optimal fluency, children should reread three or four times. Give feedback on children's oral reading and use of the blending strategy. See Routine Cards 1 and 4.

MORE PRACTICE

Instead of rereading just pp. 86–89, have children reread the entire selection three or four times. You may want to have children read along with the AudioText.

ACTIVITY 2 Word Work

Spiral Review Consonant Blends

To Do	To Say	5 minutes

Review consonant blends.

Scaffold instruction.

Write *blast*.

Look at this word. You can read this word because you know how to blend consonant sounds at the beginning and end of a word. Remember, when two or more different consonants are together in a word, you usually hear the sound of each consonant. What consonant blend is at the beginning of the word? *(bl)* **What consonant blend is at the end of the word?** *(st)* **What is the word?** *(blast)*

Write *splits*.

Look at this word. You can read this word because you know how to read words with consonant blends and -s endings. Cover up the -s ending. Let's blend the base word. How many consonants are at the beginning of the base word? *(3)* **What consonant blend do these letters stand for?** *(/spl/)* **What is the base word?** *(split)* **Now blend the base word with the -s ending. Remember, the -s ending can stand for either /s/ or /z/. What is the word?** *(splits)*

On the board, write the words with consonant blends in three columns as shown in the chart.

Sort Words **How are the words in each column alike?** Have children describe the sorting rule and suggest a heading for each column. (Beginning Blends, Ending Blends, Beginning and Ending Blends)

Call on children to read the words in each column and use them in a sentence.

Beginning Blends	Ending Blends	Beginning and Ending Blends
stem	best	plant
spell	desk	blend
frog	hand	blast
	camp	crust
		spring

CORRECTIVE FEEDBACK

MONITOR PROGRESS

If . . . children have difficulty reading the words,
then . . . have them use sound-by-sound blending.

For more practice, see next page.

Continued Spiral Review

MORE PRACTICE

Model reading words in sentences.	When I read a sentence, I read each word without stopping between the words. If I come to a word I don't know, I blend it. Then I read the sentence again. Model reading this sentence, stopping to blend *scrap: We fed a scrap of ham to Spot.*
Write practice sentences.	Have each child read a sentence. **Britt makes crafts and sells the best ones.** **Pick up the rest of the twigs and sticks.** **Clem has string and ten blocks on his desk.**
Phonological and Phonemic Awareness	Optional practice activities, pp. 226–229.

ACTIVITY 3 Read Together

Choral Reading "Did You Know?" p. 94

To Do — **To Say** — *10 minutes*

	To Do	To Say
Develop language and concepts.	Display p. 94.	**Before Reading** This page tells more about deserts. What have you learned about deserts? (Allow children to share what they know.) Do you think a very cold place could be a desert? Share information about the South Pole. The South Pole is a very cold place at the most southern part of Earth. It is a desert because it is very dry. It gets less than an inch of precipitation (rain or snow) each year.
Model fluent reading.		Read the title of the selection. Ask children to predict what it is about. When I read a group of facts, I read the facts in order from top to bottom. I pause at the end of sentences. Read the selection, emphasizing the pause at the end of each sentence. Read it a second time, having children point to each word.
	Build fluency through choral reading.	**Choral Reading** Now read the facts aloud with me. Remember to pause at the end of each sentence. Reread the group of facts several times with children.
Develop concepts.	Monitor listening comprehension.	**After Reading** How much rain do deserts get each year? Is that a lot of rain or a little? Are all deserts hot places? What kind of landform is the South Pole? How are the South Pole and Death Valley alike?

ACTIVITY 4 Build Concepts

Oral Vocabulary *arid, cactus, dune, landform, precipitation*

To Do — **To Say** — *5–10 minutes*

	To Do	To Say
Review oral vocabulary.	Read the words on the Amazing Words board.	**Focus on Letter-Sounds** Remember, you can find sounds you know in big words. • Which words have the letter *d?* • What word has the word *land* in it? • What word begins with a two-letter consonant blend? • What word ends with /s/? What word ends with /d/?

	Provide Multiple Contexts Review the meanings of the words. Then ask questions to place the words in diverse contexts.
Encourage discussion.	• Which *arid landform* are you reading about this week? This *landform* is *arid* because it gets very little *precipitation*. What is another word for *arid*? What is another word for *precipitation*? Do we live in an *arid* place? Do we get a lot of *precipitation* here?
	• *Cactuses* and *dunes* are two things that you can see in many deserts. Describe a *cactus*. Describe a *dune*. Where else can you see *cactuses* besides deserts? Where else can you see *dunes*?

MORE PRACTICE

Apply oral vocabulary to new situations.	• Tell me how you would feel in an *arid* place. • Tell me about a *landform* you would like to visit. • Tell me what you might wear or use in a place that gets a lot of *precipitation*. • Tell me some ways *cactuses* are different from other plants. • Tell me some things you might see on a *dune*.

ACTIVITY **5** Write

Response to Literature Interactive Writing

To Do   **To Say**   *5–10 minutes*

Generate ideas.

Share the pen.

Review the story "Sand Blast!"	**What do the children on the bus see and feel on their trip in the desert?** Discuss desert plants and animals and the effects of a sand blast.
Have children participate in writing a list of items that can be found in deserts.	Write *Deserts can have _____.* Have children read the words you wrote. Then have them supply endings for the sentence. Invite individuals to write familiar letter-sounds, word parts, and high-frequency words. Have them find the spelling of high-frequency words on the Word Wall. Ask questions such as: • What is the first sound in *dens*? (/d/) What is the letter for /d/? *(d)* • What is the vowel sound in *dens*? (/e/) What is the letter for /e/? *(e)* • What sound do you hear after the vowel sound in *dens*? (/n/) What is the letter for /n/? *(n)* • What is the last sound in *dens*? (/z/) What is the letter for it? *(s)*
Writing elements: conventions	Frequently reread what has been written while tracking the print. Point out that each sentence starts with a capital letter and ends with a period. Point out that words that name more than one of something usually end with *-s*. Read the completed list aloud, having children read with you. (For example, *Deserts can have fox dens. Deserts can have rocks. Deserts can have sand blasts. Deserts can have bucks. Deserts can have dunes. Deserts can have cactuses. Deserts can have people.*)

MORE PRACTICE

Prompt independent writing.	**Journal Writing** Tell about a trip you have taken with your family or friends.

Homework	Practice Book, p. 19, High-Frequency Words

ACTIVITY 1 · Assessment Options

Sentence Reading

| | **To Do** | **To Say** | *5 minutes* |

Assess sentence reading.

To Do: Use reproducible p. 248.

To Say: Have each child read the sentences. Record scores on the Sentence Reading Chart, p. 252. Work with one child as others complete Write Sentences below.

Draw a picture of ten red tents.
Peg tells Fred to wink his left eye.
Who read about the hen and her nest of eggs?

CORRECTIVE FEEDBACK

MONITOR PROGRESS

If . . . children have trouble reading words with short *e* or words with *-s,*
then . . . reteach the blending strategy lessons on pp. 52 and 56.

If . . . children cannot read a high-frequency word,
then . . . mark the missed word or words on a high-frequency word list and send the list home for additional practice or have them practice with a fluent reader.

If . . . children misread a word in the sentence,
then . . . correct the error and have them reread the word and then the sentence.

Practice sentence writing.

To Do: Provide white boards.

Write Sentences Have children copy the sentences from reproducible p. 248 on white boards. Have them confirm their spellings by comparing the words they wrote to the words in the sentences.

Phonological and Phonemic Awareness

Optional practice activities, pp. 280–283

Passage Reading

| | **To Do** | **To Say** | *5–10 minutes* |

Assess fluency and comprehension.

To Do: Determine which children to assess this week.

To Say: Choose from these options: monitoring fluency (see pp. 244–245) and/or monitoring retelling (p. 246). Have children reread "Sand Blast!" Be sure each child is assessed every other week.

If you have time, assess every child.

ACTIVITY 2 · Use Concepts

Oral Vocabulary *arid, cactus, dune, landform, precipitation*

| | **To Do** | **To Say** | *5 minutes* |

Check under-standing of oral vocabulary.

To Do: Use the Amazing Words to wrap up the week's concept.

Monitor understanding of oral vocabulary, using Routine Card 5.

To Say: As time allows, ask questions such as these.

- Tell me about the pictures on pp. 74–76 using some of the week's Amazing Words.
- Would you need a raincoat in an *arid* place?
- Are all *landforms* alike? Why or why not?
- Do animals and plants need *precipitation?* Can a place get too much *precipitation?*
- In what ways are *cactuses* unusual plants?
- What is the same about every *dune?* (They are made of sand.) Would it be easy or hard for a person to walk across *dunes?* Why?

Preview next week's concept.

Next week you will read about people we can ask when we are searching for answers to our questions.

ACTIVITY 3 Read to Connect

Reread "Sand All Around," pp. 74–81

	To Do	**To Say**	*10 minutes*

Monitor comprehension: main idea.

Have children reread "Sand All Around" silently.

As you read, think about the main idea and the details. Remember, details are small pieces of information that tell more about the main idea. After rereading, ask:

- **What is the main idea of the selection?** (The desert is a special place with animals, plants, sand, and rocks.)
- **Name a few details that tell why the desert is a special place.** (very hot, little rain, cactuses, camels)

Make connections.

Have children make connections across texts.

We also read "A Report About the Desert." Find that. **What is the main idea? What are some important details?** Record children's ideas in a main idea/details chart on the board. (For example: main idea—People live in the desert; important details—Some desert people move often; desert people make crafts.) Children will use the chart for Activity 4.

We also read "Sand Blast!" Find that. **What is the main idea? What are some important details?** Record ideas in the chart.

What were all the selections we read this week about? (deserts) **What is the big idea?** (Deserts have lots of interesting things to explore.)

ACTIVITY 4 Write

Response to Literature Independent Writing

	To Do	**To Say**	*5–10 minutes*

Assign expository writing.

Today you will write about deserts. **What are some exciting things you might see on a trip to a desert?** Encourage children to use words you wrote on the board for Activity 3 as they write.

Guide sentence correction.

Writing elements: conventions, focus, support

Have children check their writing by asking themselves these questions.

- **Did I begin each sentence with a capital letter?**
- **Did I end each sentence with a period or question mark?**
- **Did I use good describing words to tell about the desert?**
- **Are all my sentences about the desert?**
- **Did I give details about the desert?**

MORE PRACTICE

Have children share their sentences with the group. Write each child's sentences on the board and have children ask questions about the information in each other's sentences.

Homework   Practice Book, p. 20, Writing

Unit 1 Week 5 *Who Can We Ask?*

When we are searching for answers, who can we ask?

Objectives *This week students will...*

Phonemic Awareness
- segment and count sounds in words

Phonics
- blend and read words with short *u*, *sh*/sh/, and *th*/th/
- apply knowledge of letter-sounds to decode unknown words when reading
- recognize high-frequency words *also, among, early, today*

Fluency
- practice fluency with oral rereading

Vocabulary
- build concepts and oral vocabulary: *curious, delicate, information, inquire, sturdy*

Text Comprehension
- read connected text
- draw conclusions to improve comprehension
- write in response to literature

Word Work *This week's phonics focus is . . .*

Short *u*   Digraphs *sh, th*

High-Frequency Words *Tested Vocabulary*

The first appearance of each word in the Student Reader is noted below.

also   He has a dog, but he **also** likes cats. (p. 99)

among   Divide the fruit **among** all of us. (p. 101)

early   If something happens **early,** it happens near the beginning. (p. 104)
       She got up **early** in the morning.

today   **Today** is my uncle's birthday. (p. 104)

Amazing Words *Oral Vocabulary*

The week's vocabulary is related to the concept of searching for answers.

curious   eager to know

delicate   easily broken

information   knowledge given or received of some fact or event

inquire   to ask

sturdy   strong, solid

Student Reader Unit 1 *This week students will read the following selections.*

Daily Lesson Plan

	ACTIVITIES	MATERIALS
Day 1	**Word Work** Phonemic Awareness: Segment and Count Sounds Phonics: Blend Words with Short *u* High-Frequency Words *also, among, early, today* **Build Concepts** *delicate, inquire, sturdy* **Read a Passage** "Who Can We Ask?" pp. 98–105 Comprehension: Use Strategies Reread for Fluency	Student White Boards Sound-Spelling Card 35 Tested Vocabulary Cards *Sing with Me Big Book* and Audio CD Student Reader: Unit 1 Routine Cards 1, 2, 3, 4, 6, 7 AudioText Practice Book, p. 21, Short *u*
Day 2	**Reread for Fluency** **Word Work** Phonemic Awareness: Segment and Count Sounds Phonics: Blend Words with *sh*/sh/, *th*/th/ High-Frequency Words *also, among, early, today* **Read a Passage** "A Bird Trick," pp. 106–113 Comprehension: Use Strategies **Write** Response to Literature: Shared Writing	Student Reader: Unit 1 Student White Boards Sound-Spelling Cards 32, 34 Tested Vocabulary Cards Routine Cards 1, 2, 3, 4, 6, 7 AudioText Practice Book, p. 22, Consonant Digraphs *sh*/sh/, *th*/th/
Day 3	**Reread for Fluency** **Word Work** Phonemic Awareness: Segment and Count Sounds Phonics: Fluent Word Reading High-Frequency Words *also, among, early, today* **Build Concepts** *curious, information* **Read a Passage** "The Just Facts Club," pp. 114–125 Comprehension: Draw Conclusions	Student Reader: Unit 1 Student White Boards Tested Vocabulary Cards Sound-Spelling Card 4 Routine Cards 1, 2, 3, 4, 6 AudioText Practice Book, p. 23, Draw Conclusions
Day 4	**Reread for Fluency** **Word Work** Phonics: Spiral Review Phonological and Phonemic Awareness Activities, pp. 280–283 **Read Together** "A Visit to the Library," p. 126 Comprehension: Listening **Build Concepts** *curious, delicate, information, inquire, sturdy* **Write** Response to Literature: Interactive Writing	Student Reader: Unit 1 Routine Cards 1, 4 AudioText Practice Book, p. 24, High-Frequency Words
Day 5	**Assessment Options** Fluency, Comprehension Sentence Reading; End-of-Unit Test Phonological and Phonemic Awareness Activities, pp. 280–283 **Use Concepts** *curious, delicate, information, inquire, sturdy* **Read to Connect** "Who Can We Ask?" pp. 98–105 Comprehension: Draw Conclusions **Write** Response to Literature: Independent Writing	Reproducible p. 248 Sentence Reading Chart, p. 252 Assessment Book, p. 24 Student White Boards Student Reader: Unit 1 Routine Card 5 Practice Book, p. 25, Writing

See pp. xvi–xvii for how *My Sidewalks* integrates instructional practices for ELL.

Word Work

Phonemic Awareness Segment and Count Sounds

	To Do	To Say	*2 minutes*
Scaffold instruction.	Distribute white boards. Write *mud*.	**Model** Listen to the sounds in *mud.* Stretch the sounds /mmm/ /uuu/ /d/ as you write *m, u, d.* Repeat. This time have children write the letters as you write. **Now let's count the sounds in** *mud.* **I will say the word slowly and hold up a finger for each sound: /m/ /u/ /d/. There are three sounds in** *mud.*	
	Write *duck*. Lead children in counting sounds as they write.	**Teach and Practice** Now let's say and count the sounds in *duck.* Have children say the sounds with you as you point to the letters. (/d/ /u/ /k/) **Hold up a finger for each sound. How many sounds in** *duck?* **(3) How many letters in** *duck?* **(4)** Continue counting sounds with these words:	

up (2)   fun (3)   hunt (4)   pups (4)   truck (4)   jumps (5)

Blending Strategy Short *u*

	To Do	To Say	*5–10 minutes*
Use the blending routine.	See Routine Card 1. Write *bag* and *big*.	**1 Connect** You can read words with these short vowel sounds. What are the words? What is the vowel sound in *bag?* (/a/) in *big?* (/i/) Now let's learn about short *u*.	*Routine*
	Display Sound-Spelling Card 35.	**2 Use Sound-Spelling Card** This is an umbrella. What sound do you hear at the beginning of *umbrella?* (/u/) Say it with me: /u/. The letter *u* can stand for the sound /u/ in *umbrella.*	
		3 Listen and Write Write the letter *u* for /u/. As you write, say the sound to yourself: /u/. Now say the sound aloud.	
Scaffold instruction.	Write *bug*.	**4 Model** The letter *u* can stand for /u/. This is how I blend this word: /b/ /u/ /g/, *bug.* Now you try: /b/ /u/ /g/, *bug.*	

When *u* is the only vowel at the beginning or in the middle of a word, it usually stands for its short sound, /u/.

$$\underrightarrow{b} \; \underrightarrow{u} \; \underrightarrow{g}$$

CORRECTIVE FEEDBACK	Write each practice word. Monitor student practice.	**5 Group Practice** Let's try the same thing with these words. Give feedback, using the *if . . . then* statements on Routine Card 1.

run   slug*   cups   drums   stuck   scrub

6 Individual Practice Write the words; have each child blend two of them.

sun   gum   cut   luck   junk   club   stump*   plucks*

Check understanding of practice words.	*Children need to make sense of words that they segment and blend. If needed, help children with meanings. A *slug* is like a snail, but it doesn't have a shell. (Point to picture on p. 102.) If you *stump* someone, you've asked something the person can't answer. *Plucks* means picks or pulls something off. (Demonstrate plucking something off a desk.)

MORE PRACTICE	Model spelling short *u* words.	**Spell and Write** What sounds do you hear in *bus?* (/b/ /u/ /s/) What is the letter for /b/? Let's all write *b.* What is the letter for /u/? Write *u.* What is the letter for /s/? Write *s.* Continue practice as time allows. Have children confirm their spelling by comparing it to what you've written.

hut   gum   tub   rugs   plus   lump   just   grunt   stung

High-Frequency Words *also, among, early, today*

To Do	To Say	
		3 minutes

Teach high-frequency words.

Display *also*.

1 Say, Spell, Write Use the Tested Vocabulary Cards. Display *also*. Here are some words that we won't sound out. We'll spell them. This word is *also*: *a, l, s, o* (point to each letter), *also*. What is this word? What are the letters in the word? Now you write *also*.

Point to the second and third letters in *also*.

2 Identify Letter-Sounds Let's look at the sounds in *also* that you do know. What is this letter? *(l)* What is the sound for this letter? *(/l/)* Continue with *s*.

3 Demonstrate Meaning Tell me a sentence using *also*. Model a sentence if children need help.

Display *among, early, today*.

Repeat the Routine with *among, early,* and *today*. Children can identify these letter-sounds: *among* (*m*/m/, *ng*/ng/), *early* (*l*/l/), *today* (*t*/t/, *d*/d/). Have children write the words in their word banks. Add the words to the Word Wall.

ACTIVITY **2** Build Concepts

Oral Vocabulary *delicate, inquire, sturdy*

To Do	To Say	
		5–10 minutes

Introduce oral vocabulary.

Scaffold instruction.

Display p. 5 of *Sing with Me Big Book*. Play audio CD.

This week you will learn how to search for answers to questions. Listen for the Amazing Words *sturdy, delicate,* and *inquire* as I sing this song. Play or sing the song. Then have children sing it with you.

Follow the Routine to teach *delicate, inquire,* and *sturdy*.

1 Introduce, Demonstrate, and Apply

sturdy, delicate The song talks about a *sturdy* oak and *delicate* spider webs. Have children say each word. *Sturdy* is another way to say "strong." Picture a *sturdy* oak tree in your mind. What does the *sturdy* tree look like? Does it have thin or thick branches? Can you climb on it? Now picture a spider web. Does the spider web look as *sturdy* as a tree does? No, a spider web looks *delicate*, or easily broken. A spider web is not as *sturdy* as an oak tree. What other things are *sturdy*? What things are *delicate*?

inquire The title of the song is "Where to Inquire." The word *inquire* means "ask," so the title "Where to Inquire" means "where to ask." The child in the picture has some questions and is *inquiring*, or searching for answers. The song says the more you *inquire*, the smarter you get. Do you agree?

Display the words on the Amazing Words board.

2 Display the Words Have children say each word as they look at it. You can find sounds you know in big words. Read *stur/dy* as you run your hand under the syllables. What consonant blend do you hear at the beginning of this word? *(st)* What sounds do these letters stand for? *(/s/ /t/)* For *delicate* and *inquire*, children can identify these letter-sounds and words parts: *delicate* (*del, i*/i/, *c*/k/, *t*/t/), *inquire* (*in, qu*/kw/).

Monitor understanding.

3 Use the Words Ask children to use each word in a sentence. Model a sentence if children need help.

MORE PRACTICE

Use oral vocabulary to discuss the song. Are books the only places people go to *inquire*? How else could you find answers to questions about *sturdy* oaks? about spider webs that look *delicate*?

ACTIVITY 3 Read a Passage

Build Background "Who Can We Ask?" pp. 98–105

To Do	To Say	
		10 minutes

Develop language and concepts.

See Routine Card 7. Read aloud p. 97 of the student book.

Preview the Week The selections this week tell about different ways people find answers to their questions. Read aloud the selection titles and descriptions on p. 97. Ask children what they think each selection will be about.

Scaffold instruction.

See Routine Card 6. Display pp. 98–105.

Ask questions and elaborate on answers to develop language.

Key concepts: *inquire, questions, answer, library, facts, computer, information, librarians, Internet, news, television, newspaper*

Before Reading Read the title aloud. Do a structured picture walk.

pp. 98–99 Where are the kids on the second page? (in class) Why do some have their hands up? (They're asking questions.) Yes, you raise your hand in class to inquire, or ask, about something. Who can help answer the kids' questions? (teacher, aide, classmates) Kids can also ask people in their families for help. Why do you think there is an owl on both pages? (Owls are thought to be wise.)

pp. 100–101 Why do you think there is a picture of an ant and some ducks on the first page? (The selection might tell where to find information about ants or ducks.) Where are the kids on the second page? (in a library) How can a library help kids answer their questions? (Kids can look in books.) Yes, you can look up facts in books. You can ask librarians to help you find information.

pp. 102–103 This is a slug. How is the boy finding out about slugs? (by using a computer) Yes, you can search the Internet to find information quickly. Where else can you find out about slugs? (books, magazines, television, DVDs)

pp. 104–105 You can get information about the weather by watching the news on television. You can also look at a map in the newspaper. Let's read about how to find answers to questions.

Guide comprehension.

Read pp. 98–105.

Model strategic reading. Use Routine Card 2.

During Reading Ask children to read along with you. As we read, ask yourself: What did I learn about getting answers? What is this mainly about? Read pp. 98–105 aloud with the group. Stop on each page to model asking questions. For example, for pp. 100–101: After I read, I ask myself: What is this page mainly about? The author asks questions such as "Can ants lift rocks?" The picture shows a library and the words say, "Kids can go here." I think this page is mainly about using the library to get facts that answer questions.

Monitor independent reading.

Use Routine Card 3.

Reread Have children read the selection aloud together without you. Then have them read it on their own in a whisper. Listen in on each child. Monitor reading, using Routine Card 3.

Summarize.

Use oral vocabulary to develop the concept.

After Reading Where can you *inquire* to get answers to questions? Some things you use, such as books, are *sturdy*, but others, such as maps, are *delicate*. Do you need to be more careful with something that is *sturdy* or something that is *delicate*?

Reread for Fluency "Who Can We Ask?" pp. 98–101

To Do	To Say	
		5–10 minutes

CORRECTIVE FEEDBACK

Monitor oral reading.

Read pp. 98–101 aloud. Read them three or four times so your reading gets better each time. Give feedback on children's oral reading and use of the blending strategy. See Routine Cards 1 and 4.

MORE PRACTICE

Instead of rereading just pp. 98–101, have children reread the entire selection three or four times. You may want to have children read along with the AudioText.

Homework Practice Book, p. 21, Phonics: Short *u*

ACTIVITY 1 · Reread for Fluency

Paired Reading "Who Can We Ask?" pp. 102–105

To Do	To Say	
		5–10 minutes

CORRECTIVE FEEDBACK

Pair children. Monitor paired reading.

Children read pp. 102–105 orally, switching readers at the end of the first page. Have partners reread; now the other partner begins. For optimal fluency, children should reread three or four times. Give feedback on children's oral reading and use of the blending strategy. See Routine Cards 1 and 4.

MORE PRACTICE

Instead of rereading just pp. 102–105, have children reread the entire selection three or four times. You may want to have children read along with the AudioText.

ACTIVITY 2 · Word Work

Phonemic Awareness Segment and Count Sounds

To Do	To Say	
		2 minutes

Scaffold instruction.

Distribute white boards. Write *thin.*

Model Listen to the sounds in *thin.* Stretch the sounds /th/ /iii/ /nnn/ as you write *th, i, n.* Repeat. This time have children write the letters as you write. Now let's count the sounds in *thin.* I will say the word slowly and hold up a finger for each sound: /th/ /i/ /n/. There are three sounds in *thin.*

Write *brush.* Lead children in counting sounds as they write.

Teach and Practice Now let's say and count the sounds in *brush.* Have children say the sounds with you as you point to the letters. (/b/ /r/ /u/ /sh/) Hold up a finger for each sound. How many sounds in *brush?* (4) How many letters in *brush?* (5) Continue counting sounds with these words:

that (3)   cash (3)   with (3)   ship (3)   thick (3)   splash (5)

Blending Strategy Consonant Digraphs sh/sh/, th/th/

5–10 minutes

Routine

	To Do	To Say
Use the blending routine. **Scaffold instruction.**	Write *trip* and *desk*.	**1 Connect** You already can read words like these. What are the words? *(trip, desk)* What two sounds are at the beginning of *trip*? (/t/ /r/) What letters stand for the sounds? *(t, r)* What two sounds are at the end of *desk*? (/s/ /k/) What letters stand for the sounds? *(s, k)* In consonant blends like *tr* and *sk*, each letter stands for a different sound. Today we are learning about pairs of letters that each stand for one sound.
	Display Sound-Spelling Cards 32 and 34.	**2 Use Sound-Spelling Cards** This is a shark. What sound do you hear at the beginning of *shark*? (/sh/) Say it with me: /sh/. The two letters *sh* stand for one sound, /sh/, when they are together. This is a thermometer. What sound do you hear at the beginning of *thermometer*? (/th/) Say it with me: /th/. The two letters *th* stand for one sound, /th/, when they are together.
		3 Listen and Write Write the letters *sh* for /sh/. As you write, say the sound to yourself: /sh/. Now say the sound aloud. Repeat for *th*/th/.
	Write *shop* and *dish*.	**4 Model** The two letters *sh* stand for /sh/. This is how I blend this word: /sh/ /o/ /p/, *shop*. Now you try it: /sh/ /o/ /p/, *shop*. Repeat with *dish*. Point out that *sh* can come at the beginning or end of a word.
	Write *that* and *path*.	The two letters *th* stand for /th/. This is how I blend this word: /th/ /a/ /t/, *that*. Now you try it: /th/ /a/ /t/, *that*. Repeat with *path*. Point out that *th* can come at the beginning or end of a word.
		My Sidewalks does not require children to distinguish between the two sounds of *th*, as in *then* and *think*. This distinction will not affect children's ability to decode.

s h o p   d i s h   t h a t   p a t h

	To Do	To Say
CORRECTIVE FEEDBACK	Write each practice word. Monitor student practice.	**5 Group Practice** Let's try the same thing with these words. Give feedback, using the *if . . . then* statements on Routine Card 1.
		shell dash bath them thing flash*
		6 Individual Practice Write the words; have each child blend two of them.
		fish shut than math slush* thump*
	Check understanding of practice words.	*Children need to make sense of words as they segment and blend. If needed, help children with meanings. Shiny things *flash*, or give off light, in the sun. *Slush* is snow that is partly melted. A *thump* is a heavy knock, like this. (Demonstrate thumping fist on desk.)
MORE PRACTICE	Model spelling *sh* and *th* words.	**Spell and Write** What sounds do you hear in *shop*? (/sh/ /o/ /p/) What are the letters for /sh/? Let's all write *sh*. What is the letter for /o/? Write *o*. What is the letter for /p/? Write *p*. Continue practice as time allows. Have children confirm their spelling by comparing it to what you've written.
		ship bush then with crash thank splash

High-Frequency Words *also, among, early, today*

3 minutes

	To Do	To Say
Teach high-frequency words. **Lead cumulative review.**	Display *also, among, early,* and *today*.	Use the Tested Vocabulary Cards. Point to a word. Say and spell it. Have children say and spell the word. Ask children to identify familiar letter-sounds. Have them take turns reading the words.
		Use the Tested Vocabulary Cards to review high-frequency words from previous weeks.

ACTIVITY 3 Read a Passage

Reading "A Bird Trick," pp. 106–113

	To Do	**To Say**	*10–15 minutes*

Develop language and concepts.

Scaffold instruction.

See Routine Cards 6 and 7. Display pp. 106–113.

Ask questions and elaborate on answers to develop language.

Key concepts: *car wash, coins, machine, camera*

Before Reading Have children recall what they learned about how people find answers. Read the title. Do a structured picture walk.

pp. 106–107 What happens at this place? Yes, at this car wash, people put coins, such as quarters, in this machine. Then water, suds, and brushes wash the car.

pp. 108–109 This camera (point to it) takes pictures of the coin box. What is the man doing in the first picture? (opening the coin box) This man takes the coins out each day and probably puts them in the bank.

pp. 110–111 The camera at the car wash took these pictures of the coin machine. What kind of camera do you think it is? (a video camera)

pp. 112–113 Where are the birds with all the coins? (by the coin box, then on the roof) What do you think is happening? (The birds are taking the coins to the roof.) Let's read to find out if our predictions are correct.

Teach story words.

Write *coin.*

You will read this word in the selection. It is *coin.* Have children say the word and spell it. Review its meaning.

Guide comprehension.

Read pp. 106–113. See Routine Card 2.

During Reading Ask children to read along with you. As we read, ask yourself: What did I learn? What is this selection mainly about? Read pp. 106–109 aloud with the group. Then ask: Who is this man? Where does he work? Yes, Bill works at the car wash. He collects the coins from the machine. What problem does Bill have? (The coins are gone.) What is Bill's plan? (to take pictures)

Read pp. 110–113 aloud with the group. Then ask: What happens on these pages? How did the pictures help get answers? (The pictures show birds taking the coins.)

Monitor independent reading.

Use Routine Card 3.

Reread Have children read the selection aloud together without you. Then have them read it on their own in a whisper. Listen in on each child. Monitor reading, using Routine Card 3.

Model summarizing.

Think aloud.

After Reading What happened in the selection? Model how to summarize. We read that the coins at the car wash were missing. Then Bill took pictures of the coin machine. The pictures show that birds were taking the coins.

MORE PRACTICE

Develop oral vocabulary.

How did Bill *inquire* about the missing coins? Would it be difficult to break into the *sturdy* coin box? Were you surprised that small, *delicate* birds were taking the coins?

ACTIVITY 4 Write

Response to Literature Shared Writing

	To Do	**To Say**	*5 minutes*

Guide shared writing.

Write sentence frames. Read the questions.

What does Bill want to know? Bill wants to know _____.
What does Bill find out? The birds _____.

Invite children to suggest answers. Discuss and record answers to complete the sentence frames. While writing, model connecting sounds to letters and forming letters (see pp. 257–259). Have children read answers aloud as you track print.

Homework

Practice Book, p. 22, Phonics: Digraphs *sh*/sh/ and *th*/th/

3

ACTIVITY 1 Reread for Fluency

Oral Reading "A Bird Trick," pp. 106–109

	To Do	**To Say**	*5–10 minutes*
CORRECTIVE FEEDBACK	Monitor oral reading.	Read pp. 106–109 aloud. Read them three or four times so your reading gets better each time. Give feedback on children's oral reading and use of the blending strategy. See Routine Cards 1 and 4.	
MORE PRACTICE		Instead of rereading just pp. 106–109, have children reread the entire selection three or four times. You may want to have children read along with the AudioText.	

ACTIVITY 2 Word Work

Phonemic Awareness Segment and Count Sounds

	To Do	**To Say**	*2 minutes*
Scaffold instruction.	Distribute white boards. Write *rush*.	**Model** Listen to the sounds in *rush*. Stretch the sounds /rrr/ /uuu/ /sh/ as you write *r, u, sh*. Repeat. This time have children write the letters as you write. Now let's count the sounds in *rush*. I will say the word slowly and hold up a finger for each sound: /r/ /u/ /sh/. There are three sounds in *rush*.	
	Lead children in counting sounds as they write.	**Teach and Practice** Have children say the sounds with you as you point to the letters. (/r/ /u/ /sh/) Hold up a finger for each sound. How many sounds in *rush*? (3) How many letters in *rush*? (4) Continue counting sounds with these words:	
		hush (3)　　shell (3)　　math (3)　　crush (4)　　thump (4)　　scrub (5)	

Fluent Word Reading Short *u*, Consonant Digraphs *sh*/sh/, *th*/th/

	To Do	**To Say**	*5–10 minutes*
Use the word-reading routine.	Write *hush*.	**1 Connect** You can read this word because you know that *u* can stand for /u/ and *sh* stands for /sh/. What is the word? *(hush)*	*Routine*
Scaffold instruction.	Write *thud, shrunk,* and *moth*.	**2 Model** When you come to a new word, look at all the letters in the word and think about its vowel sound. Say the letter-sounds in the word to yourself and then read the word. Model reading *thud, shrunk,* and *moth* in this way. When you come to a new word, what are you going to do?	
	Write each practice word.	**3 Group Practice** Let's read these words. Look at all the letters, think about the vowel sound, and say the letter-sounds to yourself. We will read words with short *u, sh,* and *th*. When I point to the word, let's read it together. Allow 2–3 seconds previewing time for each word.	
		suds　　mush　　math　　that　　flush　　thick　　trash　　shrub　　thrill	
CORRECTIVE FEEDBACK	**MONITOR PROGRESS**	**If . . .** children have difficulty previewing and reading whole words, **then . . .** have them use sound-by-sound blending.	
		If . . . children can't read the words fluently at a rate of 1–2 seconds per word, **then . . .** continue practicing the list.	

MORE PRACTICE	Model reading words in sentences.	When I read a sentence, I read each word without stopping between the words. If I come to a word I don't know, I blend it. Then I read the sentence again. Model reading this sentence, stopping to blend *brush: I brush the moth off my shin.*
	Write practice sentences.	Have each child read a sentence. **Did this pup splash in mud?** **That shop sells thick buns with jam.** **Seth had fresh fish and a cup of milk for lunch.**

High-Frequency Words *also, among, early, today*

	To Do	**To Say**	*3 minutes*
Review high-frequency words.	Display *also, among, early,* and *today.*	Use the Tested Vocabulary Cards. Point to a word. Say and spell it. Have children say and spell the word. Ask children to identify familiar letter-sounds and word parts. Have them take turns reading the words.	

ACTIVITY 3 Build Concepts

Oral Vocabulary *curious, information*

	To Do	**To Say**	*5–10 minutes*
Teach oral vocabulary.	Display p. 114 of the student book.	Today you will read about some *curious* kids who want *information.*	Routine
	Follow the Routine to teach *curious* and *information.*	**1 Introduce, Demonstrate, and Apply** *curious* When people are *curious,* they ask questions. *Curious* people want answers. Have children say *curious.* The kids in this story are *curious* about many things. What are you *curious* about? *information* This story is about the Just Facts Club. Kids in the club know lots of facts. Facts are kinds of *information.* Have children say the word. People can give you *information.* Where else can you get *information?*	
	Display the words on the Amazing Words board.	**2 Display the Words** Have children say each word as they look at it. You can find sounds you know in big words. What letter do you see at the beginning of *curious? (c)* What sound does it stand for? *(/k/)* Which letter is at the end of *curious? (s)* What sound does it stand for? *(/s/)* Read *in/for/ma/tion* as you run your hand under the syllables. Children can identify *in, f/f/, m/m/,* and *n/n/.*	
	Monitor understanding.	**3 Use the Words** Ask children to use each word in a sentence. Model a sentence if children need help.	
MORE PRACTICE		Use oral vocabulary to discuss searching for answers. Are you *curious* about things you already know or about things you want to know more about? What kinds of *information* can you find in a telephone book? If you're *curious* about something, how can you find *information* to answer your questions?	

ACTIVITY 4 Read a Passage

Reading "The Just Facts Club," pp. 114–125

	To Do	To Say	*10 minutes*

Teach draw conclusions.

Scaffold instruction.

Introduce the skill.

Model the skill.

Today you are going to learn how to draw conclusions. To draw conclusions, use what you know about life and what you read to figure out more about the characters and what happens in a story. For example, if I read a story about a puppy, I can use what I know about puppies and what the story tells me to draw conclusions about what the puppy in the story is like and what it may do.

Apply the skill. Display pp. 112–113.

Remember the ending of "A Bird Trick"? How do you think Bill felt when he saw the pictures of the birds taking the car wash coins? Think about what you read about Bill and Bill's plan. Think about what you know about animals that play tricks or do funny things.

Develop language and concepts.

See Routine Card 6. Display pp. 114–125.

Model using key words and concepts.

Key concepts: *facts, club, members, kindergarten, thinking, puzzled, stumped, photograph*

Monitor children's use of vocabulary.

Before Reading Read the title. Do a structured picture walk.

pp. 114–115 The sign says *The Just Facts Club.* What kind of club do you think that is? Yes, these club members must like facts! They probably like to find information.

pp. 116–117 This sign says "Kindergarten," so these kids must be kindergarteners. What are they doing? What questions would you ask a club that likes facts?

pp. 118–121 Point to a boy on p. 118 who seems to be thinking hard. On p. 120 the same boy grins, or smiles. He and the other club members must be answering everyone's questions.

pp. 122–123 Which character on p. 122 looks puzzled? Maybe a question has him stumped. When you're stumped, you don't know the answer.

pp. 124–125 All the kids are grinning in this photograph. They look thrilled. I wonder why this happened. What is your prediction?

Now turn to your partner and talk about the pictures, using the same words I did.

Guide comprehension.

Read pp. 114–125. Use Routine Card 2.

During Reading Ask children to read along with you. As we read, ask yourself: What do I know about clubs? What conclusions can I draw about the characters and what happens in the story? Read pp. 114–117 aloud with the group. Then ask: What conclusions can you draw about the club members? (They like facts. They know how to find information.)

Read pp. 118–121 aloud with the group. Then ask: What do you know about questions and answers like these? (They are riddles.)

Read pp. 122–125 aloud with the group. Then ask: What conclusions can you draw about the kindergarteners' feelings? (They're excited.) How do you know? (They grin. The author says "This thrills the K kids.")

Monitor independent reading.

Use Routine Card 3.

Reread Have children read the selection aloud together without you. Then have them read it on their own in a whisper. Listen in on each child. Monitor reading, using Routine Card 3.

Guide retelling.

Prompt children as they retell the story.

After Reading Have one child retell the story while the others assist. What happens at the beginning of the story? in the middle? at the end? (The K kids ask some questions. The club gives fun answers. Then the K kids finally stump the club. For their wish, the kids get their picture taken with the club.) See Monitoring Retelling, p. 246.

Homework

Practice Book, p. 23, Draw Conclusions

ACTIVITY 1 Reread for Fluency

Paired Reading "The Just Facts Club," pp. 114–117

5–10 minutes

	To Do	To Say
CORRECTIVE FEEDBACK	Pair children. Monitor paired reading.	Children read pp. 114–117 orally, switching readers at the end of the first page. Have partners reread; now the other partner begins. For optimal fluency, children should reread three or four times. Give feedback on children's oral reading and use of the blending strategy. See Routine Cards 1 and 4.
MORE PRACTICE		Instead of rereading just pp. 114–117, have children reread the entire selection three or four times. You may want to have children read along with the AudioText.

ACTIVITY 2 Word Work

Spiral Review Short Vowels a, e, i, o, u

5–10 minutes

	To Do	To Say
Review short vowels.	Write *map, tell, thin, pot,* and *hush.*	Look at these words. You can read these words because you know the sounds of short vowels: short a/a/, short e/e/, short i/i/, short o/o/, and short u/u/. Remember, when there is only one vowel at the beginning or in the middle of the word, it usually stands for its short sound. Blend the letter-sounds in each word and read each one aloud. *(map, tell, thin, pot, hush)*
	Distribute white boards.	**Sort Words** Use a chart to sort words with short vowels. Read the words and have children copy each word under the correct short vowel heading. Call on individuals to choose a word from the chart, read it aloud, and use it in sentences.

Routine

Words: *dig, bus, cats, that, brush, hot, up, wish, moth, shed*

Short *a*	Short *e*	Short *i*	Short *o*	Short *u*
cats	shed	dig	hot	bus
that		wish	moth	brush
				up

CORRECTIVE FEEDBACK	**MONITOR PROGRESS**	*If . . .* children have difficulty identifying vowel sounds, *then . . .* say the words, emphasizing each sound. Have them echo you.
MORE PRACTICE	Model reading words in sentences.	When I read a sentence, I read each word without stopping between the words. If I come to a word I don't know, I blend it. Then I read the sentence again. Model reading this sentence, stopping to blend *splash: My pet frog jumps in the bath with a big splash!*
	Write practice sentences.	Have each child read a sentence. Miss Hill tells Tom to shush in math class. Bob drinks a cup of fresh milk with his snack. The fat pigs dash into the wet mud.
	Phonological and Phonemic Awareness	Optional practice activities, pp. 280–283

ACTIVITY 3 Read Together

Echo Reading "A Visit to the Library," p. 126

	To Do	To Say	10 minutes
Develop language and concepts.	Display p. 126.	**Before Reading** This diagram shows parts of a library. What can you find in a library? (Allow children to share what they know.) How could you use a diagram like this? (to know where to go in the library) The computers area is here. Point. You use computers to find information quickly. Repeat for other labels.	
Model fluent reading.		Read the title. Ask children to predict what the words under the diagram will be about. Listen as I read this question. When I read questions, I often raise my voice near the end of them. Read the question, raising your voice on *first.*	
	Build fluency through echo reading.	**Echo Reading** I'll read the question again. Then you repeat it back to me. Try to make your voice sound like mine. Repeat a few times, having children point to words as they read. Read the diagram labels using questions and answers like these: Where are (the magazines)? (The magazines) are here. Point to the label as you say it in your question. Have children use the same terms in their answer and point to the appropriate diagram label.	
Develop concepts.	Monitor listening comprehension.	**After Reading** What are these circles? (tables) Where is the librarian's desk? If you drew a diagram of a room in your house, what would you show?	

ACTIVITY 4 Build Concepts

Oral Vocabulary *curious, delicate, information, inquire, sturdy*

	To Do	To Say	5–10 minutes
Review oral vocabulary.	Read the words on the Amazing Words board.	**Focus on Letter-Sounds** Remember, you can find sounds you know in big words.	
		• Which word begins with *s?* Which word ends with *s?* In these words, does *s* stand for /s/ or /z/?	
		• What two words begin with *in?* Which word begins with /d/?	
	Encourage discussion.	**Ask for Reasons and Examples** Review the meanings of the words. Then ask questions and give directives to elicit reasons and examples.	
		• What are some *sturdy* things? What are some *delicate* things?	
		• Why would someone *inquire* about something? What are you *curious* about? Where or how would you *inquire* about it?	
		• Give an example of *information.* Tell where you might find this *information.*	
MORE PRACTICE	Apply oral vocabulary to new situations.	• Raise your hand when you hear a word that means almost the same as *sturdy:* funny (no), strong (yes), silly (no). Raise your hand when you hear a word that means almost the same as *delicate:* wild (no), sweet (no), thin (yes).	
		• Answer *yes* or *no.* Give reasons for your answers. Would you *inquire* if you wanted to learn someone's address? (yes) Would you *inquire* if you wanted to tell someone how much fun you had at a party? (no) Would a *curious* cat look in a box? (yes)	
		• Tell me where you would find *information* about these things: television program times, weather reports, word spellings.	

ACTIVITY 5 | Write

Response to Literature Interactive Writing

| To Do | To Say | *5–10 minutes* |

Generate ideas.

Review the story "The Just Facts Club."

What do the kids in the Just Facts Club like to do? Discuss the reasons the Just Facts Club members like to answer questions. Invite children to share other riddles or silly questions/answers they have heard.

Share the pen.

Have children participate in writing silly questions.

Write *Which hens are wet?* Have children read the sentence you wrote. Then have them write their own silly questions. Invite individuals to write familiar letter-sounds, word parts, and high-frequency words. Have them find the spelling of high-frequency words on the Word Wall. Ask questions such as:

- **What is the first sound in** *hen?* (/h/) **What is the letter for /h/?** *(h)*
- **What is the vowel sound in** *hen?* (/e/) **What is the letter for /e/?** *(e)*
- **What is the last sound in** *hen?* (/n/) **What is the letter for that sound?** *(n)*

Writing elements: conventions

Frequently reread what has been written while tracking the print. Point out that each question starts with a capital letter and ends with a question mark. Point out the extra space between words.

Read the completed questions aloud, having children read with you. (For example, *When is grass not green? Which pigs are thin?*)

MORE PRACTICE

Prompt independent writing.

Journal Writing Tell about a funny joke you have heard.

Homework Practice Book, p. 24, High-Frequency Words

ACTIVITY 1 — Assessment Options

Sentence Reading

To Do | **To Say**

5 minutes

Assess sentence reading.

Use reproducible p. 248.

Have each child read the sentences. Record scores on the Sentence Reading Chart, p. 252. Work with one child as others complete Write Sentences below.

They have a pup, but they also want a fish.
Today we rush and get to math class early.
Hunt for shells among the wet rocks.

CORRECTIVE FEEDBACK

MONITOR PROGRESS

If . . . children have trouble reading words with short *u, sh*/sh/, or *th*/th,
then . . . reteach the blending strategy lessons on pp. 68 and 72.

If . . . children cannot read a high-frequency word,
then . . . mark the missed word or words on a high-frequency word list and send the list home for additional practice or have them practice with a fluent reader.

If . . . children misread a word in the sentence,
then . . . correct the error and have them reread the word and then the sentence.

Practice sentence writing.

Provide white boards.

Write Sentences Have children copy the sentences from reproducible p. 248 on white boards. Have them confirm their spellings of the words they wrote by comparing them to the words in the sentences.

Phonological and Phonemic Awareness

Optional practice activities, pp. 280–283

End-of-Unit Test

To Do | **To Say**

5–10 minutes

Assess fluency and comprehension.

Use Assessment Book, p. 24.

Options for end-of-unit assessment are available in the Assessment Book.

ACTIVITY 2 — Use Concepts

Oral Vocabulary *curious, delicate, information, inquire, sturdy*

To Do | **To Say**

5 minutes

Check understanding of oral vocabulary.

Use the Amazing Words to wrap up the week's concept.

Monitor understanding of oral vocabulary, using Routine Card 5.

As time allows, ask questions such as these.

- Tell me about the pictures on pp. 98–105 using some of the week's Amazing Words.
- Tell me what a *sturdy* necklace might look like. Tell me what a *delicate* necklace might look like. In what ways is a *sturdy* necklace different from a *delicate* one?
- What is an animal that you are very *curious* about? Why are you *curious* about it?

Preview next week's concept.

- Who would you ask or where would you look to find *information* about rules for a game or sport?

Next week you will read about what to do in dangerous situations.

ACTIVITY 3 Read to Connect

Reread "Who Can We Ask?" pp. 98–105

To Do | **To Say** | 5 minutes

Monitor comprehension: draw conclusions.

Have children reread "Who Can We Ask?" silently.

As you read, draw conclusions by thinking about what you already know about real life and what you read. After rereading, ask:

- Are there lots of different people you can ask if you have questions, or are there just a few people you can ask?
- Are there just a few places where you can find information, or are there many places to find information?

Ask children who they can ask and where they can go to get answers to their questions. List their responses on the board. (For example: I can ask a pal; I can look at a map.) Children will use the list for Activity 4.

Make connections.

Have children make connections across texts.

We also read "A Bird Trick." Find that. What is Bill curious about? How does Bill get information? What does Bill learn? Record ideas in a chart.

We also read "The Just Facts Club." Draw conclusions about the club and the K kids. Why do you think the club likes to give answers? Why do the K kids like to ask the club questions? Record ideas in webs.

What did all the selections we read this week show us about searching for answers to questions? What is the big idea? (There are many different ways to get answers to questions.)

ACTIVITY 4 Write

Response to Literature Independent Writing

To Do | **To Say** | 5–10 minutes

Assign narrative writing.

Today you will write about finding answers to questions. First, think about something you are curious about. Write a story about some people who were curious about the same thing and tell how they found answers to their questions. Encourage children to use words you wrote on the board for Activity 3 as they write.

Guide sentence correction.

Writing elements: conventions, focus, support

Have children check their writing by asking themselves these questions.

- Did I begin each sentence with a capital letter?
- Did I use periods and question marks correctly?
- Are all the sentences about my topic?
- Did I add details?

MORE PRACTICE

Have children share their sentences with the group. Write their sentences on the board. Have children compare their ideas about finding answers and write any facts they know that can answer their classmates' questions.

Homework Practice Book, p. 25, Writing

Unit 2 Week 1 *Danger!*

What can we do in a dangerous situation?

Objectives *This week students will...*

Phonemic Awareness
- segment, count, and delete sounds in words

Phonics
- blend and read words with *ch*/ch/, *tch*/ch/, *wh*/hw/, and the inflected ending *-ing*
- apply knowledge of letter-sounds to decode unknown words when reading
- recognize high-frequency words *around, eight, enough, nothing*

Fluency
- practice fluency with oral rereading

Vocabulary
- build concepts and oral vocabulary: *courageous, hazard, prevent, rescue, wildfire*

Text Comprehension
- read connected text
- identify sequence to improve comprehension
- write in response to literature

Word Work *This week's phonics focus is . . .*

Consonant Digraphs *ch, tch, wh*   Ending *-ing*

High-Frequency Words *Tested Vocabulary*

The first appearance of each word in the Student Reader is noted below.

around	The new kids walk **around** school. (p. 7) The top spins **around.**
eight	The number between seven and nine is **eight.** (p. 10)
enough	We have **enough** snacks for all. (p. 9)
nothing	There is **nothing** in the empty closet. (p. 8)

Amazing Words *Oral Vocabulary*

The week's vocabulary is related to the concept of knowing what to do in a dangerous situation.

courageous	brave
hazard	something that may cause danger
prevent	to keep from happening
rescue	to save a person from danger or get her or him out of trouble
wildfire	a fire in nature that is not planned

Student Reader Unit 2 *This week students will read the following selections.*

Daily Lesson Plan

	ACTIVITIES	MATERIALS
Day 1	**Word Work** Phonemic Awareness: Segment and Count Sounds Phonics: Blend Words with *ch*/ch/, *tch*/tch, *wh*/wh/ High-Frequency Words *around, eight, enough, nothing* **Build Concepts** *courageous, hazard, rescue* **Read a Passage** "Danger!" pp. 6–11 Comprehension: Use Strategies Reread for Fluency	Student White Boards Sound-Spelling Cards 7, 41 Tested Vocabulary Cards *Sing with Me Big Book* and Audio CD Student Reader: Unit 2 Routine Cards 1, 2, 3, 4, 6, 7 AudioText Practice Book, p. 26, Digraphs *ch, tch, wh*
Day 2	**Reread for Fluency** **Word Work** Phonemic Awareness: Delete Ending Sounds Phonics: Blend Words with -*ing* High-Frequency Words *around, eight, enough, nothing* **Read a Passage** "Danger on the Job," pp. 12–15 Comprehension: Use Strategies **Write** Response to Literature: Shared Writing	Student Reader: Unit 2 Student White Boards Tested Vocabulary Cards Routine Cards 1, 2, 3, 4, 6, 7 AudioText Practice Book, p. 27, Ending -*ing*
Day 3	**Reread for Fluency** **Word Work** Phonemic Awareness: Delete Ending Sounds Phonics: Fluent Word Reading High-Frequency Words *around, eight, enough, nothing* **Build Concepts** *prevent, wildfire* **Read a Passage** "Fire on the Hill," pp. 16–23 Comprehension: Sequence	Student Reader: Unit 2 Student White Boards Tested Vocabulary Cards Routine Cards 1, 2, 3, 4, 6 AudioText Practice Book, p. 28, Sequence
Day 4	**Reread for Fluency** **Word Work** Phonics: Spiral Review Phonological and Phonemic Awareness Activities, pp. 280–283 **Read Together** "Fire Safety at Home," p. 24 Comprehension: Listening **Build Concepts** *courageous, hazard, prevent, rescue, wildfire* **Write** Response to Literature: Interactive Writing	Student Reader: Unit 2 Routine Cards 1, 4 AudioText Student White Boards Practice Book, p. 29, High-Frequency Words
Day 5	**Assessment Options** Fluency, Comprehension Sentence Reading; Passage Reading Phonological and Phonemic Awareness Activities, pp. 280–283 **Use Concepts** *courageous, hazard, prevent, rescue, wildfire* **Read to Connect** "Danger!" pp. 6–11 Comprehension: Sequence **Write** Response to Literature: Independent Writing	Reproducible p. 248 Sentence Reading Chart, p. 253 Fluency Progress Chart, p. 245 Student White Boards Student Reader: Unit 2 Routine Card 5 Practice Book, p. 30, Writing

See pp. xvi–xvii for how *My Sidewalks* integrates instructional practices for ELL.

1

Word Work

Phonemic Awareness Segment and Count Sounds

To Do	To Say	

2 minutes

Scaffold instruction.

Distribute white boards. Write *inch*.

Model Listen to the sounds in *inch*. Stretch the sounds /iii/ /nnn/ /ch/ as you write *i, n, ch*. Repeat. This time have children write the letters as you write. **Now let's count the sounds in *inch*. I will say the word slowly and hold up a finger for each sound: /i/ /n/ /ch/. There are three sounds in *inch*.**

Lead children in counting sounds as they write.

Teach and Practice Have children say the sounds with you as you point to the letters. (/i/ /n/ /ch/) **Hold up a finger for each sound. How many sounds in *inch*?** (3) **How many letters in *inch*?** (4) Continue counting sounds with these words:

such (3)	when (3)	catch (3)	which (3)	chest (4)	switch (4)

Blending Strategy Digraph *ch/ch/, tch/ch/, wh/hw/*

To Do	To Say	

Routine

Use the blending routine.

Write *ship*.

1 Connect You already can read this word. What is it? What is the beginning sound in *ship*? (/sh/) What two letters represent this sound? *(sh)* Now let's look more at pairs or groups of letters that stand for one sound when they are together.

Display Sound-Spelling Card 7.

2 Use Sound-Spelling Card This is chalk. What sound do you hear at the beginning of *chalk*? (/ch/) Say it with me: /ch/. The two letters *ch* stand for one sound, /ch/, when they are together. The letters *tch* can also stand for /ch/, as in *watch*. Point to a wristwatch.

Scaffold instruction.

3 Listen and Write Write the letters *ch* for /ch/. As you write, say the sound to yourself: /ch/. Now say the sound aloud. Repeat for *tch*/ch/.

Write *chin, branch,* and *catch*.

4 Model The letters *ch* stand for /ch/. This is how I blend this word: /ch/ /i/ /n/, *chin*. Now you try: /ch/ /i/ /n/, *chin*. Repeat with *branch* and *catch*. Point out that *ch* can come at the beginning or end of a word. The letters *tch* can come at the end of a word, but not at the beginning.

Display Sound-Spelling Card 41. Write *when*.

Repeat steps 2 and 3 for *wh*/hw/. Use Sound-Spelling Card 41, depicting a whale, and explain that the letters *wh* can stand for the sound /hw/ at the beginning of *whale*. Then model blending *when*: /hw/ /e/ /n/, *when*.

$$\underrightarrow{c\ h\ i\ n} \qquad \underrightarrow{b\ r\ a\ n\ c\ h} \qquad \underrightarrow{c\ a\ t\ c\ h} \qquad \underrightarrow{w\ h\ e\ n}$$

CORRECTIVE FEEDBACK

Write each practice word. Monitor student practice.

5 Group Practice Let's try the same thing with these words. Give feedback, using the *if . . . then* statements on Routine Card 1.

chin	itch	munch*	whip	fetch*

6 Individual Practice Write the words; have each child blend two of them.

rich	check	lunch	stitch	which	pitch	whiz*	ditch

Check understanding of practice words.

*Children need to make sense of words that they segment and blend. If needed, help children with meanings. When I *munch* a chip, I chew it. A dog can *fetch*, or go get, a ball. Jo is a *whiz* at math. She's great at it.

MORE PRACTICE

Model spelling *ch, tch,* and *wh* words.

Spell and Write What sounds do you hear in *chin*? (/ch/ /i/ /n/) What are the letters for /ch/? Let's all write *ch*. What is the letter for /i/? Write *i*. What is the letter for /n/? Write *n*. Continue practice as time allows. Have children confirm their spelling by comparing it to what you've written.

chip	such	when	bunch	ditch	hatch	which	patch	chick

High-Frequency Words *around, eight, enough, nothing*

To Do	To Say	
		3 minutes

Teach high-frequency words.

Display *around.*

1 Say, Spell, Write Use the Tested Vocabulary Cards. Display *around.* Here are some words that we won't sound out. We'll spell them. This word is *around: a, r, o, u, n, d* (point to each letter), *around.* What is this word? What are the letters in the word? Now you write *around.*

Point to the last two letters in *around.*

2 Identify Letter-Sounds Let's look at the sounds in *around* that you do know. What consonant blend do you see at the end of *around?* (nd) What sounds do these letters stand for? (/nd/)

3 Demonstrate Meaning Tell me a sentence using *around.* Model a sentence if children need help.

Display *eight, enough,* and *nothing.*

Repeat the Routine with *eight, enough,* and *nothing.* Children can identify these letter-sounds and word parts: *eight* (t/t/), *enough* (n/n/), *nothing* (n/n/, *thing*). Have children write the words in their word banks. Add the words to the Word Wall.

Routine

ACTIVITY **2** Build Concepts

Oral Vocabulary *courageous, hazard, rescue*

To Do	To Say	
		5–10 minutes

Introduce oral vocabulary.

Scaffold instruction.

Display p. 6 of *Sing with Me Big Book.* Play audio CD.

This week you will learn about what we can do in dangerous situations. Listen for the Amazing Words *courageous, hazard,* and *rescue* as I sing this song. Play or sing the song. Then have children sing it with you.

Routine

Follow the Routine to teach *courageous, hazard,* and *rescue.*

1 Introduce, Demonstrate, and Apply

courageous The girl who helps save her friend is *courageous. Courageous* means brave. Have children say the word. The girl in the song helps make a *courageous rescue.* When a person does something that takes courage, that person is *courageous.*

hazard In the song, the girl's friend is facing a *hazard.* A *hazard* is something that may cause danger. A *hazard* might hurt someone or damage something. Have children say the word. Lightning can be a *hazard.* Poison can be a *hazard.* What other things can be *hazards?*

rescue The title of this song is "To the Rescue." When you *rescue* someone, you save the person from danger or get her or him out of trouble. Have children say the word. Forest rangers *rescue* hikers who get hurt or lost in the woods, and firefighters *rescue* people from fires. What other workers might *rescue* people or animals?

Display the words on the Amazing Words board.

2 Display the Words Have children say each word as they look at it. You can find sounds you know in big words. Read *res/cue* as you run your hand under the syllables. What letters are in the first part of *rescue?* (res) What sound does this word part make? (/res/) What sound does the letter *c* stand for in *rescue?* (/k/) For *hazard* and *courageous,* children can identify these letter-sounds and word parts: *hazard* (haz, d/d/), *courageous* (c/k/, r/r/, s/s/).

Monitor understanding.

3 Use the Words Ask children to use each word in a sentence. Model a sentence if children need help.

MORE PRACTICE

Use oral vocabulary to discuss the song. How does the girl help *rescue* her friend? How can calling 9-1-1 help *rescue* someone from a *hazard?* Tell me about a *courageous rescue* you've seen on TV or heard about.

ACTIVITY 3 Read a Passage

Build Background "Danger!" pp. 6–11

	To Do	To Say	10 minutes

Develop language and concepts.

See Routine Card 7. Read aloud pp. 1–5 of the student book.

Preview the Book Read aloud the title on p. 1. The selections in this book are about working together. Use pp. 2–3 to preview the weeks in this unit and p. 5 to preview the selections in this week. Ask children what they think each selection will be about.

Scaffold instruction.

See Routine Card 6. Display pp. 6–11.

Ask questions and elaborate on answers to develop language.

Key concepts: *sign, danger, dangerous, poison, harmful, symbol, warning*

Before Reading Read the title aloud. Do a structured picture walk with children.

pp. 6–7 What do these boys want to do? (swim) Look at the picture on the sign. Do you think they found a good spot to swim? Right, the sign shows a line crossing out a swimmer. It says, "Danger, No Swimming." This is not a safe spot for swimming. It is dangerous.

pp. 8–9 This girl wants a snack. Are these boxes and bottles safe to open? Why not? (No, they are dangerous.) When you see a picture of a skull and crossbones (point to it), it means there is poison inside. Poison is harmful to eat, drink, or touch. What should you do if you see something with this poison symbol? (Leave it alone.)

pp. 10–11 Have you seen warning signs like these before? They show dangers to watch out for or things you shouldn't do. What do these signs tell you? Which sign tells you not to light a campfire?

Teach story words.

Write *danger* and *fire*.

You will read these words in the selection: *danger* and *fire*. Have children say each word and spell it. Review their meanings. Now let's read to find out more about signs that warn people about dangers.

Guide comprehension.

Monitor independent reading. Model strategic reading. Use Routine Cards 2 and 3.

During Reading Read each page in a whisper. Raise your hand if you need help with a word. Stop at the end of each page to model asking questions. For example, for p. 7: After I read, I ask myself: What is this mainly about? The author says, "Much danger is in this pond." I think this page is mainly about a dangerous pond that people shouldn't swim in.

Summarize.

Use oral vocabulary to develop the concept.

After Reading What *hazards* do the signs warn people about? How can you stay safe from *hazards,* like falling rocks? Might you need a *rescue* if you didn't obey a warning sign? Why? Name some *courageous* people who might *rescue* someone from a burning forest.

Reread for Fluency "Danger!" pp. 6–8

	To Do	To Say	5–10 minutes

CORRECTIVE FEEDBACK

Monitor oral reading.

Read pp. 6–8 aloud. Read them three or four times so your reading gets better each time. Give feedback on children's oral reading and use of the blending strategy. See Routine Cards 1 and 4.

MORE PRACTICE

Instead of rereading just pp. 6–8, have children reread the entire selection three or four times. You may want to have children read along with the AudioText.

Homework Practice Book, p. 26, Phonics: Digraphs *ch*/ch/, *tch*/ch/, *wh*/hw/

ACTIVITY 1 Reread for Fluency

Paired Reading "Danger!" pp. 9–11

| To Do | To Say | *5–10 minutes* |

CORRECTIVE FEEDBACK

To Do: Pair children. Monitor paired reading.

To Say: Children read pp. 9–11 orally, switching readers at the end of the first page. Have partners reread; now the other partner begins. For optimal fluency, children should reread three or four times. Give feedback on children's oral reading and use of the blending strategy. See Routine Cards 1 and 4.

MORE PRACTICE

Instead of rereading just pp. 9–11, have children reread the entire selection three or four times. You may want to have children read along with the AudioText.

ACTIVITY 2 Word Work

Phonemic Awareness Delete Ending Sounds

| To Do | To Say | *2 minutes* |

Scaffold instruction.

To Do: Distribute white boards. Write *helping*.

Lead children in deleting ending sounds /ing/ as they write.

To Say:

Model Listen to the sounds in *helping*. Stretch the sounds /hhh/ /eee/ /lll/ /p/ /ing/ as you write *h, e, l, p, ing*. Repeat. This time have children write the letters as you write. **Now let's take off the ending sounds /ing/. Erase** *-ing*. **Listen to the sounds that are left: /h/ /e/ /l/ /p/.**

Teach and Practice Have children say the sounds with you as you point to the letters. (/h/ /e/ /l/ /p/) **What is** *helping* **without /ing/?** (*help*) Continue the activity with these words:

fixing (fix)	**resting** (rest)	**spilling** (spill)
checking (check)	**packing** (pack)	**drinking** (drink)

Blending Strategy Inflected Ending -ing

To Do	To Say	5–10 minutes

Use the blending routine.

Scaffold instruction.

Write *helps*.

Write *help*. Then add *-ing* to form *helping*.

1 Connect You can read words like this already because you know how to blend base words with the ending *-s*. What is the word? What is the base word for *helps?* (*help*) Today we will learn about adding the ending *-ing to* words.

2 Model I can add the ending *-ing* to *help* to make a new word. To blend this word, I cover the ending and read the base word: *help*. Then I uncover and read the ending: *-ing*. Finally, I blend the two parts together: *help, ing, helping*. Now you try it: *help, ing, helping*.

h e l p i n g

3 Listen and Write Write the word *catch*. Then add the ending *-ing* to make a new word. As you write, silently blend the base word and the ending together: *catch, ing*. Now say the new word aloud: *catching*.

CORRECTIVE FEEDBACK

Write each practice word. Monitor student progress.

4 Group Practice Let's try reading these words and then saying the base word without the ending *-ing*. Give feedback, using the *if . . . then* statements on Routine Card 1.

drilling* (drill)   buzzing* (buzz)   standing (stand)   munching (munch)

5 Individual Practice Write the words. Have each child blend two of them.

lifting   asking   yelling   pitching*   pinching   stinging   splashing

Check understanding of practice words.

*Children need to make sense of words that they segment and blend. If needed, help children with meanings. When a worker is *drilling*, he or she is using a tool to make a hole. (Point to p. 13.) Bees make a *buzzing* sound as they fly around. (Demonstrate.) *Pitching* a ball means throwing it to a batter.

MORE PRACTICE

Distribute white boards.
Model adding the ending *-ing*.

Build Words Write base words that do not change spelling when the ending *-ing* is added. Have children copy the words on their white boards. For the first word, model adding the ending *-ing*. Have children continue the activity by adding *-ing* to each word. Then have them read the words and use them in sentences.

act   jump   dash   hunt   sing   stack   punch   scratch

High-Frequency Words *around, eight, enough, nothing*

To Do	To Say	3 minutes

Teach high-frequency words.

Display *around*, *eight*, *enough*, and *nothing*.

Use the Tested Vocabulary Cards. Point to *nothing*. Say and spell it. *Nothing* is not formed from a base word and the ending *-ing*. Cover up *-ing* to show that the remaining letters don't form a base word. *Nothing* combines the words *no* and *thing*. Have children say and spell *nothing*. Ask children to identify familiar letter-sounds. Repeat for *around, eight*, and *enough*. Then have children take turns reading all the words.

Lead cumulative review.

Use the Tested Vocabulary Cards to review high-frequency words from previous weeks.

ACTIVITY **3** Read a Passage

Reading "Danger on the Job," pp. 12–15

To Do	To Say	*10–15 minutes*

Develop language and concepts.

Scaffold instruction.

See Routine Cards 6 and 7. Display pp. 12–15.

Ask questions and elaborate on answers to develop language.

Key concepts: *protect, beekeeper, danger, hazard, drilling, safe, crossing guard*

Before Reading Have children recall what they learned about checking for danger. Read the title. Do a structured picture walk with children.

pp. 12–13 Why does this worker wear a special suit and a mask? Right, these things protect the beekeeper from the danger of stinging bees. What danger, or hazard, can come from drilling in a street? (loud noise, flying rocks, getting hit) What does the worker wear to be safe? (Help children name clothing items and safety gear.) Name things you wear to stay safe when you play or do jobs.

pp. 14–15 How do the workers' hard hats and gloves protect them from hazards? (falling branches, getting cut) What does the crossing guard use to help drivers see her? (stop sign, colored vest) How does she keep children safe? (She stops traffic so they won't get hit by a car.)

Teach story words.

Write *danger*.

You will read this word in the selection. It is *danger*. Have children say the word and spell it. Review its meaning.

Guide comprehension.

Monitor independent reading.

Use Routine Cards 2 and 3.

During Reading Read the pages in a whisper. Raise your hand if you need help with a word. As you read, ask yourself: What am I learning about dangers that some workers face? What is this mainly about?

pp. 12–14 What did you learn about staying safe on the job? What are these pages mainly about? (Workers wear special clothing and other things to protect themselves from dangers on their jobs.)

p. 15 What did you learn about how the crossing guard keeps herself and the children safe? (She stops drivers so she and the children can cross streets safely.)

Model summarizing.

Think aloud.

After Reading What did you learn about workers on the job? What was the selection mainly about? Model how to summarize. The first part tells what workers wear to keep them safe. The last page tells how a crossing guard keeps herself and children safe. The selection is mainly about how workers stay safe on the job.

MORE PRACTICE

Develop oral vocabulary.

What are some other ways workers protect themselves from *hazards* at their jobs? Name some jobs where workers *rescue* people in danger. Do you have to be *courageous* to be a *rescue* worker?

ACTIVITY **4** Write

Response to Literature Shared Writing

To Do	To Say	*5 minutes*

Guide shared writing.

Write sentence frames. Read the questions.

What is the danger at Ben's job? The danger is _____.
What helps Ben? Ben puts on _____.

Invite children to suggest answers. Change the names in the sentence frames to include other jobs. Discuss and record answers to complete the sentence frames. While writing, model connecting sounds to letters and forming letters. (See pp. 257–259.) Have children read answers aloud as you track print.

Homework   Practice Book, p. 27, Phonics: Ending *-ing*

3

ACTIVITY 1 Reread for Fluency

Oral Reading "Danger on the Job," pp. 12–14

	To Do	To Say	5–10 minutes
CORRECTIVE FEEDBACK	Monitor oral reading.	Read pp. 12–14 aloud. Read them three or four times so your reading gets better each time. Give feedback on children's oral reading and use of the blending strategy. See Routine Cards 1 and 4.	
MORE PRACTICE		Instead of rereading just pp. 12–14, have children reread the entire selection three or four times. You may want to have children read along with the AudioText.	

ACTIVITY 2 Word Work

Phonemic Awareness Delete Ending Sounds

	To Do	To Say	2 minutes
Scaffold instruction.	Distribute white boards. Write *matching*.	**Model** Listen to the sounds in *matching*. Stretch the sounds /mmm/ /aaa/ /ch/ /ing/ as you write *m, a, tch, ing*. Repeat. This time have children write the letters as you write. **Now let's take off the ending sounds /ing/.** Erase *-ing*. **Listen to the sounds that are left: /m/ /a/ /ch/.**	
	Lead children in counting sounds as they write.	**Teach and Practice** Have children say the sounds with you as you point to the letters. (/m/ /a/ /ch/) **What is *matching* without /ing/?** (*match*) Continue: pinching (pinch) itching (itch) catching (catch) checking (check) hatching (hatch)	

Fluent Word Reading ch/ch/, tch/ch/, wh/hw/, Inflected Ending -ing

	To Do	To Say	5–10 minutes
Use the blending routine.	Write *hitching*.	**1 Connect** You can read this word because you know that *tch* stands for /ch/ and you know how to blend a base word and the ending *-ing*. What is the word? *(hitching) Hitching* means hooking up to.	*Routine*
Scaffold instruction.	Write *fetching*, *crunching*, and *whip*.	**2 Model** When you come to a new word, look at all the letters in the word and think about its consonant sounds. Model reading *fetching*, *crunching*, and *whip* in this way. When you come to a new word, what are you going to do?	
		3 Group Practice Let's read these words. Look at all the letters, think about the consonant sounds, and say the sounds to yourself. We will read words with *ch*, *tch*, *wh*, and *-ing*. When I point to the word, let's read it together. Allow 2–3 seconds previewing time for each word. chunk bench crutch whisk* which sketching* whacking* swinging stamping	
	Check understanding of practice words.	*Children need to make sense of words that they segment and blend. If needed, help children with meanings. You *whisk*, or sweep, crumbs off a table. *Sketching* means drawing. *Whacking* means hitting loudly.	
CORRECTIVE FEEDBACK	**MONITOR PROGRESS**	**If . . .** children have difficulty previewing and reading whole words, **then . . .** have them use sound-by-sound blending.	
		If . . . children can't read the words fluently at a rate of 1–2 seconds per word, **then . . .** continue practicing the list.	

Model reading words in sentences.	When I read a sentence, I read each word without stopping between the words. If I come to a word I don't know, I blend it. Then I read the sentence again. Model reading this sentence, stopping to blend *hatching: A chick is hatching from an egg.*
Write practice sentences.	Have each child read a sentence.
	When I get an itch, I cannot stop scratching it. **We had fun pitching and catching.** **Chuck and Whit are munching their lunch on a bench.**

High-Frequency Words *around, eight, enough, nothing*

To Do	To Say	3 minutes

Review high-frequency words.

| Display *around, eight, enough,* and *nothing.* | Use the Tested Vocabulary Cards. Point to a word. Say and spell it. Have children say and spell the word. Ask children to identify familiar letter-sounds. Have them take turns reading the words. |

ACTIVITY 3 Build Concepts

Oral Vocabulary *prevent, wildfire*

To Do	To Say	5–10 minutes

Teach oral vocabulary.

Scaffold instruction.

Display p. 16 of the student book.	Today you will read about a *wildfire* that people cannot *prevent*.
Follow the Routine to teach *prevent* and *wildfire*.	**1 Introduce, Demonstrate, and Apply** ***prevent*** People in this story could not *prevent* the *wildfire* on the hill. *Prevent* means to keep from happening. Have children say the word. Sometimes you cannot *prevent* a *wildfire* from starting, such as when lightning strikes dry woods. But campers can *prevent wildfires* by not making campfires. What else can people do to *prevent wildfires*? ***wildfire*** This story is about a *wildfire* that burns on a hill. A fire in nature that is not planned is a *wildfire*. Have children say the word. *Wildfires* can happen when woods are very dry. What might happen if a *wildfire* burns near homes?
Display the words on the Amazing Words board.	**2 Display the Words** Have children say each word as they look at it. You can find sounds you know in big words. Read *pre/vent* as you run your hand under the syllables. What two letters do you see at the beginning of *prevent*? (pr) What sounds do these letters make? (/pr/) at the end of prevent? (*nt*/nt/) Read *wild/fire* as you run your hand under the syllables. Children can identify *w*/w/, *ld*/ld/, *f*/f/, *r*/r/.
Monitor understanding.	**3 Use the Words** Ask children to use each word in a sentence. Model a sentence if children need help.

| | Use oral vocabulary to discuss the dangers of wildfires and how to prevent them. Why are *wildfires* dangerous? What should you do if you see a *wildfire*? How can people *prevent wildfires* if they burn leaves or trash? Who helps put out a *wildfire*? Is it safer to *prevent* a *wildfire* or to put out a *wildfire*? Why? |

ACTIVITY 4 Read a Passage

Reading "Fire on the Hill," pp. 16–23

To Do	To Say	10 minutes

Teach sequence.

Scaffold instruction.

Introduce the skill.

Model the skill.

Apply the skill.

Today you are going to learn about sequence. Sequence is what happens first, next, and last. In the story "Three Little Pigs," first the wolf blows down a straw house. Then he blows down the house made of twigs. Last, he tries to blow down the brick house, but he can't do it.

Walk over to a child. Shake his or her hand. Sit down. **What did I do first?** (walked up) **What did I do next?** (shook a hand) **What did I do last?** (sat down) **When you read "Fire on the Hill," think about sequence—what happens first, next, and last in the story?**

Develop language and concepts.

See Routine Card 6. Display pp. 16–23.

Model using key words and concepts.

Key concepts: *hills, danger, hazard, fire, wildfire, helicopter, police officer, safe, firefighter, rescued, burned*

Monitor children's use of vocabulary.

Before Reading Read the title. Do a structured picture walk.

pp. 16–17 Point to hills. **What danger, or hazard, is happening on the hills?** (a fire) Yes, there is a dangerous wildfire near the boy's home. Point to the helicopter. **How is it trying to help?** (drops water on fire) **Should the boy try to help?**

pp. 18–19 The fire is burning hot and fast. (Point to the smoke.) The police officer tells about the danger. **What do you think he is saying?** (get to a safe place) The boy's family goes to the school to be safe. **How does the boy feel? How do his parents help?**

pp. 20–21 The firefighter says the danger is ending. **How do you think the family feels about the people who rescued their home?**

pp. 22–23 The hill is burned. (Point to burnt area.) But finally the fire is over. **How does the boy feel now? How would you feel?**

Now turn to your partner and talk about the pictures, using the same words I did.

Teach story words.

Write *danger* and *fire*.

You will read these words in the story: *danger* and *fire*. Have children say each word and spell it. Review their meanings. **Now let's read to find out what happens when a fire starts on the hill.**

Guide comprehension.

Monitor independent reading.

Use Routine Cards 2 and 3.

During Reading Read the pages in a whisper. Raise your hand if you need help with a word. As you read, ask yourself: What happens first, next, and last?

pp. 16–17 What is the first important thing that happens in the selection? (Chuck spots a fire on the hill.)

pp. 18–19 What happens next? (Men in trucks tell Chuck to get away fast.) What happens after that? (Chuck, his mom, and his dad run to the school.)

pp. 20–23 What happens at the end? (The fire ends. Chuck and his parents go home. Chuck is happy everyone is safe.)

Guide retelling.

Prompt children as they retell the story.

After Reading Have one child retell the story while the others assist. **What important things happened first, next, and last?** (First, Chuck saw the fire. Then police told the family to get away, so they went to the school. Next, the fire ended. Finally, the family went home. They felt glad they were safe and their home didn't burn.) See Monitoring Retelling, p. 246.

Homework   Practice Book, p. 28, Sequence

ACTIVITY 1 Reread for Fluency

Paired Reading "Fire on the Hill," pp. 16–18

5–10 minutes

	To Do	To Say
CORRECTIVE FEEDBACK	Pair children. Monitor paired reading.	Children read pp. 16–18 orally, switching readers at the end of the first page. Have partners reread; now the other partner begins. For optimal fluency, children should reread three or four times. Give feedback on children's oral reading and use of the blending strategy. See Routine Cards 1 and 4.
MORE PRACTICE		Instead of rereading just pp. 16–18, have children reread the entire selection three or four times. You may want to have children read along with the AudioText.

ACTIVITY 2 Word Work

Spiral Review Consonant Digraphs *ch, sh, tch, th, wh*

5–10 minutes

	To Do	To Say
Review consonant digraphs. **Scaffold instruction.**	Write *chest, dish, with, which,* and *patch.*	**Look at these words. You can read these words because you know that sometimes two or more letters together stand for just one sound. For example, the letters *ch* in this first word stand for the single sound /ch/. Now blend each word silently. When I point at a word, read it aloud.** As needed, review the sound of each digraph: *ch*/ch/, *sh*/sh/, *th*/th/, *wh*/hw/, and *tch*/ch/. Use *chest* to point out the difference between a consonant digraph (two or more consonants that represent one sound) and a consonant blend (two or more consonants whose sounds are blended together).
	Distribute white boards.	**Sort Words** Have children copy the words *chick, rush, thin,* and *when* at the tops of their white boards. Then have them copy and place the following words in the correct column according to their consonant digraph sounds: *shell, bunch, match, check, fish, bath, whip, thick, scratch, then.* **What sound do you hear at the beginning of *chick*?** (/ch/) **What other words have /ch/?** Repeat for each of the other digraphs. Have children read each column aloud.

chick	rush	thin	when
bunch	shell	bath	whip
match	fish	thick	
check		then	
scratch			

My Sidewalks does not require children to distinguish between the two sounds of *th,* as in *thin* and *then.* This distinction will not affect children's ability to decode.

CORRECTIVE FEEDBACK	**MONITOR PROGRESS**	**If . . .** children have difficulty identifying consonant digraph sounds, **then . . .** say the words, emphasizing each sound. Have them echo you.

For more practice, see next page.

MORE PRACTICE

Model reading words in sentences.	When I read a sentence, I read each word without stopping between the words. If I come to a word I don't know, I blend it. Then I read the sentence again. Model reading this sentence, stopping to blend *bunch: Whit let a bunch of fish swim in the bathtub.*
Write practice sentences.	Have each child read a sentence. **Which shop sells such a thin watch? Trish is a whiz at checking math answers. When will Seth chop this thick branch?**

Phonological and Phonemic Awareness Optional practice activities, pp. 280–283

ACTIVITY 3 Read Together

Choral Reading "Fire Safety at Home," p. 24

To Do	To Say	*10 minutes*

Develop language and concepts.

Display p. 24.

Before Reading This is a fire truck. What do you know about fire trucks? (Allow children to share what they know.) What would you do if a fire started at home? Share information about fire safety. Smoke alarms warn you when a fire starts. Make a plan to get out quickly. Then call for help.

Model fluent reading.

Read the title of the poster. Ask children to predict what information the poster will have. When I read a poster like this, I read more slowly to make sure I understand important information. I pause before I read the next tip. Read the poster at an appropriate rate, pausing at the end of sentences and between tips. Read the poster a second time, having children point to each word.

Build fluency through choral reading.

Choral Reading Now read the poster aloud with me. Try to make your voice sound like mine as we read. Reread the poster several times with children.

Develop concepts.

Monitor listening comprehension.

After Reading What is "Fire Safety at Home" all about? How many fire safety tips are on the poster? (four) Why are fire safety tips important?

ACTIVITY 4 Build Concepts

Oral Vocabulary *courageous, hazard, prevent, rescue, wildfire*

To Do	To Say	*5–10 minutes*

Review oral vocabulary.

Read the words on the Amazing Words board.

Focus on Letter-Sounds Remember, you can find sounds you know in big words.

- Which words have an *s?* What sound does *s* make in these words?
- Which word has *fire* in it?
- Which word ends with /d/? Which word ends with /t/?

Encourage discussion.

Provide Examples Review the meanings of the words. Give examples. Then ask questions to elicit examples from children.

- Firefighters are *courageous,* or brave, when they *rescue* people from fires. What other workers act *courageously?*
- A *hazard* is something that may be dangerous. One *hazard* you read about is a *wildfire.* What are some other *hazards?*
- Park workers *prevent,* or stop, fires from happening by removing dead trees and dry bushes. What other ways can fires be *prevented?*

MORE PRACTICE

Apply oral vocabulary to new situations.

- If the example I give could be a *hazard,* raise your hand. I will call on someone to explain why it may be a hazard: Flowers (not), snowstorm (hazard), tornado (hazard), sunset (not), wildfire (hazard).
- I think that everyone is *courageous,* or brave, at one time or another. Could trying something for the first time be *courageous?* Why or why not? Could speaking in front of a group be *courageous?* Why or why not?
- Lots of dangers or problems can be *prevented.* Suppose you have a cold. How can you help *prevent* other people from catching it?

ACTIVITY **5** | Write

Response to Literature Interactive Writing

| To Do | To Say | *5–10 minutes* |

Generate ideas.

Share the pen.

Review the story "Fire on the Hill."

What does Chuck do after he sees the fire? Discuss the family's departure and eventual return home.

Write: *1. Chuck ___ the fire.*

Have children participate in listing the events in the story in order.

Have children read the number and words you wrote. Then have them supply verbs. Invite individuals to write familiar letter-sounds, word parts, and high-frequency words. Have them find the spelling of high-frequency words on the Word Wall. Ask questions such as:

- Cover the -*s* ending in *spots.* What base word do you see? *(spot)*
- What sound does the -*s* ending make? (/s/) What is the whole word? *(spots)*

Provide similar sentence frames for the other sequence of events.

2. The men ___ at Chuck.

3. Chuck ___ to school.

4. The fire ___.

5. Chuck ___ back home.

Writing elements: conventions

Frequently reread what has been written while tracking the print. Point out that each sentence starts with a capital letter and ends with a period. Point out the extra space between words.

Read the completed list aloud, having children read with you. (For example, *1. Chuck spots the fire. 2. The men yell at Chuck. 3. Chuck runs to school. 4. The fire ends. 5. Chuck runs back home.*)

MORE PRACTICE

Prompt independent writing.

Journal Writing Tell about a fire you have seen.

Homework

Practice Book, p. 29, High-Frequency Words

ACTIVITY 1 Assessment Options

Sentence Reading

	To Do	**To Say**	*5 minutes*
Assess sentence reading.	Use reproducible p. 248.	Have each child read the sentences. Record scores on the Sentence Reading Chart, p. 253. Work with one child as others complete Write Sentences below.	

Will eight chests be enough for all this cash?
Which chimp is swinging around the branch?
Mitch is bringing nothing to the boxing match.

CORRECTIVE FEEDBACK

MONITOR PROGRESS

If . . . children have trouble reading words with *ch*/ch/, *tch*/ch/, *wh*/hw/, or *-ing*,
then . . . reteach the blending strategy lessons on pp. 84 and 88.

If . . . children cannot read a high-frequency word,
then . . . mark the missed word or words on a high-frequency word list and send the list home for additional practice or have them practice with a fluent reader.

If . . . children misread a word in the sentence,
then . . . correct the error and have them reread the word and then the sentence.

Practice sentence writing. Provide white boards. **Write Sentences** Have children copy the sentences from reproducible p. 248 on white boards. Have them confirm spellings by comparing the words they wrote to the words in the sentences.

Phonological and Phonemic Awareness Optional practice activities, pp. 280–283

Passage Reading

	To Do	**To Say**	*5–10 minutes*
Assess fluency and comprehension.	Determine which children to assess this week.	Choose from these options: monitoring fluency (see pp. 244–245) and/or monitoring retelling (see p. 246). Have children reread "Fire on the Hill." Be sure each child is assessed every other week.	

If you have time, assess every child.

ACTIVITY 2 Use Concepts

Oral Vocabulary *courageous, hazard, prevent, rescue, wildfire*

	To Do	**To Say**	*5 minutes*
Check understanding of oral vocabulary.	Use the Amazing Words to wrap up the week's concept. Monitor understanding of oral vocabulary, using Routine Card 5.	As time allows, ask questions such as these.	

- Tell me about the pictures on pp. 6–11 using some of the week's Amazing Words.
- Tell me about some *hazards* that can cause danger. How do people *prevent* these *hazards*?
- Why are people who climb high mountains *courageous*? Why are workers who *rescue* people from *wildfires courageous*?
- What *courageous* things can children do? What *courageous* things have you done?

To Do	To Say
Preview next week's concept.	Next week you will read about what makes a team.

ACTIVITY 3 Read to Connect

Reread "Danger!" pp. 6–11

10 minutes

	To Do	To Say
Monitor comprehension: sequence.	Have children reread "Danger!" silently.	As you read, think about what happens first, next, and last. After rereading, ask: • What is the first thing Chad and Mitch do? After they read the sign, what must they do next? • What is the first thing Whit does? After Whit sees the danger signs, what must she do next? What will she do last?
Make connections.	Have children make connections across texts.	We also read "Danger on the Job." Find that. What are some of the dangers the workers face? What do they do to stay safe? Record children's ideas in a T-chart on the board. We also read about Chuck and the fire in "Fire on the Hill." What danger does Chuck see? What does he do first, next, and last? Record ideas in a list on the board. (For example: Chuck sees a fire; Chuck listens to the men; Chuck runs to the school; the fire stops so Chuck goes home.) Children will use the list for Activity 4. What do all the selections we read this week tell us about danger? What is the big idea? (We can protect ourselves from danger.)

ACTIVITY 4 Write

Response to Literature Independent Writing

5–10 minutes

	To Do	To Say
Assign expository writing.		Today you will write directions telling someone what to do if there is a fire. Write what the person should do first, next, and last. Encourage children to use words you wrote on the board for Activity 3 as they write.
Guide sentence correction.	Writing elements: organization, support	Have children check their writing by asking themselves these questions. • Did I begin directions with action words? • Did I use the correct order, telling what to do first, next, and last? • Did I use details to explain what to do?
MORE PRACTICE		Have children share their directions with the group. Write their sentences on the board. Children can compare directions and compile a class list. Then have them practice reading and writing sentences from the list.
Homework		Practice Book, p. 30, Writing

Unit 2 Week 2 *Team Spirit*

What makes a team?

Objectives *This week students will...*

Phonemic Awareness
- add ending sounds to words

Phonics
- blend and read words with inflected endings *-ed* and *-ing*
- apply knowledge of letter-sounds to decode unknown words when reading
- recognize high-frequency words *build, carry, heavy, water*

Fluency
- practice fluency with oral rereading

Vocabulary
- build concepts and oral vocabulary:
  ability, compete, contribute, recreation, victory

Text Comprehension
- read connected text
- identify sequence to improve comprehension
- write in response to literature

Word Work *This week's phonics focus is . . .*

Ending *-ed*   Inflected Endings

High-Frequency Words *Tested Vocabulary*

The first appearance of each word in the Student Reader is noted below.

build   To **build** is to make something by putting things together. (p. 31)

carry   When you **carry** something, you take it from one place to another. (p. 30)

heavy   If something is **heavy,** it is hard to lift or carry. It weighs a lot. (p. 30)

water   **Water** is liquid that fills oceans, rivers, lakes, and ponds. (p. 30)
             Water falls from the sky as rain.

Amazing Words *Oral Vocabulary*

The week's vocabulary is related to the concept of what makes a team.

ability   a special skill or talent

compete   to try to win a game, contest, or prize

contribute   to help or give advice

recreation   something people do for fun

victory   a win

Student Reader Unit 2 *This week students will read the following selections.*

Daily Lesson Plan

	ACTIVITIES	MATERIALS
Day 1	**Word Work** Phonemic Awareness: Add Ending Sounds Phonics: Blend Words with Inflected Ending *-ed* High-Frequency Words *build, carry, heavy, water* **Build Concepts** *compete, contribute, recreation* **Read a Passage** "Team Spirit," pp. 28–31 Comprehension: Use Strategies Reread for Fluency	Student White Boards Tested Vocabulary Cards *Sing with Me Big Book* and Audio CD Student Reader: Unit 2 Routine Cards 1, 2, 3, 4, 6, 7 AudioText Practice Book, p. 31, Ending *-ed*
Day 2	**Reread for Fluency** **Word Work** Phonemic Awareness: Add Ending Sounds Phonics: Blend Base Words and Endings High-Frequency Words *build, carry, heavy, water* **Read a Passage** "The Red Fins," pp. 32–35 Comprehension: Use Strategies **Write** Response to Literature: Shared Writing	Student Reader: Unit 2 Student White Boards Tested Vocabulary Cards Routine Cards 1, 2, 3, 4, 6, 7 AudioText Practice Book, p. 32, Base Words and Endings
Day 3	**Reread for Fluency** **Word Work** Phonemic Awareness: Add Ending Sounds Phonics: Fluent Word Reading High-Frequency Words *build, carry, heavy, water* **Build Concepts** *ability, victory* **Read a Passage** "Jon and Jen," pp. 36–45 Comprehension: Sequence	Student Reader: Unit 2 Student White Boards Tested Vocabulary Cards Routine Cards 1, 2, 3, 4, 6 AudioText Practice Book, p. 33, Sequence
Day 4	**Reread for Fluency** **Word Work** Phonics: Spiral Review Phonological and Phonemic Awareness Activities, pp. 280–283 **Read Together** "Be a Good Sport!" p. 46 Comprehension: Listening **Build Concepts** *ability, compete, contribute, recreation, victory* **Write** Response to Literature: Interactive Writing	Student Reader: Unit 2 Routine Cards 1, 4 AudioText Student White Boards Practice Book, p. 34, High-Frequency Words
Day 5	**Assessment Options** Fluency, Comprehension Sentence Reading; Passage Reading Phonological and Phonemic Awareness Activities, pp. 280–283 **Use Concepts** *ability, compete, contribute, recreation, victory* **Read to Connect** "Team Spirit," pp. 28–31 Comprehension: Sequence **Write** Response to Literature: Independent Writing	Reproducible p. 249 Sentence Reading Chart, p. 253 Fluency Progress Chart, p. 245 Student White Boards Student Reader: Unit 2 Routine Card 5 Practice Book, p. 35, Writing

See pp. xvi–xvii for how *My Sidewalks* integrates instructional practices for ELL.

Word Work

Phonemic Awareness Add Ending Sounds

To Do	To Say	*2 minutes*

Scaffold instruction.

Distribute white boards.
Write *spell/spelled, help/helped,* and *lift/lifted.*

Lead children in identifying ending sounds as they write.

Model Listen to the sounds in *spell.* Stretch the sounds /sss/ /p/ /eee/ /lll/ as you write *s, p, e, ll.* Repeat. This time have children write the letters as you write. **Now let's add the ending -ed. Listen to the sounds in *spelled.* Stretch the sounds** /sss/ /p/ /eee/ /lll/ /d/ as you add *-ed* to *spell.* Repeat. This time have children write *-ed* at the end of *spell.* Repeat with *help/helped* and *lift/lifted.*

Teach and Practice Have children say the sounds with you as you point to the letters in *spelled, helped,* and *lifted.* (/s/ /p/ /e/ /l/ /d/; /h/ /e/ /l/ /p/ /t/; /l/ /i/ /f/ /t/ /ed/) **What sound do you hear at the end of *spelled?* (/d/) *helped?* (/t/) *lifted?* (/ed/)** Continue the activity with these words:

jumped (/t/)   yelled (/d/)   wished (/t/)   filled (/d/)   planted (/ed/)

Blending Strategy Inflected Ending *-ed*

To Do	To Say	*5–10 minutes*

Use the blending routine.

Scaffold instruction.

See Routine Card 1.
Write *spills.*

1 Connect You already can read this word. What is it? What is the base word? *(spill)* What is the ending? *(-s)* Today we will learn about adding the ending *-ed* to base words.

Routine

Write *spill.* Add *-ed* to form *spilled.*

2 Model Add *-ed* to *spill.* The ending *-ed* shows that something happened in the past: *I spilled some milk yesterday.* To blend this word, I cover the ending. Then I read the base word: *spill.* Then I uncover and read the ending: /d/. Finally, I blend the two parts together: *spilled.* Now you try it: *spill, /d/, spilled.* What sound does *-ed* stand for in *spilled?* (/d/)

Write *pinched* and *dusted.*

Repeat with *pinched* and *dusted.* Point out that the ending *-ed* can also stand for the sound /t/ or /ed/.

s p i l l e d   p i n c h e d   d u s t e d

3 Listen and Write Write the word *smell.* As you write, say the sounds to yourself: /s/ /m/ /e/ /l/. Now add *-ed.* Blend the base word and the ending together: *smell, /d/.* Now say the word aloud: *smelled.*

CORRECTIVE FEEDBACK

Write each practice word.
Monitor student practice.

4 Group Practice Let's try reading these words. Give feedback, using the *if . . . then* statements on Routine Card 1.

melted   limped*   filled   checked   rested   rocked*

5 Individual Practice Write the words; have each child blend two of them.

kicked   ended   yelled   hunted   rushed*   banged

Check understanding of practice words.

*Children need to make sense of words that they segment and blend. If needed, help children with meanings. *Limped* means walked in a painful way. (Demonstrate.) Mom *rocked* the baby to sleep. (Demonstrate.) *Rushed* means moved quickly. We *rushed* to the ballgame.

MORE PRACTICE

Model building words with *-ed* endings.

Build Words Have children add *-ed* to the base words below and read the new words. Discuss how the ending of the base word may help them figure out if *-ed* stands for /d/, /t/, or /ed/. For example, a base word that ends in *ck* will usually have an *-ed* ending that stands for /t/. Model with *pick/picked.*

stack(ed)   add(ed)   spill(ed)   fix(ed)   dash(ed)   hatch(ed)

High-Frequency Words *build, carry, heavy, water*

To Do	To Say	

Teach high-frequency words.

Display *build.*

1 Say, Spell, Write Use the Tested Vocabulary Cards. Display *build.* Here are some words that we won't sound out. We'll spell them. This word is *build: b, u, i, l, d* (point to each letter), *build.* What is this word? What are the letters in the word? Now you write *build.*

Point to *b* and *ld* in *build.*

2 Identify Letter-Sounds Let's look at the sounds in *build* that you do know. Point to *b.* What is this letter? *(b)* What is the sound for this letter? *(/b/)* Continue with final consonant blend *ld.*

3 Demonstrate Meaning Tell me a sentence using *build.* Model a sentence if children need help.

Display *carry, heavy,* and *water.*

Repeat the Routine with *carry, heavy,* and *water.* Children can identify these letter-sounds: *carry* (*c/k/*), *heavy* (*h/h/*, *v/v/*), *water* (*w/w/*, *t/t/*). Have children write the words in their word banks. Add the words to the Word Wall.

Routine

ACTIVITY 2 Build Concepts

Oral Vocabulary *compete, contribute, recreation*

To Do	To Say	

Introduce oral vocabulary.

Scaffold instruction.

Display p. 7 of *Sing with Me Big Book.* Play audio CD.

This week you will learn about team spirit. Listen for the Amazing Words *compete, contribute,* and *recreation* as I sing this song. Play or sing the song. Then have children sing it with you.

Follow the Routine to teach *compete, contribute,* and *recreation.*

1 Introduce, Demonstrate, and Apply

compete The kids on the team in the song know how to *compete.* When a team *competes,* the teammates try to win a game, contest, or prize. Have children say *compete.* People *compete* when they play sports or when they enter spelling bees. What things do you *compete* in?

contribute The song explains that all the team members *contribute* to the team, or do their part to help the team do well. Have children say *contribute.* Each of you *contributes* to this class. You work together on projects. You help keep the room clean. What are some ways you *contribute* at home?

recreation The song says that the soccer game is *recreation. Recreation* is something people do for fun. Have children say *recreation.* Some kinds of *recreation,* like playing sports, are active. Other kinds of *recreation,* such as reading, are quiet. What kinds of *recreation* do you like most?

Display the words on the Amazing Words board.

2 Display the Words Have children say each word as they look at it. You can find sounds you know in big words. Read *com/pete* as you run your hand under the syllables. Look at the *c.* What sound does it make? What sounds do the letters *m, p,* and *t* make? For *contribute* and *recreation,* children can identify these letter-sounds and word parts: *contribute* (*con, trib*), *recreation* (*rec, r/r/, n/n/*).

Monitor understanding.

3 Use the Words Ask children to use each word in a sentence. Model a sentence if children need help.

MORE PRACTICE

Use oral vocabulary to discuss the song. In what sport does the team *compete?* How do team members *contribute* to the team? Why is the game *recreation,* even though team members work hard?

Read a Passage

Build Background "Team Spirit," pp. 28–31

	To Do	To Say	*10 minutes*

Develop language and concepts.

See Routine Card 7. Read aloud p. 27 of the student book.

Preview the Week Use the illustration on p. 26 to introduce this week's concept of team spirit. **Why might the child be holding a trophy? How can team spirit help a team?** Read aloud the titles and descriptions on p. 27. Ask children what they think each selection will be about.

Scaffold instruction.

See Routine Card 6. Display pp. 28–31.

Ask questions and elaborate on answers to develop language.

Key concepts: *uniforms, basketball, soccer, baseball, competes, prize, trophy, team spirit, contribute, build, builders*

Before Reading Read the title aloud. Do a structured picture walk with children.

pp. 28–29 Look at the balls the teams have and the uniforms they wear. **What kinds of teams are shown?** (basketball, soccer, baseball) Sometimes when a team competes, it wins a prize—like a trophy. (point to trophy) Look at the grins on everyone's faces. They have team spirit. They have fun playing together. **What makes a team fun?**

p. 30 **What is this team doing?** (planting) **How does everyone on the team contribute?** (by digging, carrying pots, and planting) The author says that one kid can't carry the heavy pot so the team lifts it together. Working together shows team spirit.

p. 31 The selection explains that a team of kids helped build this playground. They had fun putting the swings and other equipment together. Now everyone has fun playing here. **Did the builders of the playground have team spirit? Why or why not?**

Teach story word.

Write *team*.

You will read this word in the story. It is *team*. Have children say the word and spell it. Review its meaning. Now let's read to learn more about team spirit.

Guide comprehension.

Monitor independent reading.

Model strategic reading. Use Routine Cards 2 and 3.

During Reading Read each page in a whisper. Raise your hand if you need help with a word. Stop at the end of each page to model asking questions. For example, for p. 30: After I read, I asked myself: What is this page mainly about? The author writes, "This team dug and planted." I think this page is mainly about how a team of kids and adults works together to plant a garden.

Summarize.

Use oral vocabulary to develop the concept.

After Reading What did you learn about ways people *contribute* to teams? Must teams always *compete*? What kinds of *recreation* do the teams in the selection enjoy? When everyone *contributes*, does the work seem easier? Why?

Reread for Fluency "Team Spirit," pp. 28–30

	To Do	To Say	*5–10 minutes*

CORRECTIVE FEEDBACK

Monitor oral reading.

Read pp. 28–30 aloud. Read them three or four times so your reading gets better each time. Give feedback on children's oral reading and use of the blending strategy. See Routine Cards 1 and 4.

MORE PRACTICE

Instead of rereading just pp. 28–30, have children reread the entire selection three or four times. You may want to have children read along with the AudioText.

Homework

Practice Book, p. 31, Phonics: Ending *-ed*

ACTIVITY **1** # Reread for Fluency

Paired Reading "Team Spirit," pp. 29–31

5–10 minutes

	To Do	To Say
CORRECTIVE FEEDBACK	Pair children. Monitor paired reading.	Children read pp. 29–31 orally, switching readers at the end of the first page. Have partners reread; now the other partner begins. For optimal fluency, children should reread three or four times. Give feedback on children's oral reading and use of the blending strategy. See Routine Cards 1 and 4.
MORE PRACTICE		Instead of rereading just pp. 29–31, have children reread the entire selection three or four times. You may want to have children read along with the AudioText.

ACTIVITY **2** # Word Work

Phonemic Awareness Add Ending Sounds

2 minutes

	To Do	To Say
Scaffold instruction.	Distribute white boards. Write *smash/smashing*, *jump/jumped*, and *yell/yelled*. Lead children in counting sounds as they write.	**Model** Listen to the sounds in *smash.* Stretch the sounds /sss/ /mmm/ /aaa/ /shshsh/ as you write *s, m, a, sh.* Repeat. This time have children write the letters as you write. Now let's add the ending *-ing.* Listen to the sounds in *smashing.* Stretch the sounds /sss/ /mmm/ /aaa/ /shshsh/ /iiinnng/ as you add *-ing* to *smash.* Repeat. This time have children write *-ing* at the end of *smash.* Repeat with *jump/jumped* and *yell/yelled.* **Teach and Practice** Have children say the sounds with you as you point to the letters in *smashing, jumped,* and *yelled.* (/s/ /m/ /a/ /sh/ /ing/; /j/ /u/ /m/ /p/ /t/; /y/ /e/ /l/ /d/) What sounds do you hear at the end of *smashing?* (/ing/) *helped?* (/t/) *filled?* (/d/) Continue the activity with these words: rested (/ed/) lifted (/ed/) kicking (/ing/) winked (/t/) filled (/d/) planting (/ing/)

Blending Strategy Base Words and Endings

To Do	To Say	
		Routine
		5–10 minutes

Use the blending routine.

Write *helped* and *helping*.

1 Connect The endings *-ed* and *-ing* can be added to base words to describe actions: *I helped Tom yesterday. I am helping Jan now.* What have you learned about blending these words? (Cover the ending. Read the base word. Then read the ending. Finally, blend the parts.) What are these words? Today we will learn about base words whose spelling changes when *-ed* or *-ing* is added.

Scaffold instruction.

Write *hop, hopped,* and *hopping.*

2 Model Look at the spelling of these words. The *p* in *hop* is doubled before the endings *-ed* and *-ing* are added. This happens in short-vowel words that end with a single consonant. This is how to blend these words. For *hopped* and *hopping*, cover the added consonant and ending and read the base word. Then uncover and read the ending. Finally, blend the two parts. Let's blend these words together: *hop, ped, hopped; hop, ping, hopping.*

h o p p e d   h o p p i n g

Point out that *-ed* makes the sound /t/ in *hopped*. It can also make the sound /d/ or /ed/.

3 Listen and Write Write the word *grab.* Double the final consonant. Then add the ending *-ed* to the base word. Now blend the base word and the ending together: *grab, bed.* Say the word aloud: *grabbed.*

Repeat, adding *-ing* to *grab.* Remind children to double the final consonant before adding the ending.

CORRECTIVE FEEDBACK

Write each practice word. Monitor student practice.

4 Group Practice Let's try reading these words and saying the base word for each one. Give feedback, using the *if . . . then* statements on Routine Card 1.

getting	rubbed	stopping	clapped	swimming	chatted*
(get)	(rub)	(stop)	(clap)	(swim)	(chat)

5 Individual Practice Write the words; have each child blend two of them.

batted*	winning	grinned*	shopped	hugged	dropping

Check understanding of practice words.

*Children need to make sense of words as they segment and blend. If needed, help children with meanings. *I chatted,* or talked, with Ann last night. The player *batted,* or hit, the baseball a long way. (Demonstrate.) *Grinned* means smiled.

MORE PRACTICE

Model adding *-ed* and *-ing* endings to base words.

Build Words Write base words whose final consonant doubles when the endings *-ed* and *-ing* are added. Have children copy the base words on their white boards. For the first word, model doubling the final consonant and adding *-ed* and *-ing*. Have children continue the activity by adding the endings *-ed* and *-ing* to the base words.

chip	pet	spot	trip	scrub	plan	slip	drag

High-Frequency Words *build, carry, heavy, water*

To Do	To Say	
		3 minutes

Teach high-frequency words.

Display *build, carry, heavy,* and *water.*

Use the Tested Vocabulary Cards. Point to a word. Say and spell it. Have children say and spell the word. Ask children to identify familiar letter-sounds. Have them take turns reading the words.

Lead cumulative review.

Use the Tested Vocabulary Cards to review high-frequency words from previous weeks.

ACTIVITY 3 Read a Passage

Reading "The Red Fins," pp. 32–35

To Do	To Say

10–15 minutes

Develop language and concepts.

See Routine Cards 6 and 7. Display pp. 32–35.

Before Reading Have children recall what they learned about team spirit. Read the title. Do a structured picture walk with children.

Scaffold instruction.

Ask questions and elaborate on answers to develop language.

Key concepts: *swimming pool, lanes, compete, team, fins, race, team spirit, trophy, medal*

pp. 32–33 What place is shown? (a swimming pool) This swimming pool has lanes where swimmers compete to be the fastest swimmer. This girl is on the swimming team called the Red Fins. Why is that a good name for a swimming team?

p. 34 Why does the girl stretch out her arms? (to dive into the water) How can the rest of the team show team spirit while the girl races? (cheer for her)

p. 35 Which swimmer do you think won the race? (the girl in the middle) Yes, this girl holds a trophy and wears a medal. The team works hard, but they have fun.

Teach story word.

Write *team*.

You will read the word *team* in the story. Have children say the word and spell it. Now let's read to learn more about the Red Fins.

Guide comprehension.

Monitor independent reading.

During Reading Read the pages in a whisper. Raise your hand if you need help with a word. As you read, ask yourself: What did I learn about the Red Fins? What is this mainly about?

Use Routine Cards 2 and 3.

pp. 32–33 What did you learn about the Red Fins? What are these pages mainly about? (The Red Fins want to be a winning team.) They build a winning team by working hard and cheering for each other.

pp. 34–35 What do you learn about Beth? What are these pages mainly about? (Beth wins the race.) Beth helps her team by winning a race, but they will keep working hard to build a winning team.

Model summarizing.

Think aloud.

After Reading What did you learn about the Red Fins? What was the selection mainly about? Model how to summarize. The first two pages describe how hard the Red Fins work and how everyone on the swimming team contributes. The next pages describe a race that Beth, a member of the Red Fins team, wins. The selection is mainly about how the Red Fins are building a winning team.

MORE PRACTICE

Develop oral vocabulary.

Do you think the Red Fins like to *compete?* How do the team members who are not swimming *contribute* to the team? How can swimming on the Red Fins team be hard work and also *recreation?*

ACTIVITY 4 Write

Response to Literature Shared Writing

To Do	To Say

5 minutes

Guide shared writing.

Write sentence frames. Read the questions.

What does a swimming team do? A swimming team _____.
How does a swimming team win? A swimming team wins by _____.

Invite children to suggest answers. Discuss and record answers to complete the sentence frames. While writing, model connecting sounds to letters and forming letters (see pp. 257–259). Have children read answers aloud as you track print.

Homework

Practice Book, p. 32, Phonics: Base Words and Endings

3

ACTIVITY 1 | Reread for Fluency

Oral Reading "The Red Fins," pp. 34–35

	To Do	To Say	
			5–10 minutes
CORRECTIVE FEEDBACK	Monitor oral reading.	Read pp. 34–35 aloud. Read them three or four times so your reading gets better each time. Give feedback on children's oral reading and use of the blending strategy. See Routine Cards 1 and 4.	
MORE PRACTICE		Instead of rereading just pp. 34–35, have children reread the entire selection three or four times. You may want to have children read along with the AudioText.	

ACTIVITY 2 | Word Work

Phonemic Awareness Add Ending Sounds

	To Do	To Say	
			2 minutes
Scaffold instruction.	Distribute white boards. Write *grill/grilled, ask/asked,* and *rest/resting.* Lead children in identifying sounds as they write.	**Model** Listen to the sounds in *grill.* Stretch the sounds /g/ /rrr/ /iii/ /lll/ as you write *g, r, i, ll.* Repeat. This time have children write the letters as you write. Now let's add the ending *-ed.* Listen to the sounds of *grilled.* Stretch the sounds /g/ /rrr/ /iii/ /lll/ /d/ as you add *-ed* to *grill.* Repeat. This time have children write *-ed* at the end of *grill.* Repeat with *ask/asked* and *rest/resting.* **Teach and Practice** Have children say the sounds with you as you point to the letters in *grilled, asked,* and *resting.* (/g/ /r/ /i/ /l/ /d/; /a/ /s/ /k/ /t/; /r/ /e/ /s/ /t/ /ing/) What sound do you hear at the end of *grilled?* (/d/) *asked?* (/t/) *resting?* (/ing/) Continue the activity with these words: picked (/t/) yelled (/d/) camping (/ing/) missed (/t/) spilled (/d/) lifting (/ing/)	

Fluent Word Reading Base Words and Endings

	To Do	To Say	
			5–10 minutes
Use the blending routine.	Write *petted.*	**1 Connect** You can read this word because you know how to read base words with endings. What is the base word? *(pet)* What happened to the base word before the *-ed* ending was added? *(t* was doubled) What is the word? *(petted)* Remember, when the base word has a short vowel sound and ends in a single consonant, the final consonant is doubled before endings are added.	*Routine*
Scaffold instruction.	Write *sobbed,* and *running.*	**2 Model** When you come to a new word that has a base word and an ending, read the base word. Next, read the ending. Then blend the two parts. Model reading *sobbed* and *running* in this way. When you see a new word, what are you going to do?	
		3 Group Practice Let's read words that have base words and endings. For each word, first find the base word. Next, find the ending. Then blend the two parts silently. When I point to the word, we will read it together. Allow 2–3 seconds previewing time for each word. batting clapping stepped jogged grinning dragged ripping spinning	
CORRECTIVE FEEDBACK	**MONITOR PROGRESS**	**If . . .** children have difficulty previewing and reading whole words, **then . . .** have them use sound-by-sound blending. **If . . .** children can't read the words fluently at a rate of 1–2 seconds per word, **then . . .** continue practicing the list.	

| Model reading words in sentences. | When I read a sentence, I read each word without stopping between the words. If I come to a word I don't know, I blend it. Then I read the sentence again. Model reading this sentence, stopping to blend *shopping: They hopped in the van and went shopping.* |
| Write practice sentences. | Have each child read a sentence.
We clapped for the winning team.
Dan grabbed some lunch after swimming.
I hugged my friend because she was sobbing. |

High-Frequency Words *build, carry, heavy, water*

To Do	To Say	3 minutes

Review high-frequency words.

| Display *build, carry, heavy,* and *water.* | Use the Tested Vocabulary Cards. Point to a word. Say and spell it. Have children say and spell the word. Ask children to identify familiar letter-sounds. Have them take turns reading the words. |

ACTIVITY **3** | Build Concepts

Oral Vocabulary *ability, victory*

To Do	To Say	5–10 minutes

Teach oral vocabulary.

Display p. 36 of the student book.	Today you will read about two best friends, Jon and Jen. Each has an *ability* that leads their teams to *victory*.	Routine
Follow the Routine to teach *ability* and *victory*.	**1 Introduce, Demonstrate, and Apply** ***ability*** Jon and Jen both have athletic *ability*. That means they are good at sports. Have children say the word. An *ability* is a special skill or talent. Jon's *ability* is in batting. His batting is tops. Jen's *ability* is in running. She runs really fast. Name an *ability* that you have. ***victory*** This story is about how people's abilities lead to *victory* for their teams. A *victory* is a win. Have children say the word. A sports team earns a *victory* when it beats the other team. People have a *victory* party to celebrate a win. How does it feel to be victorious?
Display the words on the Amazing Words board.	**2 Display the Words** Have children say each word as they look at it. You can find sounds you know in big words. Read *a/bil/i/ty* as you run your hand under the syllables. What sound does the letter *b* make? (/b/) What vowel sound comes after the *b?* (/i/) Read *vic/tor/y* as you run your hand under the syllables. Children can identify *vic* and *t*/t/.
Monitor understanding.	**3 Use the Words** Ask children to use each word in a sentence. Model a sentence if children need help.

| | Use oral vocabulary to discuss talent and competition. Does everyone have an *ability* of some kind? What kind of *ability* might a tiny baby have? What *ability* might someone have in art or music? Does a person's *ability* always lead to a *victory*? How would it feel to never have a *victory*? |

ACTIVITY 4 Read a Passage

Reading "Jon and Jen," pp. 36–45

	To Do	**To Say**
Teach sequence. **Scaffold instruction.**	Introduce the skill. Model the skill.	Today you are going to learn how to keep track of sequence while you read. As you read, think about what happens first, next, and last. For example, we read "Fire on the Hill" last week. First, Chuck sees a fire. Next, the police tell everyone to run away from the danger. Finally, Chuck and his parents run to the school to be safe.
	Apply the skill.	Suppose you are reading about two friends who build a giant sandcastle for a contest. What might happen first, next, and last? (First, they make a sandcastle. Next, judges look at all the castles. Finally, the friends win a prize.)
Develop language and concepts.	See Routine Card 6. Display pp. 36–45.	**Before Reading** Read the title. Do a structured picture walk.
	Model using key words and concepts.	**pp. 36–39** The Cubs team plays baseball. What is Jon doing? (running) Yes, Jon batted, or hit, the baseball and is now running the bases. The story says Jen swung, but missed. Now Jen watches Jon bat.
	Key concepts: *team, batted, baseball, bases, abilities, missed, hit, track, runners*	**pp. 40–41** Jon and Jen are also on another kind of team. What does the Jets team do? (run) A track team has fast runners.
		pp. 42–45 Jen shows Jon how to run fast. Teammates help each other. Jon and Jen carry water jugs. This will help their team. You need to drink lots of water when you play sports.
	Monitor children's use of vocabulary.	Now turn to your partner and talk about the pictures, using the same words I did.
Teach story word.	Write *team*.	You will read this word in the story. It is *team.* Have children say the word and spell it.
Guide comprehension.	Monitor independent reading.	**During Reading** Read the pages in a whisper. Raise your hand if you need help with a word. As you read, ask yourself: What happens first in the story? What happens next? last?
	Use Routine Cards 2 and 3.	**pp. 36–39** What happened first in the story? (Jon hit well, but Jen did not. Jon helped Jen.) Jon showed Jen how to hit the ball.
		pp. 40–43 What happened next in the story? (Jen ran fast, but Jon did not. Jen helped Jon.) Jen showed Jon how to run fast.
		pp. 44–45 What happens at the end of the story? (Jen and Jon will build top teams.) They will build top teams by helping each other. It takes different abilities to make a great team.
Guide retelling.	Prompt children as they retell the selection.	**After Reading** Have one child retell the story while the others assist. What happened first in the story? Then what happened? What happened last? See Monitoring Retelling, p. 246.
Homework		Practice Book, p. 33, Sequence

ACTIVITY **1** Reread for Fluency

Paired Reading "Jon and Jen," pp. 36–39

	To Do	To Say	*5–10 minutes*
CORRECTIVE FEEDBACK	Pair children. Monitor paired reading.	Children read pp. 36–39 orally, switching readers at the end of the first page. Have partners reread; now the other partner begins. For optimal fluency, children should reread three or four times. Give feedback on children's oral reading and use of the blending strategy. See Routine Cards 1 and 4.	
MORE PRACTICE		Instead of rereading just pp. 36–39, have children reread the entire selection three or four times. You may want to have children read along with the AudioText.	

ACTIVITY **2** Word Work

Spiral Review Base Words and Endings -s, -ed, -ing

	To Do	To Say	*5–10 minutes*
Use the word-reading routine.	Write *swings*.	You can read this word because you know how to blend the base word and the ending -s together. What is the base word? *(swing)* What sound does -s make in this word? */z/* Remember that -s can stand for /s/ or /z/. Blend *swing* and /z/. What is the word? *(swings)*	
Scaffold instruction.	Write *batting*.	You can read this word because you know how to blend the base word and the ending -ing. You know that some base words double the last consonant before the ending is added. What is the base word? *(bat)* Blend the base word and the -ing ending. What is the word? *(batting)*	
	Distribute white boards.	**Build Words** Use a chart to make new words. Write *plan, hunt, drag,* and *help* under the heading Base Words. Write the headings -s, -ed, and -ing. Have children copy the base words and rewrite them with any necessary spelling changes and corresponding ending in each column. Call on volunteers to read the new words aloud and use them in sentences.	

Base Words	-s	-ed	-ing
plan	plans	planned	planning
hunt	hunts	hunted	hunting
drag	drags	dragged	dragging
help	helps	helped	helping

CORRECTIVE FEEDBACK	**MONITOR PROGRESS**	*If . . .* children have difficulty reading the new words, *then . . .* have them use sound-by-sound blending.

For more practice, see next page.

MORE PRACTICE	Model reading words in sentences.	When I read a sentence, I read each word without stopping between the words. If I come to a word I don't know, I blend it. Then I read the sentence again. Model reading this sentence, stopping to blend *bragged: Lin bragged about running fast.*
	Write practice sentences.	Have each child read a sentence. Who loves skipping and jumping? We stopped and chatted with our pals. Some milk spilled, so the cat is licking it up.
	Phonological and Phonemic Awareness	Optional practice activities, pp. 280–283

ACTIVITY 3 Read Together

Choral Reading "Be a Good Sport!" p. 46

	To Do	**To Say**	*10 minutes*
Develop language and concepts.	Display p. 46.	**Before Reading** This page has four boxes with pictures and words. The words in ovals tell what the characters say. Where have you seen pages like this before? Allow children to share what they know. How can you tell which character is speaking? (Part of the oval points to a character.) Read the title and ask children to predict what it is about. What does it mean to be a good sport? (Possible answer: Don't get mad if you lose.) Share information about being a good sport. Good sports play fair. They don't cheat.	
Model fluent reading.	Model prosody.	When I read the words the characters say, I speak as though I'm talking. When I read comic strips, I read the boxes in order. Point out the order: top row, left to right; bottom row, left to right. Read the strip in a conversational tone of voice. Read it a second time, having children point to each word.	
	Build fluency through choral reading.	**Choral Reading** Now read the comic strip aloud with me. Try to make your voice sound like mine as we read. Reread the strip several times with children.	
Develop concepts.	Monitor listening comprehension.	**After Reading** What did you learn about being a good sport? How does it feel to play with someone who isn't a good sport?	

ACTIVITY 4 Build Concepts

Oral Vocabulary *ability, compete, contribute, recreation, victory*

	To Do	**To Say**	*5–10 minutes*
Review oral vocabulary.	Read the words on the Amazing Words board.	**Focus on Letter-Sounds** You can find sounds you know in big words. • Which word begins with a vowel? Which two words end with *y*? • Which word begins with *com*? Which word begins with *con*?	
	Encourage discussion.	**Provide Multiple Contexts** Review the meanings of the words. Then ask questions to place the words in diverse contexts. • Why do people *compete?* Can you *compete* at school? Where else might you *compete?* • What *ability* would help you earn a *victory* at a spelling bee? How can fans' cheering *contribute* to a team's *victory?* • What kinds of *recreation* do you like? Do you sometimes *compete* against others doing your favorite kind of *recreation?*	

MORE PRACTICE | Apply oral vocabulary to new situations.

- Let's make a list of things people do for *recreation.* I'll start the list with one of my favorite kinds of *recreation,* reading. Record children's suggestions. **What is the same about all these different kinds of *recreation?*** (They are all things people do for fun.)
- Let's make a list of ways we *contribute* to the classroom. I'll start the list with one way I *contribute.* I come to school early and get supplies ready for the day. Record children's suggestions. Each one of you *contributes* to our class in your own way.
- **What does this sentence mean?** *If you* compete *to the best of your* ability, *we can earn a* victory. **Can you say the ideas in this sentence without using the words *compete, ability,* and *victory?***

ACTIVITY **5** Write

Response to Literature Interactive Writing

| To Do | To Say | 5–10 minutes |

Generate ideas.

Share the pen.

To Do	**To Say**
Review the story "Jon and Jen."	**What can Jon and Jen do well? How do they help each other?** Discuss how Jon and Jen improve each other's batting and running skills.
Have children participate in writing a list of skills Jon and Jen demonstrate in the story.	Write these sentence starters: *Jon can* _____. *Jen can* _____. Have children read the words you wrote. Then have them supply endings for the sentence. Invite individuals to write familiar letter-sounds, word parts, and high-frequency words. Have them find the spelling of high-frequency words on the Word Wall. Ask questions such as:
	• **What are the first two sounds in swing?** (/s/ /w/) **What letters stand for them?** *(sw)*
	• **What is the vowel sound in *swing?*** (/i/) **What is the letter for /i/?** *(i)*
	• **What is the last sound in *swing?*** (/ng/) **What letters stand for this sound?** *(ng)*
Writing elements: conventions	Frequently reread what has been written while tracking the print. Point out that each sentence starts with a capital letter and ends with a period. Point out the extra space between words.
	Read the completed list aloud, having children read with you. (For example, *Jon can swing. Jon can help Jen. Jen can run fast. Jen can help Jon.*)

MORE PRACTICE | Prompt independent writing. | **Journal Writing** Tell about a team you are on. |

Homework | Practice Book, p. 34, High-Frequency Words

ACTIVITY 1 — Assessment Options

Sentence Reading

To Do	To Say	5 minutes

Assess sentence reading.

Use reproducible p. 249.

Have each child read the sentences. Record scores on the Sentence Reading Chart, p. 253. Work with one child as others complete Write Sentences below.

Ben is planning to build a big hut.
Can you carry these heavy branches?
Lin dropped the jug of water, and it spilled on the rug.

CORRECTIVE FEEDBACK

MONITOR PROGRESS

If . . . children have trouble reading base words with endings,
then . . . reteach the blending strategy lessons on pp. 100 and 104.

If . . . children cannot read a high-frequency word,
then . . . mark the missed word or words on a high-frequency word list and send the list home for additional practice or have them practice with a fluent reader.

If . . . children misread a word in the sentence,
then . . . correct the error and have them reread the word and then the sentence.

Practice sentence writing.

Provide white boards.

Write Sentences Have children copy the sentences from reproducible p. 249 on white boards. Have them confirm spellings by comparing the words they wrote to the words in the sentences.

Phonological and Phonemic Awareness

Optional practice activities, pp. 280–283

Passage Reading

To Do	To Say	5–10 minutes

Assess fluency and comprehension.

Determine which children to assess this week.

Choose from these options: monitoring fluency (see pp. 244–245) and/or monitoring retelling (see p. 246). Have children reread "Jon and Jen." Be sure each child is assessed every other week.

If you have time, assess every child.

ACTIVITY 2 — Use Concepts

Oral Vocabulary *ability, compete, contribute, recreation, victory*

To Do	To Say	5 minutes

Check understanding of oral vocabulary.

Use the Amazing Words to wrap up the week's concept.

Monitor understanding of oral vocabulary, using Routine Card 5.

As time allows, ask questions such as these.

- Tell me about the pictures on pp. 28–31 using some of the week's Amazing Words.
- What *ability* do you wish you had? Can you learn this *ability* from someone else?
- Tell me about some ways people like to *compete*.
- What could you *contribute* if someone forgot his or her lunch? What could you *contribute* to a lonely person?
- How are the things you do for *recreation* in the summer different from the things you do for *recreation* in the winter?
- How would a good sport behave after a *victory?*

To Do	To Say
Preview next week's concept.	Next week you will read about times when sharing makes good sense.

ACTIVITY 3 Read to Connect

Reread "Team Spirit," pp. 28–31

10 minutes

	To Do	To Say
Monitor comprehension: sequence.	Have children reread "Team Spirit" silently.	As you read, think about which teams are described first, next, and last. Think about what each team does. After rereading, ask: • **Did you read about sports teams first or the gardening team first?** (sports teams) • **Think about the gardening team. What does the team do first to start the garden?** (They dig holes.) **What do they do after that?** (They plant bushes.) • **Which team did you read about last?** (the building team) **What happened after the kids helped build the playground?** (The kids run and jump. They have fun.)
Make connections.	Have children make connections across texts.	We also read "The Red Fins." Find that. What did you learn about what swimming teams do to win and have fun? Record children's ideas in a list on the board. (For example: they work hard; they practice; they compete; they cheer each other; they win races; they build a winning team.) Children will use the list for Activity 4. We also read "Jon and Jen," about how the friends help each other win. What can Jon do well at first? What can Jen do well? How do the pals help each other? Record ideas in a chart. What do all the stories we read this week show us about winning teams? What is the big idea? (Members on a winning team work hard and help each other.)

ACTIVITY 4 Write

Response to Literature Independent Writing

5–10 minutes

	To Do	To Say
Assign narrative writing. **Guide sentence correction.**	 Writing elements: conventions, support organization	Today you will write a story about a team. Write what kind of team it is. Explain what the team does first, next, and last to have fun and to win. Encourage children to use words you wrote on the board for Activity 3 as they write. Have children check their writing by asking themselves these questions. • **Did I begin each sentence with a capital letter?** • **Did I use correct marks at the ends of sentences?** • **Did I use good action words to describe what the team does?** • **Did I explain what the team does in the correct order?**
MORE PRACTICE		Have children share their sentences with the group. List the various kinds of teams on the board and have children practice reading and writing the list.
Homework		Practice Book, p. 35, Writing

Unit 2 Week 3 *Sharing*

When does sharing make sense?

Objectives *This week students will...*

Phonemic Awareness
- segment, count, and blend sounds in words

Phonics
- blend and read words with long *a* (CVC*e*), *c*/s/, and *g*/j/
- apply knowledge of letter-sounds to decode unknown words when reading
- recognize high-frequency words *another, enjoy, few, toward*

Fluency
- practice fluency with oral rereading

Vocabulary
- build concepts and oral vocabulary: *conflict, greedy, inhabit, portion, resolve*

Text Comprehension
- read connected text
- compare and contrast to improve comprehension
- write in response to literature

Word Work *This week's phonics focus is . . .*

Long *a* (CVC*e*)   *c*/s/, *g*/j/

High-Frequency Words *Tested Vocabulary*

The first appearance of each word in the Student Reader is noted below.

another	I chose **another** game. (p. 54)
enjoy	If you **enjoy** something, it makes you happy. (p. 50)
few	If you have a **few,** you do not have many. (p. 52)
toward	He walked **toward** the door. (p. 54)

Amazing Words *Oral Vocabulary*

The week's vocabulary is related to the concept of sharing.

conflict	a struggle or fight
greedy	wanting more than your share of something
inhabit	to live in a place
portion	an amount of something
resolve	to make a decision; solve or fix a problem

Student Reader Unit 2 *This week students will read the following selections.*

Daily Lesson Plan

	ACTIVITIES	MATERIALS
Day 1	**Word Work** Phonemic Awareness: Segment and Count Sounds Phonics: Blend Words with Long *a* (CVC*e*) High-Frequency Words *another, enjoy, few, toward* **Build Concepts** *conflict, inhabit, resolve* **Read a Passage** "Sharing," pp. 50–57 Comprehension: Use Strategies Reread for Fluency	Student White Boards Sound-Spelling Card 2 Tested Vocabulary Cards *Sing with Me Big Book* and Audio CD Student Reader: Unit 2 Routine Cards 1, 2, 3, 4, 6, 7 AudioText Practice Book, p. 36, Long *a* (CVC*e*)
Day 2	**Reread for Fluency** **Word Work** Phonemic Awareness: Segment and Blend Sounds Phonics: Blend Words with *c*/s/, *g*/j/ High-Frequency Words *another, enjoy, few, toward* **Read a Passage** "Who Can Share a Tree?" pp. 58–63 Comprehension: Use Strategies **Write** Response to Literature: Shared Writing	Student Reader: Unit 2 Student White Boards Tested Vocabulary Cards Sound-Spelling Cards 17, 31 Routine Cards 1, 2, 3, 4, 6, 7 AudioText Practice Book, p. 37, *c*/s/; *g*/j/
Day 3	**Reread for Fluency** **Word Work** Phonemic Awareness: Segment and Blend Sounds Phonics: Fluent Word Reading High-Frequency Words *another, enjoy, few, toward* **Build Concepts** *greedy, portion* **Read a Passage** "A Snack for Grace," pp. 64–69 Comprehension: Sequence	Student Reader: Unit 2 Student White Boards Tested Vocabulary Cards Routine Cards 1, 2, 3, 4, 6 AudioText Practice Book, p. 38, Sequence
Day 4	**Reread for Fluency** **Word Work** Phonics: Spiral Review Phonological and Phonemic Awareness Activities, pp. 280–283 **Read Together** "Share with a Brother," p. 70 Comprehension: Listening **Build Concepts** *conflict, greedy, inhabit, portion, resolve* **Write** Response to Literature: Interactive Writing	Student Reader: Unit 2 Routine Cards 1, 4 AudioText Student White Boards Practice Book, p. 39, High-Frequency Words
Day 5	**Assessment Options** Fluency, Comprehension Sentence Reading; Mid-Unit Passage Reading Phonological and Phonemic Awareness Activities, pp. 280–283 **Use Concepts** *conflict, greedy, inhabit, portion, resolve* **Read to Connect** "Sharing," pp. 50–57 Comprehension: Sequence **Write** Response to Literature: Independent Writing	Reproducible p. 249 Sentence Reading Chart, p. 253 Assessment Book, p. 80 Fluency Progress Chart, p. 245 Student White Boards Student Reader: Unit 2 Routine Card 5 Practice Book, p. 40, Writing

See pp. xvi–xvii for how *My Sidewalks* integrates instructional practices for ELL.

ACTIVITY **1** ## Word Work

Phonemic Awareness Segment and Count Sounds

	To Do	To Say	*2 minutes*

Scaffold instruction.

Distribute white boards. Write *mad*. Then add *e* to form *made*.

Model Listen to the sounds in *mad*. Stretch the sounds /mmm/ /aaa/ /d/ as you write *m, a, d*. Repeat. This time have children write the letters as you write. Now let's count the sounds in *mad*. I will say the word slowly and hold up a finger for each sound: /m/ /a/ /d/. There are three sounds in *mad*. Now listen to the sounds in *made*: /mmm/ /āāā/ /d/.

Lead children in counting sounds as they write.

Teach and Practice Have children say the sounds with you as you point to the letters. (/m/ /ā/ /d/) Hold up a finger for each sound. How many sounds in *made*? (3) How many letters? (4) Continue counting sounds with these words:

tap (3)   tape (3)   can (3)   cane (3)   plan (4)   plane (4)

Blending Strategy Long *a* (CVCe)

	To Do	To Say	*5–10 minutes*

Use the blending routine.

Write *tap*.

Routine

1 Connect You already can read this word. What is the word? *(tap)* What vowel sound do you hear in *tap*? (the short *a* sound) Now let's look more at the letter *a* and its long vowel sound.

Display Sound-Spelling Card 2.

2 Use Sound-Spelling Card This is an apron. What sound do you hear at the beginning of apron? (/ā/) Say it with me: /ā/. /ā/ is the long *a* sound: /ā/. It says its name: *a*/ā/.

Scaffold instruction.

Write *tape*.

3 Listen and Write Write *tape*: *t, a, p, e*. What vowels do you see in *tape*? *(a, e)* *Tape* has the long *a* sound: /ā/. As you write, say the sound to yourself: /ā/. Now say the sound aloud.

Write *tap*. Then add *e* to form *tape*.

4 Model When I add *e* to *tap*, it makes the *a* say its name. The sound of *a* in this new word is /ā/. The *e* is silent. This is how I blend this word: /t/ /ā/ /p/, *tape*. Now you try: /t/ /ā/ /p/, *tape*.

Point out that when a word has a vowel followed by consonant and *e*, the vowel usually uses its long vowel sound and the *e* is silent.

$$\underset{\rightarrow}{t}\ \underset{\rightarrow}{a}\ \underset{\rightarrow}{p}\ e$$

CORRECTIVE FEEDBACK

Write each practice word. Monitor student practice.

5 Group Practice Let's try the same thing with these words. Give feedback, using the *if . . . then* statements on Routine Card 1.

date   lake   gave   male   plate   shape

6 Individual Practice Write the words; have each child blend two of them.

wade*   game   safe   cake   quake*   grade

Check understanding of practice words.

*Children need to make sense of words that they segment and blend. If needed, help children with meanings. When you *wade*, you walk through water that is not deep. When you *quake*, you shake. I'd *quake* if I saw a bear! (Demonstrate.)

MORE PRACTICE

Model spelling long *a* (CVCe) words.

Spell and Write What sounds do you hear in *bake*? (/b/ /ā/ /k/) What is the letter for /b/? Let's all write *b*. Continue with *a*/ā/ and *k*/k/. What letter must we add to make *a* say its name? *(e)* Provide practice as time allows. Have children confirm their spelling by comparing it to what you've written.

late   wave   case   name   take   made

High-Frequency Words *another, enjoy, few, toward*

To Do	To Say	

3 minutes

Teach high-frequency words.

Display *another*.

1 Say, Spell, Write Use the Tested Vocabulary Cards. Display *another*. Here are some words that we won't sound out. We'll spell them. This word is *another: a, n, o, t, h, e, r* (point to each letter), *another*. What is this word? What are the letters in the word? Now you write *another*.

Point to *an* and *th* in *another*.

2 Identify Letter-Sounds You can find sounds you know in big words. Read *an/oth/er* as you run your hand under the syllables. Children can identify *an* and *th*/th/.

Display *enjoy, few,* and *toward*.

3 Demonstrate Meaning Tell me a sentence using *another*. Model a sentence if children need help.

Repeat the Routine with *enjoy, few,* and *toward*. Children can identify these letter-sounds and word parts: enjoy (*en, j*/j/), few (*f*/f/), and toward (*t*/t/, *d*/d/). Have children write the words in their word banks. Add the words to the Word Wall.

ACTIVITY **2** Build Concepts

Oral Vocabulary *conflict, inhabit, resolve*

To Do	To Say	

5–10 minutes

Introduce oral vocabulary.

Scaffold instruction.

Display p. 8 of *Sing with Me Big Book*. Play audio CD.

This week you will learn about sharing. Listen for the Amazing Words *conflict, inhabit,* and *resolve* as I sing this song. Play or sing the song. Then have children sing it with you.

Follow the Routine to teach *conflict, inhabit,* and *resolve.*

1 Introduce, Demonstrate, and Apply

conflict There could be a *conflict* because other animals want to inhabit Turtle's pond. A *conflict* is a struggle or fight. Have children say the word. Often brothers and sisters have a *conflict* over who gets to choose the first snack. What kinds of *conflicts* might classmates have?

inhabit Turtle *inhabits* a small pond. When you *inhabit* a place, you live in it. Have children say the word. Lots of different insects *inhabit* the tall grass near the pond. An apartment building is *inhabited* by many different people. What other sorts of places do people *inhabit*?

resolve The animals' problem is that they all want to live in the small pond. Turtle *resolves* the problem by telling the animals they can share the pond. If you *resolve* something, you make a decision or you solve or fix a problem. Have children say the word. The room was noisy until the teacher *resolved* the problem by asking children to whisper. How would you *resolve* an argument with a friend about sharing your bike?

Display the words on the Amazing Words board.

2 Display the Words Have children say each word as they look at it. You can find sounds you know in big words. Read *in/hab/it* as you run your hand under the syllables. Children can identify *in, hab, it*. For *conflict* and *resolve*, children can identify these letter-sounds and word parts: conflict (*con, flict*), resolve (*r*/r/, *s*/s/, *v*/v/).

Monitor understanding.

3 Use the Words Ask children to use each word in a sentence. Model a sentence if children need help.

MORE PRACTICE

Use oral vocabulary to discuss the song. Who *inhabits* the pond at the beginning? Who wants to *inhabit* the pond? What *conflict* do the animals have? How was the *conflict resolved*?

ACTIVITY 3 Read a Passage

Build Background "Sharing," pp. 50–57

	To Do	**To Say**	*10 minutes*

Develop language and concepts.

See Routine Card 7. Read aloud p. 49 of the student book.

Preview the Week Use the illustration on p. 48 to introduce this week's concept of sharing. **What will the girl share? When does it make sense to share food with others?** Read aloud the titles and descriptions on p. 49. Ask children what they think each selection will be about.

Scaffold instruction.

See Routine Card 6. Display pp. 50–57.

Ask questions and elaborate on answers to develop language.

Key concepts: *lake, wade, waves, share, toss, lands, bunk bed, conflict, resolve*

Before Reading Read the title aloud. Do a structured picture walk with children.

pp. 50–51 The kids are in a lake. A lake is bigger than a pond. Point to the lake. **What are the kids doing in the lake?** (playing) Yes, they are wading, or walking in the water. The kids jump in the waves. Point to waves. The kids share the lake. When you share, you let someone use something with you.

pp. 52–53 The kids help Mom bake. **What do they bake?** (a cake) The kids want to save a plate of cake for Dad. **Why do you think they want to share the cake with Dad?** (It is fun to share things with others.)

pp. 54–55 The kids play a game. They must toss, or throw, a bag gently. Point to the kid who tosses the bag. The boy hopes the bag comes down, or lands, in a spot. Point to a spot. **What might happen next? How will the kids share this game?**

pp. 56–57 The girls sit on a bunk bed. A bunk bed has two beds stacked one above the other. Point to the bunk bed. Suppose there was a conflict because both girls wanted the top bunk bed. **How could the girls share to resolve the problem?**

Teach story words.

Write *share*.

You will read this word in the story. It is *share*. Have children say the word and spell it. Review its meaning. **Let's read to find out more about sharing.**

Guide comprehension.

Monitor independent reading. Model strategic reading. Use Routine Cards 2 and 3.

During Reading Read the page in a whisper. Raise your hand if you need help with a word. Stop at the end of each page to model asking questions. For example, for p. 51: After I read, I ask myself: What did I learn about sharing? The author tells how kids can swim, wade, and jump in the waves at the lake. I learned that it is fun to share a lake.

Summarize.

Use oral vocabulary to develop the concept.

After Reading **Do the kids enjoy the lake or *inhabit* the lake? What kind of place might the kids *inhabit*? Does sharing with others cause *conflicts* or *resolve conflicts*?**

Reread for Fluency "Sharing," pp. 50–53

	To Do	**To Say**	*5–10 minutes*

CORRECTIVE FEEDBACK

Monitor oral reading.

Read pp. 50–53 aloud. Read them three or four times so your reading gets better each time. Give feedback on children's oral reading and use of the blending strategy. See Routine Cards 1 and 4.

MORE PRACTICE

Instead of rereading just pp. 50–53, have children reread the entire selection three or four times. You may want to have children read along with the AudioText.

Homework

Practice Book, p. 36, Phonics: Long *a* (CVC*e*)

ACTIVITY **1** Reread for Fluency

Paired Reading "Sharing," pp. 54–57

To Do	To Say	
		5–10 minutes

CORRECTIVE FEEDBACK

Pair children. Monitor paired reading.

Children read pp. 54–57 orally, switching readers at the end of the first page. Have partners reread; now the other partner begins. For optimal fluency, children should reread three or four times. Give feedback on children's oral reading and use of the blending strategy. See Routine Cards 1 and 4.

MORE PRACTICE

Instead of rereading just pp. 54–57, have children reread the entire selection three or four times. You may want to have children read along with the AudioText.

ACTIVITY **2** Word Work

Phonemic Awareness Segment and Blend Sounds

To Do	To Say	
		2 minutes

Scaffold instruction.

Distribute white boards. Write *face*.

Write *cage.* Lead children in blending sounds as they write.

Model Listen to the sounds in *face.* Stretch the sounds /fff/ /ā ā ā/ /sss/ as you write f, a, c, e. Repeat. This time have children write the letters as you write.

Teach and Practice Have children say the sounds with you as you point to the letters (/f/ /ā/ /s/) and blend the sounds to say the word. *(face)* Now listen to the sounds in *cage.* Say /k/ /ā/ /j/. Have children say sounds as you point to letters and then blend the sounds to say the word. Continue with these words:

age   race   page   place

Blending Strategy *c/s/*, *g/j/*

5–10 minutes

Routine

To Do	To Say
Use the blending routine. Write *safe* and *jam*.	**1 Connect** You already can read words like these. What are the words? What sounds do they start with? (/s/, /j/) What letter stands for the sound /s/ at the beginning of *safe*? *(s)* What letter stands for the sound /j/ at the beginning of *jam*? *(j)* Today we are learning about other letters that stand for the sounds /s/ and /j/.
Scaffold instruction. Display Sound-Spelling Card 31.	**2 Use Sound-Spelling Card** This is a submarine. What sound do you hear at the beginning of *submarine*? (/s/) Say it with me: /s/. The letter *s* stands for the /s/ at the beginning of *submarine*. The letter *c* can also stand for /s/.
	3 Listen and Write Write the letter *c* for /s/. As you write, say the sound to yourself: /s/. Now say the sound aloud.
Write *race*.	**4 Model** In this word, the letter *c* stands for /s/. Point out that the letter *c* usually stands for the sound /s/ when *e*, *i*, or *y* comes after it. In this word, the letter *e* comes after *c,* so *c* has the sound /s/. This is how I blend this word: /r/ /ā/ /s/, *race*. Now you try it: /r/ /ā/ /s/, *race*.
Display Sound-Spelling Card 17. Write *page*.	Repeat steps 2 and 3 for the sound /j/. Use Sound-Spelling Card 17, depicting a jet. Explain that *jet* begins with *j*/j/, but *g* can also stand for /j/. Then model blending *page*: /p/ /ā/ /j/, *page*. Point out that the letter *g* often has the sound /j/ when *e* or *i* comes after it.

$$\underset{\rightarrow}{r}\ \underset{\rightarrow}{a}\ \underset{\rightarrow}{c}\ e \qquad\qquad \underset{\rightarrow}{p}\ \underset{\rightarrow}{a}\ \underset{\rightarrow}{g}\ e$$

To Do	To Say
CORRECTIVE FEEDBACK Write each practice word. Monitor student practice.	**5 Group Practice** Let's try the same thing with these words. Give feedback, using the *if . . . then* statements on Routine Card 1.
	ace* face trace age wage* stage
	6 Individual Practice Write the words; have each child blend two of them.
	cage lace* rage* pace* place space
Check understanding of practice words.	*Children need to make sense of words as they segment and blend. If needed, help children with meanings. An *ace* is a person who is very good at something. I'd like to be an *ace* at dancing. A *wage* is money you get paid for work. *Lace* is thin threads spun into a pattern. *Rage* can mean very angry or done with a lot of force, like winds that *rage* during a storm. (Make sounds of wind.) When you *pace*, you walk back and forth. (Demonstrate.)
MORE PRACTICE Distribute white boards. Build words with *ace* and *age*.	**Build Words** Have children write *ace* and *age* at the tops of their boards. Have them build new words by adding the letters *r*, *f*, *l*, *pl*, and *sp* to the front of *ace*, and *c*, *p*, *r*, and *st* to the front of *age*. Model adding *r* to *ace* to form *race*. Call on children to read each word and use it in a sentence or tell what it means.

High-Frequency Words *another, enjoy, few, toward*

3 minutes

To Do	To Say
Teach high-frequency words. Display *another, enjoy, few,* and *toward*.	Use the Tested Vocabulary Cards. Point to a word. Say and spell it. Have children say and spell the word. Ask children to identify familiar letter-sounds. Have them take turns reading the words.
Lead cumulative review.	Use the Tested Vocabulary Cards to review high-frequency words from previous weeks.

ACTIVITY 3 Read a Passage

Reading "Who Can Share a Tree?" pp. 58–63

	To Do	**To Say**	*10–15 minutes*

Routine

Develop language and concepts.

Scaffold instruction.

See Routine Cards 6 and 7. Display pp. 58–63.

Ask questions and elaborate on answers to develop language.

Key concepts: *inhabit, tree, trunk, branches, nest, twigs, web, trap, shade*

Before Reading Have children recall what they learned about animals sharing a pond. Read the title. Do a structured picture walk with children.

pp. 58–59 What place do the bird and spider inhabit? (a tree) This bird's nest rests on a branch. Where is the spider's web? (on another branch) The web will trap, or catch, bugs for the spider to eat.

pp. 60–61 Where did the nuts come from (the tree) What is the squirrel doing in the second picture? (digging) It will bury the nuts to eat all winter long.

pp. 62–63 Where is the boy reading? (under the tree) The boy is reading in the shade of the tree.

Write story words.

Write *tree* and *share*.

You will read these words in the story: *tree* and *share*. Point to each word. Have children say and spell each word. Review their meanings.

Guide comprehension.

Monitor independent reading.

During Reading Read the pages in a whisper. Raise your hand if you need help with a word. As you read, ask yourself: What am I learning about sharing a tree? What is this mainly about?

Use Routine Cards 2 and 3.

pp. 58–61 What did you learn about creatures sharing a tree? (A bird, a spider, and a squirrel share parts of a tree.) The creatures use the tree as a place to live or as a way to get food.

pp. 62–63 What did you learn about a child sharing a tree? (A child shares a tree's trunk and a tree's shade.)

Model summarizing.

Think aloud.

After Reading What did you learn about sharing a tree? What was the selection mainly about? Model how to summarize. The first few pages told about creatures who use the tree as a home and as a way to get food. The last two pages told how a boy gets shade from a tree. I put that all together and pick the most important ideas. The selection is mainly about how creatures and a boy all share a tree.

MORE PRACTICE

Develop oral vocabulary.

Why is the tree a good place for creatures to *inhabit?* Suppose someone wanted to chop down the tree. What kind of *conflict* might this cause? How might the problem be *resolved?*

ACTIVITY 4 Write

Response to Literature Shared Writing

	To Do	**To Say**	*5 minutes*

Guide shared writing.

Write sentence frames. Read the questions.

Who can share a tree? A tree can be shared by _____.
What does a tree share? A tree shares _____.

Invite children to suggest answers. Discuss and record answers to complete the sentence frames. While writing, model connecting sounds to letters and forming letters. (See pp. 257–259.) Have children read answers aloud as you track print.

Homework

Practice Book, p. 37, Phonics: *c*/s/; *g*/j/

3

ACTIVITY 1 Reread for Fluency

Oral Reading "Who Can Share a Tree?" pp. 58–60

5–10 minutes

	To Do	**To Say**
CORRECTIVE FEEDBACK	Monitor oral reading.	**Read pp. 58–60 aloud. Read them three or four times so your reading gets better each time. Give feedback on children's oral reading and use of the blending strategy. See Routine Cards 1 and 4.**
MORE PRACTICE		Instead of rereading just pp. 58–60, have children reread the entire selection three or four times. You may want to have children read along with the AudioText.

ACTIVITY 2 Word Work

Phonemic Awareness Segment and Blend Sounds

2 minutes

	To Do	**To Say**
Scaffold instruction.	Distribute white boards. Write *lake*.	**Model** Listen to the sounds in *lake*. Stretch the sounds /lll/ /ā ā ā/ /k/ as you write *l, a, k, e*. Repeat. Have children write the letters as you write.
	Write *race* and *page*. Lead children in blending sounds.	**Teach and Practice** Have children say the sounds with you as you point to the letters (/l/ /ā/ /k/) and blend the sounds to say the word. *(lake)* Repeat the process with *race* and *page*. Continue practicing with these words.
		same lace sale wage date face made age

Fluent Word Reading Long *a* (CVCe), *c*/s/, *g*/j/

5–10 minutes

	To Do	**To Say**
Use the word-reading routine.	Write *name*.	**1 Connect** You can read this word because you know how to read long *a* words. Remember, when you see *a* followed by a consonant and the letter *e*, you know *a* stands for /ā/. What sound does *a* in this word stand for? (/ā/) What is the word? *(name)*
Scaffold instruction.	Write *game, face,* and *cage*.	**2 Model** When you come to a new word, look at all the letters in the word and think about its vowel sound. Say the sounds in the word to yourself, and then read the word. Model reading *game, face,* and *cage* in this way. Remind children that the letter *c* usually stands for the sound /s/ when followed by *e, i,* or *y*. The letter *g* usually stands for the sound /j/ when followed by *e* or *i*. When you come to a new word, what are you going to do?
	Write each practice word.	**3 Group Practice** Let's read these words. Look at all the letters, think about the vowel sound, and say the letter-sounds to yourself. We will read words with long *a, c,* and *g*. When I point to the word, let's read it together. Allow 2–3 seconds previewing time for each word.
		age take came wave made Grace grapes place stage
CORRECTIVE FEEDBACK	**MONITOR PROGRESS**	*If . . .* children have difficulty previewing and reading whole words, *then . . .* have them use sound-by-sound blending.
		If . . . children can't read the words fluently at a rate of 1–2 seconds per word, *then . . .* continue practicing the list.

Routine

MORE PRACTICE	Model reading words in sentences.	When I read a sentence, I read each word without stopping between the words. If I come to a word I don't know, I blend it. Then I read the sentence again. Model reading this sentence, stopping to blend *lace: Mom makes a dress with lace for Sage.*
	Write practice sentences.	Have each child read a sentence.
		The tame rats race out of the cage.
		Jane will save my place on the stage.
		Dave made a black spot on the page.

High-Frequency Words *another, enjoy, few, toward*

	To Do	**To Say**	*3 minutes*
Review high-frequency words.	Display *another, enjoy, few,* and *toward.*	Use the Tested Vocabulary Cards. Point to a word. Say and spell it. Have children say and spell the word. Ask children to identify familiar letter-sounds. Have them take turns reading the words.	

ACTIVITY 3 Build Concepts

Oral Vocabulary *greedy, portion*

	To Do	**To Say**	*5–10 minutes*
Teach oral vocabulary.	Display p. 64 of the student book.	Today you will read a story about a girl who is not *greedy* because she shares *portions* of her snack.	*Routine*
	Follow the Routine to teach *greedy* and *portion.*	**1 Introduce, Demonstrate, and Apply**	
		greedy This story is about a girl who is not *greedy*. Someone who is *greedy* wants more than his or her share of something. Have children say the word. A *greedy* child asks his parents for lots of birthday presents. A *greedy* person does not like to share. Name a word that means the opposite of *greedy*. (*sharing, generous, giving*)	
		portion The girl in this story gives a *portion* of grapes to each of her friends. A *portion* is an amount of something. It is often the amount of food served at one time. Have children say the word. I sometimes eat an extra *portion* of mashed potatoes. What is your favorite food? Do you ever ask for another *portion* of it?	
	Display the words on the Amazing Words board.	**2 Display the Words** Have children say each word as they look at it. You can find sounds you know in big words. What two letters do you see at the beginning of *greedy?* (gr) What sounds do they make? (/gr/) Read *por/tion* as you run your hand under the syllables. Children can identify p/p/, r/r/, and n/n/.	
	Monitor understanding.	**3 Use the Words** Ask children to use each word in a sentence. Model a sentence if children need help.	
MORE PRACTICE		Use oral vocabulary to discuss sharing. If a classmate offered to share her new crayons with you, how could you show that you aren't *greedy?* Would you share a big *portion* or small *portion* of pancakes with your brother or sister? Why?	

Reading "A Snack for Grace," pp. 64–69

To Do	To Say	
		10 minutes

Teach sequence.

Scaffold instruction.

Introduce the skill.

Model the skill.

Apply the skill.

Today you are going to keep track of the order in which things happen in a story. Remember that when you put events in order, you tell what happened first, next, and last. For example, I can tell you what I did at home last night in order from first to last. First, I ate dinner. Next, I read the newspaper. Last, I went to sleep.

Think about what happened when you got home from school yesterday. What did you do first? next? last? (Possible answer: ate dinner, played a game, went to sleep)

Develop language and concepts.

See Routine Card 6. Display pp. 64–69.

Model using key words and concepts.

Key concepts: *bunch, out back, portion, share, gate, greedy, generous, lots, few, conflict, resolve*

Monitor children's use of vocabulary.

Before Reading Read the title. Do a structured picture walk.

pp. 64–65 What does Grace do with the grapes? Yes, she washes a big bunch, or group, of grapes and then takes them out in her backyard. Grace puts a portion of grapes on a plate. Do you think this portion is big enough to share with her friend at the gate? Why?

pp. 66–67 Is Grace a greedy person? No, Grace isn't greedy. She is generous. She shares her grapes with more friends. Point to the portions of grapes Grace shares.

p. 68 How many grapes are left, a lot or a few? (a few) Grace gave most of the grapes to her friends. Do you think she will be upset? Will there be a conflict?

p. 69 What is this boy doing? (bringing more grapes) How might the boy resolve a problem? (Now Grace will get a fair share of grapes.)

Now turn to your partner and talk about the pictures, using the same words I did.

Guide comprehension.

Monitor independent reading.

Use Routine Cards 2 and 3.

During Reading Read the pages in a whisper. Raise your hand if you need help with a word. As you read, ask yourself: What happens first, next, and last in this story?

pp. 64–67 What happens first in the story? (Grace shares the big bunch of grapes with her friends.)

p. 68 What happens next in the story? What do Grace's friends notice? (Grace has shared most of her grapes, so there are only a few grapes left for Grace.)

p. 69 What happens last in the story? (Rafe brings another big bunch of grapes to share. Grace's friends make sure she gets lots of grapes.)

Guide retelling.

Prompt children as they retell the story.

After Reading Have one child retell the story while the others assist. What happened first? next? last? (First, Grace shared her grapes with friends. Next, Grace shared most of her grapes, so there were only a few grapes left for Grace. Last, Rafe brought more grapes to share.) See Monitoring Retelling, p. 246.

Homework | Practice Book, p. 38, Sequence

ACTIVITY 1 Reread for Fluency

Paired Reading "A Snack for Grace," pp. 64–66

To Do	To Say	
		5–10 minutes

CORRECTIVE FEEDBACK

Pair children. Monitor paired reading.

Children read pp. 64–66 orally, switching readers at the end of the first page. Have partners reread; now the other partner begins. For optimal fluency, children should reread three or four times. Give feedback on children's oral reading and use of the blending strategy. See Routine Cards 1 and 4.

MORE PRACTICE

Instead of rereading just pp. 64–66, have children reread the entire selection three or four times. You may want to have children read along with the AudioText.

ACTIVITY 2 Word Work

Spiral Review Short *a* and Long *a* (CVC*e*)

To Do	To Say	
		5–10 minutes

Review short *a* and long *a*.

Write *tap*.

You can read this word because you know what sounds *a* can stand for. What sound does *a* have in this word? (/a/) Remember, when *a* is the only vowel at the beginning or in the middle of a word, it usually stands for its short sound, /a/. Now let's blend the sounds to say the word: /t/ /a/ /p/, *tap*.

Scaffold instruction.

Add *e* to *tap* to form *tape*.

How does the vowel sound /a/ change when the letter *e* is added to the end of *tap*? (It changes to the long *a* sound, /ā/.) Remember, when you see the letter *a* followed by a consonant and the letter *e*, the *a* usually stands for its long sound, /ā/, and the *e* is silent. Now let's blend the sounds to say the word: /t/ /ā/ /p/, *tape*.

Distribute white boards. Write tap and *tape* at top of two-column chart.

Sort Words Let's sort words by their vowel sounds. Point to and read *tap* and *tape*. Then display this list of words: *cap, cape, rag, rage, plan, plane, fact,* and *face*. Call on children to read each word in the list and tell whether it has a vowel sound like *tap* or *tape*. Write the word in an appropriate column on a class chart as children write on their boards.

How are the words in the first column alike? (They're all short *a* words. They all show only one vowel.) How are the words in the second column alike? (They're all long *a* words. They all show *a* followed by a consonant and a silent *e*.)

Short *a*	Long *a*
tap	tape
cap	cape
rag	rage
plan	plane
fact	face

CORRECTIVE FEEDBACK

MONITOR PROGRESS

If . . . children have difficulty reading the words,
then . . . review the effect of *e* at the end of the words and blend the words sound-by-sound.

For more practice, see next page.

4

MORE PRACTICE

Model reading words in sentences.	When I read a sentence, I read each word without stopping between the words. If I come to a word I don't know, I blend it. Then I read the sentence again. Model reading this sentence, stopping to blend *makes: Shane makes a good wage at this place.*
Write practice sentences.	Have each child read a sentence. **Grace and Sage ate grapes in the shade.** **I race past the stage in my cape.** **I trace the shape on the page.**

Phonological and Phonemic Awareness — Optional practice activities, pp. 280–283

ACTIVITY 3 Read Together

Choral Reading "Share with a Brother," p. 70

	To Do	**To Say**	*10 minutes*
Develop language and concepts.	Display p. 70.	**Before Reading** This is a comic strip about sharing with a new baby. What do you know about new babies? (Allow children to share what they know.) Babies need soft toys, so they don't get hurt. They can't eat what you eat because they don't have teeth yet.	
Model fluent reading.	Model prosody.	Read the title of the comic strip. Ask children to predict what it is about. The sentences in these circles tell what the characters are saying. When I read words the characters say, I speak like I am talking to my friends. When I read comic strips, I read each box in order: top row, left to right, and then bottom row, left to right. Read the sentences using a conversational tone. Read them a second time, having children point to each word.	
	Build fluency through choral reading.	**Choral Reading** Now read the comic strip aloud with me. Try to make your voice sound like mine as we read. Reread the comic strip several times with children.	
Develop concepts.	Monitor listening comprehension.	**After Reading** What does the boy want to share with the new baby? Does it make sense to share these things with a little baby? Why or why not? How is the problem *resolved?*	

ACTIVITY 4 Build Concepts

Oral Vocabulary *conflict, greedy, inhabit, portion, resolve*

	To Do	**To Say**
Review oral vocabulary.	Read the words on the Amazing Words board.	**Focus on Letter-Sounds** Remember, you can find sounds you know in big words. • What word begins with *c?* What word ends with *n?* • Which word begins with the sounds /gr/? What letters stand for /gr/? • Which word has *in* in it? Which word has *it* in it?
	Encourage discussion.	**Provide Multiple Contexts** Review the meanings of the words. Then ask questions to place the words in diverse contexts. • Describe a place that you would like to *inhabit.* Why? Who would *inhabit* the place with you? What kinds of things would you share? • Think about two dogs that *inhabit* the same house. Suppose one dog is *greedy* and takes the other dog's *portion* of food. How would you *resolve* the *conflict* in a peaceful way? (feed them separately)

MORE PRACTICE

Apply oral vocabulary to new situations.

- **Which word means about the same as** *conflict*—*war* **or** *peace?* (war)
- **If you give a friend a** *portion* **of your toys, do you give your friend all of the toys or some of them?** (some)
- **Green plants can't** *inhabit* **a place that is cold and icy all the time. Why?** (They need to live in places with sun, soil, and water.) **Name places green plants do** *inhabit.* (Possible answer: forest, garden, park)
- **Suppose a friend asks for a drink out of your glass. Does it make sense to share?** (no) **Are you** *greedy* **if you say no?** (no) **Why?** (It is unhealthy to share a drink from the same glass.)

ACTIVITY **5** | Write

Response to Literature Interactive Writing

To Do	To Say	5–10 minutes

Generate ideas.

Review the story "A Snack for Grace."

Why do you think Grace shared most of her grapes with her friends? Discuss reasons Grace shared so many of her grapes.

Share the pen.

Have children participate in writing reasons why someone shares.

Write *Grace shares because* _____. Have children read the words you wrote. Then have them supply endings for each sentence. Invite individuals to write familiar letter-sounds, word parts, and high-frequency words. Have them find the spelling of high-frequency words on the Word Wall. Ask questions such as:

- **What is the first sound in** *made?* (/m/) **What is the letter for /m/?** *(m)*
- **What is the vowel sound in** *made?* (/ā/) **What is the letter for /ā/?** *(a)*
- **What is the last sound in** *made?* (/d/) **What is the letter for /d/?** *(d)*
- **Which letter do we add to the end of** *m, a, d,* **to make** *a* **say its name?** *(e)*

Writing elements: conventions

Frequently reread what has been written while tracking the print. Point out that each sentence starts with a capital letter and ends with a period. Point out the extra space between words.

Read the completed sentences aloud, having children read with you. (For example, *Grace shares because her friends came. Grace shares because she has many grapes.*)

MORE PRACTICE

Prompt independent writing.

Journal Writing Tell about a time when you shared something with someone.

Homework

Practice Book, p. 39, High-Frequency Words

ACTIVITY 1 | Assessment Options

Sentence Reading

To Do **To Say** *5 minutes*

Assess sentence reading.

Use reproducible p. 249.

Have each child read the sentences. Record scores on the Sentence Reading Chart, p. 253. Work with one child as others complete Write Sentences below.

My name is on another page.
I enjoy a few games.
We race toward the gate.

CORRECTIVE FEEDBACK

MONITOR PROGRESS

If . . . children have trouble reading words with long *a* (CVC*e*), *c*/s/, or *g*/j/,
then . . . reteach the blending strategy lessons on pp. 116 and 120.

If . . . children cannot read a high-frequency word,
then . . . mark the missed word or words on a high-frequency word list and send the list home for additional practice or have them practice with a fluent reader.

If . . . children misread a word in the sentence,
then . . . correct the error and have them reread the word and then the sentence.

Practice sentence writing.

Provide white boards.

Write Sentences Have children copy the sentences from reproducible p. 249 on white boards. Have them confirm spellings by comparing the words they wrote to the words in the sentences.

Phonological and Phonemic Awareness

Optional practice activities, pp. 226–229

Mid-Unit Passage Reading

To Do **To Say** *5–10 minutes*

Assess fluency and comprehension.

Determine which children to assess. Use Assessment Book, p. 80.

Choose from these options: monitoring fluency (see pp. 244–245) and/or monitoring retelling (see p. 246). Have children read the Unit 2 Mid-Unit Fluency Passage in the Assessment Book. Be sure each child is assessed every other week.

If you have time, assess every child.

ACTIVITY 2 | Use Concepts

Oral Vocabulary *conflict, greedy, inhabit, portion, resolve*

To Do **To Say** *5 minutes*

Check understanding of oral vocabulary.

Use the Amazing Words to wrap up the week's concept.

Monitor understanding of oral vocabulary, using Routine Card 5.

As time allows, ask questions such as these.

- Tell me about the pictures on pp. 50–57 using some of the week's Amazing Words.
- Name animals that *inhabit* your neighborhood.
- How could you *resolve* a *conflict* with a friend over sharing a swing on the playground?
- If you are *greedy*, you might not have many friends. Why?
- In a grocery store, workers often share little *portions* of food with customers. What kinds of food *portions* have you seen? (portions of meat, salad, cheese, fish, snacks, and so on) Does it make sense to share *portions* with customers?

	To Do	To Say
Preview next week's concept.		Next week you will read about working together and alone.

ACTIVITY **3** Read to Connect

Reread "Sharing," pp. 50–57

	To Do	To Say	
Monitor comprehension: sequence.	Have children reread "Sharing" silently.	As you read, think about the order in which the author describes things that are fun for kids to share. After rereading, ask:	*10 minutes*

Routine

- What place that is fun to share is described first? What can kids share at this place?
- What thing that is fun to share is described last? How do kids share this thing?

Make connections.	Have children make connections across texts.	**Why is it fun for kids to share?** Record children's ideas in a list on the board. (For example: You get to be with other people; you can make friends.) Children will use the list for Activity 4.

We also read "Who Can Share a Tree?" Find that. **What does a tree have that can be shared with creatures and people?** (branches, twigs, space for nests and webs, a safe place, nuts, a place to rest, shade) **Why is it good that a tree shares?** (For example: It has something that others need; it helps others.) Record children's ideas in a T-chart on the board. Children will use the list for Activity 4.

We also read "A Snack for Grace," about a girl who shares with her friends. **What happens first, next, and last in the story?** Have children help you make a list of the correct sequence of events. **How do Grace and her friends feel when they share?** Record children's ideas at the end of the sequential list.

What did all the selections we read this week show us about sharing? What is the big idea? (Sharing can be fun and helpful. It makes sense to share.)

ACTIVITY **4** Write

Response to Literature Independent Writing

	To Do	To Say	
Assign expository writing.		Today you will write about why it is good to share. Write reasons that show why sharing makes sense. Encourage children to use words you wrote on the board for Activity 3 as they write.	*5–10 minutes*
Guide sentence correction.	Writing elements: conventions, support	Have children check their writing by asking themselves these questions.

- Did I begin each sentence with a capital letter?
- Does each sentence make sense?
- Did I add details from my own experience?

MORE PRACTICE		Have children share their sentences with the group. Write their sentences on the board and have children practice reading and writing each other's sentences.
Homework		Practice Book, p. 40, Writing

Unit 2 Week 4 *Side by Side*

When should we work together? When should we work alone?

Objectives *This week students will...*

Phonemic Awareness
- segment, count, and add sounds in words

Phonics
- blend and read words with long *i* (CVC*e*) and inflected endings *-ed* and *-ing*
- apply knowledge of letter-sounds to decode unknown words when reading
- recognize high-frequency words *across, instead, moon, through*

Fluency
- practice fluency with oral rereading

Vocabulary
- build concepts and oral vocabulary: *companion, independent, partnership, solution, survival*

Text Comprehension
- read connected text
- identify main idea to improve comprehension
- write in response to literature

Word Work *This week's phonics focus is . . .*

Long *i* (CVC*e*)   Inflected Endings

High-Frequency Words *Tested Vocabulary*

The first appearance of each word in the Student Reader is noted below.

across	My friend lives **across** the street. (p. 76)
instead	**Instead** means in place of something else. (p. 74)
moon	The **moon** moves around the Earth. (p. 78)
through	The kitten ran **through** the house. (p. 77) We learned a new song all the way **through.**

Amazing Words *Oral Vocabulary*

The week's vocabulary is related to the concept of working together and working alone.

companion	someone who shares in what you are doing
independent	thinking or doing things by yourself, not with other people
partnership	two or more people joined together to share something
solution	a way to solve or fix a problem
survival	continuing to live or keep going

Student Reader Unit 2 *This week students will read the following selections.*

Daily Lesson Plan

	ACTIVITIES	MATERIALS
Day 1	**Word Work** Phonemic Awareness: Segment and Count Sounds Phonics: Blend Words with Long *i* (CVC*e*) High-Frequency Words *across, instead, moon, through* **Build Concepts** *partnership, solution, survival* **Read a Passage** "Side by Side," pp. 74–79 Comprehension: Use Strategies Reread for Fluency	Student White Boards Sound-Spelling Card 16 Tested Vocabulary Cards *Sing with Me Big Book* and Audio CD Student Reader: Unit 2 Routine Cards 1, 2, 3, 4, 6, 7 AudioText Practice Book, p. 41, Long *i* (CVC*e*)
Day 2	**Reread for Fluency** **Word Work** Phonemic Awareness: Add Ending Sounds Phonics: Blend Base Words and Endings High-Frequency Words *across, instead, moon, through* **Read a Passage** "Animals Together, Animals Alone," pp. 80–87 Comprehension: Use Strategies **Write** Response to Literature: Shared Writing	Student Reader: Unit 2 Student White Boards Tested Vocabulary Cards Routine Cards 1, 2, 3, 4, 6, 7 AudioText Practice Book, p. 42, Base Words and Endings
Day 3	**Reread for Fluency** **Word Work** Phonemic Awareness: Add Ending Sounds Phonics: Fluent Word Reading High-Frequency Words *across, instead, moon, through* **Build Concepts** *companion, independent* **Read a Passage** "Sliding Boxes," pp. 88–95 Comprehension: Main Idea	Student Reader: Unit 2 Student White Boards Tested Vocabulary Cards Routine Cards 1, 2, 3, 4, 6 AudioText Practice Book, p. 43, Main Idea
Day 4	**Reread for Fluency** **Word Work** Phonics: Spiral Review Phonological and Phonemic Awareness Activities, pp. 280–283 **Read Together** "All Work Together," pp. 96–98 Comprehension: Listening **Build Concepts** *companion, independent, partnership, solution, survival* **Write** Response to Literature: Interactive Writing	Student Reader: Unit 2 Routine Cards 1, 4 AudioText Student White Boards Practice Book, p. 44, High-Frequency Words
Day 5	**Assessment Options** Fluency, Comprehension Sentence Reading; Passage Reading Phonological and Phonemic Awareness Activities, pp. 280–283 **Use Concepts** *companion, independent, partnership, solution, survival* **Read to Connect** "Side by Side," pp. 74–79 Comprehension: Main Idea **Write** Response to Literature: Independent Writing	Reproducible p. 249 Sentence Reading Chart, p. 253 Student White Boards Fluency Progress Chart, p. 245 Student Reader: Unit 2 Routine Card 5 Practice Book, p. 45, Writing

Word Work

Phonemic Awareness Segment and Count Sounds

| **To Do** | **To Say** | *2 minutes* |

Scaffold instruction.

Distribute white boards.
Write *fin.* Then add *e* to form *fine.*

Model You see a fin on a fish. Listen to the sounds in *fin.* Stretch the sounds /fff/ /iii/ /nnn/ as you write *f, i, n.* Repeat. This time have children write the letters as you write. **Now let's count the sounds in *fin.* I will say the word slowly and hold up a finger for each sound: /f/ /i/ /n/. There are three sounds in *fin.* Now listen to the sounds in *fine:* /fff/ /īī/ /nnn/.**

Lead children in counting sounds as they write.

Teach and Practice Have children say the sounds with you as you point to the letters. (/f/ /ī/ /n/) **Hold up a finger for each sound. How many sounds in *fine?* (3) How many letters? (4)** Continue counting sounds with these words:

hid (3)   hide (3)   rip (3)   ripe (3)   slid (4)   slide (4)

Blending Strategy Long *i* (CVC*e*)

| **To Do** | **To Say** | *5–10 minutes* |

Routine

Use the blending routine.

Write *hid.*

1 Connect You already can read this word. What is the word? *(hid)* What vowel sound do you hear in *hid?* (the short *i* sound) Today we'll learn another sound for the letter *i*—the long *i* sound.

Display Sound-Spelling Card 16.

2 Use Sound-Spelling Card This is ice cream. What sound do you hear at the beginning of *ice cream?* (/ī/) Say it with me: /ī/. /ī/ is the long *i* sound: /ī/. It says its name: *i*/ī/.

Scaffold instruction.

Write *hide.*

3 Listen and Write Write *hide: h, i, d, e.* What vowels do you see in *hide?* (*i, e*) *Hide* has the long *i* sound: /ī/. As you write, say the sound to yourself: /ī/. Now say the sound aloud.

Write *hid.* Then add *e* to form *hide.*

4 Model When I add *e* to *hid,* it makes the *i* say its name. The sound of *i* in this new word is /ī/. The *e* is silent. This is how I blend this word: /h/ /ī/ /d/, *hide.* Now you try: /h/ /ī/ /d/, *hide.*

Point out that when a word has the vowel *i* followed by a consonant and *e,* the *i* usually has its long sound and the *e* is silent.

$$\underset{\rightarrow}{h} \; \underset{\rightarrow}{i} \; \underset{\rightarrow}{d} \; e$$

CORRECTIVE FEEDBACK

Write each practice word. Monitor student practice.

5 Group Practice Let's try the same thing with these words. Give feedback, using the *if . . . then* statements on Routine Card 1.

dive   wipe   nine   pile   slice*   shine

6 Individual Practice Write the words; have each child blend two of them.

line   dime   side   tile*   nice   white   smile   stripe

Check understanding of practice words.

*Children need to make sense of words that they segment and blend. If needed, help children with meanings. A *slice* is a thin piece cut from something. A *tile* is a thin piece of hard clay or stone. Some floors are made of *tile.*

MORE PRACTICE

Model spelling long *i* (CVC*e*) words.

Spell and Write What sounds do you hear in *like?* (/l/ /ī/ /k/) What is the letter for /l/? Let's all write *l.* Continue with *i*/ī/ and *k*/k/. What letter must we add to make *i* say its name? *(e)* Provide practice as time allows. Have children compare their spellings to what you've written.

five   time   wide   bike   ride   while   prize

High-Frequency Words *across, instead, moon, through*

To Do	To Say	*3 minutes*

Teach high-frequency words.

Display *across.*

1 Say, Spell, Write Use the Tested Vocabulary Cards. Display *across.* Here are some words that we won't sound out. We'll spell them. This word is *across: a, c, r, o, s, s* (point to each letter), *across.* What is this word? What are the letters in the word? Now you write *across.*

Point to *cr, o,* and *ss* in *across.*

2 Identify Letter-Sounds Let's look at the sounds in *across* that you do know. What are these letters? *(cr)* What are the sounds for these letters? *(/kr/)* Continue with *o/o/* and *ss/s/.*

3 Demonstrate Meaning Tell me a sentence using *across.* Model a sentence if children need help.

Display *instead, moon,* and *through.*

Repeat the Routine with *instead, moon,* and *through.* Children can identify these letter-sounds and word parts: *instead (in, st/ st/, d/d/), moon (m/m/, n/n/),* and *through (thr/thr/).* Have children write the words in their word banks. Add the words to the Word Wall. Point out that the words they are learning are on p. 99.

ACTIVITY **2** Build Concepts

Oral Vocabulary *partnership, solution, survival*

To Do	To Say	*5–10 minutes*

Introduce oral vocabulary.

Scaffold instruction.

Display p. 9 of *Sing with Me Big Book.* Play audio CD.

This week you will learn about working together. Listen for the Amazing Words *partnership, solution,* and *survival* as I sing this song. Play or sing the song. Then have children sing it with you.

Follow the Routine to teach *partnership, solution,* and *survival.*

1 Introduce, Demonstrate, and Apply

partnership The friend hopes to form a *partnership* to solve a problem. A *partnership* happens when two or more people join together to share something. Have children say the word. Best friends have a *partnership.* They get together to have fun and help one another. What *partnerships* do you have? What do you share in these *partnerships?*

solution In the song, one friend had a problem and couldn't find a *solution.* A *solution* is a way to solve, or fix, a problem. Have children say the word. A doctor can help you find the *solution* to a health problem. Who else can help you find *solutions* to problems?

survival One friend thought a partnership would be good for *survival. Survival* means something continues to live or keep going. Have children say the word. Water is good for a plant's *survival.* What is something that is good for your *survival?*

Display the words on the Amazing Words board.

2 Display the Words Have children say each word as they look at it. You can find sounds you know in big words. Read *part/ner/ship* as you run your hand under the syllables. What smaller word do you see at the end of *partnership?* (ship) For *solution* and *survival,* children can identify these letter-sounds: *solution (s/s/, l/l/, n/n/), survival (s/s/, v/v/, l/l/).*

Monitor understanding.

3 Use the Words Ask children to use each word in a sentence. Model a sentence if children need help.

MORE PRACTICE

Use oral vocabulary to discuss the song. Why does one friend want to form a *partnership* with the other friend? How do the friends find a *solution* to the problem? The friends in the song are good for each other's *survival.* How are your friends good for your *survival?*

ACTIVITY 3 Read a Passage

Build Background "Side by Side," pp. 74–79

	To Do	To Say	10 minutes

Develop language and concepts.

See Routine Card 7. Read aloud p. 73 of the student book.

Preview the Week Use the illustration on p. 72 as a starting point to discuss this week's concept of side by side. How are the children working side by side? Why is it better for them to work together instead of alone? Read aloud the titles and descriptions on p. 73. Ask children what they think each selection will be about.

Scaffold instruction.

See Routine Card 6. Display pp. 74–79.

Ask questions and elaborate on answers to develop language.

Key concepts: *ant hill, inhabit, survival, solution, problem, spittlebug, alone, partnership, set*

Before Reading Read the title aloud. Do a structured picture walk with children.

p. 74 What insects do you see? (ants) The ants are making an ant hill to inhabit. An ant hill is important for the ants' survival. Point to one ant. One ant cannot dig a big ant hill in the sand. What is the solution to the problem? (Lots of ants work together to make the ant hill.)

p. 75 This is a spittlebug. Where is it? (in a wet nest) The spittlebug makes its own bubbles to build its nest. Does the spittlebug have help from other spittlebugs? (no) The spittlebug works alone. When do you work alone? When is it good to work with others?

pp. 76–77 Point to the kids with the bag. They have formed a partnership. What are they working together to do? (fill a bag with leaves) What are the other kids working together to do? (rake leaves)

pp. 78–79 The sun has set, or gone down. It is night. What is this boy doing? (homework) The boy works to find a solution to a math problem. How will the boy feel if he finds the solution on his own? (happy, proud) If he can't figure out a solution, what should he do?

Let's read to find out about working together and working alone.

Guide comprehension.

Monitor independent reading. Model strategic reading. Use Routine Cards 2 and 3.

During Reading Read the page in a whisper. Raise your hand if you need help with a word. Stop at the end of each page to model asking questions. For example, for p. 74: After I read, I ask myself: What did I learn about how ants work? The author tells how lots of ants dig piles of sand to make an ant hill. I learned that ants like to work together.

Summarize.

Use oral vocabulary to develop the concept.

After Reading Which of these things shows a *partnership:* a spittlebug making a nest by itself or lots of ants making an ant hill? Explain. Why is working together good for the *survival* of ants? Do you think it's good to work alone to find *solutions* to math problems? Why or why not?

Reread for Fluency "Side by Side," pp. 74–75

	To Do	To Say	5–10 minutes

CORRECTIVE FEEDBACK

Monitor oral reading.

Read pp. 74–75 aloud. Read them three or four times so your reading gets better each time. Give feedback on children's oral reading and use of the blending strategy. See Routine Cards 1 and 4.

MORE PRACTICE

Instead of rereading just pp. 74–75, have children reread the entire selection three or four times. You may want to have children read along with the AudioText.

Homework

Practice Book, p. 41, Phonics: Long *i* (CVC*e*)

ACTIVITY 1 Reread for Fluency

Paired Reading "Side by Side," pp. 76–79

| To Do | To Say | 5–10 minutes |

CORRECTIVE FEEDBACK

To Do: Pair children. Monitor paired reading.

To Say: Children read pp. 76–79 orally, switching readers at the end of the first page. Have partners reread; now the other partner begins. For optimal fluency, children should reread three or four times. Give feedback on children's oral reading and use of the blending strategy. See Routine Cards 1 and 4.

MORE PRACTICE

Instead of rereading just pp. 76–79, have children reread the entire selection three or four times. You may want to have children read along with the AudioText.

ACTIVITY 2 Word Work

Phonemic Awareness Add Ending Sounds

| To Do | To Say | 2 minutes |

Scaffold instruction.

To Do: Distribute white boards. Write *fill*, *filled*, and *filling*.

To Say: **Model** Listen to the sounds in *fill.* Stretch the sounds /ffff/ /iii/ /lll/ as you write *f, i, ll.* Repeat. This time have children write the letters as you write. Now let's add the ending *-ed.* Listen to the sounds in *filled.* Stretch the sounds /fff/ /iii/ /lll/ /d/ as you add *-ed* to *fill.* Repeat. Have children write the letters as you write. Now let's add the ending *-ing.* Listen to the sounds in *filling.* Stretch the sounds /fff/ /iii/ /lll/ /ing/ as you add *-ing* to *fill.* Repeat. Have children write the letters as you write.

To Do: Lead children in identifying ending sounds as they write.

To Say: **Teach and Practice** Have children say the sounds as you point to the letters and then blend the sounds to say each word. What sound do you hear at the end of *filled?* (/d/) What sounds do you hear at the end of *filling?* (/ing/) Continue adding *-ed* and *-ing* to form the words below. Have children blend each new word and identify its ending sound.

wished (/t/) wishing (/ing/) drilled (/d/) drilling (/ing/) kicked (/t/) kicking (/ing/)

Blending Strategy Base Words and Endings

Use the blending routine.

Write *kicked* and *kicking*.

1 Connect You already can read words like these. What do you know about reading these words? (Both have a base word and an ending. Read the base word; read the ending; blend the two parts.) What are these words? Today we'll learn about words whose spelling changes before the ending *-ed* or *-ing* is added.

Scaffold instruction.

Write *like*. Then erase the final *e* and add *-ed* to form *liked*.

2 Model This word is *like*. Before adding the ending *-ed*, I need to drop the *e* from *like*. Erase *e* from *like* and add *-ed*. This is how I blend this word. Read the base word and then read the ending. Blend the two parts. Let's blend this word together: *like, ed, liked.* Point out that *-ed* stands for /t/ in *liked*. It can also stand for /d/ or /ed/.

Write *smile*. Then erase the final *e* and add *-ing* to form *smiling*.

Repeat, adding *-ing* to *smile*. When the base word ends with *e*, and the ending you're adding starts with a vowel like *-ed* and *-ing*, drop the final *e* from the base word before adding the ending. Use *likes* and *smiles* to point out that base words don't change their spellings when the *-s* ending is added, since *s* is a consonant.

l i k e d   s m i l i n g

Write *wave*.

3 Listen and Write Write the word *wave*. Now erase the *e* from *wave* and add the ending *-ed*. As you write, say the word to yourself: *waved*. Now say the word aloud. Repeat with *waving*.

CORRECTIVE FEEDBACK

Write each practice word. Monitor student practice.

4 Group Practice Let's try reading these words and saying the base word for each one. Give feedback, using the *if . . . then* statements on Routine Card 1.

baked	riding	piled	racing	chasing	smiled
(bake)	(ride)	(pile)	(race)	(chase)	(smile)

5 Individual Practice Write the words; have each child blend two of them.

making	wiped	trading	shined	slicing	placed
(make)	(wipe)	(trade)	(shine)	(slice)	(place)

MORE PRACTICE

Model building words by dropping final *e* and adding *-ed* and *-ing*.

Build Words Write each of these base words twice: *hike, name, bike, skate*. Have children copy each pair of words on their white boards. With the first pair of words, model erasing the *e* and adding the ending *-ed* to the first word in the pair. Then add *-ing* to the other word in the pair. Have children continue the activity, writing the endings *-ed* and *-ing* on each base word. Then have them read the words with endings.

High-Frequency Words *across, instead, moon, through*

Teach high-frequency words.

Display *across, instead, moon,* and *through*.

Use the Tested Vocabulary Cards. Point to a word. Say and spell it. Have children say and spell the word. Ask children to identify familiar letter-sounds. Have them take turns reading the words.

Lead cumulative review.

Use the Tested Vocabulary Cards to review high-frequency words from previous weeks.

ACTIVITY **3** Read a Passage

Reading "Animals Together, Animals Alone," pp. 80–87

10–15 minutes

	To Do	To Say
Develop language and concepts. **Scaffold instruction.**	See Routine Cards 6 and 7. Display pp. 80–87. Ask questions and elaborate on answers to develop language. Key concepts: *wolf, pup, pack, cougar, survival, elk, penguin, sloth*	**Before Reading** Have children recall what they learned about how the ants worked together and the spittlebug worked alone. Read the title. Do a structured picture walk with children. **pp. 80–83** A wolf looks like a dog, but it is wild. Point to the wolf. A young wolf is called a pup. Point to the pup. Wolves work together in a pack. Point to the pack. What is this big cat? It is a cougar. It needs food for survival, so it hunts elk. Does it hunt with other cougars? **pp. 84–87** What animals do you see on the ice? (penguins) How can you tell the penguins like being together? (They are having fun sliding, swimming, and diving.) This animal is a sloth. Point to the sloth. The sloth likes to be alone. Let's read to learn more about these animals.
Guide comprehension.	Monitor independent reading. See Routine Cards 2 and 3.	**During Reading** Read the pages in a whisper. Raise your hand if you need help with a word. As you read, ask yourself: What am I learning about how animals work? What is this mainly about? **pp. 80–83** What did you learn about how a wolf works? (A wolf hunts with other wolves in a pack. Wolves hunt together.) What did you learn about how a cougar works? (A cougar hunts without other cats. Cougars work alone.) **pp. 84–87** What did you learn about how a penguin works? (A penguin dives and fishes with other penguins. Penguins work together.) What did you learn about how a sloth works? (A sloth doesn't work much. A sloth likes to be alone.)
Model summarizing.	Think aloud.	**After Reading** What did you learn about how animals work? What was the selection mainly about? Model how to summarize. The first few pages were about wolves working together and a cougar working alone. The last few pages told how penguins work and play together and how a sloth spends its time alone. I put that all together and pick the most important ideas. The selection is mainly about how some animals work together and some animals work alone.
MORE PRACTICE	Develop oral vocabulary.	Do wolves in a pack have a kind of *partnership?* Does a cougar need other cougars for its *survival?* How might a *partnership* among the penguins be good for their *survival?* Napping in trees could be a problem for a sloth. How might its long nails be a *solution?*

ACTIVITY **4** Write

Response to Literature Shared Writing

5 minutes

	To Do	To Say
Guide shared writing.	Write sentence frames. Read the questions.	Who works together? _____ work together. They _____. Who does not work together? _____ do not work together. They _____. Invite children to suggest answers. Discuss and record answers to complete the sentence frames. While writing, model connecting sounds to letters and forming letters (see pp. 257–259). Have children read answers aloud as you track print.
Homework		Practice Book, p. 42, Phonics: Base Words and Endings

3

ACTIVITY 1 Reread for Fluency

Oral Reading "Animals Together, Animals Alone" pp. 80–83

5–10 minutes

	To Do	To Say
CORRECTIVE FEEDBACK	Monitor oral reading.	**Read pp. 80–83 aloud. Read them three or four times so your reading gets better each time. Give feedback on children's oral reading and use of the blending strategy.** See Routine Cards 1 and 4.
MORE PRACTICE		Instead of rereading just pp. 80–83, have children reread the entire selection three or four times. You may want to have children read along with the AudioText.

ACTIVITY 2 Word Work

Phonemic Awareness Add Ending Sounds

2 minutes

	To Do	To Say
Scaffold instruction.	Distribute white boards. Write *miss, missed,* and *missing.*	**Model** Listen to the sounds in *miss.* Stretch the sounds /mmm/ /iii/ /sss/ as you write *m, i, ss.* Repeat. Have children write the letters as you write. **Now let's add -ed.** Listen to the sounds in *missed.* Say /mmm/ /iii/ /sss/ /t/ as you add *-ed* to *miss.* Repeat; have children write. **Now let's add -ing.** Listen to the sounds in *missing.* Say /mmm/ /iii/ /sss/ /ing/ as you add *-ing* to *miss.* Repeat; have children write.
	Lead children in adding and identifying ending sounds as they write.	**Teach and Practice** Have children say the sounds as you point to the letters. **What sound do you hear at the end of *missed*?** (/t/) **at the end of *missing*?** (/ing/) Write the words below. Have children blend the words and identify the ending sounds. fixed (/t/) fixing (/ing/) spilled (/d/) spilling (/ing/) thrilled (/d/) thrilling (/ing/)

Fluent Word Reading Long *i* (CVC*e*), Base Words and Endings

5–10 minutes

	To Do	To Say
Use the word-reading routine. **Scaffold instruction.**	Write *wipe.*	**1 Connect** You can read this word because you know how to read long *i* words. When you see *i* followed by a consonant and *e,* the *e* makes the *i* say its name: /ī/. What is the word? *(wipe)*
	Write *hike, hiked,* and *hiking.*	**2 Model** When you come to a new word, look at all the letters in the word and think about its vowel sound. Say the letter-sounds in the word to yourself, and then read the word. Model reading *hike, hiked,* and *hiking.* When you come to a new word, what are you going to do?
	Write each practice word.	**3 Group Practice** Let's read these words. Look at all the letters, think about the vowel sound, and say the letter-sounds to yourself. We will read words with long *i* and the endings *-ed* and *-ing.* When I point to the word, let's read it together. Allow 2–3 seconds previewing time for each word. biked shining sliced rising faced sliding chased striking chimed
CORRECTIVE FEEDBACK	**MONITOR PROGRESS**	*If . . .* children have difficulty previewing and reading whole words, *then . . .* have them use sound-by-sound blending. *If . . .* children can't read the words fluently at a rate of 1–2 seconds per word, *then . . .* continue practicing the list.

MORE PRACTICE	Model reading words in sentences.	When I read a sentence, I read each word without stopping between the words. If I come to a word I don't know, I blend it. Then I read the sentence again. Model reading this sentence, stopping to blend *slicing: It is wise to take your time when you are slicing a cake.*
	Write practice sentences.	Have each child read a sentence.
		Mike smiled with pride at his nine prizes. **Are you wiping that tile with a white cloth?** **Miss Fine hiked five miles to get to the big pine.**

High-Frequency Words *across, instead, moon, through*

	To Do	**To Say**	3 minutes
Review high-frequency words.	Display *across, instead, moon,* and *through.*	Use the Tested Vocabulary Cards. Point to a word. Say and spell it. Have children say and spell the word. Ask children to identify familiar letter-sounds. Have them take turns reading the words.	

ACTIVITY 3 | Build Concepts

Oral Vocabulary *companion, independent*

	To Do	**To Say**	5–10 minutes
Teach oral vocabulary.	Display p. 88 of the student book.	Today you will read a story about an *independent* boy and girl who become *companions.*	*Routine*
	Follow the Routine to teach *companion* and *independent.*	**1 Introduce, Demonstrate, and Apply**	
		companion The girl and boy in this story become *companions.* A *companion* is someone who shares in what you are doing. Have children say the word. Classmates are your *companions* at school. You work and play together. Who are your *companions* at home? What do you do together?	
		independent The boy and girl in this story are each *independent.* Someone who is *independent* does not want help from other people. Have children say the word. An *independent* two-year-old wants to dress and feed herself without help from her parents. Suppose you have math homework. If you are *independent*, what would you do first: ask for help or try to do it on your own?	
	Display the words on the Amazing Words board.	**2 Display the Words** Have children say each word as they look at it. You can find sounds you know in big words. Read *com/pan/ion* as you run your hand under the syllables. What sound does *c* stand for at the beginning of *companion?* (/k/) What sounds do *p, a, n* stand for in the middle of this word? (/pan/) Read *in/de/pen/dent.* Children can identify *in, d*/d/, *pen,* and *dent.*	
	Monitor understanding.	**3 Use the Words** Ask children to use each word in a sentence. Model a sentence if children need help.	
MORE PRACTICE		Use oral vocabulary to discuss working together. How can working with *companions* help you finish a job more quickly? Which would you likely do *independently*: paint a picture or paint a house? Explain.	

ACTIVITY 4 Read a Passage

Reading "Sliding Boxes," pp. 88–95

| To Do | To Say | 10 minutes |

Teach main idea.

Scaffold instruction.

Introduce the skill.

Model the skill.

Today you are learning about the main idea and details of a story. The main idea is the most important idea. It tells what the whole story is about. Details tell more about the main idea. For example, last week we read "A Snack for Grace." Grace put grapes on a plate. She gave some to her friends. A friend brought more grapes. They all had fun sharing. The main idea is they all had fun sharing. Grace giving grapes is a detail that tells what they shared.

Apply the skill.

Suppose you read a story about a family working together for Dad's party. Mom bakes a cake, Gram blows up balloons, and the kids wrap gifts. What is the main idea? What is a detail? Have children explain their answers.

Develop language and concepts.

See Routine Card 6. Display pp. 88–95.

Model using key words and concepts.

Key concepts: *independent, problem, solution, companions*

Before Reading Read the title. Do a structured picture walk.

pp. 88–89 Where does this story happen? (at school) The school will sell the things in this box. The boy's job is to take the box across the room.

pp. 90–91 The girl's job is to take the box of prizes across the room. What problem does she have? (It's too heavy for her to lift.) The girl tries to lift it on her own. Is that a good solution? Why or why not?

pp. 92–93 Point to the companions on p. 93. What are they doing? (working together to move the box) They tie a rope around the box and pull together to make the box slide.

pp. 94–95 The companions got the job done. How can you tell? (They've unpacked their boxes.) Working together is a good solution.

Monitor children's use of vocabulary.

Now turn to your partner and talk about the pictures, using the same words I did.

Guide comprehension.

Monitor independent reading.

Use Routine Cards 2 and 3.

During Reading Read the pages in a whisper. Raise your hand if you need help with a word. As you read, ask yourself: What is the main idea of the story?

pp. 88–91 What is Mike's job? What is his problem? (He must take a big box across the room. He can't lift the box on his own.) What is Kate's job? What is her problem? (She must take a big box across the room. She can't lift the box by herself.)

pp. 92–93 How do Mike and Kate solve their problems? (They tie rope around each box and work together to slide them across the room.)

pp. 94–95 What is the main idea of the story? (Children can work together to get a big job done.) What are some details that tell more about working together? (Mike can't move his box. Kate can't move her box. They use a rope and work together to move each box.)

Guide retelling.

Prompt children as they retell the story.

After Reading Have one child retell the story while the others assist. What happens first? next? last? What is the main idea? (Kids can work together to get a big job done.) See Monitoring Retelling, p. 246.

Homework

Practice Book, p. 43, Main Idea

ACTIVITY **1** Reread for Fluency

Paired Reading "Sliding Boxes," pp. 88–90

| To Do | To Say | *5–10 minutes* |

CORRECTIVE FEEDBACK

Pair children. Monitor paired reading.

Children read pp. 88–90 orally, switching readers at the end of the first page. Have partners reread; now the other partner begins. For optimal fluency, children should reread three or four times. Give feedback on children's oral reading and use of the blending strategy. See Routine Cards 1 and 4.

MORE PRACTICE

Instead of rereading just pp. 88–90, have children reread the entire selection three or four times. You may want to have children read along with the AudioText.

ACTIVITY **2** Word Work

Spiral Review Short *i* and Long *i* (CVC*e*)

| To Do | To Say | *5–10 minutes* |

Review short *i* and long *i*.

Write *bit*.

You can read this word because you know the letter *i* can stand for the sounds /i/ and /ī/. What sound does *i* have in this word? (/i/) Remember, when *i* is the only vowel at the beginning or middle of a word, it usually stands for its short sound, /i/. Now let's blend the sounds to say the word: /b/ /i/ /t/, *bit*.

Scaffold instruction.

Add *e* to *bit* to form *bite*.

How does the vowel sound /i/ change when the letter *e* is added to the end of *bit?* (It changes to the long *i* sound. The *e* makes the *i* say its name: /ī/.) Remember, when you see *i* followed by a consonant and the letter *e*, the *i* usually stands for its long sound, /ī/, and the *e* is silent. Now let's blend the sounds to say the word: /b/ /ī/ /t/, *bite*.

Distribute white boards. Write *bit* and *bite* at top of two-column chart.

Sort Words Let's sort words by their vowel sounds. Point to and read *bit* and *bite*. Then display this list of words: *rid, ride, slid, slide, strip, stripe, slim, slime*. Call on children to read each word in the list and tell whether it has a vowel sound like *bit* or *bite*. Write the word in an appropriate column on a class chart as children write on their boards.

How are the words in the first column alike? (They're all short *i* words. They all have only one vowel.) How are the words in the second column alike? (They're all long *i* words. They all have *i* followed by a consonant and a silent *e*.) Have children suggest a heading for each column. (Short *i*, Long *i*)

Short *i*	Long *i*
bit	bite
rid	ride
slid	slide
strip	stripe
slim	slime

CORRECTIVE FEEDBACK

MONITOR PROGRESS

If . . . children have difficulty reading the words,
then . . . review the effect of *e* at the end of the words and blend the words sound-by-sound.

For more practice, see next page.

Continued Spiral Review

MORE PRACTICE

Model reading words in sentences.	When I read a sentence, I read each word without stopping between the words. If I come to a word I don't know, I blend it. Then I read the sentence again. Model reading this sentence, stopping to blend *vine: Jim will pick the ripe grapes from the vine.*
Write practice sentences.	Have each child read a sentence. **Tim liked to ride his bike to Pine Lake.** **The nice bride is smiling at the big white cake.** **Is there still time to make a kite from this kit?**
Phonological and Phonemic Awareness	Optional practice activities, pp. 280–283

ACTIVITY **3** Read Together

Choral Reading "All Work Together," pp. 96–98

To Do **To Say** *10 minutes*

Develop language and concepts.	Display pp. 96–98.	**Before Reading** This is a song about kids working together with others to get jobs done more quickly. When have you worked with others to get a big job done more quickly? (Allow children to share their experiences.) The people in this song work together with a wiggle and a giggle and a grin. Show me how you wiggle, giggle, and grin.
Model fluent reading.	Model prosody.	Read the title of the song. Ask children to predict what it is about. Listen to my voice as I read. When I read words from a song, I try to keep a rhythm as I read. Read the song lyrics with expression, keeping a steady rhythm. You may wish to tap the beat with your foot. Read it a second time, having children point to each word.
	Build fluency through choral reading.	**Choral Reading** Now read aloud with me. Try to make your voice sound like mine as we read. Reread the song several times with children. You can also play or sing the song to children and then have them sing along with you.
Develop concepts.	Monitor listening comprehension.	**After Reading** What kinds of work does the song say the kids can do? How can the kids get jobs done more quickly? What is the *solution?* How does this song show that working together with *companions* can be fun?

ACTIVITY **4** Build Concepts

Oral Vocabulary *companion, independent, partnership, solution, survival*

To Do **To Say** *5–10 minutes*

Review oral vocabulary.	Read the words on the Amazing Words board.	**Focus on Letter-Sounds** Remember, you can find sounds you know in big words. • What words begin with *s?* What words end with *n?* • Which word ends with the sounds /nt/? What letters stand for /nt/? • Which word has *ship* in it? Which word has *pan* in it?

Encourage discussion.	**Use Personal Contexts** Review the meanings of the words. Then ask children to use the words in personal contexts.

- Tell about a time you formed a *partnership* to make or do something. What did you and your partners make or do?

- Think of a problem you or a friend had. What *solution* helped you solve the problem?

- Which things must you have for your *survival*—games, food, television, air, water? (food, air, water)

- Describe a time when you felt *independent.* Describe a time when you had fun working with a *companion.*

Apply oral vocabulary to new situations.	- Suppose you couldn't find a *companion* to play catch. What might be a *solution* to the problem? (ask someone new; shoot some baskets) - Clap to show how much you would like to be *independent* (not at all, a little bit, a lot). Why? - Why does the *survival* of people in a fire sometimes depend on firefighters? (People may need to be rescued to stay alive.)

ACTIVITY 5 ## Write

Response to Literature Interactive Writing

	To Do	To Say	*5–10 minutes*
Generate ideas.	Review the story "Sliding Boxes."	Do you think that Mike and Kate had fun working together? Discuss whether Mike and Kate enjoyed working together. Have children give reasons for their conclusions.	
Share the pen.	Have children participate in writing about times when work is fun.	Write *Work is fun when _____.* Have children read the words you wrote. Then have them supply endings for the sentence. Invite individuals to write familiar letter-sounds, word parts, and high-frequency words. Have them find the spelling of high-frequency words on the Word Wall. Ask questions such as:	

- What is the first sound in *time?* (/t/) What is the letter for /t/? *(t)*

- What is the vowel sound in *time?* (/ī/) What is the letter for /ī/? *(i)*

- What is the last sound in *time?* (/m/) What is the letter for /m/? *(m)*

- Which letter do we add to the end of *t, i, m,* to make the *i* say its name: /ī/? *(e)*

Writing elements: conventions	Frequently reread what has been written while tracking the print. Point out that each sentence starts with a capital letter and ends with a period. Point out the extra space between words. Read the completed sentences aloud, having children read with you. (For example, *Work is fun when the job does not take much time. Work is fun when you work with friends. Work is fun when it is over!*)

MORE PRACTICE Prompt independent writing.	**Journal Writing** Tell about working with another person.

Homework	Practice Book, p. 44, High-Frequency Words

ACTIVITY 1 Assessment Options

Sentence Reading

To Do	To Say	5 minutes

Assess sentence reading.

To Do: Use reproducible p. 249.

To Say: Have each child read the sentences. Record scores on the Sentence Reading Chart, p. 253. Work with one child as others complete Write Sentences below.

I piled white rice on my plate.
The moon is shining through the vines.
Mike liked hiking across hills instead of riding on them.

CORRECTIVE FEEDBACK

MONITOR PROGRESS

If . . . children have trouble reading long *i* (CVC*e*) words and base words with endings,
then . . . reteach the blending strategy lessons on pp. 132 and 136.

If . . . children cannot read a high-frequency word,
then . . . mark the missed word or words on a high-frequency word list and send the list home for additional practice or have them practice with a fluent reader.

If . . . children misread a word in the sentence,
then . . . correct the error and have them reread the word and then the sentence.

Practice sentence writing.

To Do: Provide white boards.

Write Sentences Have children copy the sentences from reproducible p. 249 on white boards. Have them confirm spellings by comparing the words they wrote to the words in the sentences.

Phonological and Phonemic Awareness

Optional practice activities, pp. 280–283

Passage Reading

To Do	To Say	5–10 minutes

Assess fluency and comprehension.

To Do: Determine which children to assess this week.

To Say: Choose from these options: monitoring fluency (see pp. 244–245) and/or monitoring retelling (see p. 246). Have children read "Sliding Boxes." Be sure each child is assessed every other week.

If you have time, assess every child.

ACTIVITY 2 Use Concepts

Oral Vocabulary *companion, independent, partnership, solution, survival*

To Do	To Say	5 minutes

Check understanding of oral vocabulary.

To Do: Use the Amazing Words to wrap up the week's concept.

Monitor understanding of oral vocabulary, using Routine Card 5.

To Say: As time allows, ask questions such as these.

- Describe the pictures on pp. 74–79 using some of the week's Amazing Words.
- If you are *independent,* you might not know when you should work with *companions.* Why?
- When you put on a school play, why is it best to form a *partnership* with others?
- When might you work a long time to find a *solution* to a math problem? (when the math problem is hard, when I don't ask for help)
- *Survival* in a cold, icy place is difficult. Name some animals that are adapted for *survival* in icy places. (penguins, seals)

Preview next week's concept.

Next week you will read about fun celebrations.

ACTIVITY 3 Read to Connect

Reread "Side by Side," pp. 74–79

	To Do	To Say	10 minutes

Monitor comprehension: main idea.

To Do: Have children reread "Side by Side" silently.

To Say: As you read, think about the ways creatures and people work. What is the main, or most important, idea? What details tell more about the main idea? After rereading, ask:

- What is the main idea of this selection? (Sometimes it is good to work together. Sometimes it is good to work alone.)

- Describe some details that tell more about working together and working alone. (Ants work together to build an ant hill. A spittlebug works alone to build a nest. Kids work together to pick up piles of leaves. Mike works alone on his math homework.)

- When does it make sense to work together? When does it make sense to work alone? Record children's ideas in a T-chart on the board. Children will use the chart for Activity 4.

Make connections.

To Do: Have children make connections across texts.

To Say: We also read "Animals Together, Animals Alone." Find that. Which animals like to be together? How does being together help them? Which animals like to be alone? Why? In two webs, record children's ideas about animals together and animals alone.

We also read "Sliding Boxes," about a boy and a girl who each try to move a heavy box across a room. Why was it best for Mike and Kate to work together? (They couldn't do the job alone. It helped them get the job done.) Add children's ideas in the T-chart above.

What did all the selections we read this week show us about working together? (Working together helps some creatures survive. When people work together, they can get big jobs done.)

ACTIVITY 4 Write

Response to Literature Independent Writing

	To Do	To Say	5–10 minutes

Assign personal narrative.

Guide sentence correction.

To Do: Writing elements: conventions, support

To Say: Today you will write about when we should work together. Describe a time when working together is better than working alone. Encourage children to use words you wrote on the board for Activity 3 as they write.

Have children check their writing by asking themselves these questions.

- Did I begin each sentence with a capital letter?

- Did I use the correct mark at the end of each sentence?

- Did I think about the spelling of base words before adding endings?

- Did I use details from my own experience?

MORE PRACTICE

Have children share their sentences with the group. Write their sentences on the board and have children practice reading and writing each other's sentences.

Homework Practice Book, p. 45, Writing

Unit 2 Week 5 *Let's Celebrate*

How can we contribute to a celebration?

Objectives *This week students will...*

Phonemic Awareness
- segment, count, and add sounds in words

Phonics
- blend and read words with long *o* (CVC*e*) and possessive nouns
- apply knowledge of letter-sounds to decode unknown words when reading
- recognize high-frequency words *father, mother, remember, touch*

Fluency
- practice fluency with oral rereading

Vocabulary
- build concepts and oral vocabulary: *decorate, dine, float, holiday, participate*

Text Comprehension
- read connected text
- draw conclusions to improve comprehension
- write in response to literature

Word Work *This week's phonics focus is . . .*

Long *o* (CVC*e*)   Possessives

High-Frequency Words *Tested Vocabulary*

The first appearance of each word in the Student Reader is noted below.

father	A **father** is a man who has a child or children. (p. 102)
mother	A **mother** is a woman who has a child or children. (p. 102)
remember	When you **remember** something, you keep it in your mind. (p. 103)
touch	When you **touch** something, you feel it. (p. 106)

Amazing Words *Oral Vocabulary*

The week's vocabulary is related to the concept of celebrations.

decorate	to make something beautiful by adding ornaments
dine	to eat a meal
float	a low, flat car that carries something to show in a parade
holiday	a day when people celebrate something special
participate	to join in

Student Reader Unit 2 *This week students will read the following selections.*

102	**Let's Find Out: Let's Celebrate**	Narrative Nonfiction
110	**Big, Big Balloon**	Narrative Nonfiction
116	**The Balloon Ride**	Fantasy
124	**Make a Greeting Card**	Directions

Daily Lesson Plan

	ACTIVITIES	MATERIALS
Day 1	**Word Work** Phonemic Awareness: Segment and Count Sounds Phonics: Blend Words with Long *o* (CVC*e*) High-Frequency Words *father, mother, remember, touch* **Build Concepts** *dine, holiday, participate* **Read a Passage** "Let's Celebrate," pp. 102–109 Comprehension: Use Strategies Reread for Fluency	Student White Boards Sound-Spelling Card 24 Tested Vocabulary Cards *Sing with Me Big Book* and Audio CD Student Reader: Unit 2 Routine Cards 1, 2, 3, 4, 6, 7 AudioText Practice Book, p. 46, Long *o* (CVC*e*)
Day 2	**Reread for Fluency** **Word Work** Phonemic Awareness: Add Phonemes Phonics: Blend Possessive Nouns High-Frequency Words *father, mother, remember, touch* **Read a Passage** "Big, Big Balloon," pp. 110–115 Comprehension: Use Strategies **Write** Response to Literature: Shared Writing	Student Reader: Unit 2 Student White Boards Tested Vocabulary Cards Routine Card 4 AudioText Practice Book, p. 47, Possessives
Day 3	**Reread for Fluency** **Word Work** Phonemic Awareness: Add Phonemes Phonics: Fluent Word Reading High-Frequency Words *father, mother, remember, touch* **Build Concepts** *decorate, float* **Read a Passage** "The Balloon Ride," pp. 116–123 Comprehension: Draw Conclusions	Student Reader: Unit 2 Student White Boards Tested Vocabulary Cards Routine Cards 1, 2, 3, 4, 6 AudioText Practice Book, p. 48, Draw Conclusions
Day 4	**Reread for Fluency** **Word Work** Phonics: Spiral Review Phonological and Phonemic Awareness Activities, pp. 280–283 **Read Together** "Make a Greeting Card," pp. 124–125 Comprehension: Listening **Build Concepts** *decorate, dine, float, holiday, participate* **Write** Response to Literature: Interactive Writing	Student Reader: Unit 2 Student White Boards Routine Cards 1, 4 AudioText Practice Book, p. 49, High-Frequency Words
Day 5	**Assessment Options** Fluency, Comprehension Sentence Reading; End-of-Unit Test Phonological and Phonemic Awareness Activities, pp. 280–283 **Use Concepts** *decorate, dine, float, holiday, participate* **Read to Connect** "Let's Celebrate," pp. 102–109 Comprehension: Draw Conclusions **Write** Response to Literature: Independent Writing	Reproducible p. 250 Sentence Reading Chart, p. 253 Assessment Book, p. 33 Student White Boards Student Reader: Unit 2 Routine Card 5 Practice Book, p. 50, Writing

See pp. xvi–xvii for how *My Sidewalks* integrates instructional practices for ELL.

Word Work

Phonemic Awareness Segment and Count Sounds

2 minutes

	To Do	To Say
Scaffold instruction.	Distribute white boards. Write *rod.* Then add *e* to form *rode.* Lead children in counting sounds as they write.	**Model** You fish with a rod. Listen to the sounds in *rod.* Stretch the sounds /rrr/ /ooo/ /d/ as you write *r, o, d.* Repeat. This time have children write the letters as you write. Now let's count the sounds in *rod.* I will say the word slowly and hold up a finger for each sound: /r/ /o/ /d/. There are three sounds in *rod.* Now listen to the sounds in *rode:* /rrr/ /ōōō/ /d/. **Teach and Practice** Have children say the sounds with you as you point to the letters. (/r/ /ō/ /d/) Hold up a finger for each sound. How many sounds in *rode?* (3) How many letters? (4) Continue counting sounds with these words: not (3) note (3) hop (3) hope (3) rob (3) robe (3)

Blending Strategy Long *o* (CVC*e*)

5–10 minutes

Routine

	To Do	To Say
Use the blending routine.	Write *not.*	**1 Connect** You already can read this word. What is the word? *(not)* What vowel sound do you hear in *not?* (the short *o* sound) Today we'll learn another sound for the letter *o*—the long *o* sound.
	Display Sound-Spelling Card 24.	**2 Use Sound-Spelling Card** This is an ocean. What sound do you hear at the beginning of *ocean?* (/ō/) Say it with me: /ō/. /ō/ is the long *o* sound: /ō/. It says its name: *o*/ō/.
Scaffold instruction.	Write *note.*	**3 Listen and Write** Write *note: n, o, t, e.* What vowels do you see in *note?* (*o, e*) *Note* has the long *o* sound: /ō/. As you write, say the sound to yourself: /ō/. Now say the sound aloud.
	Write *not.* Then add *e* to form *note.*	**4 Model** When I add *e* to *not,* it makes the *o* say its name. The sound of *o* in this new word is /ō/. The *e* is silent. This is how I blend this word: /n/ /ō/ /t/, *note.* Now you try: /n/ /ō/ /t/, *note.* Point out that when a word has the vowel *o* followed by consonant and *e,* the *o* usually has its long sound and the *e* is silent. <p align="center">n o t e</p>
CORRECTIVE FEEDBACK	Write each practice word. Monitor student practice.	**5 Group Practice** Let's try the same thing with these words. Give feedback, using the *if . . . then* statements on Routine Card 1. robe nose home pose* close throne*
		6 Individual Practice Write the words; have each child blend two of them. rose hole poke froze stone choke
	Check understanding of practice words.	*Children need to make sense of words that they segment and blend. If needed, help children with meanings. When you *pose,* you hold your body in one place. This is how I *pose* for a photo. (Demonstrate.) Show how you *pose.* A *throne* is a big chair on which a king or queen sits.
MORE PRACTICE	Model spelling long *o* (CVC*e*) words.	**Spell and Write** What sounds do you hear in *note?* (/n/ /ō/ /t/) What is the letter for /n/? Let's all write *n.* Continue with *o*/ō/ and *t*/t/. What letter must we add to make *o* say its name? *(e)* Provide practice as time allows. Have children compare their spellings to what you've written. cone pole hope joke spoke drove

High-Frequency Words *father, mother, remember, touch*

To Do	To Say	3 minutes

Teach high-frequency words.

Display *father*.

1 Say, Spell, Write Use the Tested Vocabulary Cards. Display *father*. Here are some words that we won't sound out. We'll spell them. This word is *father*: *f, a, t, h, e, r* (point to each letter), *father*. What is this word? What are the letters in the word? Now you write *father*.

Point to *f* and *th* in *father*.

2 Identify Letter-Sounds Let's look at the sounds in *father* that you do know. What is this letter? *(f)* What is the sound for this letter? *(/f/)* Continue with *th*/th/.

3 Demonstrate Meaning Tell me a sentence using *father*. Model a sentence if children need help.

Display *mother, remember,* and *touch*.

Repeat the Routine with *mother, remember,* and *touch.* Children can identify these letter-sounds and word parts: *mother* (*m*/m/, *th*/th), *remember* (*mem, b*/b/), and *touch* (*t*/t/, *ch*/ch/). Have children write the words in their word banks. Add the words to the Word Wall. Point out that the words they are learning are on pp. 126–127.

Routine

ACTIVITY **2** Build Concepts

Oral Vocabulary *dine, holiday, participate*

To Do	To Say	5–10 minutes

Introduce oral vocabulary.

Scaffold instruction.

Display p. 10 of *Sing with Me Big Book.* Play audio CD.

This week you will learn about celebrating. Listen for the Amazing Words *dine, holiday,* and *participate* as I sing this song. Play or sing the song. Then have children sing it with you.

Routine

Follow the Routine to teach *dine, holiday,* and *participate.*

1 Introduce, Demonstrate, and Apply

dine The table is set for the people to *dine.* When you *dine,* you eat a meal. Have children say the word. We *dined* at a restaurant on New Year's Day. When you *dine,* what kinds of food do you eat?

holiday The song tells why *holidays* are fun to celebrate. A *holiday* is a day when people celebrate something special. Have children say the word. Independence Day is a *holiday* on the Fourth of July. It's special because on this *holiday* we celebrate the start of the United States as an independent country. What *holidays* do you celebrate at your home?

participate In the song, friends and family members *participate* in the *holiday* celebration. When you *participate* in something, you join in. Have children say the word. Some children like to *participate* by serving food on a *holiday.* In what ways do you *participate* in your family's *holiday* celebrations?

Display the words on the Amazing Words board.

2 Display the Words Have children say each word as they look at it. You can find sounds you know in big words. Read *hol/i/day* as you run your hand under the syllables. Children can identify *h*/h/, *d*/d/. Repeat for *par/tic/i/pate.* Children can identify *p*/p/, *t*/t/, *pate.* Then have children read *dine.*

Monitor understanding.

3 Use the Words Ask children to use each word in a sentence. Model a sentence if children need help.

MORE PRACTICE

Use oral vocabulary to discuss the song. Who gathers to celebrate the *holiday?* How do the visitors *participate* in the celebration? Will the people *dine* at this *holiday* celebration? How do you know?

Read a Passage

Build Background "Let's Celebrate," pp. 102–109

To Do	To Say

10 minutes

Develop language and concepts.

See Routine Card 7. Read aloud p. 101 of the student book.

Preview the Week Use the illustration on p. 100 as a starting point to discuss this week's concept of celebrating. **What is the girl holding? Do you think she might be going to a celebration? Why?** Read aloud the titles and descriptions on p. 101. Ask children what they think each selection will be about.

Scaffold instruction.

See Routine Card 6. Display pp. 102–109.

Ask questions and elaborate on answers to develop language.

Key concepts: *prepare, participate, pose, photo, throne, float* (n.), *banner, celebration, surprised*

Before Reading Read the title aloud. Do a structured picture walk with children.

pp. 102–103 This family works together to prepare, or get ready for, a party. **How do Mom and Dad help prepare?** (Mom hangs a piñata; Dad pours punch.) **How do you think the kids participate?** The family will pose, or stay still, for a photo of this happy time. **Point to their photo.**

pp. 104–105 These kids prepare for a parade. Someone will sit on a throne, or big chair. **Point to the throne.** A float will carry the throne in the parade. **Point to the float. How do the kids work together to make the float?** (They stick flowers in holes.) **How will the kids remember this time?** (They'll look at the photo.)

pp. 106–107 What are these kids doing? Yes, they are working together to make a big sign, or a banner. The banner says, "Welcome to Grade 2." **Do you think they are preparing for a celebration at school? What kind?** (Possible answers: open house, family night, fun fair)

pp. 108–109 Point to the kid who looks surprised. What are the other kids doing? (jumping up from behind things and yelling) **What kind of celebration is this?** (a surprise party) Let's read to find out how people get ready to celebrate.

Guide comprehension.

Monitor independent reading. Model strategic reading. Use Routine Cards 2 and 3.

During Reading Read the page in a whisper. Raise your hand if you need help with a word. Stop at the end of each page to model asking questions. For example, for p. 102: After I read, I ask myself: What is this mainly about? The author tells how Mom hangs a rope for games, Dad fills cups with punch, and the kids made a cake. This is mainly about how a family works together to get ready for a party.

Summarize.

Use oral vocabulary to develop the concept.

After Reading What foods will the family eat as they *dine* at their party? Suppose the kids ride on the float in a *holiday* parade. Which *holiday* might they be celebrating? How do the kids *participate* in making the banner? How do kids *participate* in a surprise party?

Reread for Fluency "Let's Celebrate," pp. 102–105

To Do	To Say

5–10 minutes

CORRECTIVE FEEDBACK

Monitor oral reading.

Read pp. 102–105 aloud. Read them three or four times so your reading gets better each time. Give feedback on children's oral reading and use of the blending strategy. See Routine Cards 1 and 4.

MORE PRACTICE

Instead of rereading just pp. 102–105, have children reread the entire selection three or four times. You may want to have children read along with the AudioText.

Homework

Practice Book, p. 46, Phonics: Long *o* (CVC*e*)

ACTIVITY 1 Reread for Fluency

Paired Reading "Let's Celebrate," pp. 106–109

To Do	To Say

5–10 minutes

CORRECTIVE FEEDBACK

Pair children. Monitor paired reading.

Children read pp. 106–109 orally, switching readers at the end of the first page. Have partners reread; now the other partner begins. For optimal fluency, children should reread three or four times. Give feedback on children's oral reading and use of the blending strategy. See Routine Cards 1 and 4.

MORE PRACTICE

Instead of rereading just pp. 106–109, have children reread the entire selection three or four times. You may want to have children read along with the AudioText.

ACTIVITY 2 Word Work

Phonemic Awareness Add Phonemes

To Do	To Say

2 minutes

Scaffold instruction.

Distribute white boards. Write *rat*. Add *'s* to form *rat's nose*.

Write *pig*. Add *'s* to form *pig's pen*. Lead children in adding sounds as they write.

Model Listen to the sounds in *rat*. Stretch the sounds /rrr/ /aaa/ /t/ as you write *r, a, t*. Repeat and have children write the letters as you write. The rat's nose wiggled. Listen to the sounds when I add /s/ to *rat*. Say /rrr/ /aaa/ /t/ /s/ as you add *'s* to *rat*. Repeat and have children add *'s* as you write.

Teach and Practice Have children say the sounds with you as you point to the letters in *rat's*. (/r/ /a/ /t/ /s/) What sound did we add to *rat?* (/s/) What new word did we make? *(rat's)* Repeat the process by adding /z/ to *pig* to form *pig's*. Continue adding /s/ and /z/ to form these phrases:

can's lid   cat's dish   dog's bone   hill's stones   duck's pond   frog's legs

Blending Strategy Possessive Nouns

5–10 minutes

Routine

	To Do	To Say
Use the blending routine.	Write *pig* and *pigs*.	**1 Connect** You studied words like these already. What are these words? Which word names one animal? Which word is a singular noun? *(pig)* Which word names more than one animal? Which word is a plural noun? *(pigs)* Today we'll learn about possessive nouns.
Scaffold instruction.	Write *pig's pen*.	**2 Model** A possessive noun shows who or what owns something. It can be singular or plural. The apostrophe and *s* in *pig's* shows that something belongs to one pig. The pen belongs to the pig. This is how I blend this word: /p/ /i/ /g/ /z/, *pig's*. Let's read the phrase together: *pig's pen*.
	Write *pigs' pen*.	The *s* and the apostrophe in *pigs'* means that something belongs to more than one pig. The pen belongs to the pigs. When a word ends with *s* and means "more than one," the apostrophe comes after the *s*. This is how I blend this word: /p/ /i/ /g/ /z/, *pigs'*. Let's read the phrase together: *pigs' pen*.
	Write *rat nose*.	**3 Listen and Write** Write *rat*. Write *nose* next to it, leaving some space between the words. Now make *rat* a possessive noun. Show that the nose belongs to one rat. Add an apostrophe and *s* to the end of *rat*. As you write, say the possessive noun to yourself: *rat's*. Now say the word aloud. Let's read the phrase: *rat's nose*.
		Remind children that *s* can stand for /z/ as in *pigs'* or /s/ as in *rat's*.
CORRECTIVE FEEDBACK	Write each practice phrase. Monitor student practice.	**4 Group Practice** Let's try reading these phrases with possessive nouns. Give feedback, using the *if . . . then* statements on Routine Card 1.
		friends' game man's hat snakes' hole dad's note bat's cave
		5 Individual Practice Write these phrases; have each child blend two of them.
		Mike's gift frogs' pond bride's dress vets' pets dogs' bones
		Have children explain the meanings of each possessive noun, telling who owns what and whether there is one or more than one owner.
MORE PRACTICE	Model building possessive nouns.	**Build Words** Write the pairs of nouns shown below. Have children copy the pairs on their white boards with space between each word. With the first example, model how to make the first noun possessive by adding an apostrophe and *s*. Have children continue the activity, adding an apostrophe and *s* to each singular noun and an apostrophe to each plural noun. Then have them read and explain what the phrases mean.
		mom plates bugs web cats snack king throne apes grapes

High-Frequency Words *father, mother, remember, touch*

3 minutes

	To Do	To Say
Teach high-frequency words.	Display *father, mother, remember,* and *touch*.	Use the Tested Vocabulary Cards. Point to a word. Say and spell it. Have children say and spell the word. Ask children to identify familiar letter-sounds. Have them take turns reading the words.
Lead cumulative review.		Use the Tested Vocabulary Cards to review high-frequency words from previous weeks.

Read a Passage

Reading "Big, Big Balloon," pp. 110–115

To Do	To Say

10–15 minutes

Develop language and concepts.

Scaffold instruction.

See Routine Cards 6 and 7. Display pp. 110–115.

Ask questions and elaborate on answers to develop language. Key concepts: *model, balloon, skin, floats* (v.)

Before Reading Have children recall what they learned about making a float for a parade. Read the title. Do a structured picture walk.

pp. 110–111 What did the man draw? (a clown) Yes, then the man used his drawing to make a model, or small copy, of the clown.

pp. 112–115 The man used the clown model to make a clown balloon. Point to the balloon. Its outside covering, or skin, is made of cloth. It floats in the sky. Where is the big, big balloon now? (in a parade)

Write story word.

Write *balloon*.

You will read this word in the selection. It is *balloon*. Have children say the word and spell it. Review its meaning. Let's read to find out more about the big balloon.

Guide comprehension.

Monitor independent reading.

During Reading Read the pages in a whisper. Raise your hand if you need help with a word. As you read, ask yourself: What am I learning about a big balloon? What is this mainly about?

pp. 110–111 What did you learn about planning a big balloon? (First, the man makes a drawing. Next, he makes a little model.)

pp. 112–115 What did you learn about making a big balloon? (The man cuts cloth shapes and puts them together.) What did you learn about showing a big balloon? (Men use long ropes to show the balloon in the parade. People like the balloon.)

Model summarizing.

Think aloud.

After Reading What did you learn about a big balloon? What was the selection mainly about? Model how to summarize. The first few pages told about planning and making the balloon. The last two pages told how the balloon is shown in a parade. I put that all together and pick the most important ideas. The selection is mainly about how to plan, make, and show a big balloon for a parade.

MORE PRACTICE

Develop oral vocabulary.

Did the man *dine* on or paint the clown model? (paint) The big balloon can be used in *holiday* parades. On which *holiday* might you see the big parade balloon? Would you like to *participate* in planning, making, or showing the big balloon? Why?

Write

Response to Literature Shared Writing

To Do	To Say

5 minutes

Guide shared writing.

Write sentence frames. Read the questions.

How do you plan a big balloon? To plan a big balloon, you _____.
How do you make a big balloon? To make a big balloon, you _____.

Invite children to suggest answers. Discuss and record answers to complete the sentence frames. While writing, model connecting sounds to letters and forming letters (see pp. 257–259). Have children read answers aloud as you track print.

Homework Practice Book, p. 47, Possessives

ACTIVITY **1** Reread for Fluency

Oral Reading "Big, Big Balloon," pp. 110–112

To Do	To Say	*5–10 minutes*

CORRECTIVE FEEDBACK

Monitor oral reading.

Read pp. 110–112 aloud. Read them three or four times so your reading gets better each time. Give feedback on children's oral reading and use of the blending strategy. See Routine Cards 1 and 4.

MORE PRACTICE

Instead of rereading just pp. 110–112, have children reread the entire selection three or four times. You may want to have children read along with the AudioText.

ACTIVITY **2** Word Work

Phonemic Awareness Add Phonemes

To Do	To Say	*2 minutes*

Scaffold instruction.

Distribute white boards. Write *snake*. Add *'s* to form *snake's hole.* Write *cub.* Add *'s* to form *cub's den.* Lead children in adding sounds.

Model This is *snake.* Now listen to the sounds when I add /s/ to the end of *snake.* Say /sss/ /nnn/ /āāāā/ /k/ /sss/ as you add *'s* to *snake.* Repeat and have children add *'s.*

Teach and Practice What sound did we add to *snake?* (/s/) What new word did we make? *(snake's)* Let's read the phrase: *snake's hole.* Repeat, adding /z/ to *cub* and reading *cub's den.* Continue adding /s/ and /z/ to form these phrases:

man's nose	hen's nest	rat's cage	crab's legs	kid's jokes	bike's tire

Fluent Word Reading Long *o* (CVCe), Possessive Nouns

To Do	To Say	*5–10 minutes*

Use the word-reading routine.

Scaffold instruction.

Write *robe.*

1 Connect You can read this word because you know how to read long *o* words. Remember, when you see *o* followed by a consonant and *e,* the *e* makes the *o* say its name, /ō/, and the *e* is silent. What is the word? *(robe)*

Write *moles' hole.*

2 Model When you come to a new word, look at all the letters in the word and think about its vowel sound. Say the letter-sounds in the word to yourself, and then read the word. Model reading *moles' hole.* When you come to a new word, what are you going to do?

Write each practice word.

3 Group Practice Let's read these words. Look at all the letters, think about the vowel sound, and say the letter-sounds to yourself. We will read words with long *o* and possessive nouns. When I point to the word, let's read it together. Allow 2–3 seconds previewing time for each word.

kids' rope	Dad's hose	chicks' home	Mom's rose	Mike's stones

CORRECTIVE FEEDBACK

MONITOR PROGRESS

If . . . children have difficulty previewing and reading whole words,
then . . . have them use sound-by-sound blending.

If . . . children can't read the words fluently at a rate of 1–2 seconds per word,
then . . . continue practicing the list.

MORE
PRACTICE

Model reading words in sentences.	When I read a sentence, I read each word without stopping between the words. If I come to a word I don't know, I blend it. Then I read the sentence again. Model reading this sentence, stopping to blend *smoke: I hope the man does not choke on the fire's smoke.*
Write practice sentences.	Have each child read a sentence. **The man's dog stole the hens' eggs.** **Rose drove in Dad's truck up the hill's paths.** **The kids' jokes made the class laugh.**

High-Frequency Words *father, mother, remember, touch*

To Do	To Say	3 minutes

Review high-frequency words.

Display *father, mother, remember,* and *touch.*	Use the Tested Vocabulary Cards. Point to a word. Say and spell it. Have children say and spell the word. Ask children to identify familiar letter-sounds. Have them take turns reading the words.

ACTIVITY **3** | Build Concepts

Oral Vocabulary *decorate, float*

To Do	To Say	5–10 minutes

Teach oral vocabulary.

Display p. 116 of the student book.	Today you will read a story about a girl who floats away with some decorations. *Routine*
Follow the Routine to teach *decorate* and *float* (v.).	**1 Introduce, Demonstrate, and Apply** *decorate* The girl in this story brings balloons to a friend's party. The girl could *decorate* the friend's house with the balloons. When you *decorate* something, you make it as pretty as you can. Have children say the word. I like to *decorate* birthday cakes with pink roses. How would you *decorate* our classroom for a party? *float* Some big kids in "Let's Celebrate" worked on a *float* together. A *float* carries something to show in a parade. *Floats* are sometimes shaped with wire, then *decorated* with bits of thin, colorful paper. Some *floats* are *decorated* with real flowers! Have children say the word. Have you ever seen a *float* in a parade?
Display the words on the Amazing Words board.	**2 Display the Words** Have children say each word as they look at it. You can find sounds you know in big words. Read *dec/o/rate* as you run your hand under the syllables. Children can identify *dec* and *rate.* For *float,* children can identify *fl*/fl/ and *t*/t/.
Monitor understanding.	**3 Use the Words** Ask children to use each word in a sentence. Model a sentence if children need help.

MORE
PRACTICE | Use oral vocabulary to discuss celebrating. How does *decorating* make a celebration better? Have you ever been at a celebration where confetti, small bits of paper, drop from the ceiling and *float* down on your head?

ACTIVITY 4 Read a Passage

Reading "The Balloon Ride," pp. 116–123

	To Do	To Say	*10 minutes*

Teach draw conclusions.

Scaffold instruction.

Introduce the skill.

Model the skill.

Today you are going to use what you have read, what you see in pictures, and what you know about real life to draw conclusions. Authors don't tell us everything, so we have to draw conclusions to figure out things on our own. For example, the author of "Big, Big Balloon" doesn't tell why the men hope the balloon's ropes won't snap. I see the balloon is big. I read that it is filled with gas. I know it can float. So I draw the conclusion that the men hope the ropes won't snap because they don't want the balloon to float away.

Apply the skill.

Why do the mothers, fathers, and kids clap and yell when they see the big balloon? (It is special to see a big balloon. They are excited.)

Develop language and concepts.

See Routine Card 6. Display pp. 116–123. Model using key words and concepts. Key concepts: *party, balloons, floats* (v.), *gulls*

Monitor children's use of vocabulary.

Before Reading Read the title. Do a structured picture walk.

pp. 116–118 This girl is going to a party. How can you tell? (She has a gift. She gets balloons.) The balloons float because they're full of gas.

pp. 119–121 The girl floats up. How do you think she feels? (afraid, worried) Birds called gulls pop the balloons. Why do you think they do this? (They like to peck at colorful things.)

pp. 122–123 Where is the girl now? (on the ground at a party)

Now turn to your partner and talk about the pictures, using the same words I did.

Teach story words.

Write *balloon*.

You will read this word in the story: *balloon*. Have children say and spell it. Review its meaning. **Let's read more about the balloon ride.**

Guide comprehension.

Monitor independent reading.

Use Routine Cards 2 and 3.

During Reading Read the pages in a whisper. Raise your hand if you need help with a word. As you read, ask yourself: What have I read and what do I know that will help me draw conclusions about the characters and what happens in the story?

pp. 116–118 Meg gets a gift and lots of balloons for Rose. What does this tell you about Meg? (She is a kind and generous friend.)

pp. 119–121 Why does Meg float into the sky? (She holds so many balloons filled with gas that they are able to lift her up.) Why does Meg come down again? (The gulls pop so many balloons that the few balloons left can't keep Meg in the air.)

pp. 122–123 When she gets to the party, how does Meg feel? (happy, relieved) How do her friends feel? (happy, excited) Why does Meg say that she will get just five balloons next time? (She won't float away with just five balloons.)

Guide retelling.

Prompt children as they retell the story.

After Reading Have one child retell the story while the others assist. **What happens at the beginning? in the middle? at the end? How does Meg feel about her balloon ride?** (It was exciting, but a bit scary. She doesn't want to take another one.) See Monitoring Retelling Chart, p. 246.

Homework

Practice Book, p. 48, Draw Conclusions

ACTIVITY 1 Reread for Fluency

Paired Reading "The Balloon Ride," pp. 116–119

To Do	To Say	
		5–10 minutes

CORRECTIVE FEEDBACK

Pair children. Monitor paired reading.

Children read pp. 116–119 orally, switching readers at the end of the first page. Have partners reread; now the other partner begins. For optimal fluency, children should reread three or four times. Give feedback on children's oral reading and use of the blending strategy. See Routine Cards 1 and 4.

MORE PRACTICE

Instead of rereading just pp. 116–119, have children reread the entire selection three or four times. You may want to have children read along with the AudioText.

ACTIVITY 2 Word Work

Spiral Review Short *o* and Long *o* (CVCe)

To Do	To Say	
		5–10 minutes

Review short *o* and long *o*.

Write *hop*.

You can read this word because you know what sounds *o* can stand for. What sound does *o* have in this word? (/o/) Remember, when *o* is the only vowel at the beginning or in the middle of a word, it usually stands for its short sound, /o/. Now let's blend the sounds to say the word: /h/ /o/ /p/, *hop*.

Scaffold instruction.

Add *e* to *hop* to form *hope*.

How does the vowel sound /o/ change when the letter *e* is added to the end of *hop*? (It changes to the long *o* sound, /ō/.) Remember, when you see the letter *o* followed by a consonant and the letter *e*, the *o* usually stands for its long sound, /ō/, and the *e* is silent. Now let's blend the sounds to say the word: /h/ /ō/ /p/, *hope*.

Distribute white boards. Write *hop* and *hope* at the top of a T-chart.

Sort Words Let's sort words by their vowel sounds. Point to and read *hop* and *hope*. Then display this list of words: *not, note, rod, rode, glob, globe, slop, slope*. Call on children to read each word and tell whether its vowel sound is like *hop* or *hope*. Write the word in the appropriate column as children write on their boards.

How are the words in the first column alike? (all short *o* words; all have one vowel) How are the words in the second column alike? (all long *o* words; all have *o*, a consonant, and a silent *e*) Have children suggest a heading for each column.

Short *o*	Long *o*
hop	hope
not	note
rod	rode
glob	globe
slop	slope

CORRECTIVE FEEDBACK

MONITOR PROGRESS

If . . . children have difficulty reading the words,
then . . . review the effect of *e* at the end of the words and blend the words sound-by-sound.

For more practice, see next page.

Continued Spiral Review

MORE PRACTICE

Model reading words in sentences.	When I read a sentence, I read each word without stopping between the words. If I come to a word I don't know, I blend it. Then I read the sentence again. Model reading this sentence, stopping to blend *slope: Bob rode on an ox up the hill's slope.*
Write practice sentences.	Have each child read a sentence. Tom got those votes for the top job. Smoke rose from the pot on the hot stove. Do not poke Dot's pole in the moles' hole!

Phonological and Phonemic Awareness — Optional practice activities, pp. 280–283

ACTIVITY 3 Read Together

Choral Reading "Make a Greeting Card," pp. 124–125

	To Do	**To Say**	
			10 minutes
Develop language and concepts.	Display pp. 124–125.	**Before Reading** This is a card for a friend. When have you made cards for others? (Allow children to share their experiences.) Share information about greeting cards. A greeting is a friendly wish. A greeting card might wish a friend good luck or happy birthday, or just say hello.	
Model fluent reading.		Read the title of the directions. Ask children to predict what the selection is about. The words by these dots tell what you'll need to make the card. The numbered steps tell how to make the card. When I read how to make something, I read the steps in order. Point to show the order 1–5. I read carefully and not too fast to make sure I understand what I'm reading. Then read the text at the appropriate rate. Read it a second time, having children point to each word.	
	Build fluency through choral reading.	**Choral Reading** Now read the selection with me. Try to make your voice sound like mine as we read. Reread several times with children.	
Develop concepts.	Monitor listening comprehension.	**After Reading** What do you need to make a greeting card? What is the first step? the last step? How would you *decorate* the card? What greeting would you write on a *holiday* card?	

ACTIVITY 4 Build Concepts

Oral Vocabulary *decorate, dine, float, holiday, participate*

	To Do	**To Say**	
			5–10 minutes
Review oral vocabulary.	Read the words on the Amazing Words board.	**Focus on Letter-Sounds** Remember, you can find sounds you know in big words. • Which words begin with *d?* What word ends with *t?* • What word begins with the sounds /fl/? What letters stand for /fl/? • Which words have *ate* in them?	

Encourage discussion.	**Ask for Examples** Review the meanings of the words. Then ask children to create examples related to the words.	

- If someone likes animals, how might the person *decorate* his or her bedroom? What kinds of *decorations* might you see in the room?
- If you *dined* at a restaurant, what types of things would you order?
- Think of a *holiday* parade you've seen. What kinds of *floats* were in the parade? What did the *floats* look like?
- In what ways do you *participate* in class?

MORE PRACTICE — Apply oral vocabulary to new situations.

- If you *participated* in a parade, what kind of *float* could you make? How would you *decorate* it?
- Do you like to eat hot dogs when you *dine?* Why?
- Name a *holiday* and tell how you could *decorate* to celebrate it.

ACTIVITY **5** Write

Response to Literature Interactive Writing

To Do	To Say	*5–10 minutes*

Generate ideas.

Review the story "The Balloon Ride."

How does Meg contribute to Rose's party? Discuss ways Meg helped make Rose's birthday party special.

Share the pen.

Have children participate in writing about what kids can bring to celebrations.

Write *Kids can bring* _____. Have children read the words you wrote. Then have them supply endings for each sentence. Invite individuals to write familiar letter-sounds, word parts, and high-frequency words. Have them find the spelling of high-frequency words on the Word Wall. Ask questions such as:

- What is the first sound in *rose?* (/r/) What is the letter for /r/? *(r)*
- What is the vowel sound in *rose?* (/ō/) What is the letter for /ō/? *(o)*
- What is the last sound in *rose?* (/z/) Is the letter for /z/ in *rose s or z?* *(s)*
- What letter do we add to the end of *r, o, s* to make the long *o* vowel sound, /ō/? *(e)*

Writing elements: conventions

Frequently reread what has been written while tracking the print. Point out that each sentence starts with a capital letter and ends with a period. Point out the extra space between words.

Read the completed sentences aloud, having children read with you. (For example, *Kids can bring a rose. Kids can bring a gift. Kids can bring balloons.*)

MORE PRACTICE — Prompt independent writing.

Journal Writing Tell about a party you have been to and what you did there.

Homework — Practice Book, p. 49, High-Frequency Words

ACTIVITY **1** Assessment Options

Sentence Reading

To Do	To Say	*5 minutes*

Assess sentence reading.

Use reproducible p. 250.

Have each child read the sentences. Record scores on the Sentence Reading Chart, p. 237. Work with one child as others complete Write Sentences below.

Remember not to touch my mother's rose.
Father's fishing pole is close to those stones.
We woke up and Hope drove us to our pals' home.

CORRECTIVE FEEDBACK

MONITOR PROGRESS

If . . . children have trouble reading words with long *o* (CVC*e*) or possessive nouns,
then . . . reteach the blending strategy lessons on pp. 148 and 152.

If . . . children cannot read a high-frequency word,
then . . . mark the missed word or words on a high-frequency word list and send the list home for additional practice or have them practice with a fluent reader.

If . . . children misread a word in the sentence,
then . . . correct the error and have them reread the word and then the sentence.

Practice sentence writing.

Provide white boards.

Write Sentences Have children copy the sentences from reproducible p. 250 on white boards. Have them confirm spellings by comparing the words they wrote to the words in the sentences.

Phonological and Phonemic Awareness

Optional practice activities, pp. 280–283

End-of-Unit Test

To Do	To Say	*5–10 minutes*

Assess fluency and comprehension.

Use Assessment Book, p. 33.

Options for end-of-unit assessment are available in the Assessment Book.

ACTIVITY **2** Use Concepts

Oral Vocabulary *decorate, dine, float, holiday, participate*

To Do	To Say	*5 minutes*

Check understanding of oral vocabulary.

Use the Amazing Words to wrap up the week's concept.

Monitor understanding of oral vocabulary, using Routine Card 5.

As time allows, ask questions such as these.

- Describe the pictures on pp. 102–109 using some of the week's Amazing Words.
- School is often closed on *holidays* because _____.
- On Thanksgiving Day, what might you *dine* on? (turkey, yams, pumpkin pie)
- What might happen to a parade *float* if it rained?
- How might kids *participate* in a school fun fair?
- Why would someone *decorate* their table?

Preview next week's concept.

Next week you will read about how ideas turn into inventions.

ACTIVITY 3 Read to Connect

Reread "Let's Celebrate," pp. 102–109

To Do	To Say	5 minutes

Monitor comprehension: draw conclusions.

Have children reread "Let's Celebrate" silently.

As you read, use the words, pictures, and what you know to draw conclusions about what happens in the selection. Figure out more about the people and the different celebrations. After rereading, ask:

- **How do the family members contribute to the celebration?** Record children's responses in a chart. (For example, they set up games, serve drinks, and make a cake.) Children will use the chart for Activity 4. **Why do you think they all participate?** Add children's ideas to the chart.

- **The kids had to stick roses in many holes to decorate the float. What does this tell you about the kids?** Add children's ideas to the chart.

- **After the surprise party, how do you think the kids could help?** Add children's ideas to the chart.

Make connections.

Have children make connections across texts.

We also read "Big, Big Balloon." Find that. Why do you think the man makes big balloons? How does he help make the parade special? Record children's ideas in a list.

We also read "The Balloon Ride," about a girl who brings balloons to a party. Why do you think Meg kept getting more and more balloons? How did Meg's arrival make Rose's party special? Record children's reasons in a list.

What did all the selections we read this week show us about celebrations? (People help make celebrations special in many ways.)

ACTIVITY 4 Write

Response to Literature Independent Writing

To Do	To Say	5–10 minutes

Assign descriptive writing.

Guide sentence correction.

Writing elements: conventions, support

Today you will write about how people can contribute to a celebration. Describe ways people can participate before, during, and after celebrations. Encourage children to use words you wrote on the board for Activity 3 as they write.

Have children check their writing by asking themselves these questions.

- **Did I begin each sentence with a capital letter?**
- **Did I use correct marks at the end of sentences?**
- **Did I write possessive nouns correctly?**
- **Did I use describing words?**

MORE PRACTICE

Have children share their sentences with the group. Write their sentences on the board and have children practice reading and writing each other's sentences.

Homework — Practice Book, p. 50, Writing

Unit 3 Week 1 *Ideas Become Inventions*

How do inventors turn ideas into inventions?

Objectives *This week students will...*

Phonemic Awareness
- segment, count, and blend sounds in words

Phonics
- blend and read words with long *u* and long *e* (CVC*e*) and the contractions *'s* and *n't*
- apply knowledge of letter-sounds to decode unknown words when reading
- recognize high-frequency words *house, idea, machine, sign*

Fluency
- practice fluency with oral rereading

Vocabulary
- build concepts and oral vocabulary: *construct, contraption, project, sidekick, unique*

Text Comprehension
- read connected text
- draw conclusions to improve comprehension
- write in response to literature

Word Work *This week's phonics focus is . . .*

Long *u* and Long *e* (CVC*e*)   Contractions *'s, n't*

High-Frequency Words *Tested Vocabulary*

The first appearance of each word in the Student Reader is noted below.

house	A **house** is a building where people live. (p. 8)
idea	An **idea** is a thought or plan. (p. 6)
machine	A **machine** is something with moving parts that does work for you. (p. 7)
sign	A **sign** has pictures or words that tell you something important. (p. 7) A **sign** can also tell of something to come or something to look for.

Amazing Words *Oral Vocabulary*

The week's vocabulary is related to the concept of turning ideas into inventions.

construct	to build or put something together
contraption	something that is put together in an odd or strange way
project	something you plan and then do
sidekick	a good friend and partner
unique	something that is the only one of its kind

Student Reader Unit 3 *This week students will read the following selections.*

Daily Lesson Plan

	ACTIVITIES	MATERIALS
Day 1	**Word Work** Phonemic Awareness: Segment and Count Sounds Phonics: Blend Words with Long *u* and Long *e* (CVC*e*) High-Frequency Words *house, idea, machine, sign* **Build Concepts** *construct, sidekick, unique* **Read a Passage** "Ideas Become Inventions," pp. 6–11 Comprehension: Use Strategies Reread for Fluency	Student White Boards Sound-Spelling Cards 10 and 36 Tested Vocabulary Cards *Sing with Me Big Book* and Audio CD Student Reader: Unit 3 Routine Cards 1, 2, 3, 4, 6, 7 AudioText Practice Book, p. 51, Long *u*, Long *e* (CVC*e*)
Day 2	**Reread for Fluency** **Word Work** Phonemic Awareness: Blend Sounds Phonics: Blend Contractions *'s, n't* High-Frequency Words *house, idea, machine, sign* **Read a Passage** "In-Line Skates," pp. 12–17 Comprehension: Use Strategies **Write** Response to Literature: Shared Writing	Student Reader: Unit 3 Student White Boards Tested Vocabulary Cards Routine Cards 1, 2, 3, 4, 6, 7 AudioText Practice Book, p. 52, Contractions *'s, n't*
Day 3	**Reread for Fluency** **Word Work** Phonemic Awareness: Blend Sounds Phonics: Fluent Word Reading High-Frequency Words *house, idea, machine, sign* **Build Concepts** *contraption, project* **Read a Passage** "Zute," pp. 18–25 Comprehension: Draw Conclusions	Student Reader: Unit 3 Student White Boards Tested Vocabulary Cards Routine Cards 1, 2, 3, 4, 6 AudioText Practice Book, p. 53, Draw Conclusions
Day 4	**Reread for Fluency** **Word Work** Phonics: Spiral Review Phonological and Phonemic Awareness Activities, pp. 280–283 **Read Together** "A Time Line of Fun!" p. 26 Comprehension: Listening **Build Concepts** *construct, contraption, project, sidekick, unique* **Write** Response to Literature: Interactive Writing	Student Reader: Unit 3 Student White Boards Routine Cards 1, 4 AudioText Practice Book, p. 54, High-Frequency Words
Day 5	**Assessment Options** Fluency, Comprehension Sentence Reading; Passage Reading Phonological and Phonemic Awareness Activities, pp. 280–283 **Use Concepts** *construct, contraption, project, sidekick, unique* **Read to Connect** "Ideas Become Inventions," pp. 6–11 Comprehension: Draw Conclusions **Write** Response to Literature: Independent Writing	Reproducible p. 250 Sentence Reading Chart, p. 254 Student White Boards Fluency Progress Chart, p. 245 Student Reader: Unit 3 Routine Card 5 Practice Book, p. 55, Writing

See pp. xvi–xvii for how *My Sidewalks* integrates instructional practices for **ELL.**

Word Work

Phonemic Awareness Segment and Count Sounds

Scaffold instruction.

To Do	To Say	*2 minutes*

Distribute white boards.

Write *us*. Then add *e* to form *use*.

Lead children in counting sounds as they write.

Model Listen to the sounds in *us*. Stretch the sounds /uuu/ /sss/ as you write *u*, *s*. Repeat. This time have children write the letters as you write. **Now let's count the sounds in *us*. I will say the word slowly and hold up a finger for each sound: /u/ /s/. There are two sounds in *us*. Now listen to the sounds in *use*: /ūūū/ /zzz/.**

Teach and Practice Have children say the sounds with you as you point to the letters. (/ū/ /z/) **Hold up a finger for each sound. How many sounds in *use*?** (2) **How many letters in *use*?** (3) Continue counting sounds:

pet (3)　Pete (3)　cut (3)　cute (3)　them (3)　these (3)

Blending Strategy Long *u*, Long *e* (CVCe)

Use the blending routine.

To Do	To Say	*5–10 minutes*

Write *cut* and *pet*.

Routine

1 Connect You already can read these words. What are the words? What vowel sound do you hear in *cut*? (short *u*) in *pet*? (short *e*) Today we'll learn about long vowel sounds for *u* and *e*.

Display Sound-Spelling Card 36.

2 Use Sound-Spelling Cards This is a uniform. What sound do you hear at the beginning of *uniform*? (/ū/) Say it with me: /ū/. /ū/ is the long *u* sound. It says its name: *u*/ū/.

Scaffold instruction.

Write *cute*.

3 Listen and Write Write *cute*: *c*, *u*, *t*, *e*. What vowels do you see in *cute*? (*u*, *e*) *Cute* has the long *u* sound: /ū/. As you write, say the sound to yourself: /ū/. Now say the sound aloud.

Write *cut*. Then add *e* to form *cute*.

4 Model When I add *e* to *cut*, it makes the *u* say its name. The sound of *u* in this new word is /ū/. The *e* is silent. This is how I blend it: /k/ /ū/ /t/, *cute*. Now you try it: /k/ /ū/ /t/, *cute*.

Display Sound-Spelling Card 10. Write *Pete*.

Repeat steps 2 and 3 for long *e*. Use Sound-Spelling Card 10 to introduce the long *e* sound heard at the beginning of *easel*. Then model blending *Pete*, /p/ /ē/ /t/, *Pete*. Point out that when a vowel is followed by a consonant and then the letter *e*, the first vowel is usually long and the *e* is silent.

c u t e　　　P e t e

CORRECTIVE FEEDBACK

Write each practice word. Monitor student practice.

5 Group Practice Let's try the same thing with these words. Give feedback, using the *if . . . then* statements on Routine Card 1.

rule　Gene　dune*　rude　Luke　these

6 Individual Practice Write the words; have each child blend two of them.

Eve　cube　huge　Zeke　prune*　theme*

Check understanding of practice words.

*Children need to make sense of words that they segment and blend. If needed, help children with meanings. A *dune* is a large hill of sand. A *prune* is a dried plum. The *theme* of a story is the main idea.

MORE PRACTICE

Model spelling long *u* and long *e* (CVC*e*) words.

Spell and Write What sounds are in *tune*? (/t/ /ū/ /n/) What is the letter for /t/? Let's all write *t*. Continue with *u*/ū/ and *n*/n/. What letter must we add to make *u* say its name? *(e)* Provide practice as time allows. Have children compare their spellings to what you've written.

| tube | Steve | mule | Gene | flute | these |

High-Frequency Words *house, idea, machine, sign*

Teach high-frequency words.

To Do	To Say	

3 minutes

Routine

Display *house*.

1 Say, Spell, Write Use the Tested Vocabulary Cards. Display *house*. Here are some words that we won't sound out. We'll spell them. This word is *house*: h, o, u, s, e (point to each letter), *house*. What is this word? What are the letters in the word? Now you write *house*.

Point to the *h* and *s* in *house*.

2 Identify Letter-Sounds Let's look at the sounds in *house* that you do know. What is this letter? *(h)* What is the sound for this letter? *(/h/)* Continue with *s*.

3 Demonstrate Meaning Tell me a sentence using *house*. Model a sentence if children need help.

Display *idea*, *machine*, and *sign*.

Repeat the Routine with *idea*, *machine*, and *sign*. Children can identify these letter-sounds: *idea* (d/d/), *machine* (m/m/, n/n/), sign (s/s/, n/n/). Have children write the words in their word banks. Add the words to the Word Wall.

ACTIVITY **2** **Build Concepts**

Oral Vocabulary *construct, sidekick, unique*

Introduce oral vocabulary.

Scaffold instruction.

To Do	To Say	

5–10 minutes

Routine

Display p. 11 of *Sing with Me Big Book*. Play audio CD.

This week you will learn about how ideas become inventions. Listen for the Amazing Words *construct*, *sidekick*, and *unique* as I sing this song. Play or sing the song. Then have children sing it with you.

1 Introduce, Demonstrate, and Apply

Follow the Routine to teach *construct*, *sidekick*, and *unique*.

construct The song talks about people working to *construct* something original and new. When you *construct* something, you build it or put it together. Have children say the word. Builders may *construct* a new house for a family. Have you ever *constructed* something with blocks?

sidekick The song says that a *sidekick* can help an inventor. A *sidekick* is a good friend and partner. Have children say the word. Two kids who are always together are *sidekicks*. Who is your *sidekick*?

unique The song is called "Unique Inventions." Something that is *unique* is the only one of its kind. There is nothing else like it. Have children say the word. You can write a *unique* story. What is something that makes you *unique*?

Display the words on the Amazing Words board.

2 Display the Words Have children say each word as they look at it. You can find sounds you know in big words. Read *u/nique* as you run your hand under the syllables. What vowel sound do you hear at the beginning of *unique*? (/ū/) What sound does *n* stand for? (/n/) For *sidekick*, children can identify *side* and *kick*. For *construct*, they can identify these letter-sounds and word parts: (c/k/, n/n/, *struct*).

Monitor understanding.

3 Use the Words Ask children to use each word in a sentence. Model sentences if children need help.

For more practice, see next page.

MORE PRACTICE

Use oral vocabulary to discuss the song. **Who builds *unique* gadgets? Why is it helpful for an inventor to have a *sidekick*? Could the *sidekick* help the inventor *construct* something?**

ACTIVITY **3** ## Read a Passage

Build Background "Ideas Become Inventions" pp. 6–11

10 minutes

	To Do	**To Say**
Develop language and concepts.	See Routine Card 7. Read aloud pp. 1–5 of the student book.	**Preview the Book** Read aloud the title on p. 1. **The selections in this book are about creative ideas.** Use pp. 2–3 to preview the weeks in this unit and p. 5 to preview the selections in this week. Ask children what they think each selection will be about.
Scaffold instruction.	See Routine Card 6. Display pp. 6–11.	**Before Reading** Read the title aloud. Do a structured picture walk with children.
	Ask questions and elaborate on answers to develop language.	**pp. 6–7** What things do you see on these pages? (airplanes, camera, sticky notes, gum, cell phone) **These are all inventions. An invention is a unique thing that people make when they think of a good idea. Some of these inventions are machines. A machine has moving parts and does work for you. Is an airplane a machine?** (yes) **Is a cell phone a machine?** (yes) **What do these inventions help people do?** (They help people communicate, go places, and so on.)
	Key concepts: *invention, idea, machine, snack, froze, tubes, construct*	**pp. 8–9** What kind of snack are the kids eating? **It is a snack made from juice that froze on a stick when it got very cold. A boy named Frank invented a frozen snack on a stick. Even kids can be inventors!**
		pp. 10–11 What are these kids doing? (making an invention) **They are using tubes, tape, and wire to construct their invention. Point to the tubes, tape, and wire. What do you think they are making?**
Teach story word.	Write *invention.*	You will read this word in the selection. It is *invention.* **Have children say the word and spell it. Review its meaning. Let's read to find out how ideas become inventions.**
Guide comprehension.	Monitor independent reading. Model strategic reading. Use Routine Cards 2 and 3.	**During Reading** Read the pages in a whisper. Raise your hand if you need help with a word. **Stop at the end of each page to model asking questions. For example, for p. 7: After I read, I asked myself: What is this page mainly about? The author says that Alexander Graham Bell made a machine that helps us chat with pals. This page is mainly about how Alexander Graham Bell invented the telephone.**
Summarize.	Use oral vocabulary to develop the concept.	**After Reading** What are some *unique* ideas that became inventions? What do Eve and her *sidekick,* Suze, use to *construct* their invention? Do you think it is easy to come up with an idea for a *unique* invention? Would you like to be an inventor's *sidekick?*

Reread for Fluency "Ideas Become Inventions," pp. 6–8

5–10 minutes

	To Do	**To Say**
CORRECTIVE FEEDBACK	Monitor oral reading.	Read pp. 6–8 aloud. Read the pages three or four times so your reading gets better each time. Give feedback on children's oral reading and use of the blending strategy. See Routine Cards 1 and 4.
MORE PRACTICE		Instead of rereading just pp. 6–8, have children reread the entire selection three or four times. You may want to have children read along with the AudioText.
Homework		Practice Book, p. 51, Phonics: Long *u,* Long *e* (CVC*e*)

ACTIVITY 1 Reread for Fluency

Paired Reading "Ideas Become Inventions," pp. 8–12

To Do	To Say	
		5–10 minutes

CORRECTIVE FEEDBACK

Pair children. Monitor paired reading.

Children read pp. 8–12 orally, switching readers at the end of the first page. Have partners reread; now the other partner begins. For optimal fluency, children should reread three or four times. Give feedback on children's oral reading and use of the blending strategy. See Routine Cards 1 and 4.

MORE PRACTICE

Instead of rereading just pp. 8–12, have children reread the entire selection three or four times. You may want to have children read along with the AudioText.

ACTIVITY 2 Word Work

Phonemic Awareness Blend Sounds

To Do	To Say	
		2 minutes

Scaffold instruction.

Distribute white boards.
Write *did, not,* and *didn't.*

Lead children in blending sounds in contractions.

Model Listen to the sounds in this word. Stretch the sounds /d/ /iii/ /d/ as you write *d, i, d.* Repeat. This time have children write the letters as you write. What is the word? *(did)* Repeat the process with *not* and *didn't.*

Teach and Practice Have children say the sounds as you point to the letters in *didn't* (/d/ /i/ /d/ /n/ /t/). Then have them blend the sounds to say the word. What is the word? *(didn't)* Point out the apostrophe does not stand for any sound. Continue with these words:

isn't   it's   can't   what's   wasn't   that's

Blending Strategy Contractions 's, n't

To Do | **To Say** | *5–10 minutes*

Use the blending routine.

Scaffold instruction.

To Do	To Say
Write *it* and *is*.	**1 Connect** You already can read words like these. What are these words? Today we will learn about combining two words, such as *it* and *is*, to make a contraction.
Write *it's* beneath *it is.*	**2 Model** *It's* is a contraction. A contraction is a short way of writing two words as one. *It* and *is* make up the contraction *it's*. *It's* is a short way of writing *it is*. This is how I blend this word: *it, 's, it's.*
This is an apostrophe. (Point to it.) In contractions, the apostrophe takes the place of letters that get left out when two words are combined. In *it's*, the apostrophe takes the place of the *i* in *is*.
Write *didn't* beneath *did not.*	The contraction *didn't* is made from the words *did* and *not*. An apostrophe takes the place of the letter *o* in *not*. This is how I blend this word: *did, n't, didn't.*

i t 's   d i d n 't

3 Listen and Write Write the word *it*. Write *is* next to it. Now erase the *i* in *is* and put in an apostrophe. As you write, say the contraction to yourself: *it's*. Now say the word aloud.

CORRECTIVE FEEDBACK

Write each practice word. Monitor student practice.

4 Group Practice Let's try reading these words and saying the two words that form each one. Give feedback, using the *if . . . then* statements on Routine Card 1.

he's (he is)   aren't (are not)   there's (there is)

don't (do not)   where's (where is)   she's (she is)

5 Individual Practice Write the words; have each child blend two of them.

it's   isn't   she's   haven't   here's   can't   let's   weren't

MORE PRACTICE

Model building contractions.

Build Words Write pairs of words that can be combined to make contractions. Have children copy the words on their white boards. With the first word, model erasing a letter and adding an apostrophe. Have children continue the activity, writing a contraction for each pair of words. Have them read the contractions.

what + is (what's)   could + not (couldn't)

she + is (she's)   has + not (hasn't)

High-Frequency Words *house, idea, machine, sign*

To Do | **To Say** | *3 minutes*

Teach high-frequency words.

Lead cumulative review.

To Do	To Say
Display *house, idea, machine,* and *sign*.	Use Tested Vocabulary Cards. Point to a word. Say and spell it. Have children say and spell the word. Ask children to identify familiar letter-sounds. Have them take turns reading the words.
Use Tested Vocabulary Cards to review high-frequency words from previous weeks.

ACTIVITY 3 Read a Passage

Reading "In-Line Skates," pp. 12–17

	To Do	To Say	10–15 minutes

Before Reading Have children recall what they learned about inventions. Read the title. Do a structured picture walk with children.

Develop language and concepts. — See Routine Cards 6 and 7. Display pp. 12–17.

Scaffold instruction. — Ask questions and elaborate on answers to develop language.

Key concepts: *skates, blades, wheels, brake, helmets, pads*

pp. 12–13 What are the kids doing? (ice-skating, roller-skating) The kids wear skates with blades to move on ice. They use skates with wheels to skate on sidewalks and other places. The skates on p. 13 are called in-line skates. (Point to them.) The wheels are all in a line.

pp. 14–17 What is the arrow on p. 15 pointing to? (brake) An in-line skater uses the brake to slow down or stop. What do these kids wear to help them stay safe on in-line skates? Yes, helmets and pads protect them if they fall while skating.

Teach story words. — Write *wheel.*

You will read this word in the selection. It is *wheel.* Have children say the word and spell it. Review its meaning.

Guide comprehension. — Monitor independent reading.

During Reading Read the pages in a whisper. Raise your hand if you need help with a word. As you read, ask yourself: What am I learning about in-line skates? What is this mainly about?

See Routine Cards 2 and 3.

pp. 12–15 What did you learn about skates? (There are different types of skates.) What did you learn about the Olsons? (They invented in-line skates.)

pp. 16–17 What are these pages mainly about? (The Olsons made and sold a lot of skates.) The Olsons' invention did well; it was a success.

Model summarizing. — Think aloud.

After Reading What did you learn about in-line skates? What was the selection mainly about? Model how to summarize. The first two pages were about different kinds of skates and the Olsons getting an idea. The next pages told how they made and sold the skates. I put that all together and pick the most important ideas. The selection is mainly about how the Olsons invented in-line skates.

MORE PRACTICE — Develop oral vocabulary.

How did the Olsons *construct* in-line skates? Do you think one of the brothers was a *sidekick?* What makes in-line skates *unique?*

ACTIVITY 4 Write

Response to Literature Shared Writing

	To Do	To Say	5 minutes

Guide shared writing. — Write sentence frames. Read the questions.

What do in-line skates have? In-line skates have _____.

Why do people like in-line skates? People like in-line skates because _____.

Invite children to suggest answers. Discuss and record answers to complete the sentence frames. While writing, model connecting sounds to letters and forming letters (see pp. 257-259). Have children read answers aloud as you track print.

Homework — Practice Book, p. 52, Phonics: Contractions *'s, n't*

3

ACTIVITY 1 Reread for Fluency

Oral Reading "In-Line Skates," pp. 12–14

	To Do	**To Say**	*5–10 minutes*
CORRECTIVE FEEDBACK	Monitor oral reading.	**Read pp. 12–14 aloud. Read them three or four times so your reading gets better each time.** Give feedback on children's oral reading and use of the blending strategy. See Routine Cards 1 and 4.	
MORE PRACTICE		Instead of rereading just pp. 12–14, have children reread the entire selection three or four times. You may want to have children read along with the AudioText.	

ACTIVITY 2 Word Work

Phonemic Awareness Blend Sounds

	To Do	**To Say**	*2 minutes*
Scaffold instruction.	Distribute white boards. Write *mule* and *these*.	**Model Listen to the sounds in this word.** Stretch the sounds /mmm/ /ūūū/ /lll/ as you write *m, u, l, e*. Repeat. This time have children write the letters as you write. **What is the word?** *(mule)* Repeat the process with *these*.	
	Write *it's*. Lead children in blending sounds.	**Teach and Practice** Have children say the sounds as you point to the letters in *it's* (/i/ /t/ /s/). Then have them blend the sounds to say the word. **What is the word?** *(it's)* **The apostrophe does not stand for any sound.** Continue with these words: **tune Steve isn't that's prune hasn't**	

Fluent Word Reading Long *u*, Long *e* (CVCe); Contractions 's, n't

	To Do	**To Say**	*5–10 minutes*
Use the word-reading routine.	Write *huge*.	**1 Connect** You can read this word because you know how to read long *u* words. Remember, when you see a vowel followed by a consonant and an *e*, the vowel usually stands for its long sound and the *e* is silent. What sound does *u* in this word stand for? *(/ū/)* What is the word? *(huge)*	*Routine*
Scaffold instruction.	Write *theme, what's,* and *wasn't*.	**2 Model** When you come to a new word, look at all the letters in the word and think about its vowel sound. Say the sounds in the word to yourself, and then read the word. Model reading *theme, it's,* and *doesn't* in this way. Remind children that a contraction combines two words. The apostrophe takes the place of letters and doesn't stand for a sound. When you come to a new word, what are you going to do?	
	Write each practice word.	**3 Group Practice** Let's read these words. Look at all the letters, think about the vowel sound, and say the letter-sounds to yourself. We will read words with long *u* and long *e* and contractions. When I point to the word, let's read it together. Allow 2–3 seconds previewing time for each word. duke these cube hasn't flute let's Zeke haven't he's	
CORRECTIVE FEEDBACK	**MONITOR PROGRESS**	*If . . .* children have difficulty previewing and reading whole words, *then . . .* have them use sound-by-sound blending. *If . . .* children can't read the words fluently at a rate of 1–2 seconds per word, *then . . .* continue practicing the list.	

<table>
<tr><td>**MORE PRACTICE**</td><td>Model reading words in sentences.</td><td>When I read a sentence, I read each word without stopping between the words. If I come to a word I don't know, I blend it. Then I read the sentence again. Model reading this sentence, stopping to blend *what's: What's the tune Pete is singing?*</td></tr>
<tr><td></td><td>Write practice sentences.</td><td>Have each child read a sentence.

It's rude to yell at Steve.
These aren't prunes.
Gene didn't use that tube.</td></tr>
</table>

High-Frequency Words *house, idea, machine, sign*

To Do	To Say	3 minutes

Review high-frequency words.	Display *house, idea, machine,* and *sign*.	Use the Tested Vocabulary Cards. Point to a word. Say and spell it. Have children say and spell the word. Ask children to identify familiar letter-sounds. Have them take turns reading the words.

ACTIVITY **3** Build Concepts

Oral Vocabulary *contraption, project*

To Do	To Say	5–10 minutes

| **Teach oral vocabulary.**

Scaffold instruction.	Display p. 18 of the student book.	Today you will read about a brother's and sister's *project*. They made a *contraption* called Zute.
	Follow the Routine to teach *contraption* and *project*.	**1 Introduce, Demonstrate, and Apply**

contraption This story is about a *contraption* called Zute. A *contraption* is something that is put together in an odd or strange way. Have children say the word. Before airplanes, early inventors put together many odd *contraptions* to try to help people fly. What kind of *contraption* could you make to catch a spider?

project In this story, a brother and sister complete a *project* together. A *project* is something you plan and then do. Have children say the word. Use the term in a sentence describing a class project. For example: Our class is working on a big *project* to paint a mural in the hall. What other kinds of *projects* have we done in class? |
	Display the words on the Amazing Words board.	**2 Display the Words** Have children say each word as they look at it. You can find sounds you know in big words. Read *con/trap/tion* as you run your hand under the syllables. What letter do you see at the beginning of *contraption?* (c) What sound does it make? (/k/) What short word do you see in the middle? *(trap)* Read *proj/ect*. Children can identify *proj, e/e/,* and *ct/kt/*.
	Monitor understanding.	**3 Use the Words** Ask children to use each word in a sentence. Model a sentence if children need help.
MORE PRACTICE		Use oral vocabulary to discuss how ideas become inventions. How might an inventor plan and complete a *project?* What *contraption* did Scott and Brennan Olson make with wheels in a line and a brake?

Routine

Read a Passage

Reading "Zute," pp. 18–25

To Do	To Say	
		10 minutes

Teach draw conclusions.

Introduce the skill.

Today you are going to learn how to draw conclusions while you read. To draw conclusions, we use what we know about real life and what we read in the selection to figure out more about what happens. For example, in "In-Line Skates," I read that lots of kids like skating with in-line skates. I know a lot of my friends like to use them too, so I can draw the conclusion that the Olsons' invention of in-line skates was a big success.

Scaffold instruction.

Model the skill.

Apply the skill.

What other kinds of conclusions can you draw about the Olsons? Do you think they were creative? smart? lazy? How do you know?

Develop language and concepts.

See Routine Card 6. Display pp. 18–25.

Model using key words and concepts.

Key concepts: *robot, machine, chores, smashes, invention, tunes*

Before Reading Read the title. Do a structured picture walk.

pp. 18–19 The kids made a robot called Zute. A robot is a machine that helps people do work. Do you think Zute is doing a good job making beds? No, this bed is not neat. It is a mess.

pp. 20–21 The robot tries to mop the floors. Is the robot helping? No, it spills water everywhere and smashes into the furniture. Zute isn't good at this chore either.

pp. 22–23 The children are fixing the robot's tubes and wires. Is that a good solution? When an invention doesn't work well, inventors often make changes.

pp. 24–25 Now Zute will play tunes. Tunes are music. How do you think the kids and parents feel about Zute now?

Monitor children's use of vocabulary.

Now turn to your partner and talk about the pictures, using the same words I did.

Guide comprehension.

Monitor independent reading.

Use Routine Cards 2 and 3.

During Reading Read the pages in a whisper. Raise your hand if you need help with a word. As you read, ask yourself: What can I figure out about the characters and what happens in the story?

pp. 18–20 Why can't Zute help? (Zute is too big. It makes messes.)

pp. 21–22 What do Mom and Dad think about Zute? (They don't like Zute's messes. They think Zute is too big and can't help them.)

pp. 22–23 Jade and Luke fix Zute. What does that tell you about them? (They don't give up. They want to keep Zute.)

pp. 24–25 What do Mom and Dad think about Zute now? (They like Zute.) Why did they change their minds about Zute? (Zute is smaller and plays tunes. It doesn't make messes.) Will Zute be able to stay? (yes)

Guide retelling.

Prompt children as they retell the story.

After Reading Have one child retell the story while the others assist. Who are the characters? What happened at the beginning? What was Zute like at first? Did Mom and Dad like Zute? How did the children change Zute at the end? See Monitoring Retelling, p. 246.

Homework

Practice Book, p. 53, Draw Conclusions

Reread for Fluency

Paired Reading "Zute," pp. 18–20

To Do	To Say

5–10 minutes

CORRECTIVE FEEDBACK

Pair children. Monitor paired reading.

Children read pp. 18–20 orally, switching readers at the end of the first page. Have partners reread; now the other partner begins. For optimal fluency, children should reread three or four times. Give feedback on children's oral reading and use of the blending strategy. See Routine Cards 1 and 4.

MORE PRACTICE

Instead of rereading just pp. 18–20, have children reread the entire selection three or four times. You may want to have children read along with the AudioText.

Word Work

Spiral Review Short *u* and Short *e*, Long *u* and Long *e* (CVC*e*)

To Do	To Say

5–10 minutes

Review short u, short e, long u, and long e.

Scaffold instruction.

Write *tub* and *pet*.

You can read these words because you know the sounds *u* and *e* can stand for. What vowel sound do you hear in the first word? (/u/) in the second word? (/e/) Remember, when there is only one vowel at the beginning or in the middle of a word, it usually stands for its short sound. What are these words?

Add *e* to *tub* and *pet* to form *tube* and *Pete*.

How does the vowel sound change when I add *e* to *tub*? (It changes to the long *u* sound, /ū/.) How does the vowel sound change when I add *e* to *pet*? (It changes to the long *e* sound, /ē/.) Remember, when a vowel is followed by a consonant and the letter *e*, the vowel usually stands for its long sound and the final *e* is silent. What are these words? *(tube, Pete)*

Distribute white boards. Write *tub*, *tube*, *pet*, and *Pete* at the top of a four-column chart.

Sort Words Let's sort words by their vowel sounds. Point to and read *tub*, *tube*, *pet*, and *Pete*. Then display this list: *cut, them, nut, hug, theme, cute, step, rule, Steve, huge, then, these*. Call on children to read each word and tell whether it has a vowel sound like *tub*, *tube*, *pet*, or *Pete*. Write the word in the appropriate column on a class chart as children write on their boards.

Discuss how the words in each column are alike. For example, all the words in the first column are short *u* words. They all have only one vowel. Have children suggest a heading for each column. (Short *u*, Long *u*, Short *e*, Long *e*)

Short *u*	Long *u*	Short *e*	Long *e*
tub	*tube*	*pet*	*Pete*
cut	cute	them	theme
nut	rule	step	Steve
hug	huge	then	these

CORRECTIVE FEEDBACK

MONITOR PROGRESS

If . . . children have difficulty reading the words,
then . . . review the effect of *e* at the end of the words and blend the words sound-by-sound.

For more practice, see next page.

4

MORE PRACTICE

Model reading words in sentences.	When I read a sentence, I read each word without stopping between the words. If I come to a word I don't know, I blend it. Then I read the sentence again. Model reading this sentence, stopping to blend *flute: Eve places the flute on the shelf.*	
Write practice sentences.	Have each child read a sentence.	
	Steve will hug his cute pet. **These are huge red cups!** **Will Luke help Zeke get up the sand dunes?**	

Phonological and Phonemic Awareness   Optional practice activities, pp. 280–283

ACTIVITY 3 Read Together

Choral Reading "A Time Line of Fun!" p. 26

	To Do	To Say	10 minutes
Develop language and concepts.	Display p. 26.	**Before Reading** This is a time line. What do you know about time lines? (Allow children to share what they know.) What are these numbers? (dates) What kinds of pictures does the time line show? (toys and other things kids use) Share information about time lines. A time line organizes information by time. These dates tell the year something happened. The text and pictures describe what happened.	
Model fluent reading.		Read the title of the time line. Ask children to predict what it is about. When I read a time line, I read the date first and then read what happened on that date. I look at the picture that goes with the information. I read carefully and pause after each event to make sure I understand what I've read. Read the time line as described. Point out each date, entry, and picture as you read. Read it a second time, having children point to each year and word.	
	Build fluency through choral reading.	**Choral Reading** Now read the time line aloud with me. Let's read carefully and pause after each event. Reread the time line several times with children.	
Develop concepts.	Monitor listening comprehension.	**After Reading** What does the time line show? What is the first toy on the time line? What is the last toy on the time line? In what year were the first crayons invented? Tell about a new toy you would like to make.	

ACTIVITY 4 Build Concepts

Oral Vocabulary *construct, contraption, project, sidekick, unique*

	To Do	To Say	5–10 minutes
Review oral vocabulary.	Read the words on the Amazing Words board.	**Focus on Letter-Sounds** Remember, you can find sounds you know in big words. • What word begins with a long *u?* Which words begin with /k/? • Which two words end with *ct?* What sounds do *ct* make? • What word is made by putting two shorter words together? What are the shorter words?	

Encourage discussion.	**Provide Multiple Contexts** Review the meanings of the words. Then ask questions to place the words in diverse contexts.

- What kinds of projects do construction workers work on? What do they *construct?*
- Where might you find a *contraption?* What things might you use to make a *contraption?*
- Can a sister or brother be a *sidekick?* Can you think of any cartoon characters that have *sidekicks?*
- Name something that makes our classroom *unique.*

MORE PRACTICE

Apply oral vocabulary to new situations.	

- If you want to *construct* a *unique contraption,* will you use written directions to build it or will you build it on your own? Why?
- Is your *sidekick* someone you like or do not like? Why?
- If you work on a big *project,* will it take a short time or a long time to complete? Why?

ACTIVITY 5 Write

Response to Literature Interactive Writing

To Do	To Say	*5–10 minutes*

Generate ideas.

Share the pen.

Review the story "Zute."	What are some things the robot can do? What can't it do? Discuss things the robot Zute can and cannot do.
Have children participate in writing a list of things they would like a class robot to do.	Write *Our class robot will ___.* Have children read the words you wrote. Then have them supply endings for the sentence. Invite individuals to write familiar letter-sounds, word parts, and high-frequency words. Have them find the spelling of high-frequency words on the Word Wall. Ask questions such as:

- What is the first sound in *tune?* (/t/) What is the letter for /t/? *(t)*
- What is the vowel sound in *tune?* (/ū/) What is the letter for /ū/? *(u)*
- What is the last sound in *tune?* (/n/) What is the letter for /n/? *(n)*
- What letter at the end of *tune* makes the *u* say its name? *(e)*

Writing elements: conventions	Frequently reread what has been written while tracking the print. Point out that each sentence starts with a capital letter and ends with a period. Point out the extra space between words.
	Read the completed list aloud, having children read with you. (For example: *Our class robot will sing a tune. Our class robot will do math. Our class robot will make a snack.*)

MORE PRACTICE

Prompt independent writing.	**Journal Writing** Describe how a robot could help with chores at your house.

Homework	Practice Book, p. 54, High-Frequency Words

ACTIVITY 1 | Assessment Options

Sentence Reading

	To Do	**To Say**	*5 minutes*
Assess sentence reading.	Use reproducible p. 250.	Have each child read the sentences. Record scores on the Sentence Reading Chart, p. 254. Work with one child as others complete Write Sentences below. **That's a huge house!** **Wasn't it your idea to make this machine?** **Eve will use red and pink to make a cute sign for these pups.**	
CORRECTIVE FEEDBACK	**MONITOR PROGRESS**	*If . . .* children have trouble reading words with long *u* and long *e* or the contractions *'s* and *n't,* **then . . .** reteach the blending strategy lessons on pp. 164 and 168.	
		If . . . children cannot read a high-frequency word, **then . . .** mark the missed word or words on a high-frequency word list and send the list home for additional practice or have them practice with a fluent reader.	
		If . . . children misread a word in the sentence, **then . . .** correct the error and have them reread the word and then the sentence.	
Practice sentence writing.	Provide white boards.	**Write Sentences** Have children copy the sentences from reproducible p. 250 on white boards. Have them confirm spellings by comparing the words they wrote to the words in the sentences.	

Phonological and Phonemic Awareness	Optional practice activities, pp. 280–283

Passage Reading

	To Do	**To Say**	*5–10 minutes*
Assess fluency and comprehension.	Determine which children to assess this week.	Choose from these options: monitoring fluency (see pp. 244–245) and/or monitoring retelling (see p. 246). Have children reread "Zute." Be sure each child is assessed every other week.	
		If you have time, assess every child.	

ACTIVITY 2 | Use Concepts

Oral Vocabulary *construct, contraption, project, sidekick, unique*

	To Do	**To Say**	*5 minutes*
Check understanding of oral vocabulary.	Use the Amazing Words to wrap up the week's concept. Monitor understanding of oral vocabulary, using Routine Card 5.	As time allows, ask questions such as these. <ul><li>Describe the pictures on pp. 6–11 using some of the week's Amazing Words.</li><li>How hard do you think it would be to *construct* a robot? What would make this a difficult *project*?</li><li>Suppose you and a *sidekick* entered an invention contest. How would you decide what kind of *contraption* you would make?</li><li>Name some things that are *unique* about the town or city where we live.</li></ul>	
Preview next week's concept.		Next week you will read about different ways that people communicate.	

ACTIVITY 3 Read to Connect

Reread "Ideas Become Inventions," pp. 6–11

10 minutes

	To Do	To Say
Monitor comprehension: draw conclusions.	Have children reread "Ideas Become Inventions" silently.	As you read, use what you know and what you've read to draw conclusions about different kinds of inventions and inventors. After rereading, ask: • **What makes something a good invention?** • **Can anyone be an inventor? What do you need to invent something?** Record children's answers in a list on the board. (For example: a good invention helps people; it is unique; people like to use it.) Children will use the list for Activity 4.
Make connections.	Have children make connections across texts.	We also read "In-Line Skates." Find that. **How did the two brothers think of the idea for in-line skates?** (They looked at old-fashioned skates; they took blades off ice skates.) **How can you come up with new ideas by looking at something that has already been invented?** Record children's ideas in a chart. We also read "Zute," about a brother and sister who invent a robot to help out around the house. **Do you think Jade and Luke are good inventors? Is Zute a good invention? Why or why not?** Discuss the invention process, pointing out that Jade and Luke changed Zute when they discovered the robot wasn't good at chores. Add children's ideas about good inventions and inventors to the list. **What did all the selections we read this week show us about inventions? What is the big idea?** (If you have a good idea, you can invent something that people will like and use.)

ACTIVITY 4 Write

Response to Literature Independent Writing

5–10 minutes

	To Do	To Say
Assign expository writing.		Today you will write about what makes something a good invention. Encourage children to use words you wrote on the board for Activity 3 as they write.
Guide sentence correction.	Writing elements: conventions, support	Have children check their writing by asking themselves these questions. • **Did I use capital letters to begin each sentence and proper noun?** • **Did I use the correct mark at the end of each sentence?** • **Did I remember to use a final *e* for words with long vowels, like *tune*?** • **Did I describe what the invention does?**
MORE PRACTICE		Have children share their sentences with the group. Write their sentences on the board and have children practice reading and writing each other's sentences.
Homework		Practice Book, p. 55, Writing

Unit 3 Week 2 *Ways to Communicate*

How many ways can we communicate?

Objectives *This week students will...*

Phonemic Awareness
- segment and blend sounds in words
- add phonemes to make new words

Phonics
- blend and read words with vowel sounds of *y*, ending *-es*, and plural *-es*
- apply knowledge of letter-sounds to decode unknown words when reading
- recognize high-frequency words *against, found, stood, wild*

Fluency
- practice fluency with oral rereading

Vocabulary
- build concepts and oral vocabulary: *conversation, correspond, postage, reply, transport*

Text Comprehension
- read connected text
- draw conclusions to improve comprehension
- write in response to literature

Word Work *This week's phonics focus is . . .*

Vowel Sounds of *y*   Ending *-es*   Plural *-es*

High-Frequency Words *Tested Vocabulary*

The first appearance of each word in the Student Reader is noted below.

against	The ladder is leaning **against** the wall. (p. 35)
found	I **found** a dime. (p. 33)
stood	We **stood** in line. (p. 34) The three letters **stood** for her name.
wild	When something is **wild,** it is not raised or grown by people. (p. 35)

Amazing Words *Oral Vocabulary*

The week's vocabulary is related to the concept of different ways to communicate.

conversation	friendly talk between two or more people
correspond	to exchange written messages with someone
postage	the money you pay to send a letter or package
reply	to answer
transport	to carry something somewhere

Student Reader Unit 3 *This week students will read the following selections.*

Daily Lesson Plan

	ACTIVITIES	MATERIALS
Day 1	**Word Work** Phonemic Awareness: Segment and Blend Sounds Phonics: Blend Words with Vowel Sounds of *y* High-Frequency Words *against, found, stood, wild* **Build Concepts** *correspond, postage, transport* **Read a Passage** "Ways to Communicate," pp. 30–35 Comprehension: Use Strategies Reread for Fluency	Student White Boards Sound-Spelling Cards 10, 16 Tested Vocabulary Cards *Sing with Me Big Book* and Audio CD Student Reader: Unit 3 Routine Cards 1, 4, 6, 7 AudioText Practice Book, p. 56, Vowel Sounds of *y*
Day 2	**Reread for Fluency** **Word Work** Phonemic Awareness: Add Phonemes Phonics: Blend Words with Ending *-es*, Plural *-es* High-Frequency Words *against, found, stood, wild* **Read a Passage** "Dots and Dashes," pp. 36–43 Comprehension: Use Strategies **Write** Response to Literature: Shared Writing	Student Reader: Unit 3 Student White Boards Tested Vocabulary Cards Routine Cards 1, 2, 3, 4, 6, 7 AudioText Practice Book, p. 57, Ending *-es*, Plural *-es*
Day 3	**Reread for Fluency** **Word Work** Phonemic Awareness: Segment and Blend Sounds Phonics: Fluent Word Reading High-Frequency Words *against, found, stood, wild* **Build Concepts** *conversation, reply* **Read a Passage** "Gramps Learns New Things," pp. 44–51 Comprehension: Draw Conclusions	Student Reader: Unit 3 Student White Boards Tested Vocabulary Cards Routine Cards 1, 2, 3, 4, 6 AudioText Practice Book, p. 58, Draw Conclusions
Day 4	**Reread for Fluency** **Word Work** Phonics: Spiral Review Phonological and Phonemic Awareness Activities, pp. 280–283 **Read Together** "A to Z in Sign Language," p. 52 Comprehension: Listening **Build Concepts** *conversation, correspond, postage, reply, transport* **Write** Response to Literature: Interactive Writing	Student Reader: Unit 3 Student White Boards Routine Cards 1, 4 AudioText Practice Book, p. 59, High-Frequency Words
Day 5	**Assessment Options** Fluency, Comprehension Sentence Reading; Passage Reading Phonological and Phonemic Awareness Activities, pp. 280–283 **Use Concepts** *conversation, correspond, postage, reply, transport* **Read to Connect** "Ways to Communicate," pp. 30–35 Comprehension: Draw Conclusions **Write** Response to Literature: Independent Writing	Reproducible p. 250 Sentence Reading Chart, p. 238 Student White Boards Fluency Progress Chart, p. 229 Student Reader: Unit 3 Routine Card 5 Practice Book, p. 60, Writing

See pp. xvi–xvii for how *My Sidewalks* integrates instructional practices for ELL.

Phonemic Awareness Segment and Blend Sounds

To Do | **To Say** | *2 minutes*

Scaffold instruction.

Distribute white boards. Write *fly*.

Model Listen to the sounds in *fly*. Stretch the sounds /fff/ /lll/ /īīī/ as you write *f, l, y*. Repeat. Have children write letters as you write.

Write *sunny*. Lead children in blending sounds.

Teach and Practice Have children say the sounds with you as you point to the letters (/f/ /l/ /ī/) and blend sounds to say the word. *(fly)* Now listen to the sounds in *sunny*. Say /s/ /u/ /n/ /ē/ as you write *s, u, nn, y*. Have children say sounds as you point to letters and blend sounds to say the word. Continue with these words.

by   funny   sky   happy   try   sandy

Blending Strategy Vowel Sounds of *y* (/ī/, /ē/)

To Do | **To Say** | *5–10 minutes*

Use the blending routine.

Write *hide* and *these*.

1 Connect You already can read words like these. What are these words? What vowel sound do your hear in *hide?* (/ī/) in *these?* (/ē/) Today we will learn about another letter that can stand for either /ī/ or /ē/.

Routine

Display Sound-Spelling Card 16.

2 Use Sound-Spelling Cards This is ice cream. What sound do you hear at the beginning of *ice cream?* (/ī/) Say it with me: /ī/.

Scaffold instruction.

3 Listen and Write Write the letter *y* for /ī/. As you write, say the sound to yourself: /ī/. Now say the sound aloud.

Write *try*.

4 Model The letter *y* stands for /ī/ in this word. This is how I blend it: /t/ /r/ /ī/, *try*. Now you blend it: /t/ /r/ /ī/, *try*.

Display Sound-Spelling Card 10. Write *happy*.

Repeat steps 2 and 3 for the sound /ē/. Use Sound-Spelling Card 10 and explain the letter *y* can also stand for the sound /ē/ heard at the beginning of *easel*. Then model blending *happy*. Point out that when *y* is at the end of a word, it stands for either /ī/ or /ē/. When *y* ends a word that has two or more syllables, the *y* usually stands for /ē/.

$$\underset{\rightarrow}{t}\ \underset{\rightarrow}{r}\ \underset{\longrightarrow}{y} \qquad \underset{\rightarrow}{h}\ \underset{\rightarrow}{a}\ \underset{\rightarrow}{p}\ \underset{\rightarrow}{p}\ \underset{\longrightarrow}{y}$$

CORRECTIVE FEEDBACK

Write each practice word. Monitor student practice.

5 Group Practice Let's try the same thing with these words. Give feedback, using the *if . . . then* statements on Routine Card 1.

by   puppy   cry   nanny*   shy   tummy

6 Individual Practice Write the words; have each child blend two of them.

my   buddy*   why   spy*   silly   skinny   candy

Check understanding of practice words.

*Children need to make sense of words that they segment and blend. If needed, help children with meanings. A *nanny* is paid to take care of a child. Your *buddy* is your close friend. To *spy* is to watch secretly.

MORE PRACTICE

Model spelling *y* words.

Spell and Write What sounds do you hear in *dry?* (/d/ /r/ /ī/) What is the letter for /d/? Let's all write *d*. What is the letter for /r/? Write *r*. What is the letter for /ī/ at the end of *dry?* Write *y*. Continue practice as time allows. Have children compare their spellings to what you've written.

fry   Andy   sky   bunny   fly   fancy

High-Frequency Words *against, found, stood, wild*

To Do	To Say	3 minutes

Teach high-frequency words.

Display *against.*

1 Say, Spell, Write Use the Tested Vocabulary Cards. Display *against.* Here are some words that we won't sound out. We'll spell them. This word is *against: a, g, a, i, n, s, t* (point to each letter), *against.* What is this word? What are the letters in the word? Now you write *against.*

Point to *g* and *nst* in *against.*

2 Identify Letter-Sounds Let's look at the sounds in *against* that you do know. What is this letter? *(g)* What is the sound for this letter? *(/g/)* Continue with *n/n/, s/s/,* and *t/t/.*

3 Demonstrate Meaning Tell me a sentence using *against.* Model a sentence if children need help.

Display *found, stood,* and *wild.*

Repeat the Routine with *found, stood,* and *wild.* Children can identify these letter-sounds: *found (f/f/, nd/nd/), stood (st/st/, d/d/), wild (w/w/, ld/ld/).* Have children write the words in their word banks. Add the words to the Word Wall. Point out that the words they are learning are on p. 53.

ACTIVITY **2** | Build Concepts

Oral Vocabulary *correspond, postage, transport*

To Do	To Say	5–10 minutes

Introduce oral vocabulary.

Display p. 12 of *Sing with Me Big Book.* Play audio CD.

This week you will learn about ways to communicate. When you communicate, you share information or news. Listen for the Amazing Words *correspond, postage,* and *transport* as I sing this song. Play or sing the song. Then have children sing it with you.

Scaffold instruction.

Follow the Routine to teach *correspond, postage,* and *transport.*

1 Introduce, Demonstrate, and Apply

correspond The singer *corresponds* with good friends. When you *correspond* with someone, you write to each other. Have children say the word. Your mother and grandfather might *correspond* using e-mail. Who do you *correspond* with?

postage The singer asks how much the *postage* is for letters. *Postage* is the money you pay to send a letter or a package. Have children say the word. Your dad might take a package to the post office to find out how much the *postage* will be.

transport The song says that postal crews sort and *transport* letters. When you *transport* something, you carry it somewhere. Have children say the word. A mail carrier can *transport* lots of mail in big bags on a mail truck. What do you use to *transport* your books to school?

Display the words on the Amazing Words board.

2 Display the Words Have children say each word as they look at it. You can find sounds you know in big words. Read *cor/re/spond* as you run your hand under the syllables. What sound does the *c* stand for? *(/k/)* Continue with *r/r/* and *spond.* For *postage* and *transport,* children can identify these letter-sounds and word parts: *postage (p/p/, st/st/, g/j/), transport (tran, sp/sp/, t/t/).*

Monitor understanding.

3 Use the Words Ask children to use each word in a sentence. Model a sentence if children need help.

MORE PRACTICE

Use oral vocabulary to discuss the song. How does the singer *correspond* with good friends? What do you think is used for *postage* on the letters? Who will *transport* the letters to the friends?

Read a Passage

Build Background "Ways to Communicate," pp. 30–35

	To Do	**To Say**	*10 minutes*

Develop language and concepts.

See Routine Card 7. Read aloud p. 29 of the student book.

Preview the Week Use the photo on p. 28 to introduce this week's concept of communication. **How can you use a computer to communicate with others? What are some other ways people communicate with each other?** Read aloud the titles and descriptions on p. 29. Ask children what they think each selection will be about.

Scaffold instruction.

See Routine Card 6. Display pp. 30–35.

Ask questions and elaborate on answers to develop language.

Key concepts: *communicate, cell phone, walkie-talkie, buddy, note, letter, stamp, computer, e-mail, sign language*

Before Reading Read the title aloud. Do a structured picture walk with children.

pp. 30–31 What machine is the girl using to communicate with someone? (a phone) **She uses a phone to chat with a buddy, or friend. What are the boy and girl using to communicate with each other?** (walkie-talkies) **These buddies take turns talking on walkie-talkies. The kids in these pictures communicate by talking.**

pp. 32–33 How are the kids communicating without talking? (They write notes.) **They each wrote a note to a buddy. A note is a short letter. You can write a note on paper and hand it to a buddy or put a stamp on it and mail it. You can use a computer to write a note and e-mail it.**

pp. 34–35 This boy makes a sign with his hands that stands for a word. People can use sign language to communicate by moving their fingers, hands, and arms to show words. How do you think the puppy feels? How do you know? A puppy can show that it's happy by wagging its tail. Animals cannot talk or write, but they can still communicate.

Teach story word.

Write *communicate*.

You will read this word in the selection. It is *communicate*. Have children say the word and spell it. Review its meaning. **Let's read to find out about different ways to communicate.**

Guide comprehension.

Monitor independent reading. Model strategic reading.

Use Routine Cards 2 and 3.

During Reading Read the pages in a whisper. Raise your hand if you need help with a word. Stop at the end of each page to model asking questions. For example, for p. 35: **After I read, I asked myself: What is this page mainly about? The author says, "Not just kids communicate." The page is mostly about how animals can communicate in different ways too.**

Summarize.

Use oral vocabulary to develop the concept.

After Reading What are some ways that people *correspond* with each other? After a note is mailed, what is used to *transport* it to a buddy in another land? What can you add to the envelope of a note for *postage?*

Reread for Fluency "Ways to Communicate," pp. 30–32

	To Do	**To Say**	*5–10 minutes*

CORRECTIVE FEEDBACK

Monitor oral reading.

Read pp. 30–32 aloud. Read them three or four times so your reading gets better each time. Give feedback on children's oral reading and use of the blending strategy. See Routine Cards 1 and 4.

MORE PRACTICE

Instead of rereading just pp. 30–32, have children reread the entire selection three or four times. You may want to have children read along with the AudioText.

Homework

Practice Book, p. 56, Phonics: Vowel Sounds of *y*

ACTIVITY **1** Reread for Fluency

Paired Reading "Ways to Communicate," pp. 33–35

5–10 minutes

	To Do	To Say
CORRECTIVE FEEDBACK	Pair children. Monitor paired reading.	Children read pp. 33–35 orally, switching readers at the end of the first page. Have partners reread; now the other partner begins. For optimal fluency, children should reread three or four times. Give feedback on children's oral reading and use of the blending strategy. See Routine Cards 1 and 4.
MORE PRACTICE		Instead of rereading just pp. 33–35, have children reread the entire selection three or four times. You may want to have children read along with the AudioText.

ACTIVITY **2** Word Work

Phonemic Awareness Add Phonemes

2 minutes

	To Do	To Say
Scaffold instruction.	Distribute white boards. Write *mix*. Then add *-es* to form *mixes*. Lead children in adding *-es*/əz/ as they write.	**Model** Listen to the sounds in *mix.* Stretch the sounds /mmm/ /iii/ /ksss/ as you write *m, i, x*. Repeat. This time have children write the letters as you write. Add *-es* to *mix*. **Now listen as I add /əz/ to *mix*: *mix, es, mixes*.** Repeat. Have children add *-es* as you write.
		Teach and Practice Have children say the sounds as you point to the letters (/m/ /i/ /ks/ /əz/) and blend the word with you. **What word do we make when we add *-es* to the end of *mix*? (mixes) What sound do you hear at the end of *mixes*? (/əz/)** Continue adding *-es*/əz/ to form these words:

dishes   boxes   lunches   misses   rushes   foxes

Blending Strategy Ending -es, Plural -es

5–10 minutes

To Do	To Say
Use the blending routine. Write *runs* and *kids*.	**1 Connect** You studied words like these already. They each have a base word and the ending -s. What are the words? What are the base words? *(run, kid)* Sometimes we add -s to a base word to describe an action, like *runs*. Sometimes we add -s to a base word to make it plural. For example, *kids* means "more than one kid." Today we will learn about action words and plural words that end with -es.
Scaffold instruction. Write *rushes*.	**2 Model** This word has the ending -es. When I cover the ending, I see the base word *rush*. First, I read the base word: *rush*. Then I uncover and read the ending -es. Then I blend the two parts: *rush, es, rushes*. Now you try it: *rush, es, rushes*.
Write *classes*.	Repeat with *classes*. Point out that adding -es to *class* makes it mean "more than one class." Explain that we add -es to a word instead of -s when the word ends in *sh, ch, tch, s, ss, x,* or *zz*.
Write *buddies* beneath *buddy*.	We also add -es to words that end in *y*. When a word ends in *y*, we change the *y* to an *i* before we add the ending -es. The *y* in *buddy* changed to the *i* in *buddies*. To blend this word, I read one part at a time and then I blend the parts together: *bud, dies, buddies*.

r u s h e s   c l a s s e s   b u d d i e s

	3 Listen and Write Write the word *buddy*. Write the ending -es next to it. Now erase the *y* in *buddy* and write an *i* in its place. As you write, say the word to yourself: *buddies*. Now say the word aloud.
CORRECTIVE FEEDBACK Write each practice word. Monitor student practice.	**4 Group Practice** Let's try reading these words. Give feedback, using the *if . . . then* statements on Routine Card 1.
	foxes tries wishes glasses puppies switches
	5 Individual Practice Write the words; have each child blend two of them.
	flies buses presses hatches buzzes candies branches
MORE PRACTICE Model building words with -es endings and -es plurals. Write -es and -ies as headings for a T-chart.	**Build Words** Write these base words: *dish, dry, lunch, scratch, tummy, bunny, kiss, nanny, fix, fizz, cry,* and *hobby*. Have children build words by adding -es or changing *y* to *i* and adding -es. Have them write the new words under the correct heading on their white boards and read them.

-es	-ies
dishes	dries
lunches	tummies
scratches	bunnies
kisses	nannies
fixes	cries
fizzes	hobbies

High-Frequency Words *against, found, stood, wild*

3 minutes

To Do	To Say
Teach high-frequency words. Display *against, found, stood,* and *wild*.	Use the Tested Vocabulary Cards. Point to a word. Say and spell it. Have children say and spell the word. Ask children to identify familiar letter-sounds. Have them take turns reading the words.
Lead cumulative review.	Use the Tested Vocabulary Cards to review high-frequency words from previous weeks.

ACTIVITY 3 Read a Passage

Reading "Dots and Dashes," pp. 36–43

To Do	To Say	*10–15 minutes*

Develop language and concepts.

See Routine Cards 6 and 7. Display pp. 36–43.

Before Reading Have children recall what they learned about ways to communicate. Read the title. Do a structured picture walk with children.

Scaffold instruction.

Ask questions and elaborate on answers to develop language.

Key concepts: *secret, code, communicate, dots, dashes, letters, telegraph, wires, phone, computer*

pp. 36–37 The kids are writing and reading a code. A code is like a word puzzle. It can use shapes, lines, or other things to stand for letters.

pp. 38–39 This man, Samuel Morse, created a code that used dots and dashes to stand for letters. He also invented this machine, called a telegraph, to send his code. It has parts you press to make sounds travel across wires to other people.

pp. 40–41 One man taps dots and dashes on the telegraph. Others record the dots and dashes and then figure out the man's note.

pp. 42–43 Before phones and computers were invented, the telegraph helped people communicate to others far away.

Teach story words.

Write *secret, communicate,* and *letter.*

You will read these words in the selection. They are *secret, communicate,* and *letter.* Have children say each word and spell it. Review their meanings. Let's read to learn more about Morse code.

Introduce proper nouns.

You will see this name in the selection. It is Samuel Morse.

Guide comprehension.

Monitor independent reading.

During Reading Read the pages in a whisper. Raise your hand if you need help with a word. As you read, ask yourself: What am I learning about codes? What is this mainly about?

See Routine Cards 2 and 3.

pp. 36–39 What is a code? (a secret way to spell out a message) What did you learn about Samuel Morse? (He created a code and invented the telegraph.)

pp. 40–43 What did you learn about how people used Morse code? (They used a telegraph to send notes in code fast to people far away.)

Model summarizing.

Think aloud.

After Reading What did you learn about codes? What was the selection mainly about? Model how to summarize. The first part told how Samuel Morse created a code and invented the telegraph. The next part told how people used Morse code. I pick the most important ideas. The selection is mainly about using Morse code to communicate.

MORE PRACTICE

Develop oral vocabulary.

How did people *correspond* using Morse code? How did a telegraph help them *transport* messages to others? Did they need *postage?*

ACTIVITY 4 Write

Response to Literature Shared Writing

To Do	To Say	*5 minutes*

Guide shared writing.

Write sentence frames. Read the questions.

What might be in a code? A code could have _____.
Why would you use a code? I would use a code to _____.

Invite children to suggest answers. Discuss and record answers to complete the sentence frames. While writing, model connecting sounds to letters and forming letters (see pp. 257–259). Have children read answers aloud as you track print.

Homework

Practice Book, p. 57, Phonics: Ending *-es,* Plural *-es*

3

ACTIVITY 1 — Reread for Fluency

Oral Reading "Dots and Dashes," p. 36–38

	To Do	To Say	*5–10 minutes*
CORRECTIVE FEEDBACK	Monitor oral reading.	**Read pp. 36–38 aloud. Read the pages three or four times so your reading gets better each time.** Give feedback on children's oral reading and use of the blending strategy. See Routine Cards 1 and 4.	
MORE PRACTICE		Instead of rereading just p. 36–38, have children reread the entire selection three or four times. You may want to have children read along with the AudioText.	

ACTIVITY 2 — Word Work

Phonemic Awareness Segment and Blend Sounds

	To Do	To Say	*2 minutes*
Scaffold instruction.	Distribute white boards. Write *funny*. Write *foxes*. Lead children in blending sounds as they write.	**Model** Listen to the sounds in *funny.* Stretch the sounds /fff/ /uuu/ /nnn/ /ēēē/ as you write *f, u, nn, y.* Repeat. This time have children write the letters as you write. **Teach and Practice** Have children say the sounds with you as you point to the letters (/f/ /u/ /n/ /ē/) and blend the sounds to say the word. *(funny)* **Now listen to the sounds in *foxes: fox, es, foxes.*** Segment the word as you write *fox, es* and then blend the parts to say the word. Repeat. Continue with these words: sky happy dries switches catches buddies	

Fluent Word Reading Vowel Sounds of *y* (/ī/, /ē/); Ending *-es*, Plural *-es*

	To Do	To Say	*5–10 minutes*
Use the word-reading routine. **Scaffold instruction.**	Write *sky.*	**1 Connect** You can read this word because you know that *y* can stand for /ī/ or /ē/ at the end of a word. What sound does *y* stand for in this word? (/ī/) What is the word?	*Routine*
	Write *sunny, misses,* and *pennies.*	**2 Model** When you come to a new word, look at all the letters in the word and think about its vowel sounds and parts. Say the letter-sounds and word parts to yourself, and then read the word. Model reading *sunny, misses,* and *pennies.* When you come to a new word, what will you do?	
	Write each practice word.	**3 Group Practice** Let's read these words. Look at all the letters, think about the vowel sound or sounds, and say the letter-sounds to yourself. We will read words with *y* and the ending *-es.* When I point to the word, let's read it together. Allow 2–3 seconds previewing time for each word. shy skinny buses tries glasses cry sandy tummies flies	
CORRECTIVE FEEDBACK	**MONITOR PROGRESS**	*If . . .* children have difficulty previewing and reading whole words, *then . . .* have them use sound-by-sound blending. *If . . .* children can't read the words fluently at a rate of 1–2 seconds per word, *then . . .* continue practicing the list.	

MORE PRACTICE

	Model reading words in sentences.	When I read a sentence, I read each word without stopping between the words. If I come to a word I don't know, I blend it. Then I read the sentence again. Model reading this sentence, stopping to blend *messy: My bunnies are messy.*
	Write practice sentences.	Have each child read a sentence. **I can fly a kite with my buddies.** **Why don't we try this yummy snack Granny made?** **Jenny wishes the dishes were dry.**

High-Frequency Words *against, found, stood, wild*

To Do   **To Say**   *3 minutes*

Review high-frequency words. | Display *against*, *found*, *stood*, and *wild.* | Use the Tested Vocabulary Cards. Point to a word. Say and spell it. Have children say and spell the word. Ask children to identify familiar letter-sounds. Have them take turns reading the words.

ACTIVITY **3** Build Concepts

Oral Vocabulary *conversation, reply*

To Do   **To Say**   *5–10 minutes*

Routine

Teach oral vocabulary. | Display pp. 44–45 of the student book. | Today you will read a story in which a grandfather visits and has a *conversation* with his grandson about how to use a computer. You can use a computer to send an e-mail note or *reply* to a note someone sent you.

Scaffold instruction. | Follow the Routine to teach *conversation* and *reply*.

1 Introduce, Demonstrate, and Apply

conversation In this story, a boy and his grandfather have a *conversation* about computers. A *conversation* is a friendly talk between two or more people. Have children say the word. What kind of *conversation* might you have with a friend?

reply In this story, a boy talks about using a computer to send and *reply* to notes. When you *reply,* you answer. Have children say the word. When I ask you a question in class, you *reply* by saying the answer. How will you *reply* when your mother asks what you learned at school today?

Display the words on the Amazing Words board. | **2 Display the Words** Have children say each word as they look at it. You can find sounds you know in big words. Read *con/ver/sa/tion* as you run your hand under the syllables. What three letters do you find at the beginning of *conversation*? How do you say the first part of *conversation*? (*con*/kon/) Read *re/ply*. Children can identify *r*/r/, *pl*/pl/, and final *y*/ī/.

Monitor understanding. | **3 Use the Words** Ask children to use each word in a sentence. Model a sentence if children need help.

MORE PRACTICE | | Use oral vocabulary to discuss ways to communicate. What machine could you use to help you have a *conversation* with someone far away? How would you *reply* to an e-mail message from a friend?

ACTIVITY 4 Read a Passage

Reading "Gramps Learns New Things," pp. 44–51

	To Do	**To Say**	*10 minutes*

Teach draw conclusions.

Scaffold instruction.

Introduce the skill.

Model the skill.

Today you will draw conclusions while you read. Remember, when we draw conclusions, we think about what we read and what we know about life to figure out more about the characters and what happens in a story. For example, suppose I read a story about two girls ice-skating. The pictures show the girls smiling. I read that they laugh and chat as they skate. I know that I like doing fun things with my friends. I put that all together and draw the conclusion that the girls are friends and are happy to be skating.

Apply the skill.

If you read about a crying boy with a broken bicycle, how do you think he feels? Why do you think that? (He is sad because he's crying; you feel bad when something you own breaks.)

Develop language and concepts.

See Routine Card 6. Display pp. 44–51.

Model using key words and concepts.

Key concepts: *visit, computer, frown, Web, Internet, e-mail, communicate*

Monitor children's use of vocabulary.

Before Reading Read the title. Do a structured picture walk.

pp. 44–45 This man is visiting a family. Who do you think the man is? How does the family feel about the visitor? The boy's grandfather is visiting. The family is happy to see Gramps.

pp. 46–47 Andy and Gramps are using a computer. A computer is a machine that can store and give information.

pp. 48–49 Gramps is frowning in this picture. Point to his frown. I think he's having trouble using the computer. Look at the next picture. How does Gramps feel now? What might have happened?

pp. 50–51 Gramps and Andy use the computer to find weather information on the Web, or Internet. Gramps sent Andy and his mom an e-mail note. Now they will reply to him.

Now turn to your partner and talk about the pictures, using the same words I did.

Teach story words.

Write *computer*.

You will read this word in the story: *computer.* Have children say the word and spell it. Review its meaning. **Let's read about Gramps's visit.**

Guide comprehension.

Monitor independent reading.

Use Routine Cards 2 and 3.

During Reading Read the pages in a whisper. Raise your hand if you need help with a word. As you read, ask yourself: What conclusions can I draw about Andy and Gramps?

pp. 44–45 How does Andy feel about Gramps coming for a visit? How do you know? (He's happy. He grins. He likes chatting with him.)

pp. 46–48 How does Gramps feel when he tries to use the computer? Why? (unhappy; he can't figure out how to use it.)

pp. 49–51 How does Gramps feel by the end of the story? Why? (He's happy because he learned to use a computer. He can use it to chat with Andy.) How does the computer help Andy and Gramps chat? (They can send e-mail to each other.)

Guide retelling.

Prompt children as they retell the story.

After Reading Have one child retell the story while the others assist. Who are the characters? What happened at the beginning? in the middle? at the end? See Monitor Retelling, p. 246.

Homework   Practice Book, p. 58, Draw Conclusions

ACTIVITY 1 Reread for Fluency

Paired Reading "Gramps Learns New Things," pp. 44–45

To Do	To Say	
		5–10 minutes

CORRECTIVE FEEDBACK

Pair children. Monitor paired reading.

Children read pp. 44–45 orally, switching readers at the end of the first page. Have partners reread; now the other partner begins. For optimal fluency, children should reread three or four times. Give feedback on children's oral reading and use of the blending strategy. See Routine Cards 1 and 4.

MORE PRACTICE

Instead of rereading just pp. 44–45, have children reread the entire selection three or four times. You may want to have children read along with the AudioText.

ACTIVITY 2 Word Work

Spiral Review Base Words and Endings (-s, -es, -ed, -ing)

To Do	To Say	
		5–10 minutes

Review base words and endings.

Write *notes, rushes, helped, flying,* and *dots.*

These words each have a base word and an ending. How do you blend words like these? (Read the base word, then the ending, and then blend the two parts together.) Read each word as I point to it and tell me its base word. Did the spelling of any of these base words change? (no)

Scaffold instruction.

Write *shopped, shopping, smiled, smiling, tried,* and *bunnies.*

Sometimes the spelling of the base word must change. Review the spelling changes below. Have children read the words and identify the base words.

shopped, shopping Double the last consonant before adding *-ed* or *-ing.*

smiled, smiling Drop final *e* before adding *-ed,* or *-ing.*

tried, bunnies Change the *y* to *i* before adding *-ed* or *-es.*

Distribute white boards.

Build Words Have children copy the base words and add the endings. Remind them, if needed, when to use *-es* instead of *-s.* Have them read the new words and identify spelling changes. Discuss meanings, pointing out, for example, words describing past actions or words that mean "more than one."

Base Words	*-s/-es*	*-ed*	*-ing*
jump	jumps	jumped	jumping
chat	chats	chatted	chatting
save	saves	saved	saving
cry	cries	cried	crying
fix	fixes	fixed	fixing
class	classes		
pond	ponds		

CORRECTIVE FEEDBACK

MONITOR FEEDBACK

If . . . children have difficulty reading the words,
then . . . review the spelling changes and blend words sound-by-sound.

For more practice, see next page.

Continued Spiral Review

Model reading words in sentences.	When I read a sentence, I read each word without stopping between the words. If I come to a word I don't know, I blend it. Then I read the sentence again. Model reading this sentence, stopping to blend *glasses: Jenny dropped the glasses and cried when the milk spilled.*
Write practice sentences.	Have each child read a sentence. I waved and yelled at my pal Kenny. The shy bunnies are hopping away. Twenty gulls fly across the sunny sky.

Phonological and Phonemic Awareness — Optional practice activities, pp. 280–283

ACTIVITY 3 Read Together

Reading "A to Z in Sign Language," p. 52

	To Do	**To Say**	*10 minutes*
Develop language and concepts.	Display p. 52.	**Before Reading** What do you know about sign language? (Allow children to share what they know.) Sign language is a way of communicating. You use your hands to make signs that stand for letters or words. Often, people who are deaf use sign language to communicate.	
Model reading.	Model reading a reference source.	**Reading** Read the title. Ask children to predict what the page is about. This page shows signs that stand for each letter of the alphabet. The signs are in alphabetical order. If I want to spell the name *Tom,* I first look for the letter *T* and position my hand and fingers to look like the photograph of the hand next to the *T.* Demonstrate. Then I look for the letter *O* and make the sign for *O.* Last, I look for the letter *M* and make the sign for *M.* Demonstrate for *O* and *M.* I have spelled *Tom* in sign language. What is the sign for *A?* Make the sign for *Y.* What letter does this sign stand for? Can you spell your name in sign language? Have children attempt to sign their names.	
Develop concepts.	Monitor listening comprehension.	**After Reading** Where might you find a page like this? Do you think there are signs for entire words too? How is this page similar to a page from a dictionary?	

ACTIVITY 4 Build Concepts

Oral Vocabulary *conversation, correspond, postage, reply, transport*

	To Do	**To Say**	*5–10 minutes*
Review oral vocabulary.	Read the words on the Amazing Words board.	**Focus on Letter-Sounds** Remember, you can find sounds you know in big words. • Which words begin with /k/? What word begins with /tr/? • What word ends with *y?* What sound does the *y* stand for? • What word has a *g?* What sound does the *g* stand for?	
	Encourage discussion.	**Provide One Context for All the Words** Review the meanings of the words. Then ask questions to place all the words in one context. • How would you *correspond* with a friend from another state? • If you sent that friend a package, how would you *transport* it to her? Where would you buy the *postage* for the package? • What machine could you use to have a *conversation* with your friend? If you left her a phone message or sent her an e-mail note, how might she *reply?*	

MORE PRACTICE

Apply oral vocabulary to new situations.

- If the things I say are ways to *correspond*, wave and say, "correspond." If not, do nothing: sending an e-mail (correspond), riding a bike (not), buying a shirt (not), mailing a letter (correspond).

- If anything I say needs *postage*, smile and say, "postage." If not, frown and say nothing: an apple (not), a package (postage), an e-mail note (not), a letter (postage).

- If anything I say is a way to have a *conversation* with someone, stand up and say, "conversation." If not, stay seated and say nothing: talk on the phone (conversation), walk by yourself (not), use sign language with a friend (conversation), take a nap (not).

ACTIVITY **5** Write

Response to Literature Interactive Writing

To Do	To Say	*5–10 minutes*

Generate ideas.

Review the story "Gramps Learns New Things."

What did Gramps learn about computers? What can you do with a computer? Discuss different ways you can use a computer.

Share the pen.

Have children participate in writing a list of things you can do with a computer.

Write *I can use a computer to _____*. Have children read the words you wrote. Then have them supply endings for the sentence. Invite individuals to write familiar letter-sounds, word parts, and high-frequency words. Have them find the spelling of high-frequency words on the Word Wall. Ask questions such as:

- What is the first sound in *send*? (/s/) What is the letter for /s/? *(s)*

- What is the vowel sound in *send*? (/e/) What is the letter for /e/? *(e)*

- What are the last two sounds in *send*? (/n/ /d/) What are the letters for them? *(nd)*

Writing elements: conventions

Frequently reread what has been written while tracking the print. Point out that each sentence starts with a capital letter and ends with a period. Point out the extra space between words.

Read the completed list aloud, having children read with you. (For example, *I can use a computer to send a note to my pals. I can use a computer to get on the Web. I can use a computer to find a map.*)

MORE PRACTICE

Prompt independent writing.

Journal Writing Tell how you helped teach something new to someone.

Homework

Practice Book, p. 59, High-Frequency Words

ACTIVITY 1 — Assessment Options

Sentence Reading

To Do	To Say	5 minutes

Assess sentence reading.

Use reproducible p. 250.

Have each child read the sentences. Record scores on the Sentence Reading Chart, p. 254. Work with one child as others complete Write Sentences below.

Benny stood against my desk.
Henry flies a kite when the sky is sunny.
Sandy was happy that she found wild bunnies.

CORRECTIVE FEEDBACK

MONITOR PROGRESS

If . . . children have trouble reading words that end with *y* or *-es,*
then . . . reteach the blending strategy lessons on pp. 180 and 184.

If . . . children cannot read a high-frequency word,
then . . . mark the missed word or words on a high-frequency word list and send the list home for additional practice or have them practice with a fluent reader.

If . . . children misread a word in the sentence,
then . . . correct the error and have them reread the word and then the sentence.

Practice sentence writing.

Provide white boards.

Write Sentences Have children copy the sentences from reproducible p. 250 on white boards. Have them confirm spellings by comparing the words they wrote to the words in the sentences.

Phonological and Phonemic Awareness

Optional practice activities, pp. 280–283

Passage Reading

To Do	To Say	5–10 minutes

Assess fluency and comprehension.

Determine which children to assess this week.

Choose from these options: monitoring fluency (see pp. 244–245) and/or monitoring retelling (see p. 246). Have children read "Gramps Learns New Things." Be sure each child is assessed every other week.

If you have time, assess every child.

ACTIVITY 2 — Use Concepts

Oral Vocabulary *conversation, correspond, postage, reply, transport*

To Do

Check understanding of oral vocabulary.

Use the Amazing Words to wrap up the week's concept.

Monitor understanding of oral vocabulary, using Routine Card 5.

As time allows, ask questions such as these.

- Tell me about the pictures on pp. 30–35 using some of the week's Amazing Words.
- Would the *postage* be the same for a package as it would for a letter?
- What is something that could *transport* large bags of food across the ocean?
- Suppose you could *correspond* with someone from a different country. What would you want to say?
- What parts of your body would you use to have a *conversation* in sign language?
- If your father asked you what you wanted to eat for dinner, how would you *reply?*

Preview next week's concept.

Next week you will read about smart and creative ideas.

ACTIVITY 3 Read to Connect

Reread "Ways to Communicate," pp. 30–35

| To Do | To Say | 10 minutes |

Monitor comprehension: draw conclusions.

Have children reread "Ways to Communicate" silently.

As you read, use what you already know and what the author says to draw conclusions about ways to communicate. After rereading, ask:

- Are there just a few ways people can communicate or many ways?
- Why is it important to be able to communicate?

Record children's answers on the board. Make a list of the different ways to communicate. (For example: people communicate by talking on the phone, writing and mailing a letter, and using sign language.) Children will use the list for Activity 4.

Make connections.

Have children make connections across texts.

We also read "Dots and Dashes." Find that. Why did people use Morse code long ago? Who might still use it today? Would you use it? If not already listed, add "using code" to the list of ways to communicate.

We also read "Gramps Learns New Things," about a boy and his grandfather finding a new way to communicate. How do you think Andy felt after teaching Gramps how to use a computer? How do you know? Is e-mail a good way to communicate? Why do you think so? Record children's conclusions in the center of a web and list supporting reasons around it.

What did all the selections we read this week have to do with? What is the big idea? (There are many different ways to communicate.)

ACTIVITY 4 Write

Response to Literature Independent Writing

| To Do | To Say | 5–10 minutes |

Assign expository writing.

Today you will write about ways we communicate. Describe different ways people communicate with each other. Include information about machines and other things we use to help us communicate. Encourage children to use words you wrote on the board for Activity 3 as they write.

Guide sentence correction.

Writing elements: conventions, organization, support

Have children check their writing by asking themselves these questions.

- Did I use a capital letter to begin sentences and proper nouns?
- Did I use correct marks at the ends of sentences?
- Did I think about spelling changes to base words before adding endings?
- Did I include a variety of machines?
- Did I describe my own experience?

MORE PRACTICE

Have children share their sentences with the group. Write their sentences on the board and have children practice reading and writing each other's sentences.

Homework Practice Book, p. 60, Writing

Unit 3 Week 3 *What a Smart Idea!*

When are creative ideas good? When are they bad?

Objectives *This week students will...*

Phonemic Awareness
- add phonemes and blend sounds in words

Phonics
- blend and read words with *r*-controlled *ar, or, ore*
- apply knowledge of letter-sounds to decode unknown words when reading
- recognize high-frequency words *become, even, front, thought*

Fluency
- practice fluency with oral rereading

Vocabulary
- build concepts and oral vocabulary: *brainstorm, brilliant, consume, prey, shrewd*

Text Comprehension
- read connected text
- identify main idea to improve comprehension
- write in response to literature

Word Work *This week's phonics focus is . . .*

r-Controlled *ar*   *r*-Controlled *or, ore*

High-Frequency Words *Tested Vocabulary*

The first appearance of each word in the Student Reader is noted below.

become	It has **become** warmer. (p. 57)
even	**Even** though it was hot, she wore a jacket. (p. 60) Do you **even** know that boy you waved to?
front	The **front** part of something is the part that faces forward. (p. 57) The **front** part is also the first part or the beginning.
thought	A **thought** is something that a person thinks. (p. 60)

Amazing Words *Oral Vocabulary*

The week's vocabulary is related to the concept of formulating creative ideas.

brainstorm	to think of many ideas until you come up with one you'll use
brilliant	intelligent; splendid or magnificent
consume	to eat something or use it all up
prey	an animal that is hunted and killed by another animal for food
shrewd	very clever and smart

Student Reader Unit 3 *This week students will read the following selections.*

Daily Lesson Plan

	ACTIVITIES	MATERIALS
Day 1	**Word Work** Phonemic Awareness: Add Initial Phonemes Phonics: Blend Words with *r*-Controlled *ar* High-Frequency Words *become, even, front, thought* **Build Concepts** *consume, prey, shrewd* **Read a Passage** "What a Smart Idea!" pp. 56–63 Comprehension: Use Strategies Reread for Fluency	Student White Boards Sound-Spelling Card 3 Tested Vocabulary Cards *Sing with Me Big Book* and Audio CD Student Reader: Unit 3 Routine Cards 1, 4, 6, 7 AudioText Practice Book, p. 61, *r*-Controlled *ar*
Day 2	**Reread for Fluency** **Word Work** Phonemic Awareness: Add Initial Phonemes Phonics: Blend Words with *r*-Controlled *or, ore* High-Frequency Words *become, even, front, thought* **Read a Passage** "A Nutty Story," pp. 64–69 Comprehension: Use Strategies **Write** Response to Literature: Shared Writing	Student Reader: Unit 3 Student White Boards Sound-Spelling Card 25 Tested Vocabulary Cards Routine Cards 1, 2, 3, 4, 6, 7 AudioText Practice Book, p. 62, *r*-Controlled *or, ore*
Day 3	**Reread for Fluency** **Word Work** Phonemic Awareness: Add Initial Phonemes Phonics: Fluent Word Reading High-Frequency Words *become, even, front, thought* **Build Concepts** *brainstorm, brilliant* **Read a Passage** "Think Smart!" pp. 70–81 Comprehension: Main Idea	Student Reader: Unit 3 Student White Boards Tested Vocabulary Cards Routine Cards 1, 2, 3, 4, 6 AudioText Practice Book, p. 63, Main Idea and Supporting Details
Day 4	**Reread for Fluency** **Word Work** Phonics: Spiral Review Phonological and Phonemic Awareness Activities, pp. 280–283 **Read Together** "I Built a Fabulous Machine," p. 82 Comprehension: Listening **Build Concepts** *brainstorm, brilliant, consume, prey, shrewd* **Write** Response to Literature: Interactive Writing	Student Reader: Unit 3 Letter Tiles *a, c, e, g, i, l, n, o, p, r, s, u* Routine Cards 1, 4 AudioText Practice Book, p. 64, High-Frequency Words
Day 5	**Assessment Options** Fluency, Comprehension Sentence Reading; Mid-Unit Passage Reading Phonological and Phonemic Awareness Activities, pp. 280–283 **Use Concepts** *brainstorm, brilliant, consume, prey, shrewd* **Read to Connect** "What a Smart Idea!" pp. 56–63 Comprehension: Main Idea **Write** Response to Literature: Independent Writing	Reproducible p. 251 Sentence Reading Chart, p. 254 Fluency Progress Chart, p. 245 Student White Boards Assessment Book, p. 81 Student Reader: Unit 3 Routine Card 5 Practice Book, p. 65, Writing

See pp. xvi–xvii for how *My Sidewalks* integrates instructional practices for ELL.

Phonemic Awareness Add Initial Phonemes

	To Do	To Say	
			2 minutes

Scaffold instruction.

Distribute white boards. Write *arm*. Then add *f* to form *farm*.

Write *art*. Then add *p* to form *part*. Lead children in adding initial phonemes.

Model Listen to the sounds in *arm*. Stretch the sounds /ăăărrr/ /mmm/ as you write *a, r, m*. Repeat. Have children write letters as you write. Listen as I add /f/ to the beginning of *arm*. Say /fff/ /ăăărrr/ /mmm/ as you add *f* to *arm*. Repeat. Have children add *f* as you write. What is the new word? *(farm)*

Teach and Practice Have children say the sounds with you as you point to *f, arm* (/f/ /ärm/) and blend to say the word. *(farm)* Listen to the sounds in *art*. Say /ăăărrr/ /t/ as your write *a, r, t*. What word do we make when we add /p/ to the front of *art*? *(part)* Continue adding initial phonemes to form these words:

jar   far   mark   dark   harm   start

Blending Strategy *r*-Controlled *ar*

	To Do	To Say	
			5–10 minutes

Routine

Use the blending routine.

Write *had* and *make*.

1 Connect You already can read words like these. What are the words? What vowel sound do your hear in *had?* (the short *a* sound) What vowel sound do your hear in *make?* (the long a sound) Today we'll learn another sound for the letter *a* that is neither short nor long—the sound when *a* is followed by the letter *r*.

Scaffold instruction.

Display Sound-Spelling Card 3.

2 Use Sound-Spelling Card This is an artist. What sound do you hear at the beginning of *artist?* (/är/) Say it with me: /är/. /är/ is the *r*-controlled sound of *a*; the sound of *a* when it is followed by an *r*.

3 Listen and Write Write the letters *ar* for /är/. As you write, say the sound to yourself: /är/. Now say the sound aloud.

Write *jar*.

4 Model When the letter *a* is followed by *r*, the *a* has an *r*-controlled sound: /är/. This is how I blend this word: /j/ /är/, *jar*. Now you try it: /j/ /är/, *jar*.

Point out that when the only vowel in a word or syllable is followed by *r*, the vowel will be affected by that *r*.

$$\overrightarrow{j \; a \; r}$$

CORRECTIVE FEEDBACK

Write each practice word. Monitor student practice.

5 Group Practice Let's try the same thing with these words. Give feedback, using the *if . . . then* statements on Routine Card 1.

car   dart*   hard   bark*   yard   smart

6 Individual Practice Write the words; have each child blend two of them.

far   harp*   card   barn   chart*   sharp

Check understanding of practice words.

*Children need to make sense of words that they segment and blend. If needed, help children with meanings. When animals *dart,* they move quickly. *Bark* is the rough outside covering of a tree. A *bark* is also the sound a dog makes. A *harp* is a large stringed musical instrument. A *chart* is a list or drawing that shows facts. Show a chart from class.

MORE PRACTICE

Model spelling *r*-controlled *ar* words.

Spell and Write What sounds do you hear in *yarn?* (/y/ /är/ /n/) What is the letter for /y/? Let's all write *y*. Continue with *ar*/är/ and *n*/n/. Provide practice as time allows. Have children compare their spellings to what you've written.

art   farm   park   star   shark   march   spark

High-Frequency Words *become, even, front, thought*

To Do	To Say	
		3 minutes

Teach high-frequency words.

Display *become*.	**1 Say, Spell, Write** Use the Tested Vocabulary Cards. Display *become*. Here are some words that we won't sound out. We'll spell them. This word is *become: b, e, c, o, m, e* (point to each letter), *become*. What is this word? What are the letters in the word? Now you write *become*.
Point to *b, c,* and *m* in *become*.	**2 Identify Letter-Sounds** Let's look at the sounds in *become* that you do know. What is this letter? *(b)* What is the sound for this letter? *(/b/)* Continue with *c*/k/ and *m*/m/. Also point out the high-frequency word *come*.
	3 Demonstrate Meaning Tell me a sentence using *become*. Model a sentence if children need help.
Display *even, front,* and *thought*.	Repeat the Routine with *even, front,* and *thought*. Children can identify these letter-sounds: *even* (*v*/v/, *n*/n/), *front* (*fr*/fr/, *nt*/nt/), and *thought* (*th*/th/, *t*/t/). Have children write the words in their word banks. Add the words to the Word Wall. Point out that the words they are learning are on p. 83.

Routine

ACTIVITY **2** Build Concepts

Oral Vocabulary *consume, prey, shrewd*

To Do	To Say	
		5–10 minutes

Introduce oral vocabulary.

Display p. 13 of *Sing with Me Big Book*. Play audio CD.	This week you will learn about smart ideas. Listen for the Amazing Words *consume, prey,* and *shrewd* as I sing this song. Play or sing the song. Then have children sing it with you.

Routine

Scaffold instruction.

| Follow the Routine to teach *consume, prey,* and *shrewd*. | **1 Introduce, Demonstrate, and Apply**

consume Someone might *consume* the little fishies for dinner. When you *consume* something, you eat it or use it all up. Have children say the word. A lot of your extra time may be *consumed* by doing homework. What did you *consume* for breakfast today?

prey Someone always looks at little fishies as their *prey. Prey* is an animal that is hunted and killed by another animal for food. Have children say the word. Small fish are often the *prey* of bigger fish. What *prey* would a cat like to catch? What *prey* do some people hunt?

shrewd Little fishies need to be *shrewd* so they won't be caught and eaten. Someone or something that is *shrewd* is very clever and smart. Have children say the word. You may want to be *shrewd* about deciding what to do with money you receive. Name a character from a story that you think is *shrewd*. |
|---|---|
| Display the words on the Amazing Words board. | **2 Display the Words** Have children say each word as they look at it. You can find sounds you know in big words. Read *prey*. What two letters are at the beginning of *prey*? *(pr)* What sounds do these letters stand for? *(/pr/)* For *shrewd* and *consume*, children can identify these letter-sounds and word parts: *shrewd* (*shr*/shr/, *d*/d/), *consume* (*c*/k/, *n*/n/, *sume*). |
| Monitor understanding. | **3 Use the Words** Ask children to use each word in a sentence. Model a sentence if children need help. |

MORE PRACTICE

Use oral vocabulary to discuss the song. Why must the little fishies be *shrewd*? Who might look at them as *prey*? How can they avoid being *consumed* for someone's dinner?

Build Background "What a Smart Idea!" pp. 56–63

To Do	**To Say**	*10 minutes*

Develop language and concepts.

See Routine Card 7. Read aloud pp. 54–55 of the student book.

Preview the Week Use the picture on p. 54 to introduce this week's concept of smart ideas. **What do you think this machine does? Have you ever had an idea you thought was smart, but it didn't turn out the way you expected?** Read aloud the titles and descriptions on p. 55. Ask children what they think each selection will be about.

Scaffold instruction.

See Routine Card 6. Display pp. 56–63.

Ask questions and elaborate on answers to develop language.

Key concepts: *twigs, spider, prey, chimp, poke, stick, nest, consume, net, apple*

Before Reading Read the title aloud. Do a structured picture walk.

pp. 56–57 What creature is peeking out from the twigs and bark? (a spider) **Point to the spider. Point to the frog. What might happen to the frog if it hops in front of the spider's trap?** (It might get caught and eaten by the spider.) **The frog is the spider's prey. The spider hides its trap so its prey won't see it and run away. That is a smart way to catch prey.**

pp. 58–59 What animals are shown in these pictures? (chimps) **One chimp pokes a stick into a nest of bugs. What do you think the chimp will do with the bugs it catches on the stick?** (eat them) **The chimp will consume, or eat, the bugs. It can't get the bugs with its arm, so it uses a stick.**

pp. 60–61 Point to the fish in the lake. How did the man catch the fish? (with a net) Yes, the man did not have a fishing pole, so he caught the fish with a net. What do you think he will do with the fish? (eat them)

pp. 62–63 What is the girl using the stick for? (to get an apple) She cannot reach the fruit, so she will poke the branches with a long stick until some apples fall down. What a smart idea! Let's read to find out more about these smart ideas for getting food.

Teach story words.

Write *spider* and *apple.*

You will read these words in the selection. They are *spider* and *apple*. Have children say each word and spell it. Review their meanings.

Guide comprehension.

Monitor independent reading. Model strategic reading.

Use Routine Cards 2 and 3.

During Reading Read the pages in a whisper. Raise your hand if you need help with a word. Stop at the end of each page to model asking questions. For example, for p. 59: **After I read, I asked myself: What did I learn? I read that the chimp poked a stick in the nest and pulled it out when bugs hopped on it. I learned that a chimp can use a stick to get bugs to eat.**

Summarize.

Use oral vocabulary to develop the concept.

After Reading What are some *shrewd* ways that spiders and chimps catch their *prey*? What will the people in the selection *consume* for snacks? How did they get those snacks?

Reread for Fluency "What a Smart Idea!" pp. 56–59

To Do	**To Say**	*5–10 minutes*

CORRECTIVE FEEDBACK

Monitor oral reading.

Read pp. 56–59 aloud. Read them three or four times so your reading gets better each time. Give feedback on children's oral reading and use of the blending strategy. See Routine Cards 1 and 4.

MORE PRACTICE

Instead of rereading just pp. 56–59, have children reread the entire selection three or four times. You may want to have children read along with the AudioText.

Homework   Practice Book, p. 61, Phonics: *r*-Controlled *ar*

ACTIVITY 1 Reread for Fluency

Paired Reading "What a Smart Idea!" pp. 60–63

To Do	To Say	
		5–10 minutes

CORRECTIVE FEEDBACK

Pair children. Monitor paired reading.

Children read pp. 60–63 orally, switching readers at the end of the first page. Have partners reread; now the other partner begins. For optimal fluency, children should reread three or four times. Give feedback on children's oral reading and use of the blending strategy. See Routine Cards 1 and 4.

MORE PRACTICE

Instead of rereading just pp. 60–63, have children reread the entire selection three or four times. You may want to have children read along with the AudioText.

ACTIVITY 2 Word Work

Phonemic Awareness Add Initial Phonemes

To Do	To Say	
		2 minutes

Scaffold instruction.

Distribute white boards. Write *orn.* Then add *h* to form *horn.*

Write *ore.* Then add *m* to form *more.* Lead children in adding initial phonemes.

Model Listen to the sounds in *orn.* Stretch the sounds /ôôôrrr/ /nnn/ as you write *o, r, n.* Repeat. Have children write letters as you write. Now listen as I add /h/ in front of *orn.* Say /h/ /ôôôrrr/ /nnn/ as you add *h* to *orn.* Repeat. Have children add *h* as you write. What is the word? *(horn)*

Teach and Practice Have children say the sounds with you as you point to *h, orn* (/h/ /ôrn/) and blend to say the word. *(horn)* Write *ore.* Now listen to the sound of *ore.* The *e* at the end is silent. Say /ôôôrrr/ as your write *o, r, e.* What word do we make when we add /m/ to the front of *ore? (more)* Continue adding initial phonemes to form these words:

corn   tore   sort   thorn   sport   store

Blending Strategy *r*-Controlled *or, ore*

To Do	To Say	

5–10 minutes

Use the blending routine.

Write *spot* and *stone*.

1 Connect You already can read words like these. What are the words? What vowel sound do your hear in *spot*? (the short *o* sound) What vowel sound do you hear in *stone*? (the long *o* sound) Today we'll learn another sound for the letter *o* that is neither short nor long—the sound of *o* when it is followed by the letter *r*.

Scaffold instruction.

Display Sound-Spelling Card 25.

2 Use Sound-Spelling Card This is an orchestra. What sound do you hear at the beginning of *orchestra*? (/ôr/) Say it with me: /ôr/. /ôr/ is the *r*-controlled sound of *o*: the sound of *o* when it is followed by the letter *r*.

3 Listen and Write Write the letters *or* for /ôr/. As you write, say the sound to yourself: /ôr/. Now say the sound aloud.

Write *sport*.

4 Model When the letter *o* is followed by *r*, the *o* has an *r*-controlled sound: /ôr/. This is how I blend this word: /s/ /p/ /ôr/ /t/, *sport*. Now you try it: /s/ /p/ /ôr/ /t/, *sport*.

Write *thorn*.

You can also blend using bigger chunks of a word. This is how I blend this word: /th/ /ôrn/, *thorn*. Now you try it: /th/ /ôrn/, *thorn*.

Write *store*.

Repeat with *store*. Point out that *ore* also stands for /ôr/. Explain that when *o* is followed by *r* and then silent *e*, the *o* is not long. It is affected by the *r*.

> s p o r t   t h o r n   s t o r e

CORRECTIVE FEEDBACK

Write each practice word. Monitor student practice.

5 Group Practice Let's try the same thing with these words. Give feedback, using the *if . . . then* statements on Routine Card 1.

for   bore*   cord   fork   porch   shore*

6 Individual Practice Write the words; have each child blend two of them.

born   form*   sort   more   cork   chore   stork*   forth*

Check understanding of practice words.

*Children need to make sense of words that they segment and blend. If needed, help children with meanings. If something is a *bore*, it is not interesting. It is *boring* or dull. The *shore* is the land at the edge of a sea or lake. When you *form* something, you make it or give it a certain shape. A *stork* is a water bird with long legs. *Forth* means forward.

MORE PRACTICE

Model spelling *r*-controlled *or, ore* words.

Spell and Write What sounds do you hear in *fork*? (/f/ /ôr/ /k/) What is the letter for /f/? Let's all write *f*. Continue with *or*/ôr/ and *k*/k/. Provide practice as time allows. Have children compare their spellings to what you've written.

or   torn   fort   sore   north   storm   score

High-Frequency Words *become, even, front, thought*

To Do	To Say

3 minutes

Teach high-frequency words.

Display *become, even, front,* and *thought*.

Use the Tested Vocabulary Cards. Point to a word. Say and spell it. Have children say and spell the word. Ask children to identify familiar letter-sounds. Have them take turns reading the words.

Lead cumulative review.

Use the Tested Vocabulary Cards to review high-frequency words from previous weeks.

ACTIVITY 3 Read a Passage

Reading "A Nutty Story," pp. 64–69

To Do   **To Say**   *10–15 minutes*

Develop language and concepts.

Scaffold instruction.

See Routine Cards 6 and 7. Display pp. 64–69.

Ask questions and elaborate on answers to develop language.

Key concepts: *crow, shore, clams, crack, shells, street*

Before Reading Have children recall what they learned about smart ideas. Read the title. Do a structured picture walk with children.

pp. 64–65 What animals are sitting on the wires? These black birds are called crows. What are the crows doing? (eating) The crows drop clams on the rocks to crack the shells open and then eat the clams.

pp. 66–67 What kind of place is shown? (a street) The crow brings nuts to the middle of the street. Why might it do this?

pp. 68–69 Where does the crow drop the nuts? (in the street) The next picture shows the crow eating the nuts that have been cracked open. How do you think the nuts' shells were cracked? Yes, cars ran over them. Do you think crows are smart?

Teach story word.

Write *crow.*

You will read this word in the selection. It is *crow.* Have children say the word and spell it. Review its meaning. **Let's read more about crows.**

Guide comprehension.

Monitor independent reading.

See Routine Cards 2 and 3.

During Reading Read the pages in a whisper. Raise your hand if you need help with a word. As you read, ask yourself: What am I learning about crows? What is this mainly about?

pp. 64–67 What did you learn about how crows get food? (They crack shells open to get the food inside.)

pp. 68–69 How did one crow crack open nuts? (by putting the nuts in the street for cars to drive over and crack open) Crows have smart ideas for getting food.

Model summarizing.

Think aloud.

After Reading What did you learn about crows? What was the selection mainly about? Model how to summarize. The first two pages told that crows eat things in shells. They use rocks to open clams. The next pages told how a crow uses cars to help it eat nuts. I put that all together and pick the most important ideas. The selection is mainly about how crows use smart ideas to get food.

MORE PRACTICE

Develop oral vocabulary.

What are some *shrewd* ways crows get food to *consume?* Are clams *prey* for crows? Might crows be *prey* for another animal?

ACTIVITY 4 Write

Response to Literature Shared Writing

To Do   **To Say**   *5 minutes*

Guide shared writing.

Write sentence frames. Read the questions.

How do crows get food? Crows get food by _____.
Why do people think crows are smart? Crows are smart because _____.

Invite children to suggest answers. Discuss and record answers to complete the sentence frames. While writing, model connecting sounds to letters and forming letters. (See pp. 257–259.) Have children read answers aloud as you track print.

Homework   Practice Book, p. 62, Phonics: *r*-Controlled *or, ore*

3

ACTIVITY 1 — Reread for Fluency

Oral Reading "A Nutty Story," pp. 64–66

	To Do	**To Say**	*5–10 minutes*
CORRECTIVE FEEDBACK	Monitor oral reading.	Read pp. 64–66 aloud. Read them three or four times so your reading gets better each time. Give feedback on children's oral reading and use of the blending strategy. See Routine Cards 1 and 4.	
MORE PRACTICE		Instead of rereading just pp. 64–66, have children reread the entire selection three or four times. You may want to have children read along with the AudioText.	

ACTIVITY 2 — Word Work

Phonemic Awareness Add Initial Phonemes

	To Do	**To Say**	*2 minutes*
Scaffold instruction.	Distribute white boards. Write *ark*. Then add *m* to form *mark*. Write *orn*. Then add *w* to form *worn*. Lead children in adding initial phonemes.	**Model** Listen to the sounds in *ark*. Stretch the sounds /ăäärrr/ /k/ as you write *a, r, k*. Repeat. Have children write letters as you write. Now listen as I add /m/ in front of *ark*. Say /mmm/ /ăäärrr/ /k/ as you add *m* to *ark*. Repeat. Have children add *m* as you write. What is the new word? *(mark)* **Teach and Practice** Have children say the sounds with you as you point to *m, ark* (/m/ /ärk/) and blend to say the word. *(mark)* Write *orn*. Now listen to the sounds in *orn*. Say /ôrn/ as you write *o, r, n*. What word do we make when we add /w/ to the front of *orn*? *(worn)* Continue adding initial phonemes to form these words: dark horn far short hard chore	

Fluent Word Reading *r*-Controlled *ar, or, ore*

	To Do	**To Say**	*5–10 minutes*
Use the word-reading routine.	Write *jar*.	**1 Connect** You can read this word because you know that *ar* can stand for /är/. What sound does *ar* stand for in this word? (/är/) Remember, when the only vowel in a word or syllable is followed by *r*, the vowel will be affected by that *r*. What is the word? *(jar)*	*Routine*
Scaffold instruction.	Write *for, more,* and *park*.	**2 Model** When you come to a new word, look at all the letters in the word and think about its vowel sound and its parts. Say the letter-sounds and word parts to yourself, and then read the word. Model reading *for, more,* and *park* in this way. When you come to a new word, what are you going to do?	
	Write each practice word.	**3 Group Practice** Let's read these words. Look at all the letters, think about the vowel sound and word parts, and say the letter-sounds and word parts to yourself. We will read words with *ar, or,* and *ore*. When I point to the word, let's read it together. Allow 2–3 seconds previewing time for each word. yard harm fork charm shore scarf porch stores stormy	
CORRECTIVE FEEDBACK	**MONITOR PROGRESS**	**If . . .** children have difficulty previewing and reading whole words, **then . . .** have them use sound-by-sound blending. **If . . .** children can't read the words fluently at a rate of 1–2 seconds per word, **then . . .** continue practicing the list.	

MORE PRACTICE

Model reading words in sentences.	When I read a sentence, I read each word without stopping between the words. If I come to a word I don't know, I blend it. Then I read the sentence again. Model reading this sentence, stopping to blend *shark: A smart shark swims by the shore.*
Write practice sentences.	Have each child read a sentence. It is not far to the store or the park. The pig was born in a barn on the farm. An army of ants marches forth.

High-Frequency Words *become, even, front, thought*

	To Do	**To Say**	*3 minutes*
Review high-frequency words.	Display *become, even, front,* and *thought*.	Use the Tested Vocabulary Cards. Point to a word. Say and spell it. Have children say and spell the word. Ask children to identify familiar letter-sounds. Have them take turns reading the words.	

ACTIVITY 3 Build Concepts

Oral Vocabulary *brainstorm, brilliant*

	To Do	**To Say**	*5–10 minutes*
Teach oral vocabulary. **Scaffold instruction.**	Display p. 70 of the student book.	Today you will read a story where kids *brainstorm* and come up with a *brilliant* idea.	*Routine*
	Follow the Routine to teach *brainstorm* and *brilliant*.	**1 Introduce, Demonstrate, and Apply** **brainstorm** In this story, two brothers and a sister *brainstorm* how to catch fish without a fishing pole. When you *brainstorm*, you think of many ideas until you come up with one you'll use. Have children say the word. You might *brainstorm* with friends to come up with a solution to a problem. Describe a problem you solved by *brainstorming* different solutions until you found the best one. **brilliant** In this story, the children come up with a *brilliant* idea for catching fish. A *brilliant* idea is a wonderful idea. Have children say the word. An author may write a *brilliant* story. What is a *brilliant* idea you have had?	
	Display the words on the Amazing Words board.	**2 Display the Words** Have children say each word as they look at it. You can find sounds and word parts you know in big words. Read *brain/storm* as you run your hand under the syllables. What word with the sound /ôr/ is part of *brainstorm*? (*storm*) Read *bril/liant* as you run your hand under the syllables. Children can identify *bril* and *nt*/nt/.	
	Monitor understanding.	**3 Use the Words** Ask children to use each word in a sentence. Model a sentence if children need help.	
MORE PRACTICE		Use oral vocabulary to discuss smart ideas. How could *brainstorming* with friends help you come up with a *brilliant* idea?	

Reading "Think Smart!" pp. 70–81

| To Do | To Say | 10 minutes |

Teach main idea.

Scaffold instruction.

Introduce the skill.

Model the skill. Display p. 44.

Today you are going to find the main idea of a story. Remember, the main idea is what the whole story is mostly about. For example, I can find the main idea of the story "Gramps Learns New Things" that we read last week. I think about what happened in the story and decide on the most important idea. Gramps visits Andy. Andy teaches him to use the computer. Now Gramps uses the computer to communicate with Andy and others. What is the story mostly about? The main idea is that Gramps learns to use a computer to communicate. Gramps' visit and Andy's "lesson" are details that tell more about the main idea.

Apply the skill.

Listen to this story. Ty loves riding his new bike. It is red and goes fast. It has a horn too. What is the story's main idea? (Ty loves his new bike.) Name some details. (The bike is red. It's fast. It has a horn.)

Develop language and concepts.

See Routine Card 6. Display pp. 70–81.

Model using key words and concepts.

Key concepts: *shore, brainstorming, plan, note pad, list, form, brim, brilliant, consume*

Monitor children's use of vocabulary.

Before Reading Read the title. Do a structured picture walk.

pp. 70–71 The title of the story is in a drawing of a fish. Where are the kids in the picture? The kids are at the shore near the water.

pp. 72–73 The kids are taking turns talking. They are brainstorming ideas about how to catch fish without a fishing pole.

pp. 74–75 The girl lists ideas in a note pad. Is making a list a good way to form, or make, a plan? Point to the pictures that show what the kids are thinking. Are these smart ideas for catching fish?

pp. 76–77 The boy grabs his sister's hat. He hangs it from a branch. The hat has a big brim. The brim is the edge that sticks out from the bottom of the hat. Point to the hat's brim. Now what will he do?

pp. 78–79 The kids use the hat to catch fish. What a brilliant idea!

pp. 80–81 The kids consume, or eat, the fish they caught.

Now turn to your partner and talk about the pictures, using the same words I did.

Guide comprehension.

Monitor independent reading.

See Routine Cards 2 and 3.

During Reading Read the pages in a whisper. Raise your hand if you need help with a word. As you read, ask yourself: What is the story mostly about? What is the story's main idea?

pp. 70–75 What do the kids decide to do? (try to catch a fish) They will make a list of their ideas for how to catch a fish.

pp. 76–77 What idea will the kids use to try to catch a fish? (put a big hat on a branch) The kids pick the best idea and try it.

pp. 78–81 How did brainstorming ideas help Mark? (The others' ideas helped Mark come up with a smart plan.) What is the story's main idea? (Brainstorming ideas can help you form a smart plan.)

Guide retelling.

Prompt children as they retell the story.

After Reading Have one child retell the story while the others assist. Who are the characters? What happens at the beginning? in the middle? at the end? See Monitor Retelling, p. 246.

Homework   Practice Book, p. 63, Main Idea and Supporting Details

ACTIVITY 1 Reread for Fluency

Paired Reading "Think Smart!" pp. 70–73

	To Do	**To Say**	*5–10 minutes*
CORRECTIVE FEEDBACK	Pair children. Monitor paired reading.	Children read pp. 70–73 orally, switching readers at the end of the first page. Have partners reread; now the other partner begins. For optimal fluency, children should reread three or four times. Give feedback on children's oral reading and use of the blending strategy. See Routine Cards 1 and 4.	
MORE PRACTICE		Instead of rereading just pp. 70–73 orally, have children reread the entire selection three or four times. You may want to have children read along with the AudioText.	

ACTIVITY 2 Word Work

Spiral Review Long *a, e, i, o, u* (CVCe)

	To Do	**To Say**	*5–10 minutes*
Review long a, e, i, o, u (CVCe). **Scaffold instruction.**	Write *cage, Steve, mice, hose,* and *rule.*	You can read these words because you know how to read words with long vowels. Remember, when a vowel is followed by a consonant and silent *e*, the vowel usually stands for its long sound. Point to *cage*. What vowel sound does this word have? (the long *a* sound) You can blend this word using bigger chunks: /k/, /age/, *cage*. What is the word? *(cage)* Repeat with *Steve, mice, hose,* and *rule.*	
	Provide letter tiles *a, c, e, g, i, l, n, o, p, s,* and *u.*	**Build Words** Write *nice*. Can you blend this word? *(nice)* Spell *nice* with letter tiles. Now change the *n* in *nice* to *r*. What is the new word? *(rice)*	
		• Change the *i* in *rice* to *a*. What is the new word? *(race)*	
		• Change the *c* in *race* to *g*. What is the new word? *(rage)*	
		• Change the *ag* in *rage* to *ul*. What is the new word? *(rule)*	
		• Change the *ul* in *rule* to *op*. What is the new word? *(rope)*	
		• Change the *p* in *rope* to *s*. What is the new word? *(rose)*	
CORRECTIVE FEEDBACK	**MONITOR PROGRESS**	**If . . .** children have difficulty reading the words, **then . . .** have them blend the words sound-by-sound.	
MORE PRACTICE	Model reading words in sentences.	When I read a sentence, I read each word without stopping between the words. If I come to a word I don't know, I blend it. Then I read the sentence again. Model reading this sentence, stopping to blend *drove: Eve drove a nice car.*	
	Write practice sentences.	Have each child read a sentence. It was dark when Gene got home. Clark will trade these five huge stones. Jane rode her bike to the sand dunes by the shore.	
Phonological and Phonemic Awareness		Optional practice activities, pp. 280–283	

ACTIVITY 3 Read Together

Choral Reading "I Built a Fabulous Machine," p. 82

	To Do	**To Say**	*10 minutes*
Develop language and concepts.	Display p. 82.	**Before Reading** The title of this poem is "I Built a Fabulous Machine." What do you think *fabulous* means? (Allow children to suggest definitions.) If something is *fabulous,* it is wonderful and exciting.	
Model fluent reading.	Model prosody.	Read the title of the poem again. Have children predict what it is about. Poems often have a rhythm, or strong beat, that helps you as you read. Listen as I read this poem. Read the poem with an appropriate rhythm, tapping a soft beat as you read. Read it a second time, having children point to each word. Remind children what rhymes are and have them identify rhyming words.	
	Build fluency through choral reading.	**Choral Reading** Now read the poem aloud with me. Try to read with the same rhythm as I do. Reread the poem several times with children.	
Develop concepts.	Monitor listening comprehension.	**After Reading** What does the fabulous machine do? Does it work fast or slowly? Why does the speaker ask if anybody has seen the cat?	

ACTIVITY 4 Build Concepts

Oral Vocabulary *brainstorm, brilliant, consume, prey, shrewd*

	To Do	**To Say**	*5–10 minutes*
Review oral vocabulary.	Read the words on the Amazing Words board.	**Focus on Letter-Sounds** Remember, you can find sounds you know in big words. • Which word begins with *pr?* with *shr?* Which words begin with *br?* • Which word has a silent *e* at the end? What long vowel sound do you hear in that word? • Which word is made by putting two words together?	
	Encourage discussion.	**Provide Multiple Contexts** Review the meanings of the words. Then ask questions to place the words in diverse contexts. • How might *brainstorming* help an inventor create a *brilliant* invention? Do you think good inventors are *shrewd?* Why or why not? • Suppose a worm and a bird are in a field. Which animal is the hunter? Which is the *prey?* Can a hunter ever become *prey?* • If you are hungry, would you *consume* a snack quickly or slowly?	
MORE PRACTICE	Apply oral vocabulary to new situations.	• If you *consume* a big bowl of spaghetti, do you throw it away or eat it all up? (eat it all up) • If you think a poem is *brilliant,* do you like it or dislike it? (like it) • If you *brainstorm* to solve a problem, do you think of no solutions or many possible solutions? (many possible solutions) • If a character in a story is *shrewd,* does the character do something that is clever or boring? (clever)	

ACTIVITY 5 Write

Response to Literature Interactive Writing

	To Do	To Say	5–10 minutes

Generate ideas.

To Do: Review the story "Think Smart!"

To Say: **What did the kids want to do? How did they come up with the idea of using a hat for a net?** Discuss how the kids thought up many ideas to help them get the idea they ended up using to catch fish.

Share the pen.

To Do: Have children participate in writing a list of ideas for a class art project about the shore.

To Say: Write the heading *Ideas for a Class Art Project.* Then write *We should* _____. Have children read the words you wrote. Then have them supply endings for the sentence. Invite individuals to write familiar letter-sounds, word parts, and high-frequency words. Have them find the spelling of high-frequency words on the Word Wall. Ask questions such as:

- **What is the first sound in** *shore?* (/sh/) **What are the letters for /sh/?** *(sh)*
- **What is the last sound in** *shore?* (/ôr/) **What three letters can stand for /ôr/ at the end of a word?** *(ore)*

To Do: Writing elements: conventions

To Say: Frequently reread what has been written while tracking the print. Point out that each sentence starts with a capital letter and ends with a period. Point out the extra space between words and between sentences.

Read the completed list aloud, having children read with you. (For example: *We should draw birds at the shore. We should make nets from hats. We should put sand in a box with shells. We should use branches to make fishing poles.*)

MORE PRACTICE

To Do: Prompt independent writing.

To Say: **Journal Writing** Tell about an idea you have had.

Homework Practice Book, p. 64, High-Frequency Words

ACTIVITY 1 | Assessment Options

Sentence Reading

	To Do	**To Say**	*5 minutes*
Assess sentence reading.	Use reproducible p. 251.	Have each child read the sentences. Record scores on the Sentence Reading Chart, p. 254. Work with one child as others complete Write Sentences below.	

I thought Norm put the jars on the front porch.
Barb likes corn, but she likes rice even more.
The stars shine when it becomes dark.

CORRECTIVE FEEDBACK	**MONITOR PROGRESS**	**If . . .** children have trouble reading words with *r*-controlled *ar, or,* or *ore,* **then . . .** reteach the blending strategy lessons on pp. 196 and 200.	
		If . . . children cannot read a high-frequency word, **then . . .** mark the missed word or words on a high-frequency word list and send the list home for additional practice or have them practice with a fluent reader.	
		If . . . children misread a word in the sentence, **then . . .** correct the error and have them reread the word and then the sentence.	
Practice sentence writing.	Provide white boards.	**Write Sentences** Have children copy the sentences from reproducible p. 251 on white boards. Have them confirm spellings by comparing the words they wrote to the words in the sentences.	
	Phonological and Phonemic Awareness	Optional practice activities, pp. 280–283	

Mid-Unit Passage Reading

	To Do	**To Say**	*10 minutes*
Assess fluency and compre- hension.	Determine which children to assess. Use Assessment Book, p. 81.	Choose from these options: monitoring fluency (see pp. 244–245) and/or monitoring retelling (see p. 246). Have children read the Unit 3 Mid-Unit Fluency Passage in the Assessment Book. Be sure each child is assessed every other week.	

ACTIVITY 2 | Use Concepts

Oral Vocabulary *brainstorm, brilliant, consume, prey, shrewd*

	To Do	**To Say**	*5 minutes*
Check understand- ing of oral vocabulary.	Use the Amazing Words to wrap up the week's concept. Monitor understanding of oral vocabulary, using Routine Card 5.	As time allows, ask questions such as these. • Describe the pictures on pp. 56–63 using some of the week's Amazing Words. • Name a real person you know or have read about who you think is *shrewd.* Why is that person *shrewd?* • Describe a *brilliant* movie. Why do you think it is *brilliant?* • When is a good time to *brainstorm* ideas? • What is the best food you have ever *consumed?* • Name an animal that is the *prey* of another animal.	
Preview next week's concept.		Next week you will read about creative ways to solve problems.	

ACTIVITY 3 Read to Connect

Reread "What a Smart Idea!" pp. 56–63

To Do	To Say	10 minutes

Monitor comprehension: main idea.

To Do: Have children reread "What a Smart Idea!" silently.

To Say: As you read, think about what the selection is mostly about and figure out its main idea. After rereading, ask:

- **What is the selection's main idea?** (Animals and people use creative ideas to get food.)
- **What are some details that tell more about the main idea?** (A spider hides its trap to catch prey; a chimp uses a stick to catch bugs; the man uses a net to catch fish; the girl uses a long stick to get apples.)
- **Why are these creative ideas good?** Record children's answers in a list on a board. (For example: they get the job done well, are not hard to do, and are smart.) Children will use the list for Activity 4.

Make connections.

To Do: Have children make connections across texts.

To Say: We also read "A Nutty Story." Find that. **Was dropping nuts on rocks a good plan? Why or why not?** (No, the nuts didn't crack open when they were dropped on rocks.) **What creative idea did the crow use to eat nuts?** Record steps that show how the crow used cars to crack open the nuts. Discuss what makes the crow's plan a good idea and add to the list above.

We also read "Think Smart!" about kids who brainstorm ideas for catching fish. **Were all of their ideas good ones? Why or why not?** Discuss times when creative ideas are bad, and list children's responses next to their ideas about good creative ideas. (For example: bad ideas don't get the job done, are too hard, and are not safe.) **How did writing *all* of their ideas help the kids come up with a good plan?** Add new suggestions to the lists on the board.

What did the selections we read this week show us about creative ideas? What is the big idea? (You can brainstorm many ideas, good and bad, to help you come up with a clever plan.)

ACTIVITY 4 Write

Response to Literature Independent Writing

To Do	To Say	5–10 minutes

Assign descriptive writing.

Guide sentence correction.

To Do: Writing elements: conventions, support

To Say: Today you will write two sentences about what makes a creative idea good or bad. First, describe what makes an idea good. Then describe what makes an idea bad. Encourage children to use words you wrote on the board for Activity 3 as they write.

Have children check their writing by asking themselves these questions.

- Did I use a capital letters and end marks correctly?
- Did I leave extra space between words?
- Did I use describing words?

MORE PRACTICE

Have children share their sentences in groups. Then have group members practice reading and writing each other's sentences.

Homework   Practice Book, p. 65, Writing

Unit 3 Week 4 *Figure It Out*

When can creative ideas solve problems?

Objectives *This week students will...*

Phonemic Awareness
- segment words into syllables and syllables into sounds

Phonics
- blend and read words with syllables VC/CV
- apply knowledge of letter-sounds to decode unknown words when reading
- recognize high-frequency words *easy, follow, knew, usual*

Fluency
- practice fluency with oral rereading

Vocabulary
- build concepts and oral vocabulary: *abundant, assist, baffle, generous, struggle*

Text Comprehension
- read connected text
- identify sequence to improve comprehension
- write in response to literature

Word Work *This week's phonics focus is . . .*

Syllables VC/CV

High-Frequency Words *Tested Vocabulary*

The first appearance of each word in the Student Reader is noted below.

easy   If something is **easy,** it is not hard to do or understand. (p. 87)

follow   When you **follow** someone or something, you go after that person or thing. (p. 88)

knew   I **knew** the answer. (p. 91)

usual   If something is **usual,** it is often seen, or it often happens. (p. 89)

Amazing Words *Oral Vocabulary*

The week's vocabulary is related to the concept of formulating creative ideas.

abundant   more than you need

assist   to help others

baffle   to confuse or bewilder

generous   willing to share

struggle   to try very hard, especially at something you find difficult

Student Reader Unit 3 *This week students will read the following selections.*

Daily Lesson Plan

	ACTIVITIES	MATERIALS
Day 1	**Word Work** Phonemic Awareness: Segment Syllables Phonics: Blend Words with Syllables VC/CV High-Frequency Words *easy, follow, knew, usual* **Build Concepts** *abundant, assist, generous* **Read a Passage** "Figure It Out," pp. 86–91 Comprehension: Use Strategies Reread for Fluency	Student White Boards Tested Vocabulary Cards *Sing with Me Big Book* and Audio CD Student Reader: Unit 3 Routine Cards 1, 2, 3, 4, 6, 7 AudioText Practice Book, p. 66, Syllables VC/CV
Day 2	**Reread for Fluency** **Word Work** Phonemic Awareness: Segment Syllables Phonics: Blend and Sort Words with Syllables VC/CV High-Frequency Words *easy, follow, knew, usual* **Read a Passage** "Justin's Bikes for Kids," pp. 92–99 Comprehension: Use Strategies **Write** Response to Literature: Shared Writing	Student Reader: Unit 3 Student White Boards Tested Vocabulary Cards Routine Cards 1, 2, 3, 4, 6, 7 AudioText
Day 3	**Reread for Fluency** **Word Work** Phonemic Awareness: Segment Syllables Phonics: Fluent Word Reading High-Frequency Words *easy, follow, knew, usual* **Build Concepts** *baffle, struggle* **Read a Passage** "The Huge Turnip," pp. 100–111 Comprehension: Sequence	Student Reader: Unit 3 Student White Boards Tested Vocabulary Cards Routine Cards 1, 2, 3, 4, 6 AudioText Practice Book, p. 67, Sequence
Day 4	**Reread for Fluency** **Word Work** Phonics: Spiral Review Phonological and Phonemic Awareness Activities, pp. 280–283 **Read Together** "Pet Puzzle," p. 112 Comprehension: Listening **Build Concepts** *abundant, assist, baffle, generous, struggle* **Write** Response to Literature: Interactive Writing	Student Reader: Unit 3 Student White Boards Routine Cards 1, 4 AudioText Practice Book, p. 68, High-Frequency Words
Day 5	**Assessment Options** Fluency, Comprehension Sentence Reading; Passage Reading Phonological and Phonemic Awareness Activities, pp. 280–283 **Use Concepts** *abundant, assist, baffle, generous, struggle* **Read to Connect** "Figure It Out," pp. 86–91 Comprehension: Sequence **Write** Response to Literature: Independent Writing	Reproducible p. 251 Sentence Reading Chart, p. 254 Student White Boards Fluency Progress Chart, p. 245 Student Reader: Unit 3 Routine Card 5 Practice Book, p. 69, Writing

See pp. xvi–xvii for how *My Sidewalks* integrates instructional practices for **ELL.**

ACTIVITY 1 Word Work

Phonemic Awareness Segment Words into Syllables, Syllables into Sounds

2 minutes

Scaffold instruction.

To Do	To Say
Distribute white boards. Write *rabbit*. Lead children in segmenting words and syllables.	**Model** Listen to the sounds in *rabbit.* I hear two syllables in *rabbit.* A syllable is a word or part of a word that has one vowel sound. Point to each syllable as you read *rabbit. (rab, bit)* Listen to the sounds in each syllable. Stretch the sounds /rrraaab/ /biiit/ as you write *rab, bit.* Repeat. Have children write the letters as you write.
	Teach and Practice Have children say the sounds in each syllable as you point to the letters. **How many syllables are there?** (two) **What are they?** *(rab, bit)* **What word does** *rab/bit* **make?** *(rabbit)* Continue with these words:
	ten/nis bas/ket mit/ten nap/kin hap/pen in/vite

Blending Strategy Syllables VC/CV

5–10 minutes

Use the blending routine.

Scaffold instruction.

Routine

To Do	To Say
Write *nap* and *kin*.	**1 Connect** You already can read words like these. What are the words? How many syllables does each word have? (one) Today we will learn about words with two syllables.
Write *napkin*.	**2 Model** When you read a word with two consonants in the middle of the word, divide the word between the consonants. I see *p* and *k* together, so I'll divide between them. Draw a line between the letters.
	First I read each syllable. Cover *kin.* This is how I blend this syllable: /n/ /a/ /p/, *nap.* Cover *nap.* This is how I blend this syllable: /k/ /i/ /n/, *kin.* Then I blend the syllables together: *nap, kin, napkin.* When a word has two consonants in the middle, tell children to try a short vowel for the first syllable.
Write *escape*.	Repeat with *escape.* Remind children about the long vowel (CVC*e*) pattern and point out that some words have the stress on the second syllable.

n a p k i n   e s c a p e

To Do	To Say
Write *ribbon*.	**3 Listen and Write** Write *ribbon.* Draw a line between the two consonants in the middle of the word. As you write, say each syllable to yourself: *rib, bon.* Now blend the two syllables and say the word aloud: *ribbon.*

CORRECTIVE FEEDBACK

To Do	To Say
Write each practice word. Monitor student practice.	**4 Group Practice** Let's try reading these words. Give feedback, using the *if . . . then* statements on Routine Card 1.
	kitten pencil button garden plastic mistake
	5 Individual Practice Write the words; have each child blend two of them.
	muffin problem hidden market* insect traffic index* consume*
Check understanding of practice words.	*Children need to make sense of words that they segment and blend. If needed, help children with meanings. A *market* is a place where you can buy food and other things. An *index* is a list of things mentioned in a book. An index is usually at the end of the book. To *consume* means to eat, or to use something up. We learned *consume* last week; it was an Amazing Word in the song we sang.

MORE PRACTICE

To Do	To Say
Model building words with two syllables.	**Build Words** Write pairs of syllables that can be combined to make words. Have children copy the syllables on their white boards and write a word for each pair. Then have them read the words aloud.
	bit + ten hel + met at + tic in + vent car + pet cos + tume rep + tile

High-Frequency Words *easy, follow, knew, usual*

Teach high-frequency words.

To Do	To Say
Display *easy.*	**1 Say, Spell, Write** Use the Tested Vocabulary Cards. Display *easy.* Here are some words that we won't sound out. We'll spell them. This word is *easy:* *e, a, s, y* (point to each letter), *easy.* What is this word? What are the letters in the word? Now you write *easy.*
Point to *s* and *y* in *easy.*	**2 Identify Letter-Sounds** Let's look at the sounds in *easy* that you do know. Point to *s.* What is this letter? *(s)* What is the sound for this letter? *(/z/)* Continue with the long *e* sound for final *y.*
	3 Demonstrate Meaning Tell me a sentence using *easy.* Model a sentence if children need help.
Display *follow, knew,* and *usual.*	Repeat the Routine with *follow, knew,* and *usual.* Children can identify these letter-sounds and word parts: *follow (fol), usual (/l/l/).* Have children write the words in their word banks. Add the words to the Word Wall. Point out that the words they are learning are on p. 113.

Routine

ACTIVITY **2** Build Concepts

Oral Vocabulary *abundant, assist, generous*

Introduce oral vocabulary.

Scaffold instruction.

To Do	To Say
Display p. 14 of *Sing with Me Big Book.* Play audio CD.	This week you will learn how to figure things out. Listen for the Amazing Words *generous, abundant,* and *assist* as I sing this song. Play or sing the song. Then have children sing it with you.
Follow the Routine to teach *abundant, assist,* and *generous.*	**1 Introduce, Demonstrate, and Apply** **abundant** The boy has an *abundant* amount of apples. *Abundant* means more than you need. Have children say *abundant.* When you have an *abundance* of something, you can be *generous* and share what you have with others. What do libraries have an *abundant* amount of? **assist** The song asks, "Is there a way we can *assist* friends?" *Assist* means to help others. Have children say *assist.* How could you *assist* someone crossing the street? If you need *assistance* with your homework, who might help you? **generous** The title of this song is "Generous Friends." *Generous* friends are willing to share. The boy in this picture is *generous* because he shares his apples with the girls. Have children say *generous.* How can you be *generous* to others? What have *generous* people shared with you?
Display the words on the Amazing Words board.	**2 Display the Words** Have children say each word as they look at it. You can find sounds you know in big words. Read *gen/er/ous* as you run your hand under the syllables. What letters are in the first syllable of *generous? (gen)* What sounds do you hear in this syllable? *(/jen/)* Continue for final *s/s/.* For *abundant* and *assist,* children can identify these letter-sounds and word parts: *abundant (bun, d/d/, nt/nt/), assist (sist).*
Monitor understanding.	**3 Use the Words** Ask children to use each word in a sentence. Model a sentence if children need help.

Routine

MORE PRACTICE

Use oral vocabulary to discuss the song. **How can *generous* friends show that they care? How does the boy *assist* his friends? What would be a *generous* thing to do if you had an *abundant* amount of crayons?**

ACTIVITY 3 Read a Passage

Build Background "Figure It Out," pp. 86–91

To Do | **To Say** | *10 minutes*

Develop language and concepts.

See Routine Card 7. Read aloud p. 85 of the student book.

Preview the Week Use the illustration on p. 84 to introduce this week's concept, figuring it out. **How do you feel when you figure out the solution to a puzzle or a problem?** Read aloud the titles and descriptions on p. 85. Ask children what they think each selection will be about.

Scaffold instruction.

See Routine Card 6. Display pp. 86–91.

Ask questions and elaborate on answers to develop language.

Key concepts: *invitations, invite, map, problem, solve, stamps, postage, deliver, stepstool, sink, assist, escape, leash*

Before Reading Read the title aloud. Do a structured picture walk with children.

pp. 86–87 These pictures show a boy's problem and how he solves it. **What is his problem?** (He can't reach the sink.) **How does he solve it?** (He climbs on a stepstool.) The boy uses a stepstool to help him reach the sink. Now he can wash his hands.

p. 88 These kids are making party invitations. When you invite a pal to a party, you ask your pal to join you. **What information should a party invitation have?** (who gives the party, why, date, time, place) **Why would the kids include a map on the invitation?**

p. 89 The kids had a problem. They didn't have any stamps for postage. **How do the kids solve their problem?** (They go to their friends' houses.) The kids deliver the invitations themselves. **What might be another way to solve the problem?** (buy stamps)

pp. 90–91 **What problem does this boy have?** (The big dog is pulling on its leash so hard that it might escape.) **How does the boy's pal assist him?** (He helps hold the leash so the dog can't escape.) The huge dog is strong, but it can't escape, or get away, if both friends hold the leash. Sometimes you need to get help to solve a problem.

Guide comprehension.

Monitor independent reading. Model strategic reading. Use Routine Cards 2 and 3.

During Reading Read each page in a whisper. Raise your hand if you need help with a word. Stop at the end of each page to model asking questions. For example, for p. 86: After I read, I ask myself: What is this page mainly about? I read that the boy can't get to the sink. That is what the page is mainly about: a boy who has a problem. He can't wash his hands because he can't reach the soap.

Summarize.

Use oral vocabulary to develop the concept.

After Reading The kids all have problems to solve. What do they do about their problems? Do the kids have an *abundant* amount of stamps? Is it *generous* to give out party invitations? How does the stepstool *assist* the boy? What kind of *assistance* does the boy with the dog need? Is the pal holding the leash *generous*?

Reread for Fluency "Figure It Out," pp. 86–89

To Do | **To Say** | *5–10 minutes*

CORRECTIVE FEEDBACK

Monitor oral reading.

Read pp. 86–89 aloud. Read them three or four times so your reading gets better each time. Give feedback on children's oral reading and use of the blending strategy. See Routine Cards 1 and 4.

MORE PRACTICE

Instead of rereading just pp. 86–89, have children reread the entire selection three or four times. You may want to have children read along with the AudioText.

Homework

Practice Book, p. 66, Phonics: Syllables VC/CV

ACTIVITY 1 Reread for Fluency

Paired Reading "Figure It Out," pp. 90–91

To Do	To Say	*5–10 minutes*
CORRECTIVE FEEDBACK	Pair children. Monitor paired reading.	Children read pp. 90–91 orally, switching readers at the end of the first page. Have partners reread; now the other partner begins. For optimal fluency, children should reread three or four times. Give feedback on children's oral reading and use of the blending strategy. See Routine Cards 1 and 4.
MORE PRACTICE		Instead of rereading just pp. 90–91, have children reread the entire selection three or four times. You may want to have children read along with the AudioText.

ACTIVITY 2 Word Work

Phonemic Awareness Segment Words into Syllables, Syllables into Sounds

To Do	To Say	*2 minutes*
Scaffold instruction.	Distribute white boards. Write *trombone*.	**Model** A trombone is a musical instrument. Pantomime playing a trombone. Listen to the sounds in *trombone.* Remember, a syllable is a word or part of a word that has one vowel sound. Point to each syllable as you read *trombone. (trom, bone)* Listen to the sounds in each syllable. Stretch the sounds /trrrooommm/ /bōōōnnn/ as you write *trom, bone.* Repeat. This time have children write the letters as you write.
	Lead children in segmenting words and syllables as they write.	**Teach and Practice** Have children say the sounds in each syllable as you point to the letters. **How many syllables are there?** (two) **What are they?** *(trom, bone)* **What word does** *trom/bone* **make?** *(trombone)* Continue the activity with these words:

muf/fin   hor/net   prin/cess   ar/tist   car/ton   in/side

Blend and Sort Words Syllables VC/CV

To Do	To Say	

5–10 minutes

Review blending words with syllables VC/CV.

Write *target*.

Remember, when you read a word like this one, first divide the word into smaller parts. If there are two consonants in the middle, divide the word between them. I see the letters *r* and *g* in the middle of this word. Draw a line between the two letters. Now I read the syllables. Cover *get.* I blend the first syllable: /t/ /är/, *tar.* Cover *tar.* Next I blend the second syllable: /g/ /e/ /t/, *get.* Then I blend the syllables together: *tar, get, target.* Now you try it: *tar, get, target.*

CORRECTIVE FEEDBACK

Write the practice words. Monitor student practice.

Write the words; have each child blend two of them. Give feedback, using the *if . . . then* statements on Routine Card 1.

happen   trumpet*   garlic*   inflate*   splendid*   cactus   dentist   forget

Check understanding of practice words.

*Children need to make sense of words that they segment and blend. If needed, help children with meanings. A *trumpet* is a musical instrument. *Garlic* is part of a plant that is used to flavor foods. When you *inflate* a balloon, you fill it with air. Something *splendid* is magnificent or wonderful.

Create a T-chart. Display headings *One Syllable* and *Two Syllables.*

Distribute white boards.

Sort Words This column is for words that have one syllable. (Point to the column heading *One Syllable.*) This column is for words that have two syllables. (Point to the heading *Two Syllables.*)

List the following words on the board: *chip, chipmunk, tennis, ten, tile, reptile, car, carpet, forgave, gave, pencil, pen, rot, rotten, tadpole, pole, Pete, compete.* Call on children to read each word aloud and decide whether it fits under the heading *One Syllable* or *Two Syllables.* Have children copy words into appropriate columns on their white boards.

One Syllable	Two Syllables
chip	chipmunk
ten	tennis
tile	reptile
car	carpet
gave	forgave
pen	pencil
rot	rotten
pole	tadpole
Pete	compete

MORE PRACTICE

Model reading and sorting one- and two-syllable words.

Sort Words Write the words below. Have children read each word in a whisper and decide if it has one or two syllables. Children can add the words to the T-chart they made above. Model reading and sorting the first word.

basket   blink   advice   space   mistake   scrub   grape   harvest

High-Frequency Words *easy, follow, knew, usual*

To Do	To Say	

3 minutes

Teach high-frequency words.

Display *easy, follow, knew,* and *usual.*

Use the Tested Vocabulary Cards. Point to a word. Say and spell it. Have children say and spell the word. Ask children to identify familiar letter-sounds. Have them take turns reading the words.

Lead cumulative review.

Use the Tested Vocabulary Cards to review high-frequency words from previous weeks.

ACTIVITY **3** Read a Passage

Reading "Justin's Bikes for Kids," pp. 92–99

To Do	To Say	
		10–15 minutes

Develop language and concepts.

Scaffold instruction.

See Routine Cards 6 and 7. Display pp. 92–99.

Ask questions and elaborate on answers to develop language.

Key concepts: *fixing, new, idea, fixed-up, donate, plan, generous*

Before Reading Have children recall what they learned about figuring out solutions to problems. Read the title. Do a structured picture walk.

pp. 92–93 What is the boy doing to this old bike? (fixing it up) Yes, Justin likes to fix up bikes so they are as good as new.

p. 94 Justin fixes another bike and then gets an idea. What might Justin do with the bikes he fixes up?

pp. 95–97 What does Justin do with his bikes? (gives them away) Justin donates his bikes to the kids. These kids don't have parents to take care of them. They don't have bikes. How do you think they feel when they get Justin's bikes? How does Justin feel?

pp. 98–99 People start giving Justin bikes to fix, so he can give more bikes to more kids. How would you describe Justin's plan? Is Justin a generous boy?

Guide comprehension.

Monitor independent reading.

See Routine Cards 2 and 3.

During Reading Read the pages in a whisper. Raise your hand if you need help with a word. As you read, ask yourself: What did I learn about Justin and his bikes? What is this selection mainly about?

pp. 92–95 What did you learn about Justin's bikes? (Justin fixed up a few old bikes and gave them away.) Why did Justin give bikes away? (Justin liked his racing bike better, so he gave the fixed-up bikes to kids who needed them.)

pp. 96–99 What did you learn about Justin's bike plan? (The kids liked Justin's bikes. People gave Justin more bikes to fix up and give away.) Justin's plan made many kids happy and it made Justin happy too.

Model summarizing.

Think aloud.

After Reading What did you learn about Justin's bikes? What was the selection mainly about? Model how to summarize. The first part told how Justin got the idea to fix up old bikes and give them to kids who didn't have bikes. The rest of the pages told more about Justin's plan. People gave him old bikes. He fixed them up and gave them to many kids in many places. I put that all together and pick the most important ideas. The selection is mainly about how Justin came up with a plan to fix up bikes and give them to kids who needed them.

MORE PRACTICE

Develop oral vocabulary.

Does Justin have an *abundant* amount of bikes to fix? Is he *generous* when he gives them away? Does he like to *assist* others?

ACTIVITY **4** Write

Response to Literature Shared Writing

To Do	To Say	
		5 minutes

Guide shared writing.

Write sentence frames. Read the questions.

What does Justin do with old bikes? Justin _____.

What does Justin do with the fixed-up bikes? Justin _____.

Invite children to suggest answers. Discuss and record answers to complete the sentence frames. While writing, model connecting sounds to letters and forming letters. (See pp. 257–259.) Have children read answers aloud as you track print.

3

ACTIVITY 1 Reread for Fluency

Oral Reading "Justin's Bikes for Kids," pp. 92–95

5–10 minutes

	To Do	To Say
CORRECTIVE FEEDBACK	Monitor oral reading.	**Read pp. 92–95 aloud. Read them three or four times so your reading gets better each time. Give feedback on children's oral reading and use of the blending strategy.** See Routine Cards 1 and 4.
MORE PRACTICE		Instead of rereading just pp. 92–95, have children reread the entire selection three or four times. You may want to have children read along with the AudioText.

ACTIVITY 2 Word Work

Phonemic Awareness Segment Words into Syllables, Syllables into Sounds

2 minutes

	To Do	To Say
Scaffold instruction.	Distribute white boards. Write *suppose*.	**Model** Listen to the sounds in *suppose.* Remember, a syllable is a word or part of a word that has one vowel sound. Point to each syllable as you read *suppose. (sup, pose)* Listen to the sounds in each syllable. Stretch the sounds /sssə/ /pōōōzzz/ as you write *sup, pose.* Repeat. This time have children write the letters as you write.
	Lead children in segmenting words and syllables as they write.	**Teach and Practice** Have children say the sounds in each syllable as you point to the letters. **How many syllables are there?** (two) **What are they?** *(sup, pose)* **What word does** *sup/pose* **make?** *(suppose)* Continue the activity with these words:
		in/sect sud/den dis/cuss trac/tor com/bine rep/tile

Fluent Word Reading Syllables VC/CV

5–10 minutes

	To Do	To Say
Use the blending routine.	Write *reptile.*	**1 Connect** You can read this word because you know how to read words that have two consonants in the middle. Remember, first you divide the word between the middle consonants. Then read each syllable. Finally, blend the syllables together. What are the syllables in this word? *(rep, tile)* What is the word? *(reptile)*
Scaffold instruction.	Write *object, piglet,* and *invite.*	**2 Model** When you come to a new word, look at all the letters in the word and think about its vowel sounds and its parts. Say the sounds and word parts to yourself and then read the word. Model reading *object, piglet,* and *invite.*
		3 Group Practice Let's read these words. Look at all the letters, think about the vowel sounds and word parts, and say the letter-sounds to yourself. We will read words with two syllables. When I point to the word, let's read it together. Allow 2–3 seconds previewing time for each word.
		cotton forget problem escape helmet entire cricket inside costume
CORRECTIVE FEEDBACK	**MONITOR PROGRESS**	*If . . .* children have difficulty previewing and reading whole words, *then . . .* have them use sound-by-sound blending. *If . . .* children can't read the words fluently at a rate of 1–2 seconds per word, *then . . .* continue practicing the list.

MORE PRACTICE	Model reading words in sentences.	When I read a sentence, I read each word without stopping between the words. If I come to a word I don't know, I blend it. Then I read the sentence again. Model reading this sentence, stopping to blend *harvest: They will harvest the crops and sell them at the market.*
	Write practice sentences.	Have each child read a sentence. **Put some napkins in the picnic basket.** **We plan to invite Anton and Justin to our party.** **What will happen if rabbits get into the garden?**

High-Frequency Words *easy, follow, knew, usual*

To Do	To Say	*3 minutes*
Review high-frequency words.	Display *easy, follow, knew,* and *usual.*	Use the Tested Vocabulary Cards. Point to a word. Say and spell it. Have children say and spell the word. Ask children to identify familiar letter-sounds. Have them take turns reading the words.

ACTIVITY 3 Build Concepts

Oral Vocabulary *baffle, struggle*

To Do	To Say	*5–10 minutes*

		Routine
Teach oral vocabulary.	Display p. 100 of the student book.	Today you will read about an unusual seed that *baffles* Pops. Pops and the others *struggle* to harvest the plant that grows from the odd seed.
Scaffold instruction.	Follow the Routine to teach *baffle* and *struggle.*	**1 Introduce, Demonstrate, and Apply** **baffle** The strange seed *baffles* Pops because he has never seen one like it before. When you are *baffled* by something, it means you are confused or bewildered by it. Have children say the word. Some puzzles *baffle* me because they are hard to figure out. Is there something that *baffles* you? **struggle** The characters in this story *struggle* to get a huge plant out of the ground. To *struggle* means to try very hard, especially at something you find difficult. Have children say the word. Players *struggle* to beat the opposing team. Someone might have to *struggle* to climb a hill on a windy day. Describe a time you *struggled* to do something.
	Display the words on the Amazing Words board.	**2 Display the Words** Have children say each word as they look at it. You can find sounds you know in big words. Read *baf/fle* as you run your hand under the syllables. What sounds do you hear in the first syllable? (/baf/) Read *strug/gle* as you run your hand under the syllables. Children can identify *strug.*
	Monitor understanding.	**3 Use the Words** Ask children to use each word in a sentence. Model a sentence if children need help.
MORE PRACTICE		Use oral vocabulary to discuss problems farmers may have to figure out. Would it *baffle* a farmer if a plant grew very big or very fast? Why or why not? A farmer might *struggle* to keep out weeds or bugs that hurt the crops. What other ways might a farmer *struggle?* When you feel *baffled* by something, do you *struggle* to figure out a solution?

ACTIVITY 4 Read a Passage

Reading "The Huge Turnip," pp. 100–111

	To Do	To Say	10 minutes

Teach sequence.

Scaffold instruction.

Introduce the skill.

Model the skill.

Today you will keep track of a story's sequence, the order in which things happen. As you read, think about what happens first, second, next, and last. For example, last week we read "Think Smart!" First, the kids brainstorm ideas about catching fish. Then Mark says to use Barb's hat like a net. Next, Barb catches some fish in her hat. Finally, the kids eat the fish.

Apply the skill.

Think of a story you know, such as "Goldilocks and the Three Bears." What happens first? second? next? last?

Develop language and concepts.

See Routine Card 6. Display pp. 100–111. Model using key words and concepts.

Key concepts: *odd, seed, garden, turnip, harvest, tug, stuck, struggle, problem*

Before Reading Read the title. Do a structured picture walk.

pp. 100–101 Pops finds an odd seed and plants it in his garden. A huge turnip grows from the seed. A turnip is kind of vegetable.

pp. 102–103 Pops and Gram struggle to harvest the huge turnip.

pp. 104–105 Pops calls for more help. The boy helps tug. Even the puppy and kitten pull hard, but the turnip is stuck in the ground.

pp. 106–107 Pops and the others are tired from their struggle with the turnip. Next, mice come. Do you think the mice can help?

pp. 108–109 What happens next? When everyone pulls together, the turnip pops out. They solved the problem by working together.

Monitor children's use of vocabulary.

pp. 110–111 Pops and Gram use the huge turnip to make all this food.

Now turn to your partner and talk about the pictures, using the same words I did.

Teach story words.

Write *seed* and *turnip*.

You will read these words in the story. They are *seed* and *turnip*. Have children say the words and spell them. Review their meanings.

Guide comprehension.

Monitor independent reading.

See Routine Cards 2 and 3.

During Reading Read the pages in a whisper. Raise your hand if you need help with a word. As you read the story, ask yourself: What happens first? second? next? last?

p. 100 What happens first? (Pops finds a seed and plants it.) **Pops finds a strange seed that baffles him and he plants it.**

p. 101 What happens second? (A plant comes up.) **A huge turnip grows from the seed. Pops decides to harvest the turnip.**

pp. 102–109 What happens next? (The family and pets struggle to pull up the turnip. Then the mice help and the turnip comes up.) **The turnip is stuck. After the mice help, the turnip comes up.**

pp. 110–111 What happens last? (Everyone eats.) **At the end, everyone eats food made from the turnip.**

Guide retelling.

Prompt children as they retell the story.

After Reading Have one child retell the story while the others assist. **What happens first? second? next? last?** See Monitoring Retelling, p. 246.

Homework

Practice Book, p. 67, Sequence

ACTIVITY **1** Reread for Fluency

Paired Reading "The Huge Turnip," pp. 100–102

5–10 minutes

	To Do	To Say
CORRECTIVE FEEDBACK	Pair children. Monitor paired reading.	Children read pp. 100–102 orally, switching readers at the end of the first page. Have partners reread; now the other partner begins. For optimal fluency, children should reread three or four times. Give feedback on children's oral reading and use of the blending strategy. See Routine Cards 1 and 4.
MORE PRACTICE		Instead of rereading just pp. 100–102, have children reread the entire selection three or four times. You may want to have children read along with the AudioText.

ACTIVITY **2** Word Work

Spiral Review Possessive Nouns

5–10 minutes

	To Do	To Say
Use the word-reading routine.	Write *Mom's garden.*	Point to *Mom's.* **You can read this word because you know how to read singular possessive nouns. Remember, the apostrophe and *s* shows that something belongs to one person or thing. What is this word?** *(Mom's)* **What belongs to Mom?** (the garden) **What is the phrase?** *(Mom's garden)*
Scaffold instruction.	Write *kittens' basket.*	Point to *kittens'.* **You can read this word because you know how to read plural possessive nouns. Remember, when a word ends in *s'*, it shows that something belongs to more than one person or thing. What is the word?** (*kittens'*) **What belongs to the kittens?** (a basket) **What is the phrase?** (*kittens' basket*)
	Display headings *Singular Possessive Nouns* and *Plural Possessive Nouns.*	**Sort Words** **This column is for phrases that show something belongs to one person or thing.** (Point to the heading *Singular Possessive Nouns.*) **This column is for phrases that show something belongs to more than one person or thing.** (Point to the heading *Plural Possessive Nouns.*)
	Distribute white boards.	List the phrases shown below in a random order. Call on children to read each phrase aloud and tell whether it goes in the singular or plural column. Have children copy the phrases into appropriate columns on their white boards.

Singular Possessive Nouns	Plural Possessive Nouns
insect's hum	rabbits' noses
reptile's skin	kids' helmets
Carmen's ribbons	cooks' muffins
chipmunk's nuts	classes' pencils
Maxwell's napkin	reptiles' cages

CORRECTIVE FEEDBACK	**MONITOR PROGRESS**	*If . . .* children have difficulty distinguishing singular possessive and plural possessive nouns, *then . . .* review instruction (above and on p. 152) and blend word sound-by-sound, noting apostrophe placement.

For more practice, see next page.

MORE PRACTICE

| Model reading words in sentences. | When I read a sentence, I read each word without stopping between the words. If I come to a word I don't know, I blend it. Then I read the sentence again. Model reading this sentence, stopping to blend *cricket's: The cricket's legs help it make tunes.* |
| Write practice sentences. | Have each child read a sentence.

 Brandon's trumpet is on the carpet.
 All the kids' mittens had red buttons.
 Can you see the hornets' nest up there? |

Phonological and Phonemic Awareness   Optional practice activities, pp. 280–283

ACTIVITY 3 Read Together

Choral Reading "Pet Puzzle," p. 112

10 minutes

	To Do	**To Say**
Develop language and concepts.	Display p. 112.	**Before Reading** What pets are shown on this page? (fish, cat, dog) What do you know about these kinds of pets? (Allow children to share what they know.) Read the title and have children predict what the selection is about. This puzzle gives clues about each person's pet. We will use the clues to figure out which person owns which pet.
Model fluent reading.		I will read each clue carefully to make sure I understand what it means. I will pause after each clue to see how it helps me solve the puzzle. At the end, I will make sure my solution makes sense. Read the first clue. Read it again, having children point to each word. Discuss which pets could not be Ana's and which pet could be Ana's. Read the second clue the same way and have them tell which pet must be Ana's. Follow this procedure for the rest of the clues. Who has a dog? (Ana) Who has a cat? (Lin) Who has a fish? (Tom)
	Build fluency through choral reading.	**Choral Reading** Now read the puzzle aloud with me. This time we won't pause after each clue. Reread the puzzle several times with children.
Develop concepts.	Monitor listening comprehension.	**After Reading** What did you learn about solving puzzles? How did the clues help you solve it?

ACTIVITY 4 Build Concepts

Oral Vocabulary *abundant, assist, baffle, generous, struggle*

5–10 minutes

	To Do	**To Say**
Review oral vocabulary.	Read the words on the Amazing Words board.	**Focus on Letter-Sounds** You can find sounds you know in big words. • Which words begin with the same sound? What letter stands for that sound? • What word begins with /j/? What word begins with /b/? • What word has two *g*'s? What sound do they make in this word?
	Encourage discussion.	**Relate Multiple Words** Review the meanings of the words. Then ask questions that relate two or more of the words in the same context. • If a *generous* person had an *abundant* amount of books, what might the person do with these books? • If someone *struggles* as he carries lots of packages, how could you *assist* him? If a math problem *baffles* your friend, what could you do to *assist*?

MORE PRACTICE

Apply oral vocabulary to new situations.

Have children choose the best synonym for each word and give an explanation for their choice.

- Does *abundant* mean almost the same as *many* or *few?* (many)
- Does *assist* mean almost the same as *hurt* or *help?* (help)
- Does *baffled* mean almost the same as *understood* or *confused?* (confused)
- Does *generous* mean almost the same as *giving* or *selfish?* (giving)
- Does *struggle* mean almost the same as *try hard* or *give up?* (try hard)

ACTIVITY **5** Write

Response to Literature Interactive Writing

| To Do | To Say | 5–10 minutes |

Generate ideas.

Review the story "The Huge Turnip."

What does Pops decide to do with the huge turnip growing in the garden? How does he finally succeed? Discuss how everyone tries to help Pops pull the huge turnip out of the ground.

Share the pen.

Have children participate in writing a list of helpers from the story.

Write these sentence frames: _____ *helps tug.* _____ *help tug.* Have children read the words you wrote. Then have them supply beginnings for each sentence. Invite individuals to write familiar letter-sounds, word parts, and high-frequency words. Have them find the spelling of high-frequency words on the Word Wall. Ask questions such as:

- How do you divide *kitten* into syllables? (Put a line between the two *t*'s.)
- How many syllables does *kitten* have? (two) What are they? *(kit, ten)*
- What word does *kit/ten* make? *(kitten)*

Writing elements: conventions

Frequently reread what has been written while tracking the print. Point out that each sentence starts with a capital letter and ends with a period. Point out the extra space between words. Assist children with subject-verb agreement as needed, reminding them to use the first frame if there is one person or animal that helps and the second frame if there are two or more people or animals that help.

Read the completed list aloud, having children read with you. (For example, *Gram helps tug. The kid helps tug. The puppy and the kitten help tug. The mice help tug.*) You can arrange sentences in sequence and add words such as *First, Next, Then,* and *Last* to the beginning of the sentences.

MORE PRACTICE

Prompt independent writing.

Journal Writing Tell what you would like to grow in a garden.

Homework

Practice Book, p. 68, High-Frequency Words

ACTIVITY 1 | Assessment Options

Sentence Reading

To Do | **To Say** | *5 minutes*

Assess sentence reading.

To Do: Use reproducible p. 251.

To Say: Have each child read the sentences. Record scores on the Sentence Reading Chart, p. 254. Work with one child as others complete Write Sentences below.

When I get home from school, my usual snack is a muffin.
I knew it would be easy to get some turnips at the market.
If you follow all the rules, you will not make a mistake.

CORRECTIVE FEEDBACK

MONITOR PROGRESS

If . . . children have trouble reading words with syllables VC/CV,
then . . . reteach the blending strategy lesson on p. 212.

If . . . children cannot read a high-frequency word,
then . . . mark the missed word or words on a high-frequency word list and send the list home for additional practice or have them practice with a fluent reader.

If . . . children misread a word in the sentence,
then . . . correct the error and have them reread the word and then the sentence.

Practice sentence writing.

To Do: Provide white boards.

Write Sentences Have children copy the sentences from reproducible p. 251 on white boards. Have them confirm spellings by comparing the words they wrote to the words in the sentences.

Phonological and Phonemic Awareness

Optional practice activities, pp. 280–283

Passage Reading

To Do | **To Say** | *5–10 minutes*

Assess fluency and comprehension.

To Do: Determine which children to assess this week.

To Say: Choose from these options: monitoring fluency (see pp. 244–245) and/or monitoring retelling (see p. 246). Have children reread "The Huge Turnip." Be sure each child is assessed every other week.

If you have time, assess every child.

ACTIVITY 2 | Use Concepts

Oral Vocabulary *abundant, assist, baffle, generous, struggle*

To Do | **To Say** | *5 minutes*

Check understanding of oral vocabulary.

To Do: Use the Amazing Words to wrap up the week's concept.

Monitor understanding of oral vocabulary, using Routine Card 5.

To Say: As time allows, ask questions such as these.

- Tell me about the pictures on pp. 86–91 using some of the week's Amazing Words.
- What is *abundant* in your house? What is a word that is the opposite of *abundant?*
- What are some jobs with which people *assist* you at school?
- If you are good at math, would a math puzzle *baffle* you?
- Explain what someone who is *generous* would be like.
- Think of a sport you like. Describe how players *struggle* to win a game in that sport.

Preview next week's concept.

Next week you will read about where ideas come from.

ACTIVITY 3 # Read to Connect

Reread "Figure It Out," pp. 86–91

To Do	To Say	

10 minutes

Monitor comprehension: sequence.

To Do: Have children reread "Figure It Out" silently.

To Say: **As you read, think about which problems are described first, next, and last. Think about how the kids figure out what to do.** After rereading, ask:

- **Which did you read about first, the kids making invitations or the boy who can't reach the sink?** (the boy who can't reach the sink) **When the boy discovers he can't reach the sink, what does he do next?** (He gets a stepstool.) **What does he do after he gets the stepstool?** (He climbs the step and washes his hands.)
- **What did the kids do after they realized they didn't have any stamps?** (They went to their friends' homes and delivered the invitations themselves.)
- **What was the last problem you read about in the selection?** (the boy who can't hold on to the big dog) **What do the boy and his friend figure out that solves the problem?** (By holding on to the leash together, they can keep the dog from getting away.)
- **What did you learn about figuring out solutions to problems from this selection?** Record children's ideas in a list on the board. (For example: Think smart; come up with a plan; follow your plan; pals can help you solve a problem.) Children will use this list for Activity 4.

Make connections.

To Do: Have children make connections across texts.

To Say: **We also read "Justin's Bikes for Kids." Find that. How does Justin figure out a way to help lots of kids?** Record ideas for what Justin does and how it helps himself and others in a T-chart.

We also read "The Huge Turnip," about a farmer harvesting a giant vegetable. What problem did Pops have? What did he and the others figure out that solved the problem? Record children's responses in a list.

What do all the selections we read this week show us about figuring things out? What is the big idea? (You can figure out solutions to problems by trying hard and getting help from others.)

ACTIVITY 4 # Write

Response to Literature Independent Writing

To Do	To Say	

5–10 minutes

Assign narrative writing.

To Say: **Today you will write about figuring out how to solve a problem. Write a story about someone who solved a problem.** Encourage children to use words you wrote on the board for Activity 3 as they write.

Guide sentence correction.

To Do: Writing elements: conventions, organization

To Say: Have children check their writing by asking themselves these questions.

- **Did I begin each sentence with a capital letter?**
- **Did I use the correct punctuation mark at the end of each sentence?**
- **Did I use the words *first, next,* and *last* to show the correct order?**

MORE PRACTICE

Have children share their sentences with the group. Write them on the board and have children practice reading and writing each other's sentences.

Homework Practice Book, p. 69, Writing

Unit 3 Week 5 *Where Ideas Come From*

Where do creative ideas come from?

Objectives *This week students will...*

Phonemic Awareness
- blend sounds and add initial phonemes in words

Phonics
- blend and read words with contractions *'ll, 'm; r*-controlled *er, ir, ur;* syllable *er*
- apply knowledge of letter-sounds to decode unknown words when reading
- recognize high-frequency words *along, both, color, guess*

Fluency
- practice fluency with oral rereading

Vocabulary
- build concepts and oral vocabulary: *accomplish, excel, inspiration, process, research*

Text Comprehension
- read connected text
- identify sequence to improve comprehension
- write in response to literature

Word Work *This week's phonics focus is . . .*

Contractions *'ll, 'm*   *r*-Controlled *er, ir, ur*   Syllable *er*

High-Frequency Words *Tested Vocabulary*

The first appearance of each word in the Student Reader is noted below.

along   Trees are planted **along** the street. (p. 121)
           We took our dog **along.**
           I get **along** well with him.

both   **Both** houses are pink. (p. 120)
           Both belong to her.

color   A **color** is either red, yellow, blue, or any of these mixed together. (p. 121)

guess   A **guess** is an idea you have when you are not sure of something. (p. 118)

Amazing Words *Oral Vocabulary*

The week's vocabulary is related to the concept of creative ideas and where they come from.

accomplish   to succeed in carrying out or finishing something

excel   to be very good at doing something

inspiration   something that has a strong or good effect on what you feel or do

process   to treat or prepare something by some special method

research   a careful investigation or hunt for facts using books, computers, experiments, and other sources

Student Reader Unit 3 *This week students will read the following selections.*

Daily Lesson Plan

	ACTIVITIES	MATERIALS
Day 1	**Word Work** Phonemic Awareness: Blend Sounds Phonics: Blend Words with Contractions *'ll, 'm* High-Frequency Words *along, both, color, guess* **Build Concepts** *excel, process, research* **Read a Passage** "Where Ideas Come From," pp. 116–121 Comprehension: Use Strategies Reread for Fluency	Student White Boards Tested Vocabulary Cards *Sing with Me Big Book* and Audio CD Student Reader: Unit 3 Routine Cards 1, 2, 3, 4, 6, 7 AudioText Practice Book, p. 70, Contractions *'ll, 'm*
Day 2	**Reread for Fluency** **Word Work** Phonemic Awareness: Add Initial Phonemes Phonics: Blend Words with *r*-Controlled *er, ir, ur;* Syllable *er* High-Frequency Words *along, both, color, guess* **Read a Passage** "Beautiful Ideas," pp. 122–129 Comprehension: Use Strategies **Write** Response to Literature: Shared Writing	Student Reader: Unit 3 Student White Boards Tested Vocabulary Cards Sound-Spelling Card 11 Routine Cards 1, 2, 3, 4, 6, 7 AudioText Practice Book, p. 71, *r*-Controlled *er, ir, ur;* Syllable *-er*
Day 3	**Reread for Fluency** **Word Work** Phonemic Awareness: Add Initial Phonemes Phonics: Fluent Word Reading High-Frequency Words *along, both, color, guess* **Build Concepts** *accomplish, inspiration* **Read a Passage** "Yelp! Help!" pp. 130–141 Comprehension: Sequence	Student Reader: Unit 3 Student White Boards Tested Vocabulary Cards Routine Cards 1, 2, 3, 4, 6 AudioText Practice Book, p. 72, Sequence
Day 4	**Reread for Fluency** **Word Work** Phonics: Spiral Review Phonological and Phonemic Awareness Activities, pp. 280–283 **Read Together** "Meet Scott Gustafson," p. 142 Comprehension: Listening **Build Concepts** *accomplish, excel, inspiration, process, research* **Write** Response to Literature: Interactive Writing	Student Reader: Unit 3 Routine Cards 1, 4 AudioText Student White Boards Practice Book, p. 73, High-Frequency Words
Day 5	**Assessment Options** Fluency, Comprehension Sentence Reading; End-of-Unit Test Phonological and Phonemic Awareness Activities, pp. 280–283 **Use Concepts** *accomplish, excel, inspiration, process, research* **Read to Connect** "Where Ideas Come From," pp. 116–121 Comprehension: Sequence **Write** Response to Literature: Independent Writing	Reproducible p. 251 Sentence Reading Chart, p. 254 Student White Boards Assessment Book, p. 42 Student Reader: Unit 3 Routine Card 5 Practice Book, p. 74, Writing

See pp. xvi–xvii for how *My Sidewalks* integrates instructional practices for ELL.

Word Work

Phonemic Awareness Blend Sounds

2 minutes

	To Do	**To Say**
Scaffold instruction.	Distribute white boards. Write *we'll*.	**Model** This word means the same as "we will." *We'll* read a story later today. Listen to the sounds in *we'll*. Stretch the sounds /www/ /ēēē/ /lll/ as you write *we, 'll*. Repeat. This time have children write the letters as you write. **What is this word?** *(we'll)*
	Lead children in blending sounds as they write.	**Teach and Practice** What smaller word do you see at the beginning of *we'll*? *(we)* Point to *'ll*. What sound do these letters make? *(/l/)* Let's blend these parts together: *we, 'll, we'll*. What is the word? *(we'll)* Continue with these contractions: I'm I'll he'll she'll it'll you'll

Blending Strategy Contractions *'ll, 'm*

5–10 minutes

Routine

	To Do	**To Say**
Use the blending routine. **Scaffold instruction.**	Write *will* and *am*.	**1 Connect** You studied words like these already. What are these words? *(will, am)* Today we will learn how to combine other words with *will* and *am* to make new words.
	Write *you* and *will* beneath *you'll*. Write *I'm* beneath *I am*.	**2 Model** *You'll* is a contraction. Remember, a contraction is a short way of writing two words as one. *You* and *will* make up the contraction *you'll*. We can put the words *you* and *will* together to make the contraction *you'll*. The apostrophe takes the place of the letters *wi* in *will*. This is how I blend this word: *you, 'll, you'll*. The contraction *I'm* is made from the words *I* and *am*. An apostrophe takes the place of the letter *a* in the contraction *I'm*. Point out that these contractions contain words children already know. They say the pronoun first and then blend it with the ending sound /l/ or /m/. y o u 'l l I 'm **3 Listen and Write** Write the word *you*. Write *will* next to it. Now erase the letters *wi* in *will* and put in an apostrophe. As you write, say the contraction to yourself: *you'll*. Now say the word aloud.
CORRECTIVE FEEDBACK	Write each practice word. Monitor student practice.	**4 Group Practice** Let's try reading these contractions and saying the two words that form each one. Give feedback, using the *if . . . then* statements on Routine Card 1. we'll (we will) she'll (she will) I'm (I am) it'll (it will) **5 Individual Practice** Write the words; have each child blend two of them. he'll I'll they'll I'm you'll we'll
MORE PRACTICE	Model building contractions.	**Build Words** Write pairs of words that can be combined to make contractions. Have children copy the pairs on their white boards. With the first word, model erasing a letter and adding an apostrophe. Have children continue the activity, writing a contraction for each pair of words. Then have them read the contractions. I + am (I'm) they + will (they'll) he + will (he'll) you + will (you'll)

High-Frequency Words *along, both, color, guess*

To Do	To Say	3 minutes

Teach high-frequency words.

Display *along*.	**1 Say, Spell, Write** Use the Tested Vocabulary Cards. Display *along*. Here are some words that we won't sound out. We'll spell them. This word is *along: a, l, o, n, g* (point to each letter), *along*. What is this word? What are the letters in the word? Now you write *along*.
Point to *long* in *along*.	**2 Identify Letter-Sounds** You can find sounds and word parts you know in big words. Read *a/long* as you run your hand under the syllables. What word do you see in the second syllable of *along? (long)*
	3 Demonstrate Meaning Tell me a sentence using *along.* Model a sentence if children need help.
Display *both, color,* and *guess*.	Repeat the Routine with *both, color,* and *guess*. Children can identify these letter-sounds: *both* (*b*/b/, *th*/th/), *color* (*c*/k/, *l*/l/), *guess* (*g*/g/, *ss*/s/). Have children write the words in their word banks. Add the words to the Word Wall. Point out that the words they are learning are on p. 143.

Routine

ACTIVITY **2** Build Concepts

Oral Vocabulary *excel, process, research*

To Do	To Say	5–10 minutes

Introduce oral vocabulary.

Scaffold instruction.

Display p. 15 of *Sing with Me Big Book.* Play audio CD.	This week you will learn about where ideas come from. Listen for the Amazing Words *excel, process,* and *research* as I sing this song. Play or sing the song. Then have children sing it with you.
Follow the Routine to teach *excel, process,* and *research*.	**1 Introduce, Demonstrate, and Apply**
	excel The song says to *excel* in new ways to think. When you *excel* in something, you're very good at it. Have children say the word. What do you *excel* in?
	process You can *process* a peanut to make shampoo and other things. When you *process* something, you treat or prepare something by some special method. Have children say the word. We can *process* wood to make paper. What other things can you make by *processing* wood? When we do or make something by following a set of steps, that is also a *process*. An artist might use a certain *process* to paint a picture.
	research With *research,* you can find out what else peanuts can become. *Research* is a careful investigation or hunt for facts using books, computers, experiments, and other sources. Have children say the word. When you write a report, you should do a lot of *research* to make sure the facts you use are true. Where is a good place to look if you want to do *research* on airplanes or dinosaurs?
Display the words on the Amazing Words board.	**2 Display the Words** Have children say each word as they look at it. You can find sounds and word parts you know in big words. Read *proc/ess* as you run your hand under the syllables. Children can identify the letter-sounds *pr*/pr/, *c*/s/, and *ss*/s/. For *excel* and *research,* children can identify these letter-sounds and word parts: *excel* (*ex*/eks/, *cel*/sel/), *research* (*r*/r/, *s*/s, *ch*/ch/).
Monitor understanding.	**3 Use the Words** Ask children to use each word in a sentence. Model a sentence if children need help.

Routine

MORE PRACTICE

Use oral vocabulary to discuss the song. What can be made by *processing* peanuts in different ways? Why would a person who *excels* in *research* be able to find out how to use peanuts to make paper, milk, and ink?

ACTIVITY **3** Read a Passage

Build Background "Where Ideas Come From," pp. 116–121
10 minutes

	To Do	**To Say**
Develop language and concepts.	See Routine Card 7. Read aloud p. 115 of the student book.	**Preview the Week** Use the picture on p. 114 to introduce this week's concept, origins of creative ideas. Where do you go or what do you do to think of creative ideas? Read aloud the titles and descriptions on p. 115. Ask children what they think each selection will be about.
Scaffold instruction.	See Routine Card 6. Display pp. 116–121. Ask questions and elaborate on answers to develop language.	**Before Reading** Read the title aloud. Do a structured picture walk with children.

pp. 116–117 Point to the computer. What do you think the girls are using the computer for? (to find information) They are using the computer to do research on the Internet. What other items might the girls use to do research and get good ideas? (books) The girls can get ideas from doing research on the computer and from books. |
| | Key concepts: *computer, Internet, research, scientist, guess, experiments, painting, artist, statues* | **pp. 118–119** What is the woman looking at? (some kind of liquid in a glass container called a test tube) What do you think this woman's job is? (scientist) The woman is a scientist. What does a scientist do? (Allow children to share what they know about scientists.) A scientist tries to find out why things are the way they are. The scientist makes a guess and conducts experiments, or tests, to find out if the guess is correct. It takes many experiments and much research to get good answers.

pp. 120–121 What are the boy and girl doing? (making a list) They are making a list of party ideas. Friends can help us brainstorm good ideas. This boy is looking at a painting by another artist to get ideas for painting his own picture. Artists need creative ideas to make pictures, statues, and other kinds of art. Let's read to learn more about where ideas come from. |
| **Guide comprehension.** | Monitor independent reading. Model strategic reading. Use Routine Cards 2 and 3. | **During Reading** Read the pages in a whisper. Raise your hand if you need help with a word. Stop at the end of each page to model asking questions. For example, for p. 120: After I read, I ask myself: What did I learn about how we get ideas? I learned that we can trade ideas with a pal and make a list of all our ideas. Then we can try out the best ideas. This page is mostly about how pals can help us come up with smart ideas. |
| **Summarize.** | Use oral vocabulary to develop the concept. | **After Reading** How could you use a computer to *research* an idea? How could making guesses and testing ideas help a scientist find different ways to *process* plants? How can getting some ideas from other artists help you *excel* in painting? |

Reread for Fluency "Where Ideas Come From," p. 117–119
5–10 minutes

	To Do	**To Say**
CORRECTIVE FEEDBACK	Monitor oral reading.	Read pp. 117–119 aloud. Read them three or four times so your reading gets better each time. Give feedback on children's oral reading and use of the blending strategy. See Routine Cards 1 and 4.
MORE PRACTICE		Instead of rereading just pp. 117–119, have children reread the entire selection three or four times. You may want to have children read along with the AudioText.
Homework		Practice Book, p. 70, Phonics: Contractions *'ll, 'm*

ACTIVITY 1 Reread for Fluency

Paired Reading "Where Ideas Come From," pp. 120–121

5–10 minutes

	To Do	**To Say**
CORRECTIVE FEEDBACK	Pair children. Monitor paired reading	Children read pp. 120–121 orally, switching readers at the end of the first page. Have partners reread; now the other partner begins. For optimal fluency, children should reread three or four times. Give feedback on children's oral reading and use of the blending strategy. See Routine Cards 1 and 4.
MORE PRACTICE		Instead of rereading just pp. 120–121, have children reread the entire selection three or four times. You may want to have children read along with the AudioText.

ACTIVITY 2 Word Work

Phonemic Awareness Add Initial Phonemes

2 minutes

	To Do	**To Say**
Scaffold instruction.	Distribute white boards. Write *urn*. Then add *t* to form *turn*. Write *er*. Then add *h* to form *her*. Lead children in adding initial phonemes as they write.	**Model** Listen to the sounds in *urn.* Stretch the sounds /ėėėrrr/ /nnn/ as you write *u, r, n.* Repeat. Have children write letters as you write. Listen as I add /t/ in front of *urn* to make a word. Say /t/ /ėėėrrr/ /nnn/ as you add *t* to *urn.* Repeat. Have children add *t* as you write. What is the word? *(turn)*
		Teach and Practice Have children say the sounds with you as you point to *t, urn* (/t/ /ėrn/) and blend to say the word. *(turn)* Write *er.* Listen to the sound of *er.* Say /ėėėrrr/ as your write *e, r.* What word do we make when we add /h/ to the front of *er?* *(her)* Continue adding initial phonemes to form these words:
		burn stir dirt shirt serve swerve

Blending Strategy *r*-Controlled *er, ir, ur;* Syllable *er*

To Do | **To Say** | *5–10 minutes*

Routine

Use the blending routine.

Write *for* and *far*.

1 Connect You already can read words like these. What are the words? *(for, far)* What do you know about the vowel sounds in *for* and *far?* (Both words have *r*-controlled vowel sounds, /ôr/ and /är/.) Today we'll learn about words with another *r*-controlled vowel sound.

Scaffold instruction.

Display Sound-Spelling Card 11.

2 Use Sound-Spelling Card This is Earth. What sound do you hear at the beginning of *Earth?* (/ėr/) Say it with me: /ėr/. /ėr/ is the *r*-controlled sound you may hear when *e, i,* or *u* is followed by the letter *r.*

3 Listen and Write Write the letters *er* for /ėr/. As you write, say the sound to yourself: /ėr/. Now say the sound aloud. Repeat for *ir* and *ur.* The letters *er, ir,* and *ur* stand for /ėr/.

Write *her*.

4 Model When the letter *e* is followed by *r,* the *e* has an *r*-controlled sound: /ėr/. This is how I blend this word: /h/ /ėr/, *her.* Now you try it: /h/ /ėr/, *her.*

Write *girl, hurt,* and *serve*.

Repeat with *girl, hurt,* and *serve.* Point out that when *e, i,* or *u* are the only vowels in a word or syllable and are followed by *r,* they make the *r*-controlled sound /ėr/. In words like *serve,* the final *e* is silent.

Write *better*.

Sometimes *er* appears at the end of a bigger word. This is how I blend this word: *bet, ter, better.*

h e r   g i r l   h u r t   s e r v e   b e t t e r

CORRECTIVE FEEDBACK

Write each practice word. Monitor student practice.

5 Group Practice Let's try the same thing with these words. Give feedback, using the *if . . . then* statements on Routine Card 1.

fur   enter   first   curl   under   church   verse*

6 Individual Practice Write the words; have each child blend two of them.

sir*   verb*   matter   burst*   shirt   chapter*   curve

Check understanding of practice words.

*Children need to make sense of words that they segment and blend. If needed, help children with meanings. A *verse* is a group of lines in a poem or song. *Sir* is a polite title for a man. *Sir* is also the title for a knight. A *verb* is an action word that tells what someone or something does. Air *bursts* from a balloon when you pop it. A *chapter* is one of the main parts of a book.

MORE PRACTICE

Model sorting *r*-controlled *er, ir, ur* words.

Sort Words Write the headings *er, ir,* and *ur.* Then list these words: *bird, clerk, letter, skirt, turn, third, after, purse, curb.* Model how to sort the first word by its spelling for /ėr/. Then have children copy the words next to appropriate headings on their white boards.

er: clerk, letter, after
ir: bird, skirt, third
ur: turn, purse, curb

High-Frequency Words *along, both, color, guess*

To Do | **To Say** | *3 minutes*

Teach high-frequency words.

Display *along, both, color,* and *guess.*

Use the Tested Vocabulary Cards. Point to a word. Say and spell it. Have children say and spell the word. Ask children to identify familiar letter-sounds. Have them take turns reading the words.

Lead cumulative review.

Use the Tested Vocabulary Cards to review high-frequency words from previous weeks.

ACTIVITY 3 Read a Passage

Reading "Beautiful Ideas," pp. 122–129

To Do	To Say	10–15 minutes

Develop language and concepts.

Scaffold instruction.

See Routine Cards 6 and 7. Display pp. 122–129.

Ask questions and elaborate on answers to develop language.

Key concepts: *painting, artists, inspire, garden, subject*

Introduce proper nouns.

Before Reading Have children recall what they learned about where ideas come from. Read the title. Do a structured picture walk.

pp. 122–123 Who do you see in this painting? (children) What are the children doing? (sitting on the beach) Children inspired this artist to paint pictures of them.

pp. 124–125 What things did this artist paint? (flowers) Where do you think this artist went to get ideas? (gardens)

pp. 126–127 What kind of fruit is shown on p. 127? (watermelon) This artist painted pictures of fruits and vegetables. They were the subjects of his paintings.

pp. 128–129 What does this painting show? (women working in the yard; clothes drying on the line) Where do you think this artist may have gotten her ideas? Let's read to find out more about how artists get ideas.

You will see these artists' names in this selection: Mary Cassatt (kə/ /sät/), Claude Monet (mō/ /nā/), Rufino (rü/ /fē/ /nō) Tamayo (tä/ /mä/ /yō/), and Clementine Hunter.

Guide comprehension.

Monitor independent reading.

Use Routine Cards 2 and 3.

During Reading Read the pages in a whisper. Raise your hand if you need help with a word. As you read, ask yourself: What am I learning about where artists get their ideas? What is this mainly about?

pp. 122–125 What did you learn about how Mary Cassatt and Claude Monet got ideas for their paintings? (Cassatt—kids and moms; Monet—gardens)

pp. 126–129 What did you learn about where Rufino Tamayo and Clementine Hunter got their ideas? (Tamayo—fruit market; Hunter—things around her)

Model summarizing.

Think aloud.

After Reading What did you learn about where artists get ideas? What was the selection mainly about? Model how to summarize. The first two pages tell how Mary Cassatt got ideas from watching children. The next pages tell how Claude Monet got ideas from gardens, how Rufino Tamayo got ideas from fruits and vegetables, and how Clementine Hunter got ideas from things around her, especially things outside. I put that all together and pick the most important idea. The selection is mainly about how artists get ideas from different people, places, and things.

MORE PRACTICE

Develop oral vocabulary.

What kind of *research* did the artists do? Would a different *process* be used for different paintings? What makes an artist *excel* in art?

ACTIVITY 4 Write

Response to Literature Shared Writing

To Do	To Say	5 minutes

Guide shared writing.

Write a sentence frame. Read the question.

Where do artists get ideas? Artists get ideas from _____.

Invite children to suggest answers. Discuss and record answers to complete the sentence frame. While writing, model connecting sounds to letters and forming letters. (See pp. 257–259.) Have children read answers aloud as you track print.

Homework

Practice Book, p. 71, Phonics: *r*-Controlled *er, ir, ur;* Syllable *-er*

ACTIVITY 1 Reread for Fluency

Oral Reading "Beautiful Ideas," pp. 122–125

	To Do	To Say	5–10 minutes
CORRECTIVE FEEDBACK	Monitor oral reading.	**Read pp. 122–125 aloud. Read them three or four times so your reading gets better each time.** Give feedback on children's oral reading and use of the blending strategy. See Routine Cards 1 and 4.	
MORE PRACTICE		Instead of rereading just pp. 122–125, have children reread the entire selection three or four times. You may want to have children read along with the AudioText.	

ACTIVITY 2 Word Work

Phonemic Awareness Add Initial Phonemes

	To Do	To Say	2 minutes
Scaffold instruction.	Distribute white boards. Write *erve.* Then add *s* to form *serve.*	**Model** Listen to the sounds in *erve.* Stretch the sounds /ĕĕĕrrr/ /vvv/ as you write *e, r, v, e.* Repeat. Have children write letters as you write. **I'll add /s/ in front of *erve.*** Say /s/ /ĕĕĕrrr/ /vvv/ as you add *s* to *erve.* Repeat. Have children add *s* as you write. **What is the word?** *(serve)*	
	Lead children in adding initial phonemes as they write.	**Teach and Practice** Have children say the sounds with you as you point to *s, erve.* (/s/ /ĕrv/) Point out that the final *e* is silent. Then blend to say the word. *(serve)* Continue adding initial phonemes to form these words:	
		nerve skirt sir her turn dirt	

Fluent Word Reading Contractions *'ll, 'm; r-*Controlled *er, ir, ur;* Syllable *er*

	To Do	To Say	5–10 minutes
Use the word-reading routine.	Write *she'll.*	**1 Connect** You can read this word because you know how to read contractions. Remember, read the word before the apostrophe and then blend it with the sound after the apostrophe. What two words make this contraction? *(she will)* What is the word? *(she'll)*	*Routine*
Scaffold instruction.	Write *he'll, birth,* and *butter.*	**2 Model** When you come to a new word, look at all the letters in the word and think about their vowel sounds and its parts. Say the sounds and word parts to yourself and then read the word. Model reading *he'll, birth,* and *butter.* When you come to a new word, what are you going to do?	
	Write each practice word.	**3 Group Practice** Let's read these words. Look at all the letters, think about their vowel sounds and parts, and say the letter-sounds to yourself. When I point to a word, let's read it together. Allow 2–3 seconds previewing time for each word.	
		we'll fern stir I'm burns thunder they'll nurses crackers	
CORRECTIVE FEEDBACK	**MONITOR PROGRESS**	*If . . .* children have difficulty previewing and reading whole words, *then . . .* have them use sound-by-sound blending.	
		If . . . children can't read the words fluently at a rate of 1–2 seconds per word, *then . . .* continue practicing the list.	

MORE PRACTICE

| Model reading words in sentences. | When I read a sentence, I read each word without stopping between the words. If I come to a word I don't know, I blend it. Then I read the sentence again. Model reading this sentence, stopping to blend *chirps: I'll take the bird that chirps.* |
| Write practice sentences. | Have each child read a sentence.

He'll park at the curb, not in the dirt.
She'll ask the clerk to find a purse that matches her red skirt.
I'm getting the dirt off my dog's fur so it'll look better. |

High-Frequency Words *along, both, color, guess*

3 minutes

	To Do	**To Say**
Review high-frequency words.	Display *along, both, color,* and *guess.*	Use the Tested Vocabulary Cards. Point to a word. Say and spell it. Have children say and spell the word. Ask children to identify familiar letter-sounds. Have them take turns reading the words.

ACTIVITY **3** Build Concepts

Oral Vocabulary *accomplish, inspiration*

5–10 minutes

	To Do	**To Say**
Teach oral vocabulary.	Display pp. 130–131 of the student book.	Today you will read a story in which an elf gives a boy ideas and *inspiration* to help him *accomplish* tasks. In stories, an elf is a tiny, make-believe person who can often do things real people cannot do. Routine
Scaffold instruction.	Follow the Routine to teach *accomplish* and *inspiration.*	**1 Introduce, Demonstrate, and Apply** **accomplish** In this story, a boy *accomplishes* different things after getting ideas from an elf. When you *accomplish* something, you succeed in carrying it out or finishing it. Have children say the word. Someone might *accomplish* many tasks around the house on a Saturday afternoon, such as washing clothes or mowing the lawn. What have you *accomplished* today? **inspiration** In this story, the elf gives the boy *inspiration* to complete tasks. *Inspiration* is something that has a strong and good effect on what you feel or do. Have children say the word. A writer might get *inspiration* to write a story from something that happened in his or her own life. A child might feel *inspired* to become a firefighter after watching a movie about firefighters. What might give you *inspiration* to read a chapter book?
	Display the words on the Amazing Words board.	**2 Display the Words** Have children say each word as they look at it. You can find sounds and word parts you know in big words. Read *ac/com/plish* as you run your hand under the syllables. Children can identify *com* and *plish.* What word do you hear at the beginning of *inspiration? (in)* Children can also identify *sp/*sp/ and *n/*n/.
	Monitor understanding.	**3 Use the Words** Ask children to use each word in a sentence. Model a sentence if children need help.
MORE PRACTICE		Use oral vocabulary to discuss where ideas come from. What things might give an artist *inspiration* to paint a picture? How could having a good idea help you *accomplish* a writing assignment?

ACTIVITY 4 Read a Passage

Reading "Yelp! Help!" pp. 130–141

	To Do	**To Say**	*10 minutes*

Teach sequence.

Scaffold instruction.

Introduce the skill.

Model the skill.

Today you are going to keep track of a story's sequence. Remember, sequence is the order of events in a story. You will tell what happened first, next, and last. For example, I can tell what we did when we got to class this morning in order from first to last. Describe three things children did at the beginning of class using the terms *first, next,* and *last.*

Apply the skill. Display p. 100.

Let's tell the order of events for the story "The Huge Turnip" that we read last week. Prompt children to describe the sequence of events in order. What happened first in this story? next? after that? last?

Develop language and concepts.

See Routine Card 6. Display pp. 130–141.

Model using key words and concepts.

Key concepts: *elf, curls, tires, pump, pencil*

Before Reading Read the title. Do a structured picture walk.

pp. 130–131 Who does the boy see in the kitchen? The boy is surprised to see an elf with green curls and a funny hat.

pp. 132–133 What does the elf give to the boy? She gives him a recipe to make a lunch with crackers and jam.

pp. 134–135 What is wrong with the boy's bike? Both tires are flat. How does the boy fix both tires? The elf gives him a pump. The boy uses the pump to fill both tires with air.

pp. 136–137 Who is working hard? The boy is thinking hard and writing ideas with a pencil. Who is under the bed? (the elf)

pp. 138–139 What does the elf give the boy? She gives him a notebook. Then the boy works hard to make gifts for his pals.

pp. 140–141 Now the elf is leaving. She has finished giving the boy ideas. Do you think the elf was helpful? Why or why not?

Monitor children's use of vocabulary.

Now turn to your partner and talk about the pictures, using the same words I did.

Guide comprehension.

Monitor independent reading.

Use Routine Cards 2 and 3.

During Reading Read the pages in a whisper. Raise your hand if you need help with a word. As you read, ask yourself: What happens first, next, and last?

pp. 130–133 Who comes to help Curtis? (Yelp) Yelp, the Help Elf, will help Curtis come up with ideas. What does Yelp help Curtis do first? (make lunch)

pp. 134–137 How does Yelp help Curtis fix his bike? (She gives him a pump.) What does she help him do next? (She gives him a pencil with ideas to write his tale.)

pp. 138–141 What does Yelp give Curtis to help with a test? (pages of notes) What is the last thing that Yelp helped Curtis do? (She gives gift ideas.) Yelp comes up with ideas, but Curtis does the hard work.

Guide retelling.

Prompt children as they retell the story.

After Reading Have one child retell the story while the others assist. Who are the characters? What happened at the beginning? in the middle? at the end? See Monitoring Retelling, p. 246.

Homework

Practice Book, p. 72, Sequence

ACTIVITY 1 Reread for Fluency

Paired Reading "Yelp! Help!" pp. 130–133

To Do	To Say	5–10 minutes

CORRECTIVE FEEDBACK

Pair children. Monitor paired reading.

Children read pp. 130–133 orally, switching readers at the end of p. 131. Have partners reread; now the other partner begins. For optimal fluency, children should reread three or four times. Give feedback on children's oral reading and use of the blending strategy. See Routine Cards 1 and 4.

MORE PRACTICE

Instead of rereading just pp. 130–133 orally, have children reread the entire selection three or four times. You may want to have children read along with the AudioText.

ACTIVITY 2 Word Work

Spiral Review r-Controlled Vowels ar, or, ore, er, ir, ur

To Do	To Say	5–10 minutes

Review r-controlled vowels ar, or, ore, er, ir, ur.

Scaffold instruction.

Write *car, corn, more, her, girl,* and *burn.*

You can read these words because you know how to read words with *r*-controlled vowels. Remember, when the only vowel in a word or syllable is followed by an *r*, the vowel will be affected by that *r*. Point to *car*. What vowel sound do you hear in this word? (/är/) What is the word? *(car)* Repeat with *corn, more, her, girl,* and *burn.*

Distribute white boards.

Sort Words Use a chart to sort words by their *r*-controlled vowel sounds. Write these headings: *ar; or, ore;* and *er, ir, ur.* Say the *r*-controlled vowel sound as you point to each pair or group of letters. Then list these words on the board: *art, first, store, hurt, barn, verse, born, harm, shore, garden, stormy, hurry.* Have children copy each word under the appropriate heading. Then have them read the words and identify each vowel sound and the letters that stand for that sound.

ar	or, ore	er, ir, ur
art	store	first
barn	born	hurt
harm	shore	verse
garden	stormy	hurry

CORRECTIVE FEEDBACK

MONITOR PROGRESS

If . . . children have difficulty reading the words,
then . . . have them use sound-by-sound blending.

MORE PRACTICE

Model reading words in sentences.

When I read a sentence, I read each word without stopping between the words. If I come to a word I don't know, I blend it. Then I read the sentence again. Model reading this sentence, stopping to blend *scarf: Kurt wore a hat and scarf.*

Write practice sentences.

Have each child read a sentence.

I'm trying to turn the lid on the jar.
She'll go to the store with her pal Mark.
We'll help the girl pick corn at the farm.

Phonological and Phonemic Awareness

Optional practice activities, pp. 280–283

ACTIVITY **3** Read Together

Choral Reading "Meet Scott Gustafson," p. 142

	To Do	**To Say** 10 minutes
Develop language and concepts.	Display p. 142.	**Before Reading** This selection is an introduction. What do you know about introductions? (Allow children to share what they know.) An introduction is when you tell someone your name and a little bit about yourself.
Model fluent reading.	Model prosody.	Read the title of the selection and the introductory sentence. Have children look at the photograph and predict what the selection is about. In this introduction, the speaker, Scott Gustafson, first tells his name and then tells what his job is. Listen to how I use a conversational tone when I read this introduction. Notice how I read it to sound like he's actually speaking to the reader. Read the introduction. Read it a second time, having children point to each word.
	Build fluency through choral reading.	**Choral Reading** Now read the introduction aloud with me. Try to make your voice sound like mine and pause when I do. Reread the introduction several times with children.
Develop concepts.	Monitor listening comprehension.	**After Reading** What does Scott Gustafson do? Where does he get his ideas? Were you surprised at how he gets some of his ideas?

ACTIVITY **4** Build Concepts

Oral Vocabulary *accomplish, excel, inspiration, process, research*

	To Do	**To Say** 5–10 minutes
Review oral vocabulary.	Read the words on the Amazing Words board.	**Focus on Letter-Sounds** Remember, you can find sounds you know in big words. • Which word begins with *pr?* Which word begins with *in?* • Which word ends with *sh?* Which word ends with *ch?* • In which word does *c* have the sound /k/? In which words does *c* have the sound /s/?
	Encourage discussion.	**Ask for Reasons and Examples** Review the meanings of the words. Then ask questions that require children to give reasons or examples. • What topic would you like to *research?* Why? What could you *accomplish* after you *research* your topic? • Name something that can be *processed*. What can it be made into? • Can an old object or machine be an *inspiration* to an inventor? Why or why not? What else could be an *inspiration?* • If you really like playing soccer, will you work to *excel* in it? Why or why not? Name people who excel in other sports.
MORE PRACTICE	Apply oral vocabulary to new situations.	• If you *accomplish* a task, do you complete it or not? (complete it) • If you *excel* in a subject, are you good or bad at it? (good at it) • When you *process* something, do you throw it out or make it into something else? (make it into something else) • If you *research* a topic, do you forget about it or find out more about it? (find out more about it)

ACTIVITY **5** **Write**

Response to Literature Interactive Writing

To Do   **To Say**

Generate ideas.

Review the story "Yelp! Help!"

Yelp gave Curtis ideas to help him accomplish different tasks. What tasks did Yelp help Curtis accomplish? Discuss the various tasks that Curtis accomplished with Yelp's helpful ideas.

Share the pen.

Have children participate in writing a list of tasks they might complete on any given day.

Write *I can use ideas to ___.* Have children read the words you wrote. Then have them supply endings for the sentence. Invite individuals to write familiar letter-sounds, word parts, and high-frequency words. Have them find the spelling of high-frequency words on the Word Wall. Ask questions such as:

- **What is the first sound in** *snack?* (/s/) **What is the letter for /s/?** *(s)* **What is the second sound in** *snack?* (/n/) **What is the letter for /n/?** *(n)*

- **What is the vowel sound in** *snack?* (/a/) **What is the letter for /a/?** *(a)*

- **What is the last sound in** *snack?* (/k/) **What two letters can stand for /k/ at the end of a word?** *(ck)*

Writing elements: conventions

Frequently reread what has been written while tracking the print. Point out that each sentence starts with a capital letter and ends with a period. Point out the extra space between words.

Read the completed list aloud, having children read with you. (For example, *I can use ideas to make a snack. I can use ideas to write a story. I can use ideas to fix something.*)

MORE PRACTICE

Prompt independent writing.

Journal Writing Tell about a task that you accomplished this week.

Homework   Practice Book, p. 73, High-Frequency Words

ACTIVITY 1 — Assessment Options

Sentence Reading

	To Do	**To Say**	*5 minutes*
Assess sentence reading.	Use reproducible p. 251.	Have each child read the sentences. Record scores on the Sentence Reading Chart, p. 254. Work with one child as others complete Write Sentences below.	

I'm riding along with the farmer and his herd.
I guess he'll sit under the banner with both of those girls.
Which color do you think they'll use first?

CORRECTIVE FEEDBACK	**MONITOR PROGRESS**	*If . . .* children have trouble reading words with the contractions *'ll, 'm; r*-controlled vowels *er, ir, ur;* or syllable *er,* *then . . .* reteach the blending strategy lessons on pp. 228 and 232.
		If . . . children cannot read a high-frequency word, *then . . .* mark the missed words or words on a high-frequency word list and send the list home for additional practice or have them practice with a fluent reader.
		If . . . children misread a word in the sentence, *then . . .* correct the error and have them reread the word and then the sentence.
Practice sentence writing.	Provide white boards.	**Write Sentences** Have children copy the sentences from reproducible p. 251 on white boards. Have them confirm spellings by comparing the words they wrote to the words in the sentences.

Phonological and Phonemic Awareness	Optional practice activities, pp. 280–283

End-of-Unit Test

	To Do	**To Say**	*10 minutes*
Assess fluency and comprehension.	Use Assessment Book, p. 42.	Options for end-of-unit assessment are available in the Assessment Book.	

ACTIVITY 2 — Use Concepts

Oral Vocabulary *accomplish, excel, inspiration, process, research*

	To Do	**To Say**	*5 minutes*
Check understanding of oral vocabulary.	Use the Amazing Words to wrap up the week's concept. Monitor understanding of oral vocabulary, using Routine Card 5.	As time allows, ask questions such as these. • Describe the pictures on pp. 116–121 using some of the week's Amazing Words. • Name a person you know or have read about who *excels* in something. What does that person *excel* in? • What kind of clothing might be *processed* to make it waterproof? • What are some important things that you *accomplished* this week? • What types of things might a scientist *research*? • What might be an *inspiration* for riding a bike instead of taking the school bus?	
Preview next week's concept.		Next week you will read about how familiar things can help us deal with changes.	

ACTIVITY 3 Read to Connect

Reread "Where Ideas Come From," pp. 116–121

5 minutes

	To Do	To Say
Monitor comprehension: sequence.	Have children reread "Where Ideas Come From" silently.	As you read, think about where ideas come from. Keep track of what you read about first, next, and last. After rereading, ask: • What did you read about first? Where can kids get ideas? • Next, you read about scientists. How can making a guess and testing it help someone come up with a good idea? • Who can kids work with to get ideas? • What did you read about last? Where can artists get ideas? Record children's answers to the first and last questions in a list on the board titled "Where Ideas Come From." (For example: Kids get ideas from books and the Internet. Artists get ideas from other artists.) Children will use the list for Activity 4. Then add to the list as you review the selections below.
Make connections.	Have children make connections across texts.	We also read "Beautiful Ideas." Find that. How did the artists in this selection get their ideas? (They got their ideas from kids, gardens, fruits and vegetables, and things around them.) We also read "Yelp! Help!" about a boy who completes tasks with a little help. What lesson about good ideas did Curtis learn from Yelp, the Help Elf? (Getting good ideas is just the start. Then you have to work hard to get things done.) What did all the selections we read this week show us about where ideas come from? What is the big idea? (People get good ideas from many different places.)

ACTIVITY 4 Write

Response to Literature Independent Writing

5–10 minutes

	To Do	To Say
Assign expository writing. **Guide sentence correction.**	Writing elements: conventions, focus, support	Today you will write about where ideas come from. Write where people find ideas. Encourage children to use words you wrote on the board for Activity 3 as they write. Have children check their writing by asking themselves these questions. • Did I end each sentence with a period? • Did I leave an extra space between words and between sentences? • Are all the sentences about my topic? • Did I add details?
MORE PRACTICE		Have children share their sentences with the group. Write their sentences on the board and have children practice reading and writing each other's sentences.
Homework		Practice Book, p. 74, Writing

Resources

Contents

Monitoring Fluency

Ongoing assessment of student reading fluency is one of the most valuable measures we have of children's reading skills. One of the most effective ways to assess fluency is taking timed samples of children's oral reading and measuring the number of words correct per minute (WCPM).

Fluency Goals

Level B End-of-Year Goal = 70–90 WCPM

Target Goals by Unit:

Unit 1 25 to 45 WCPM

Unit 2 34 to 54 WCPM

Unit 3 43 to 63 WCPM

Unit 4 52 to 72 WCPM

Unit 5 61 to 81 WCPM

Unit 6 70 to 90 WCPM

How to Measure Words Correct Per Minute—WCPM

Timed Reading of the Text

Make a copy of the text for yourself and have one for the child. Tell the child: **As you read this aloud, I want you to do your best reading. Read as quickly as you can without making mistakes. That doesn't mean it's a race. Just do your best reading. When I say *begin,* start reading.**

As the child reads, follow along in your copy. Mark words that are read incorrectly. Definitions and examples of these reading errors are given on p. 263.

Incorrect	Correct
• omissions	• self-corrections within 3 seconds
• substitutions	• repeated words
• mispronunciations	
• insertions	

After One Minute

At the end of one minute, draw a line after the last word that was read. Have the student finish reading but don't count any words beyond one minute. Arrive at the words correct per minute—WCPM—by counting the total number of words that the student read correctly in one minute.

Fluency Progress Chart

Copy the chart on the next page. Use it to record each child's progress across the year. Assist children in recording their scores on the chart and setting goals for the future.

Interpreting Results

Fluency goals are estimates, and children will vary considerably in their progress based on many factors. Also, student progress will depend greatly on where they start with respect to WCPM. Level B End-of-Year goals are the same as for children without reading difficulties at the end of Grade 2.

Fluency Progress Chart, Level B

Child's Name _____

	1	2	3*	4	5*	1	1	2	3*	4	5*	1	2	3*	4	5*	1	2	3*	4	5*	1	2	3*	4	5*	1	2	3*	4	5*
100																															
95																															
90																															
85																															
80																															
75																															
70																															
65																															
60																															
55																															
50																															
45																															
40																															
35																															
30																															
25																															
20																															
15																															
10																															
5																															

Unit 1   Unit 2   Unit 3   Unit 4   Unit 5   Unit 6

* = Fluency Assessment Using Unfamiliar Text

Monitoring Retelling

Retelling is a way to monitor and assess comprehension. Through retelling, children show whether they understand story grammar and can follow sequence, grasp main ideas, and draw conclusions about what they read. Help children learn how to retell by giving them many opportunities to retell stories and nonfiction selections. Scaffold their retellings by prompting them to tell more.

How to Do a Retelling

Have the child read quietly. If the child has difficulty with the passage, you may read it aloud.

Tell the child: **Read the story quietly to yourself. When you finish reading, I will ask you to tell me about what you read.**

When the child has finished, or when you have finished reading aloud, ask:

- (For fiction) **What happened in the story?**
- (For nonfiction) **What was the selection mostly about?**

Prompts for Retelling

If a retelling is incomplete, use prompts to encourage the child to tell more.

Narrative Prompts

- **Who is in the story?**
- **Where and when does the story take place?**
- **What happens first?**
- **Then what happens?**
- **What happens at the end?**

Expository Prompts

- **What did you learn about _____?**
- **What are the most important ideas?**

Looking Back

Encourage children to look back in the text to find answers or to confirm their answers.

- **Let's check the book to make sure.**
- **Show me where the book tells you that.**
- **Where can we look in the book to find the answer?**

See Assessment Handbook, pp. 12–13, for scoring rubrics for retelling. Use the rubrics to help children move toward fluent retelling.

Unit 1, Week 1

I always laugh with my pals.
We told Jack to pack a bag.
He can only pick one rock.

Unit 1, Week 2

Ling is afraid Tim will worry.
That fish tank is so big!
I think the bang was a surprise.

Unit 1, Week 3

Tom will learn lots of different tricks at camp.
Did Brent ever get his socks?
I put my hand up before I said the answer.

Unit 1, Week 4

Draw a picture of ten red tents.
Peg tells Fred to wink his left eye.
Who read about the hen and her nest of eggs?

- -

Unit 1, Week 5

They have a pup, but they also want a fish.
Today we rush and get to math class early.
Hunt for shells among the wet rocks.

- -

Unit 2, Week 1

Will eight chests be enough for all this cash?
Which chimp is swinging around the branch?
Mitch is bringing nothing to the boxing match.

REPRODUCIBLE PAGE

Unit 2, Week 2

Ben is planning to build a big hut.
Can you carry these heavy branches?
Lin dropped the jug of water, and it spilled on the rug.

Unit 2, Week 3

My name is on another page.
I enjoy a few games.
We race toward the gate.

Unit 2, Week 4

I piled white rice on my plate.
The moon is shining through the vines.
Mike liked hiking across hills instead of riding on them.

Unit 2, Week 5

Remember not to touch my mother's rose.
Father's fishing pole is close to those stones.
We woke up and Hope drove us to our pals' home.

Unit 3, Week 1

That's a huge house!
Wasn't it your idea to make this machine?
Eve will use red and pink to make a cute sign for these pups.

Unit 3, Week 2

Benny stood against my desk.
Henry flies a kite when the sky is sunny.
Sandy was happy that she found wild bunnies.

REPRODUCIBLE PAGE

Unit 3, Week 3

I thought Norm put the jars on the front porch.
Barb likes corn, but she likes rice even more.
The stars shine when it becomes dark.

Unit 3, Week 4

When I get home from school, my usual snack is a muffin.
I knew it would be easy to get some turnips at the market.
If you follow all the rules, you will not make a mistake.

Unit 3, Week 5

I'm riding along with the farmer and his herd.
I guess he'll sit under the banner with both of those girls.
Which color do you think they'll use first?

Child's Name _____

Unit 1 Sentence Reading Chart

| | Phonics | | High-Frequency Words | | | Reassess |
	Total Words	Words Correct	Total Words	Words Correct	Reteach ✓	Words Correct
Week 1 *Neighborhoods*						
Short *a*	5					
Final *ck*	4					
High-Frequency Words			4			
Week 2 *Outer Space*						
Short *i*	8					
Final *ng*/ng/, *nk*/ngk/	4					
High-Frequency Words			4			
Week 3 *Out in the Woods*						
Short *o*	3					
Consonant Blends	4					
High-Frequency Words			4			
Week 4 *Sand All Around*						
Short *e*	10					
Ending -*s*, Plural -*s*	3					
High-Frequency Words			4			
Week 5 *Who Can We Ask?*						
Short *u*	3					
Digraphs *sh*/sh/, *th*/th/	6					
High-Frequency Words			4			
Unit Scores	50		20			

- **RECORD SCORES** Use this chart to record scores for the Day 5 Sentence Reading Assessment.
- **RETEACH PHONICS SKILLS** If the child is unable to read all the target phonics words, then reteach the phonics skills using the Blending Strategy lessons.

- **PRACTICE HIGH-FREQUENCY WORDS** If the child is unable to read all the target high-frequency words, then provide additional practice for the week's words, using the Tested Vocabulary Cards.
- **REASSESS** Use the same set of sentences or an easier set for reassessment.

Unit 2 Sentence Reading Chart

	Phonics		High-Frequency Words			Reassess
	Total Words	Words Correct	Total Words	Words Correct	Reteach ✓	Words Correct
Week 1 *Danger!*						
ch/ch/, *tch*/ch/, *wh*/hw/	6					
Inflected Ending *-ing*	3					
High-Frequency Words			4			
Week 2 *Team Spirit*						
Inflected Ending *-ed*	2					
Base Words and Endings	3					
High-Frequency Words			4			
Week 3 *Sharing*						
Long *a* (CVCe)	5					
c/s/, *g*/j/	2					
High-Frequency Words			4			
Week 4 *Side by Side*						
Long *i* (CVCe)	9					
Base Words and Endings	5					
High-Frequency Words			4			
Week 5 *Let's Celebrate*						
Long *o* (CVCe)	9					
Possessive Nouns	3					
High-Frequency Words			4			
Unit Scores	47		20			

- **RECORD SCORES** Use this chart to record scores for the Day 5 Sentence Reading Assessment.
- **RETEACH PHONICS SKILLS** If the child is unable to read all the target phonics words, then reteach the phonics skills using the Blending Strategy lessons.
- **PRACTICE HIGH-FREQUENCY WORDS** If the child is unable to read all the target high-frequency words, then provide additional practice for the week's words, using the Tested Vocabulary Cards.
- **REASSESS** Use the same set of sentences or an easier set for reassessment.

Child's Name _____

Unit 3 Sentence Reading Chart

	Phonics		High-Frequency Words			Reassess
	Total Words	Words Correct	Total Words	Words Correct	Reteach ✓	Words Correct
Week 1 *Ideas Become Inventions*						
Long *u*, Long *e* (CVCe)	5					
Contractions *'s* and *n't*	2					
High-Frequency Words			4			
Week 2 *Ways to Communicate*						
Vowel Sounds of *y*	7					
Ending *-es*, Plural *-es*	2					
High-Frequency Words			4			
Week 3 *What a Smart Idea!*						
r-Controlled *ar*	4					
r-Controlled *or, ore*	4					
High-Frequency Words			4			
Week 4 *Figure It Out*						
Syllables VC/CV	4					
High-Frequency Words			4			
Week 5 *Where Ideas Come From*						
Contractions *'ll, 'm*	3					
r-Controlled *er, ir, ur;* Syllable *er*	6					
High-Frequency Words			4			
Unit Scores	37		20			

- **RECORD SCORES** Use this chart to record scores for the Day 5 Sentence Reading Assessment.

- **RETEACH PHONICS SKILLS** If the child is unable to read all the target phonics words, then reteach the phonics skills using the Blending Strategy lessons.

- **PRACTICE HIGH-FREQUENCY WORDS** If the child is unable to read all the target high-frequency words, then provide additional practice for the week's words, using the Tested Vocabulary Cards.

- **REASSESS** Use the same set of sentences or an easier set for reassessment.

Using End-of-Unit Assessment Results

To make instructional decisions at the end of each unit, consider scores for

- Unit Sentence Reading (Day 5 Assessments)
- Unit Test
- Benchmark Reader reading

Record Scores

Several forms are provided for recording children's progress across the year.

- Sentence Reading Charts: Record results of the weekly Day 5 assessments. See pp. 252–254.
- Record Sheet for Unit Tests: Record scores for each Unit Test. See the Assessment Book, p. 16.
- Fluency Progress Chart: Record each child's WCPM across the year. See p. 245.
- Retelling Charts: Record the child's retelling scores for each unit. See the Assessment Book, pp. 12–14.

Questions to Consider

- Has the child's performance met expectations for daily lessons?
- What can the child read alone? What can the child read with supervision?
- Is the child progressing toward grade-level goals?

Evaluate Student Progress

To move into the next unit of *My Sidewalks*, the child should

- score 80% or better on cumulative Unit scores for Sentence Reading for phonics and high-frequency words
- score 80% or better on the Unit Test
- be able to read and retell the end-of-unit Benchmark Reader accurately
- be capable of working in the Level B group based on teacher judgment

---

If . . . the child scores below 80% on the tested phonics words,
then . . . reteach the phonics skills and reassess following the reteaching.

If . . . the child scores below 80% on the tested high-frequency words,
then . . . provide additional practice for the words and reassess.

If . . . the child's scores indicate a specific weakness in one area of literacy, such as fluency or comprehension,
then . . . focus the child's instruction and practice on that area.

If . . . the child has not met the fluency benchmarks for the unit,
then . . . consider that the benchmark WCPM at the high end of a range is more typical of on-level students, and children in intensive intervention may be progressing well even if they are not meeting fluency benchmarks.

The child may be more appropriately placed in *My Sidewalks*, Level A if the child

- scores 60% or lower on Unit Tests
- is struggling to keep up with the Level B group
- is unable to decode the simplest word types

Exiting the MY SiDEWALKS Intervention Program

In Level B of *My Sidewalks,* there are two opportunities for children to exit the program—at midyear and at the end of the year. Many factors govern decisions concerning instruction for individual children. Understandably, guidelines in your school or district regarding adequate yearly progress, in addition to processes such as Individualized Education Plans, will influence each child's placement in or exit from any intervention program.

Midyear Exit Criteria

Has the child scored 80% or above on Unit Tests?

YES   NO ➡ continue in *My Sidewalks*

Is the child able to profit from instruction in the regular classroom?

YES   NO ➡ continue in *My Sidewalks*

Is the child performing successfully in a classroom reading program with or without extra support?

YES   NO ➡ continue in *My Sidewalks*

Check Reading of On-Level Material

- Select the next unread fictional passage from the classroom reading text.
- Briefly discuss the passage and preteach words identified in the program teacher's guide.
- Read aloud the title and the first paragraph.
- Ask the child to reread the first paragraph and to continue reading for three minutes.
- As the child reads, record errors.
- After reading, ask the child to retell what was read.

Determine Accuracy At the end of the reading, count the number of words read and the number of errors. Did the child read with 85% accuracy?

YES   NO ➡ continue in *My Sidewalks*

Determine Comprehension Was the child able to retell effectively?

YES   NO ➡ continue in *My Sidewalks*

Children who can read the classroom text accurately and with comprehension may exit *My Sidewalks.* If you are hesitant to exit the child, follow the Check Reading procedure on more than one occasion. If all data confirm that the child is ready to exit *My Sidewalks,* then exit the child with confidence. If results are mixed, then continue the child in the program.

End-of-Year Exit Criteria

Has the child scored 80% or above on Unit Tests?

YES   NO ➡ continue in *My Sidewalks*

Is the child able to profit from instruction in the regular classroom?

YES   NO ➡ continue in *My Sidewalks*

Is the child performing successfully in a classroom reading program with or without extra support?

YES   NO ➡ continue in *My Sidewalks*

Based on your school or district end-of-year assessment, is the child making adequate yearly progress?

YES   NO ➡ continue in *My Sidewalks*

Children who are making adequate yearly progress on school or district end-of-year assessments may be prepared to exit *My Sidewalks.*

D'Nealian™ Alphabet

a b c d e f g h i
j k l m n o p q r s t
u v w x y z

A B C D E F G
H I J K L M N O
P Q R S T U V
W X Y Z . , ' ?

1 2 3 4 5 6
7 8 9 10

Manuscript Alphabet

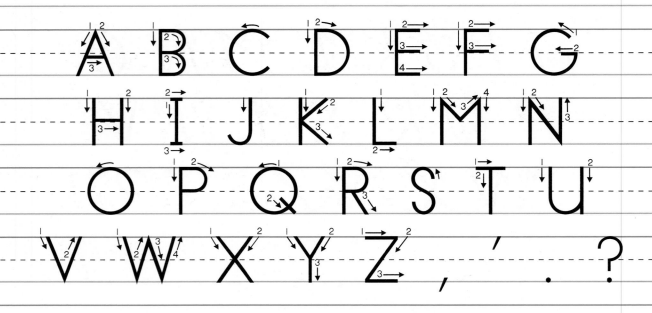

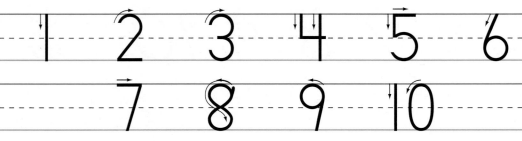

D'Nealian™ Cursive Alphabet

a b c d e f g
h i j k l m n
o p q r s t u
v w x y z

A B C D E F G
H I J K L M N
O P Q R S T U
V W X Y Z . , ' ?

1 2 3 4 5 6
7 8 9 10

Matching Students to Text

Providing children with reading materials they can and want to read is an important step toward developing fluent readers. A fluency test allows you to determine each child's instructional and independent reading level. Information on how to administer a fluency test is provided on pp. 262–263.

Instructional Reading Level

Only approximately 1 in 10 words will be difficult when reading a selection from the Student Reader for children in the *My Sidewalks* intervention program. Children reading at their instructional level need teacher support and will benefit from guided instruction.

Independent Reading Level

Children should read regularly in independent-level texts in which no more than approximately 1 in 20 words is difficult for the reader. Other factors that make a book easy to read include the child's interest in the topic, the amount of text on a page, how well illustrations support meaning, and the complexity and familiarity of the concepts.

Guide children in learning how to self-select books at their independent reading level. As you talk about a book with children, discuss the challenging concepts in it, list new words children find in sampling the book, and ask children about their familiarity with the topic. A blackline master to help children evaluate books for independent reading is provided on p. 261.

Self-Selected/Independent Reading

While oral reading allows you to assess children's reading level and fluency, independent reading is of crucial importance to children's futures as readers and learners. Children need to develop their ability to read independently for increasing amounts of time.

- Specify the amount of time you wish children to read independently each week. During the year, gradually increase the amount of time devoted to independent reading.

- Encourage children to read to a partner, to a stuffed animal, or to a family member.

- Help children track the amount of time they read independently. Tracking will help motivate them to gradually increase their duration and speed. A blackline master for tracking independent reading is provided on p. 261. Check it on a regular basis to monitor progress.

Name _____ Date _____

Choosing a Book to Read by Yourself

These questions can help you pick a book to read.

_____ 1. Is this book about something that I like?

_____ 2. This book may be about a real person, about facts, or a made-up story. Do I like reading this kind of book?

_____ 3. Have I read other things by this author? Do I like the author?

If you say "yes" to question 1, 2, or 3, go on.

_____ 4. Were there fewer than 5 hard words on the first page?

_____ 5. Does the number of words on a page look about right to me?

If you say "yes" to questions 4 and 5, the book is right for you.

Independent Reading

Write the date, the title of the book, and the number of minutes you read.

Date	Title	Minutes

Matching Students to Text

Taking a Fluency Test

A fluency test is an assessment of a child's oral reading accuracy and oral reading fluency. Reading accuracy is based on the number of words read correctly. Reading fluency is based on the reading rate (the number of words correct per minute) and the degree to which a child reads with a "natural flow."

How to Measure Reading Accuracy

1. Choose a text of about 60 to 100 words that is unfamiliar to the child.

2. Make a copy of the text for yourself. Make a copy for the child or have the child read aloud from a book.

3. Give the child the text and have the child read aloud. (You may wish to record the child's reading for later evaluation.)

4. On your copy of the text, mark any miscues or errors the child makes while reading. See the fluency test sample on p. 263, which shows how to identify and mark miscues.

5. Count the total number of words in the text and the total number of errors made by the child. Note: If a child makes the same error more than once, such as mispronouncing the same word multiple times, count it as one error. Self-corrections do not count as actual errors. Use the following formula to calculate the percentage score, or accuracy rate:

$$\frac{\text{Total Number of Words} - \text{Total Number of Errors}}{\text{Total Number of Words}} \times 100 = \text{percentage score}$$

Interpreting the Results

- A child who reads 95–100% of the words correctly is reading at an independent level and may need more challenging text.

- A child who reads 90–94% of the words correctly is reading at an instructional level and will likely benefit from guided instruction.

- A child who reads 89% or fewer of the words correctly is reading at a frustrational level and may benefit most from targeted instruction with lower-level texts and further intervention.

How to Measure Reading Rate (WCPM)

1. Follow Steps 1–3 above.

2. Note the exact times when the child begins and finishes reading.

3. Use the following formula to calculate the number of words correct per minute (WCPM):

$$\frac{\text{Total Number of Words Read Correctly}}{\text{Total Number of Seconds}} \times 60 = \text{words correct per minute}$$

Interpreting the Results

An appropriate reading rate for an on-level second-grader is 90 WCPM.

Matching Students to Text

Fluency Test Sample

Fluency Test Sample

"In that case, can you help ^me^ make my lunch?" Curtis asked.

Yelp clapped her hands (twice). Then she handed Curtis a card filled with notes.

"Crackers with butter and jam," Curtis read. "Yum. Let's try it." But when Curtis turned, he didn't ~~spot~~ ^stop^ Yelp.

After class, both tires on Curtis's bike were flat. "Yelp! Help!" Curtis cried.

Along came Yelp. She clapped her hands twice, /tĭ/ and a pump landed next to Curtis.

Then Curtis pumped up his tires.

Curtis had to admit that Yelp's pump helped.

—From *Yelp! Help!*
My Sidewalks Student Reader, Level B

Miscues

Insertion
The child inserts words or parts of words that are not in the text.

Omission
The child omits words or word parts.

Substitution
The child substitutes words or parts of words for the words in the text.

Hesitation
The child hesitates over a word, and the teacher provides the word. Wait several seconds before telling the child what the word is.

Mispronunciation/Misreading
The child pronounces or reads a word incorrectly.

Self-Correction
The child reads a word incorrectly but then corrects the error. Do not count self-corrections as actual errors. However, noting self-corrections will help you identify words the child finds difficult.

Fluency Test Results ▶	**Reading Accuracy** ▶	**Reading Rate—WCPM**
Total Number of Words: **86** Number of Errors: **5**	$\frac{86-5}{86} = \frac{81}{86} = .9418 = 94\%$	$\frac{81}{64} \times 60 = 75.9 = 76$ words correct per minute
Reading Time: **64 seconds**	Accuracy Percentage Score: **94%**	Reading Rate: **76 WCPM**

Scope and Sequence

Concepts of Print and Print Awareness	Level A	Level B	Level C	Level D	Level E
Develop awareness that print represents spoken language and conveys and preserves meaning	●				
Identify parts of a book and their functions (front cover, title, page numbers)	●				
Understand the concept of letter and word (including constancy of words and word boundaries)	●				
Track print (front to back of book, top to bottom of page, left to right on line, sweep back left for next line)	●				
Match spoken to printed words	●				
Know capital and lowercase letter names and match them	●				
Write capital and lowercase letters	●				

Phonemic Awareness	Level A	Level B	Level C	Level D	Level E
Identify sounds that are the same or different	●				
Identify and isolate initial, final, and medial sounds	●				
Blend sounds orally	●	●			
Segment a word into sounds	●	●			
Add or delete phonemes	●	●			

Phonics	Level A	Level B	Level C	Level D	Level E
Understand and apply the *alphabetic principle* that spoken words are composed of sounds that are represented by letters	●				
Know letter-sound relationships	●	●	●		
Blend sounds of letters to decode					
Consonants	●	●			
Consonant blends	●	●	●		

	1	2	3	4	5
Consonant digraphs	●	●	●		
Vowels					
Short	●	●	●	●	●
Long	●	●	●	●	●
r-Controlled	●	●	●	●	●
Digraphs	●	●	●	●	●
Diphthongs		●	●	●	●
Other vowel patterns	●	●	●	●	●
Phonograms/word families	●	●	●		
Decode words with common word parts					
Base words and inflected endings	●	●	●	●	●
Contractions	●	●	●	●	●
Possessives	●	●			
Compounds	●	●	●	●	●
Suffixes and prefixes		●	●	●	●
Blend syllables to decode words	●	●	●	●	●
VC/CV					
Consonant + *le*	●	●	●	●	●
VC/V and V/CV	●	●	●	●	●
VCCCV			●	●	●
V/V			●	●	●

Spelling					
Use sound-letter knowledge to spell	●	●	●	●	●
Use knowledge of word structure to spell	●	●	●	●	●
Blend multisyllabic words	●	●	●	●	●

Reading Fluency	**Level A**	**Level B**	**Level C**	**Level D**	**Level E**
Read aloud fluently with accuracy, comprehension, and appropriate pace/rate	●	●	●	●	●
Practice fluency in a variety of ways, including choral reading, partner/paired reading, repeated oral reading, tape-assisted reading, and Readers' Theater	●	●	●	●	●
Work toward appropriate fluency goals	40–60 WCPM	70–90 WCPM	100–120 WCPM	110–130 WCPM	120–140 WCPM

Vocabulary (Oral and Written)	**Level A**	**Level B**	**Level C**	**Level D**	**Level E**
Recognize regular and irregular high-frequency words automatically	●	●			
Recognize and understand lesson vocabulary	●	●	●	●	●
Develop vocabulary through direct instruction, concrete experiences, reading, and listening to text read aloud					
Use concept vocabulary	●	●	●	●	●
Use speaking vocabulary	●	●			
Use knowledge of word structure to figure out word meaning		●	●	●	●
Use context clues					
to confirm word identification	●	●	●		
to determine word meaning of multiple-meaning words, homonyms, homographs			●	●	●
to determine word meaning of unfamiliar words			●	●	●
Understand synonyms and antonyms			●	●	●

Text Comprehension	Level A	Level B	Level C	Level D	Level E
Comprehension Strategies					
Preview the text	●	●	●	●	●
Set and monitor purpose for reading	●	●	●	●	●
Activate and use prior knowledge	●	●	●	●	●
Make predictions	●	●	●	●	●
Ask and answer questions	●	●	●	●	●
Look back in text for answers			●	●	●
Recognize story structure: characters, plot, setting	●	●	●	●	●
Summarize text by retelling stories or identifying main ideas	●	●	●	●	●
Use graphic and semantic organizers			●	●	●
Comprehension Skills					
Compare and contrast	●	●	●	●	●
Draw conclusions		●	●	●	●
Main idea and supporting details	●	●	●	●	●
Sequence of events	●	●	●	●	●
Write in response to text	●	●	●	●	●

Unit 1 Word List

The words listed below are read and practiced each week in the *My Sidewalks* Student Readers and/or in practice activities.

Unit 1 Week 1 Neighborhoods

Short a

am	had	pass
an	has	quack
as	hat	rack
at	Jack	ran
back	jam	rap
bad	Jan	rat
bag	jazz	sack
bat	lap	sad
black	mad	sat
cab	man	tack
can	mat	tan
cap	nap	that
cat	pack	van
Dad	pal	wag
fat	pals	Zack
gab	pan	

Final ck

back	pick
black	quack
block	rack
check	Rick
chick	rock
clock	sack
deck	sick
duck	sock
Jack	tack
kick	thick
lick	truck
lock	Zack
luck	
neck	
Nick	
pack	

Sounds Reviewed

b/b/*	r/r/*
c/k/*	s/s/*
d/d/*	s/z/*
e/e/*	t/t/*
f/f/*	u/u/*
g/g/*	v/v/*
h/h/*	w/w/*
i/i/*	z/z/*
j/j/*	th/th/*
k/k/*	ch/ch/*
l/l/*	bl/bl/*
m/m/*	cl/cl/*
n/n/*	
o/o/*	
p/p/*	
qu/kw/*	

High-Frequency Words

always
laugh
only
told

Unit 1 Week 2 Outer Space

Short i

big	Jill	ring
bit	kick	rink
did	kid	rip
dig	king	sick
fig	lick	sing
fish	Ling	sink
fit	lip	sit
fix	lit	thick
give	mink	thing
hill	mix	think
him	pick	tick
his	pig	Tim
hit	pill	wig
in	pin	will
ink	pink	win
is	pit	wing
it	Rick	wink

ng/ng/

bang
gang
hang
king
Ling
lung
rang
ring
sang
sing
song
thing
wing

nk/ngk/

bank
Frank
ink
junk
mink
pink
rink
sank
sink
sunk
tank
thank
think
wink

Sounds Reviewed

a/a/	t/t/*
b/b/*	u/u/*
ck/k/	v/v/*
d/d/*	w/w/*
e/e/*	x/ks/*
f/f/*	th/th/*
g/g/*	sh/sh/*
h/h/*	fr/fr/*
j/j/*	
k/k/*	
l/l/*	
m/m/*	
o/o/*	
p/p/*	
r/r/*	
s/s/*	
s/z/*	

High-Frequency Words

afraid
so
surprise
worry

Selection Words

astronaut
space

Unit 1 Week 3 Out in the Woods

Short o

block	lock	spot
Bob	lots	stomp
box	mom	stop
clock	mop	Tom
cost	nod	top
cot	not	tromp
dock	ox	trot
dot	plop	
drop	pond	
flock	pop	
flop	pot	
fog	rob	
frog	rock	
got	rocks	
hop	shop	
hot	sob	
job	sock	

Consonant Blends

band	green	spot
best	hand	spring
block	land	stamp
brick	lost	stand
camp	mask	stick
clap	plant	stomp
clock	plants	stop
drag	plop	strap
drink	pond	string
drop	print	strip
fast	ramp	swim
flip	rocks	tromp
flock	scrap	trot
flop	shop	twig
frog	snack	twin
grab	splash	wind
grass	split	

Sounds Reviewed

a/a/	s/s/*
b/b/*	s/z/*
c/k/*	t/t/*
ck/k/	u/u/*
d/d/*	v/v/*
e/e/*	w/w/*
f/f/*	x/ks/*
g/g/*	ng/ng/
h/h/*	nk/ngk/
i/i/	
j/j/	
k/k/*	
l/l/*	
m/m/*	
n/n/*	
p/p/*	
r/r/*	

High-Frequency Words

answer
different
ever
learn

*= letter-sounds reviewed from Level A

Unit 1 Word List

Unit 1 Week 4 Sand All Around

Short e

bed	help	sled
beds	helps	slept
beg	hen	smell
bell	hens	smells
bells	jet	spell
belt	left	stem
belts	leg	stems
bends	legs	step
best	let	steps
bet	melts	Ted
blend	men	tell
Clem	mess	tells
Deb	neck	ten
den	nest	tent
dens	nets	tents
desk	next	test
dress	pecks	web
egg	Peg	webs
eggs	pet	well
fed	pets	wet
fell	red	yells
Fred	rest	yes
get	sells	
Greg	set	

Inflected Ending -s

asks	picks
bends	sells
claps	sings
drinks	sips
fills	smells
grabs	sobs
helps	spins
hits	stops
melts	taps
nods	tells
packs	yells
pecks	

Plural -s

bags
beds
bells
belts
crops
dens
eggs
hands
hens
hills
legs
maps
mats
nets
pets
rats
stems
steps
tents
webs

Sounds Reviewed

a/a/	t/t/*	pt/pt/
b/b/*	w/w/*	sk/sk/
c/k/*	y/y/*	sl/sl/
ck/k/	ng/ng/	sm/sm/
d/d/*	nk/ngk/	sp/sp/
f/f/*	cl/kl/	spr/spr/
g/g/*	cr/kr/	st/st/
h/h/*	dr/dr/	
i/i/	fr/fr/	
j/j/*	ft/ft/	
l/l/*	gr/gr/	
m/m/*	lp/lp/	
n/n/*	lt/lt/	
o/o/	mp/mp/	
p/p/*	nd/nd/	
r/r/*	nt/nt/	
s/s/*	pl/pl/	
s/z/*		

High-Frequency Words

draw
eye
picture
read /red/

Selection Words

bird
desert
rain

Unit 1 Week 5 Who Can We Ask?

Short u

brush	jumps	shush
bug	junk	shut
buns	just	slug
bus	luck	slush
club	lump	stuck
crush	lunch	stump
cup	mud	stung
cups	mush	suds
cut	plucks	sun
drums	plus	thud
duck	pup	thump
flush	pups	truck
fun	rugs	tub
grunt	run	up
gum	rush	
hunt	scrub	
hush	shrub	
hut	shrunk	

sh/sh/

brush	shop
cash	shrub
crash	shrunk
crush	shush
dash	shut
dish	slush
fish	splash
flash	trash
flush	wish
fresh	
hush	
mush	
rush	
shed	
shell	
shells	
shin	
ship	

th/th/

bath
math
moth
path
Seth
than
thank
that
them
then
thick
thin
thing
this
thrill
thud
thump
with

Sounds Reviewed

a/a/	s/z/	pl/pl/
b/b/*	t/t/*	scr/scr/
c/k/*	w/w/*	shr/shr/
ck/k/	ch/ch/	sl/sl/
d/d/*	ng/ng/	spl/spl/
e/e/	nk/ngk/	st/st/
f/f/*	th/th/	thr/thr/
g/g/*	sh/sh/	tr/tr/
h/h/*	br/br/	plural -s
i/i/	cl/cl/	-s
j/j/*	cr/cr/	
l/l/*	dr/dr/	
m/m/*	fl/fl/	
n/n/*	fr/fr/	
o/o/	gr/gr/	
p/p/*	mp/mp/	
r/r/*	nt/nt/	
s/s/		

High-Frequency Words

also
among
early
today

Selection Words

coin

Unit 2 Word List

Unit 2 Week 1 Danger!

Consonant Digraphs ch/ch/, tch/ch/, wh/hw/

bench	rich	patch
branch	such	pitch
bunch	which	pitching
check		scratch
chests	catch	scratching
chick	catching	sketching
chimp	crutch	stitch
chin	ditch	
chip	fetch	whacking
Chuck	fetching	when
chunk	hatch	which
crunching	hitching	whip
lunch	itch	whisk
munch	match	Whit
munching	Mitch	whiz

Inflected Ending -ing

asking	stamping
boxing	standing
buzzing	stinging
catching	swinging
crunching	whacking
drilling	yelling
fetching	
helping	
hitching	
lifting	
munching	
pinching	
pitching	
scratching	
sketching	
splashing	

Sounds Reviewed

a/a/	s/s/*	scr/skr/
b/b/*	t/t/*	sk/sk/
c/k/*	u/u/	spl/spl/
ck/k/	w/w/*	st/st/
d/d/*	x/ks/*	plural -s*
e/e/	y/y/*	
f/f/*	z/z/*	
h/h/*	ng/ng/	
i/i/	nk/ngk/	
k/k/*	sh/sh/	
l/l/*		
m/m/*	br/br/	
n/n/*	cr/cr/	
o/o/	dr/dr/	
p/p/*	mp/mp/	
r/r/*	nd/nd/	

High-Frequency Words

around
eight
enough
nothing

Selection Words

danger
fire

Unit 2 Week 2 Team Spirit

Inflected Ending -ed

added	grinned	rubbed
banged	hatched	rushed
batted	helped	scrubbed
bragged	hopped	shopped
chatted	hugged	slipped
checked	hunted	smelled
chipped	jogged	sobbed
clapped	kicked	spilled
dashed	limped	spotted
dragged	melted	stacked
dusted	petted	stepped
ended	pinched	stopped
filled	planned	tripped
fixed	rested	yelled
grabbed	rocked	

Inflected Ending -ing

batting	ripping
chipping	running
clapping	scrubbing
dragging	shopping
dropping	skipping
getting	slipping
grabbing	sobbing
grinning	spinning
helping	spotting
hopping	stopping
hunting	swimming
jumping	tripping
licking	winning
petting	
planning	

Sounds Reviewed

a/a/	p/p/*	dr/dr/
b/b/*	r/r/*	gr/gr/
ck/k/	s/s/*	mp/mp
d/d/*	t/t/*	nd/nd/
e/e/	u/u/	nt/nt/
f/f/*	v/v/*	pl/pl/
g/g/*	w/w/*	sc/sk/
h/h/*	x/ks/*	scr/skr/
i/i/	y/y/*	sk/sk/
j/j/*	ch/ch/	sl/sl/
k/k/*	ng/ng/	sm/sm/
l/l/*	sh/sh/	sp/sp/
m/m/*	tch/tch/	st/st/
n/n/*	br/br/	sw/sw/
o/o/	cl/cl/	tr/tr/

High-Frequency Words

build
carry
heavy
water

Selection Words

team

Unit 2 Week 3 Sharing

Long a (CVCe)

ace	lace	sale
age	lake	same
bake	late	save
cage	made	shade
cake	male	Shane
came	name	shape
cape	pace	space
case	page	stage
date	place	take
Dave	plane	tame
face	plate	tape
game	quake	trace
Grace	race	wade
grade	rage	wage
grapes	safe	wave
Jane	Sage	

c /s/

ace
face
Grace
lace
pace
place
race
space
trace

g /j/

age
cage
page
rage
Sage
stage
wage

Sounds Reviewed

a/a/	v/v/*
b/b/*	w/w/*
c/k/*	sh/sh/
d/d/*	th/th/
f/f/*	bl/bl/
g/g/*	gr/gr/
j/j/*	pl/pl/
k/k/*	pr/pr/
l/l/*	sp/sp/
m/m/*	st/st/
n/n/*	tr/tr/
p/p/*	
qu/kw/*	
r/r/*	
s/s/*	
t/t/*	

High-Frequency Words

another
enjoy
few
toward

Selection Words

share
tree

*= letter-sounds reviewed from Level A

Unit 2 Week 4 Side by Side

Long i (CVCe)

bike	ride
bite	ripe
bride	shine
dime	side
dive	slice
fine	slide
five	slime
hide	smile
kite	stripe
line	tile
miles	time
nice	vine
nine	vines
pine	while
pride	white
prize	wide
prizes	wipe
rice	wise

Inflected Endings -ed, -ing

baked	smiled	riding
biked	spilled	rising
chased	thrilled	shining
chimed	waved	skating
drilled	wiped	slicing
faced	wished	sliding
filled		smiling
fixed	biking	spilling
hiked	chasing	striking
kicked	drilling	thrilling
liked	filling	trading
missed	fixing	wiping
named	hiking	wishing
piled	kicking	
placed	making	
shined	missing	
skated	naming	
sliced	racing	

Sounds Reviewed

a/ā/	v/v/*	thr/thr/
b/b/*	w/w/*	tr/tr/
c/s/	x/ks/*	
ck/k/	z/z/*	plural -s
d/d/*	ch/ch/	
e/e/	ng/ng/	
f/f/*	sh/sh/	
h/h/*	th/th/	
i/i/	wh/hw/	
k/k/*	dr/dr/	
l/l/*	pl/pl/	
m/m/*	pr/pr/	
n/n/*	sk/sk/	
p/p/*	sl/sl/	
r/r/*	sm/sm/	
s/s/*	sp/sp/	
s/z/*	str/str/	
t/t/*		

High-Frequency Words

across
instead
moon
through

Unit 2 Week 5 Let's Celebrate

Long o (CVCe)

choke	pose
close	robe
cone	rode
drove	rope
froze	rose
globe	slope
hole	smoke
home	spoke
hope	stole
hose	stone
joke	stones
jokes	stove
moles	those
nose	throne
note	votes
poke	
pole	

Possessive Nouns

apes'	frogs'
bat's	hen's
bike's	hens'
bride's	hill's
bugs'	kid's
can's	kids'
cat's	king's
cats'	man's
chicks'	Mike's
crab's	moles'
dad's	mom's
dog's	mother's
dogs'	pals'
duck's	pig's
father's	rat's
fire's	snake's
friend's	vets'
frog's	

Sounds Reviewed

a/a/	p/p/*	nd/nd/
a/ā/	r/r/*	sl/sl/
b/b/*	s/s/	sm/sm/
c/k/*	s/z/	sn/sn/
ck/k/	t/t/*	sp/sp/
d/d/*	u/u/	st/st/
e/e/	v/v/*	thr/thr/
f/f/*	z/z/*	plural -s
g/g/*	ch/ch/	-s
h/h/*	th/th/	
i/i/	ng/ng/	
i/ī/	br/br/	
j/j/*	cl/cl/	
k/k/*	cr/cr/	
l/l/*	dr/dr/	
m/m/*	fr/fr/	
n/n/*	gl/gl/	
o/o/		

High-Frequency Words

father
mother
remember
touch

Selection Words

balloon

*= letter-sounds reviewed from Level A

Unit 3 Word List

Unit 3 Week 1 Ideas Become Inventions

Long u (CVCe)	Long e (CVCe)
cube	Eve
cute	Gene
duke	Pete
dune	Steve
flute	theme
huge	these
Luke	Zeke
mule	
prune	
rude	
rule	
tube	
use	

Contractions 's, n't

aren't	that's
can't	there's
couldn't	wasn't
didn't	weren't
don't	what's
hasn't	where's
haven't	
he's	
here's	
isn't	
it's	
let's	
she's	

Sounds Reviewed

a/a/	o/ō/	sh/sh/
b/b/*	p/p/*	wh/hw/
c/k/*	r/r/*	
d/d/*	s/s/*	
e/e/	s/z/	
e/ē/	t/t/*	
g/j/	v/v/*	
i/i/	w/w/*	
k/k/*	z/z/*	
l/l/*	pr/pr/	
m/m/*	st/st/	
n/n/*	th/th/	
o/o/		

High-Frequency Words

house
idea
machine
sign

Selection Words

invention
wheel

Unit 3 Week 2 Ways to Communicate

Vowel Sound of y (/ī/)

by	my
cry	sky
fly	spy
fry	try
shy	why

Vowel Sound of y (/ē/)

Andy	nanny
Benny	puppy
buddy	Sandy
bunny	silly
candy	skinny
fancy	sunny
funny	tummy
happy	

Ending -es, Plural -es

boxes	foxes	tummies
branches	glasses	wishes
buddies	hatches	
bunnies	hobbies	
buses	kisses	
buzzes	lunches	
candies	misses	
catches	nannies	
classes	pennies	
cries	presses	
dishes	puppies	
dries	rushes	
fixes	scratches	
fizzes	switches	
flies	tries	

Sounds Reviewed

a/a/	s/s/*	scr/skr/
b/b/*	s/z/	sk/sk/
c/k/*	t/t/*	sp/sp/
d/d/*	u/u/	sw/sw/
e/e/	w/w/*	tr/tr/
f/f/*	x/ks/*	ch/ch/
h/h/*	z/z/*	ch/tch/
i/i/	br/br/	sh/sh/
k/k/*	cl/kl/	th/th/
l/l/*	cr/kr/	wh/hw/
m/m/*	dr/dr/	-ed
n/n/*	fl/fl/	-es
o/o/	fr/fr/	-ing
p/p/*	gl/gl/	-s
r/r/*	pr/pr/	

High-Frequency Words

against
found
stood
wild

Selection Words

communicate
computer
letter
secret

Unit 3 Week 3 What a Smart Idea!

r-Controlled ar

art	jar
bark	march
barn	mark
car	park
card	scarf
charm	shark
chart	sharp
dark	smart
dart	
far	
farm	
hard	
harm	
harp	

r-Controlled or, ore

bore	north
born	or
chore	porch
cord	score
cork	shore
corn	short
for	sore
fork	sort
form	
fort	
forth	
horn	
more	
Norm	

Sounds Reviewed

a/ā/	o/ō/	rp/rp/
ar/är/	or/ôr/	rt/rt/
b/b/*	p/p/*	sc/sk/
c/k/	r/r/*	sm/sm/
d/d/*	s/s/*	sp/sp/
e/ē/	u/ū/	st/st/
f/f/*	rd/rd/	ch/ch/
h/h/*	rf/rf/	sh/sh/
i/ī/	rk/rk/	th/th/
i/i/*	rm/rm/	
m/m/*	rn/rn/	
n/n/*		

High-Frequency Words

become
even
front
thought

Selection Words

apple
crow
spider

*= letter-sounds reviewed from Level A

Unit 3 Word List

Unit 3 Week 4 Figure It Out

Syllables VC/CV

advice	forget	mittens
attic	garden	muffin
basket	happen	napkin
Brandon	harvest	pencil
button	helmet	plastic
carpet	hidden	problem
chipmunk	hornet	reptile
compete	index	ribbon
consume	insect	rotten
costume	inside	tadpole
cotton	invent	tennis
cricket	invite	traffic
entire	kitten	trumpet
escape	market	
forgave	mistake	

Sounds Reviewed

a/a/	l/l/*	ct/kt/
a/ā/	m/m/*	st/st/
ar/ä/	n/n/*	nt/nt/
b/b/*	o/o/	pl/pl/
c/k/*	o/ō/	pr/pr/
c/s/	or/ôr/	tr/tr/
d/d/*	p/p/*	ch/ch/
e/e/	r/r/*	
e/ē/	s/s/*	-'s
f/f/*	s/z/*	-s'
g/g/*	t/t/*	
h/h/*	u/u/	
i/i/	u/ū/	
i/ī/	br/br/	
k/k/*	cr/cr/	

High-Frequency Words

easy
follow
knew
usual

Selection Words

seed
turnip

Unit 3 Week 5 Where Ideas Come From

Contractions 'll, 'm

he'll
I'll
I'm
it'll
she'll
they'll
we'll
you'll

r-Controlled ir

bird
birth
dirt
first
girl
shirt
sir
skirt
stir
third

r-Controlled ur

burn
burst
church
curb
curl
curve
fur
hurry
hurt
nurses
purse
turn

Syllable er

after
better
butter
chapter
crackers
enter
letter
matter
thunder
under

r-Controlled er

clerk
fern
her
nerve
serve
swerve
verb
verse

Sounds Reviewed

ar/är/	n/n/*	st/st/
a/a/	or/ôr/	sw/sw/
b/b/*	p/p/*	ch/ch/
c/k/*	r/r/*	sh/sh/
ck/k/	s/s/	th/th/
d/d/*	s/z/	
er/ėr/	t/t/*	
e/e/	ur/ėr/	
e/ē/	v/v/	
f/f/*	w/w/*	
g/g/*	y/ē/	
h/h/*	br/br/	
i/ī/	cl/kl/	
ir/ėr/	cr/kr/	
l/l/*	nd/nd/	
m/m/*	sk/sk/	

High-Frequency Words

along
both
color
guess

Unit 4 Word List

Unit 4 Week 1 When Things Change

Sound of *a* in *ball, walk*

all	sidewalk
bald	small
ball	stalk
baseball	stall
call	talk
called	talked
chalk	tall
crosswalk	walk
eyeball	walking
fall	wall
falls	
halls	
halt	
kickball	
mall	
salt	
scald	

Compound Words

anthill	himself	something
backpack	homemade	sunrise
barnyard	homework	sunset
baseball	inside	sunshine
bathtub	kickball	
blackbird	landform	
campfire	laptop	
classmate	lipstick	
classmates	lunchbox	
crosswalk	nickname	
cupcake	pancake	
dishpan	pancakes	
eyeball	pigpen	
fireplace	popcorn	
fishpond	pothole	
flagpole	sandbox	
granddad	sidewalk	

Sounds Reviewed

a/a/	n/n/*	cr/kr/
a/ā/	o/o/	lt/lt/
ar/är/	o/ō/	lf/lf/
b/b/*	or/ôr/	mp/mp/
c/k/*	p/p/*	nd/nd/
c/s/	r/r/*	nt/nt/
ck/k/	s/s/*	sc/sc/
d/d/*	s/z/	sm/sm/
e/e/	t/t/*	st/st/
f/f/*	u/u/	
g/g/*	w/w/*	's
h/h/*	x/ks/*	n't
i/ī/		'll
i/i/	ch/ch/	'm
ir/ėr/*	th/th/	
k/k/*	sh/sh/	plural -s
l/l/*	bl/bl/	-ed
m/m/*	cl/cl/	-ing
		-s

High-Frequency Words

gone
group
move
neighbor
promise

Selection Words

camera
photo

Unit 4 Week 2 From Seed to Plant

Long *a*: *ai, ay*

brain	tail	say
frail	trail	spray
mail	trails	sprays
main	train	stay
nail	trained	stray
paid	waist	sway
pail	wait	tray
pain		way
plains	clay	
rain	day	
rains	gray	
rainy	hay	
sail	jay	
sails	lay	
snail	may	
strain	pay	
strained	play	

Long *e*: *e, ee, ea*

be	seem	meal
he	sheep	neat
me	sleep	peach
she	street	reach
we	sunscreen	real
	sweet	scream
cheek	teeth	seal
deep	tree	seat
feel	wheel	sneaky
green		squeal
jeep	beach	steal
keep	beans	stream
need	beat	teach
needs	dream	treat
queen	feast	
see	Jean	
seeds	leaf	

Sounds Reviewed

b/b/*	y/ī/	str/str/
d/d/*	ch/ch/	sw/sw/
e/e/*	sh/sh/	tr/tr/
f/f/*	th/th/	
h/h/*	wh/hw/	plural -s
j/j/*	br/br/	-ed
k/k/*	cl/kl/	-s
l/l/*	dr/dr/	
m/m/*	fr/fr/	
n/n/	gr/gr/	
p/p/*	pl/pl/	
r/r/*	scr/skr/	
s/s/*	sl/sl/	
s/z/*	sn/sn/	
t/t/*	spr/spr/	
u/u/	squ/skw/	
w/w/*	st/st/	
y/ē/		

High-Frequency Words

above
almost
change
often
straight

Unit 4 Week 3 Animals

Endings *-er, -est*

bigger	slower	messiest
bumpier	smaller	muddiest
cleaner	stronger	rainiest
colder	sunnier	safest
dirtier	thinner	shiniest
drier	wetter	sleepiest
faster	wider	sloppiest
fluffier		slowest
friskier	biggest	smallest
funnier	bravest	snowiest
happier	bumpiest	soapiest
hotter	dirtiest	strongest
longer	driest	sunniest
messier	fastest	thinnest
sadder	fluffiest	wettest
safer	happiest	widest
sillier	hottest	
sloppier	longest	

Long *o*: *o, oa, ow*

go	loan	flow
no	moan	glow
so	oats	grow
	road	grown
boat	roam	low
coach	roams	mow
coal	roast	own
coat	soap	pillow
float	soapiest	row
foam	throat	show
goats	toad	shown
groan	toast	slow
groaned	toasty	slower
groaning		slowest
groans	blow	snow
Joan	bow	snowiest
load	crow	tow

Sounds Reviewed

a/a/	l/l/*	dr/dr/
a/ā/	m/m/*	fl/fl/
ai/ā/	n/n/*	fr/fr/
al/ò/	o/o/	gl/gl/
b/b/*	p/p/*	gr/gr/
c/k/*	r/r/*	mp/mp/
d/d/*	s/s/	sl/sl/
e/e/	s/z/	sm/sm/
ea/ē/	t/t/*	sn/sn/
ee/ē/	u/u/	st/st/
f/f/*	w/w/*	str/str/
g/g/*	ng/ng/	thr/thr/
h/h/*	sh/sh/	plural -s
i/ē/	th/th/	-ed
i/i/	bl/bl/	-ing
i/ī/	cl/cl/	-s
ir/ėr/	cr/kr/	
j/j/*		

High-Frequency Words

animal
country
cover
field
warm

Selection Words

panda
pocket

*= letter-sounds reviewed from Level A

Unit 4 Word List

Unit 4 Week 4 What Changes Are Hard?

Long *i*: *igh*, *ie*

bright	sighing	lie
brighter	sighs	lied
fight	sight	lies
flight	slight	pie
flights	sunlight	pies
fright	thigh	skies
high	tight	spied
highest	tighter	spies
light		tie
lightest	cried	tied
might	cries	ties
mighty	die	tried
night	dies	tries
nights	dried	
right	dries	
sigh	flies	
sighed	fries	

Sounds Reviewed

ai/ā/	s/z/	sl/sl/
ay/ā/	u/u/	sp/sp/
c/k/*	t/t/*	spr/spr/
d/d/*	y/ē/	tr/tr/
ea/ē/	sh/sh/	plural -s
ee/ē/	ch/ch/	-er
f/f/*	th/th/	-est
h/h/*	br/br/	-ed
k/k/*	cr/kr/	-ing
l/l/*	dr/dr/	-s
m/m/*	fl/fl/	
n/n/*	fr/fr/	
oa/ō/	gr/gr/	
ow/ō/	pl/pl/	
p/p/*	scr/skr/	
r/r/*	sk/sk/	
s/s/		

High-Frequency Words

below
child
children
full
important

Selection Words

Chicago

Unit 4 Week 5 Weather Changes

Syllables VCV

acorn	lemon	project
babies	lemons	protect
bacon	lizard	rapid
cabin	lizards	river
camel	magic	robins
clever	major	robot
closet	melon	salad
comics	metal	seven
cozy	model	seventh
dragon	moment	shadow
fever	music	shadows
finished	never	shivered
flavor	open	shivers
frozen	opens	silent
habit	over	siren
hotel	paper	spiders
human	pilot	tiger
label	planet	travels
ladies	ponies	tulip
lady	pony	visit
lazy	present	visits

Sounds Reviewed

a/a/	o/o/	ct/ct/
a/ā/	o/ō/	dr/dr/
b/b/*	or/ôr/	fl/fl/
c/k/*	ow/ō/	fr/fr/
d/d/*	p/p/*	nt/nt/
e/e/	r/r/*	pl/pl/
e/ē/	s/s/	pr/pr/
f/f/*	s/z/	sp/sp/
g/g/*	t/t/*	plural -s
g/j/	u/u/	plural -es
h/h/*	u/ù/	-ed
i/i/	v/v/*	
i/ī/	y/ē/	
ee/ē/	z/z/*	
j/j/*	sh/sh/	
l/l/*	th/th/	
m/m/*	cl/kl/	
n/n/		

High-Frequency Words

head
large
poor
though
wash

Selection Words

cloud
umbrella

---

*= letter-sounds reviewed from Level A

Unit 5 Word List

Unit 5 Week 1 Good Job!

Compound Words

anthill	flagpole	rainfall
backbone	flashlight	sailboat
backpack	grapevine	sandbox
backyard	hallway	sidewalk
barnyard	herself	snowball
baseball	highway	snowflake
bathtub	homemade	snowman
bedtime	inside	spaceship
beehives	kickball	sunburn
birthday	lunchbox	sunlight
blueprint	mailbox	sunrise
campfire	nighttime	sunscreen
cannot	nutshell	sunshine
catfish	oatmeal	tightrope
classmate	pancake	treetops
cupcake	popcorn	weekday
daylight	railroad	weekend
firefly	rainbow	
fireplace	raincoat	

Sounds Reviewed

a/a/	p/p/*	pl/pl/
a/ā/	r/r/*	scr/scr/
ay/ā/	s/s/	sn/sn/
b/b/*	s/z/	sp/sp/
c/k/*	t/t/*	tr/tr/
ck/k/	u/u/	
d/d/*	w/w/*	
e/e/	y/y/*	
ee/ē/	ch/ch/	
f/f/*	sh/sh/	
g/g/*	th/th/	
h/h/*	bl/bl/	
i/ī/	cl/cl/	
ir/ėr/*	fl/fl/	
k/k/*	gr/gr/	
l/l/*	mp/mp/	
m/m/*	nd/nd/	
n/n/*	nt/nt/	
o/o/		

High-Frequency Words

book
heard
hold
listen
piece

Selection Words

skyscraper
worker

Unit 5 Week 2 Taking Care of Animals

Syllables: Consonant + le

able	gentle	scramble
apple	giggle	scribble
beagle	handle	simple
beetle	jiggle	snuggle
bottle	juggle	sparkle
bottles	jungle	stable
bubble	little	startle
bugle	maple	struggle
candle	middle	table
candles	needle	tangle
cradle	nibble	title
cradles	paddle	turtle
cuddle	puddle	turtles
cuddles	purple	wiggle
eagle	rattle	wiggled
fable	riddle	
Gable	sample	

Sounds Reviewed

a/a/	n/n/*	st/st/
a/ā/	o/o/	str/str/
b/b/*	p/p/*	plural -s
c/k/*	r/r/*	
ea/ē/	s/s/*	
ee/ē/	t/t/*	
f/f/*	u/u/	
g/g/*	u/ü/	
g/j/	ur/ėr/*	
h/h/*	w/w/*	
i/i/	cr/cr/	
i/ī/*	scr/scr/	
l/l/*	sn/sn/	
m/m/*	sp/sp/	

High-Frequency Words

boy
either
hundred
several
you're

Unit 5 Week 3 Family Jobs

Diphthongs ou, ow/ou/

bounds	south	powerful
cloud	sprout	shower
couch	town	
count	chow	
found	cow	
house	crowd	
loud	down	
mouth	flower	
out	growls	
proud	how	
proudly	howls	
shout	now	
shouts	owl	
sound	powder	
sounds	power	

Suffixes -ly, -ful

bravely	softly	thankful
correctly	sweetly	useful
easily	tightly	
gladly		
happily	frightful	
loudly	graceful	
neatly	harmful	
nicely	hopeful	
perfectly	hurtful	
proudly	mouthful	
quickly	painful	
sadly	peaceful	
safely	playful	
shyly	powerful	
simply	skillful	

Sounds Reviewed

a/ā/	l/l/*	th/th/
ay/ā/	m/m/*	br/br/
b/b/*	n/n/*	cl/cl/
c/s/	o/o/	cr/cr/
c/k/*	or/ôr/	fl/fl/
ck/k/	p/p/*	fr/fr/
d/d/*	qu/kw/*	gl/gr/
e/e/*	r/r/*	gr/gr/
ea/ē/	s/s/*	pl/pl/
ee/ē/	s/z/	pr/pr/
er/ėr/	t/t/*	sk/sk/
f/f/*	u/u/*	spr/spr/
g/g/*	ur/ėr/	sw/sw/
h/h/*	ch/ch/	plural -s
i/ī/	sh/sh/	

High-Frequency Words

ago
break
certain
probably
since

Selection Words

tool
vacuum

*= **letter-sounds reviewed from Level A**

Unit 5 Word List

Sound of oo in moon

afternoon	loop	tool
balloons	moon	tooth
bedroom	noon	zoo
bloom	poodle	zoom
boo	pool	
boost	raccoon	
boot	room	
booth	scoop	
broom	scoot	
cool	smooth	
droop	smoothly	
food	snoops	
fool	soon	
gloomy	spooky	
goofy	spoons	
hoop	too	

Prefixes un-, re-

unable	recheck
unbutton	reheat
unclean	remake
uncommon	repack
unhappy	repaint
unlike	replace
unload	replant
unlock	replay
unlucky	reread
unpack	resend
unsafe	restart
unspoken	retell
untangle	rethink
untie	reuse
unwell	revisit
unzip	

Sounds Reviewed

a/a/	n/n/*	plural -s
a/ā/	o/o/*	-ing
b/b/*	p/p/*	bl/bl/
c/k/*	r/r/*	cl/cl/
c/s/*	s/s/*	br/br/
ck/k/*	s/z/*	dr/dr/
d/d/*	t/t/*	gl/gl/
e/e/*	u/u/*	nd/nd/
er/èr/	w/w/*	nt/nt/
f/f/*	x/ks/*	pl/pl/
g/g/*	y/ē/	sc/sc/
h/h/*	z/z/*	sm/sm/
k/k/	ch/ch/	sn/sn/
l/l/*	sh/sh/	sp/sp/
m/m/*	th/th/	st/st/

High-Frequency Words

been
brother
course
special
whole

Selection Words

neighborhood

Diphthongs oi, oy

boil	pointing	joy
boiling	poison	joyful
choices	soil	joystick
coin	spoil	loyal
coins	spoiled	oyster
foil	voice	Roy
join	voices	soybean
joint		toy
joints	boy	toys
noise	boys	
noisy	cowboy	
oink	enjoy	
point	enjoys	

Silent Consonants kn/n/, wr/r/, mb/m/

knapsack	wrap	crumb
knee	wreath	crumbs
kneel	wreck	lamb
knife	wriggle	limb
knight	wrist	limbs
knights	write	plumber
knit	writing	thumb
knitting	wrong	thumbs
knob	wrote	
knock		
knocked		
knot		
know		
knuckle		
knuckles		

Sounds Reviewed*

b/b/*	l/l/	th/th/
c/k/*	m/m/*	ng/ng/
c/s/*	n/n/*	plural -s
ck/k/*	o/o/	-ing
d/d/*	ow/ō/	cr/cr/
e/e/*	p/p/*	nt/nt/
ee/ē/	r/r/*	pl/pl/
f/f/*	s/s/*	sp/sp/
g/g/*	t/t/*	st/st/
i/ī/	v/v/*	
i/i/*	y/ē/*	
k/k/*	ch/ch/	

High-Frequency Words

hour
leave
minute
sorry
watch

Unit 6 Word List

Unit 6 Week 1 Sports

Sound of *oo* in *book*

bookmark	shook
books	soot
brook	stood
brooks	took
cook	wood
cookbook	woodpecker
cooking	woof
crook	wool
foot	
football	
good	
hood	
hoof	
hook	
hooks	
look	
looking	
looks	

Suffixes *-or, -er*

actor	printer
baker	racer
batter	reader
buzzer	reporter
collector	runner
conductor	sailor
director	singer
driver	speaker
editor	swimmer
farmer	teacher
gardener	toaster
helper	visitor
inspector	winner
inventor	writer
kicker	
leader	
pitcher	
player	

Sounds Reviewed

a/a/	l/l/*	br/br/
ai/ā/	m/m/*	cr/kr/
al/ȯ/	n/n/*	dr/dr/
ar/är/	o/o/	lp/lp/
ay/ā/	oa/ō/	ng/ng/
b/b/*	p/p/*	nt/nt/
c/k/*	r/r/*	pl/pl
c/s/*	s/s/	pr/pr/
ck/k/	t/t/*	rd/rd/
d/d/*	u/u/	rm/rm/
e/e/	v/v/*	rt/rt/
e/ē/	w/w/*	sp/sp/
ea/ē/	wr/w/	st/st/
f/f/*	z/z/*	sw/sw/
g/g/*	ch/ch/	plural -s
h/h/*	tch/tch/	-s
i/i/	sh/sh/	-ing
i/ī/		
k/k/*		

High-Frequency Words

bought
buy
clothes
won
worst

Unit 6 Week 2 The American Flag

Vowel Patterns *ew, ue*

blew	blue
chew	bluebird
crew	clue
drew	clues
few	due
flew	glue
grew	Sue
knew	true
new	
news	
newt	
screw	
stew	
threw	
unscrew	

Prefixes *pre-, dis-*

disconnect	preheat
disgrace	preheating
disinfect	prepaid
dislike	prepay
disloyal	prepays
disorder	preschool
displace	preteen
displease	pretest
displeased	
disrespect	
distaste	
distrust	
precooked	
precut	
preflight	
pregame	

Sounds Reviewed

a/a/	l/l/*	cl/kl/
a/ā/	m/m/*	cr/kr/
ai/ā/	n/n/*	dr/dr/
ay/ā/	o/o/	fl/fl/
c/k/*	oo/ů/	gl/gl/
c/s/*	oo/ü/	gr/gr/
d/d/*	or/ôr/	nt/nt/
e/e/	ou/ou/	pl/pl/
e/ē/	oy/oi/	pr/pr/
ea/ē/	p/p/*	scr/scr/
ee/ē/	r/r/*	sp/sp/
f/f/*	s/s/	st/st/
g/g/*	s/z/	thr/thr/
h/h/*	t/t/*	tr/tr/
i/i/	u/u/	plural -s
i/ī/	ch/ch/	-ed
igh/ī/	th/th/	-ing
ir/ėr/	bl/bl	-s
kn/n/		

High-Frequency Words

air
America
beautiful
Earth
world

Selection Words

colonies

Unit 6 Week 3 Family Celebrations

Contractions *'re, 've, 'd*

he'd	they're	you'd
I'd	they've	you're
I've	we'd	you've
she'd	we're	
they'd	we've	

ph/f/ *dge*/j/

dolphin	badge	porridge
gopher	badger	ridge
gophers	badges	smudge
graph	bridge	wedge
Joseph	dodgeball	
nephew	edge	
orphan	fridge	
phase	fudge	
Phil	hedge	
phone	hedgehogs	
phoned	judge	
phrase	ledge	
Ralph	lodge	
Steph	Madge	
trophies	Midge	
trophy	pledge	

Sounds Reviewed

a/a/	mb/m/	y/y/*
a/ā/	n/n/*	sh/sh/
al/ȯ/	o/o/	th/th/
b/b/*	o/ō/	br/br/
d/d/*	or/ôr/	fr/fr/
e/e/	ou/ou/	gr/gr/
e/ē/	ow/ō/	pl/pl/
ew/ü/	p/p/*	sm/sm/
g/g/*	r/r/*	st/st/
h/h/*	s/s/*	tr/tr/
i/i/	s/z/	plural -s
i/ī/	u/u/	-ed
j/j/*	v/v/*	-es
kn/n/	w/w/*	
l/l/*	wr/r/	
m/m/*	y/ē/	

High-Frequency Words

believe
company
everybody
money
young

*= **letter-sounds reviewed from Level A**

Unit 6 Word List

Unit 6 Week 4 A Cowboy's Life

Short e: ea

bread	sweat
breath	sweater
dead	thread
deaf	tread
dread	unhealthiest
dreadfully	unsteadily
feather	unsteady
head	weather
health	wealthier
healthy	
Heather	
heavier	
heaviest	
heavy	
instead	
leather	
meadow	
meant	
read	
ready	
spread	
steady	

Base Words and Affixes

baker	precooked	retrimming
careful	prefaded	reused
disconnecting	preheated	reusing
discovered	prejudging	rewrapped
dislike	premixes	rewrapping
disliked	preordered	rewriting
dislikes	preplanning	sitting
disliking	presetting	thankfully
dismounted	pretreated	uneasily
displeased	prewrapped	unhappier
disregarded	rechecked	unhappily
disrespectful	remodeled	unhealthiest
distrustful	remover	unhelpful
explorer	repacking	unkindly
freezing	replaced	unluckiest
gardener	replacing	unsaddled
healthy	replanning	unsteadily
heavier	replaying	unsteady
heaviest	resaddled	untied
inventor	rescrubbed	unzipping
luckily	retied	wealthier
powerfully	retraced	

Sounds Reviewed

a/a/	n/n/*	nk/ngk/
a/ā/	o/o/	br/br/
ar/är/	oo/ù/	ct/ct/
b/b/*	or/ôr/	dr/dr/
c/k/*	ou/ou/	fr/fr/
ck/k/	ow/ō/	nd/nd/
d/d/*	ow/ou/	nt/nt/
dge/j/	p/p/*	pl/pl/
e/e/	r/r/*	pr/pr/
e/ē/	s/s/*	rd/rd/
ea/ē/	s/z/*	sp/sp/
ee/ē/	t/t/*	spr/spr/
f/f/*	u/u/	st/st/
g/g/*	v/v/*	sw/sw/
h/h/*	w/w/*	thr/thr/
i/i/	wr/r/	tr/tr/
i/ī/	x/ks/*	
j/j/*	y/ē/	
k/k/*	z/z/*	
l/l/*	th/th/	
m/m/*	ch/ch/	

High-Frequency Words

alone
between
notice
question
woman

Selection Words

barrel
bull

Unit 6 Week 5 Celebrations for Everyone

Vowel Patterns aw, au, au(gh)

August	pause
author	paused
awful	pausing
because	pawn
caught	predawn
cause	redrawing
daughter	retaught
daughters	sausage
dawn	saw
drawn	scrawnier
fault	scrawny
haul	straw
hauling	taught
lawn	thawed
naughtiest	yawn
naughty	
Paul	

Base Words and Affixes

dirtiest	remaking	unplanned
discovered	retried	unplugging
disliking	replaced	unsaddled
displease	replay	unsteadily
expected	retaught	
funniest	rethinking	
hauling	rewrap	
luckily	rewrapping	
naughtiest	scrawnier	
paused	sleepier	
pausing	smelliest	
pinning	surprising	
precooked	thankfully	
predawn	undecided	
preplan	unexpected	
preset	unhappily	
redrawing	unhelpful	

Sounds Reviewed

a/a/	ir/èr/	th/th/
a/ā/	k/k/*	nk/ngk/
ay/ā/	l/l/*	dr/dr/
b/b/*	m/m/*	lp/lp/
c/k/*	n/n/*	lt/lt/
c/s/*	or/ôr/	pl/pl/
ck/k/	oo/ù/	pr/pr/
d/d/*	p/p/*	rt/rt/
e/e/	r/r/*	scr/skr/
e/ē/	s/s/*	st/st/
ea/ē/	s/z/*	str/str/
ee/ē/	t/t/*	tr/tr/
f/f/*	u/u/	
g/g/*	v/v/*	
g/j/	wr/r/	
h/h/*	x/ks/*	
i/i/	y/y/*	
i/ī/	y/ē/	

High-Frequency Words

cold
finally
half
tomorrow
word

Selection Words

celebrate

---

*= letter-sounds reviewed from Level A

Phonological Awareness

Many of the following activities can be used at any grade level by adapting the element being practiced and the degree of difficulty.

Activity Bank

Rhyming Words

Poems and Chants

Read a poem or chant to children. Emphasize the rhymes by whispering all except rhyming words. Have children say the poems with you in the same way to help them hear the rhyming words.

Did You Ever See . . . ?

Invent rhymes and sing them to the tune of "If You're Happy and You Know It."

> Did you ever see a <u>fly</u> with a <u>tie</u>?
>
> Did you ever see a <u>fly</u> with a <u>tie</u>?
>
> Did you ever? No, I never. Did you ever? No, I never.
>
> No, I never saw a <u>fly</u> with a <u>tie</u>.

Rhyme Book

Read children a book that uses rhyme. Ask them to identify rhyming word pairs. Distribute paper and have children fold it in half width-wise. Have them draw rhyming word pairs (one in each half) from the book or that they thought of themselves.

Initial Sounds

Picture Card Sound Match

Pass out five picture cards to each child. In turn each child shows a card, telling the beginning sound and asks another player if he or she has a picture card beginning with the same sound. If the player has a picture with the same beginning sound, he or she gives it to the child who asked. When a match is made, the player shows the cards, repeats the initial sound requested, and names the two pictures.

Same Sound Silly Sentences

Display a picture card—*dog.* Guide children to identify the initial sound: This is *dog.* The first sound in dog is /d/. What is the first sound in dog? Let's say other words that begin with /d/. Take four or five suggestions; then guide children to make a potentially silly sentence. For example *dog, dinosaur, dinner,* and *dark* could be used in the sentence:

> *The dog and the dinosaur ate dinner in the dark.*

Counting Words in a Sentence

How Many Words?

Say a simple sentence. (Use monosyllabic words at first.) **Move tokens for every word you hear in the sentence. Count your tokens.** Confirm by saying the sentence again and moving tokens while you say each word.

Counting Syllables in a Word

Clapping Names

Ask a child to say his or her first name. Repeat it, clapping once for each syllable as you say it. Have children say and clap the name with you. **How many syllables (claps) did you hear?** Repeat, substituting each child's name.

Phonemic Awareness

Many of the following activities can be used at any grade level by adapting the element being practiced and the degree of difficulty.

Blending and Segmenting Sounds

What Am I?

Play a riddle game with sounds. Use items such as these:

/g/ /ā/ /t/ You open me. (gate)

/k/ /ā/ /v/ Bears sleep in me. (cave)

I Spy Some Phonemes

Choose an object in the classroom. Ask students to guess the name of your object by the clues you give them. Use clues such as these: *I spy an object with four sounds. The first sound is /t/. The last sound is /l/. The second sound is /ā/. The third sound is /b/.* Continue to provide clues until students can name the object. Repeat with other objects around the room. You may wish to have students take turns providing clues for the class.

Sound Count

Make a copy of the five-sound boxes pattern on p. 283 for each student. Supply markers, such as erasers, buttons, or checkers. Slowly say a word that has up to five sounds in it. Have each student put a marker in a box for each sound in the word.

Say the Sounds

Have a student show a picture card to another student. Ask the student to name the picture and then segment the sounds in the name of the picture (for example, *tent, /t/ /e/ /n/ /t/*).

For students who need more support with this activity, provide the appropriate number of sound boxes for the word and have students move a marker into a box for each sound.

Working with Vowels

Say a one-syllable word with a short vowel. Have students change the vowel sound to another short vowel to make a new word. Work with words such as *cab, bet, sit, log,* and *bug.* Use the Word Lists on pp. 268–279 of this book for more words.

Bubble Gum Words

Tell students you are going to slowly pull words out of your mouth, as you would pull out bubble gum. Have them identify each word as you "pull it out." Model sounding out the word *him,* /hhh/ /iii/ /mmm/, as you slowly say its sounds. Have students repeat after you as you pull other words out.

Substituting Sounds

Switcheroo

Give each student letter cards for *c, m, p, n, t,* and *a* in an envelope. Guide students in making new words by changing the letters. You may wish to begin with directions such as these:

Find the letters that make these sounds, /k/ /a/ /t/.

Blend the sounds together. What word did you spell? (cat)

Change the /k/ sound to /m/.

Blend the sounds together. What word did you spell? (mat)

Change the /t/ to /p/.

Blend the sounds together. What word did you spell? (map)

Continue substituting different sounds until you have made all of the following words: *nap, tap, cap, can, tan, man, pan,* and *pat.*

Make New Words

Have students make words that end with /t/ by changing the initial sound of *sit.* Model how to change the beginning sound and blend it with the middle and end sounds: /s/ *it* becomes /h/ *it.* Ask students to join you as you make other words, such as *pit, bit, wit, kit, lit, fit.*

This activity can be adapted for other consonant sounds by referring to the Word Lists on pp. 268–279 of this book.

Sound Switching

Tell students you will say a word. Ask them to listen carefully because you are going to switch one of the sounds and make a new word. Ask them to tell you which sound, beginning, middle, or end, was switched. For example, say *bat* and *bag,* and ask students which sound was switched. Continue the activity with these word pairs: *tab, tag; hot, hat; rake, wake; dad, sad; mad, made; red, read; page, cage; cap, cape; miss, mess; fan, fat; met, men; bug, rug.*

Sound Boxes

Oral Vocabulary Words

UNIT 1 Exploration	**UNIT 2** Working Together	**UNIT 3** Creative Ideas	**UNIT 4** Our Changing World	**UNIT 5** Responsibility	**UNIT 6** Traditions
DEVELOP LANGUAGE					
avenue investigate rural suburb urban	courageous hazard prevent rescue wildfire	construct contraption project sidekick unique	familiar keepsake preserve represent valuable	career community employee responsible teamwork	athlete challenge champion effort rival
ascend descend journey orbit universe	ability compete contribute recreation victory	conversation correspond postage reply transport	adapt annual nutrients soil sprout	concern growth litter protection veterinarian	anthem history independence patriotic symbol
camouflage galaxy mammal tranquil wildlife	conflict greedy inhabit portion resolve	brainstorm brilliant consume prey shrewd	appearance nursery stage tend transform	assign behavior cooperate obedient properly	celebration custom occasion sibling tradition
arid cactus dune landform precipitation	companion independent partnership solution survival	abundant assist baffle generous struggle	adjust ancestor courage landmark unexpected	acquaintance appreciate communicate local respect	climate herd livestock occupation rodeo
curious delicate information inquire sturdy	decorate dine float (n.) holiday participate	accomplish excel inspiration process research	blizzard condition forecast predict terrifying	apologize citizen judgment law scold	ceremony culture festival international regional

My Sidewalks provides direct instruction and daily practice in the oral vocabulary words listed above. Children learn five words per week that develop a weekly concept related to grade-level science and social studies content. These words are beyond children's reading ability but are used to expand their understanding of the concept and their ability to discuss it.

Child's Name _____ Date _____

Observation Checklist

Use this checklist to record your observations of children's reading skills and behaviors.

	Always (Proficient)	Sometimes (Developing)	Rarely (Novice)
Identifies and isolates initial sounds in words			
Identifies and isolates final sounds in words			
Blends sounds to make spoken words			
Segments one-syllable spoken words into individual phonemes			
Knows letter-sound correspondences			
Uses word structure to identify longer words			
Reads simple sentences			
Reads simple stories			
Understands simple story structure (character, setting, plot)			
Reads at an appropriate reading rate			
Reads with appropriate intonation and stress			
Summarizes plot or main ideas accurately			
Recognizes main ideas			
Recognizes sequence			
Makes comparisons and contrasts			
Draws conclusions to understand text			

Bookmarks

Fiction

- Who are the characters?

- Where does the story take place?

- When does the story take place?

- What happens . . .
  in the beginning?
  in the middle?
  at the end?

Nonfiction

- What did I learn?

- What is this mainly about?

Index

Connections Between *My Sidewalks* and *Scott Foresman Reading Street*

My Sidewalks is designed to parallel essential elements in *Scott Foresman Reading Street*. Connections between the two programs are reflected in the indexes of the Teacher's Guides.

- Corresponding **priority skills** ensure that students receive instruction in the critical elements of reading—phonemic awareness, phonics, fluency, vocabulary, and comprehension.

- Parallel **concepts and themes** enable smooth transitions between *My Sidewalks* and *Reading Street*.

- Consistency of **scaffolded instruction** promotes familiarity with routines and terminology.

- Alignment of **before, during, and after reading strategies** reinforces successful reading habits.

- **Comprehension** skill links provide Tier III readers with additional instruction and practice with main idea, compare/contrast, sequence, and drawing conclusions.

- **Vocabulary** links provide Tier III readers with additional instruction and practice with oral vocabulary.

- Consistent procedures for **corrective feedback** promptly reveal and address student needs, providing guidance for error correction.

- Connected **writing** modes offer student opportunities to respond to literature.

- **Cross-curricular** links lay out the same science and social studies foundations for Tier III readers as for students in the core program.

Index

ELL

Fluency

oa, *V2* 40, 42

ow /ō/, *V2* 40, 42

oo /ü/, *V2* 132, 138, 189

oo /u̅/, *V2* 164, 170

vowel diphthongs

oi, *V2* 148, 154, 157

ou, *V2* 116, 122, 157

ow, *V2* 116, 122, 157

oy, *V2* 148, 154, 157

vowel patterns, less common

a, al, *V2* 4, 10

au, aw, au(gh), *V2* 228, 234

ew, ue, *V2* 180, 186, 189

vowels, long

a, *V1* 116, 122, 125, 205

e, *V1* 164, 170, 173, 205; *V2* 26

i, *V1* 132, 138, 141, 205; *V2* 56

o, *V1* 148, 154, 157, 205; *V2* 40, 42

u, *V1* 164, 170, 173, 205

y, *V1* 180, 186; *V2* 29

vowels, r-controlled

ar, *V1* 196, 202, 237

er, *V1* 232, 234, 237

ir, *V1* 232, 234, 237

or/ore, *V1* 200, 202, 237

ur, *V1* 232, 234, 237

vowels, short

a, *V1* 4, 10, 42, 45, 77, 125

e, *V1* 52, 58, 77, 173

i, *V1* 20, 26, 45, 77, 141

o, *V1* 36, 42, 45, 77, 157

u, *V1* 68, 74, 77, 173

Phonological and phonemic awareness

add initial and final sounds, *V1* 39, 55, 100, 103, 106, 135, 138, 154, 183, 196, 199, 202, 231, 234

add sounds (phonemes), *V1* 100, 106, 151, 154, 183, 196; *V2* 36, 119, 135, 167, 183, 215, 218, 231, 234

blend sounds (phonemes), *V1* 4, 7, 10, 20, 23, 26, 36, 42, 167, 170, 228

count syllables, *V1* 215, 216, 280; *V2* 280

delete ending sounds (phonemes), *V1* 87, 90; *V2* 36, 196, 202

segment and blend sounds, *V1* 119, 122, 180, 186; *V2* 20, 23, 26, 39, 42, 116, 122, 132, 138, 148, 154, 164, 170, 180, 186, 212, 228

segment and count sounds, *V1* 68, 71, 74, 84, 116, 132, 148, 164, 180; *V2* 4, 10, 52, 55, 58, 151, 199

segment words into sounds (phonemes), *V1* 52, 58; *V2* 84

segment words into syllables, syllables into sounds, *V1* 212, 215, 218; *V2* 7, 68, 71, 74, 84, 87, 90, 100, 103, 106

Sound Pronunciation Guide, *Welcome to My Sidewalks,* 31–32

substitute sounds (phonemes), *V1* 13, 29; *V2* 189

Picture clues. *See* Comprehension, Strategies.

Picture walk. *See* Comprehension, Strategies.

Pictures. *See* Comprehension, Strategies, picture clues; Graphic sources, illustration.

Plot. *See* Comprehension, Strategies, story structure.

Poetic devices. *See* Sound devices and poetic elements.

Poetry. *See* Genres.

Predict. *See* Comprehension, Strategies.

Prefixes. *See* Word structure.

Prereading strategies. *See* Comprehension, Strategies, for specific strategies; Concept development.

Preview. *See* Comprehension, Strategies.

Prior knowledge. *See* Comprehension, Strategies.

Progress monitoring. *See* Assessment.

Prosody. *See* Fluency, expression/intonation (prosody).

Punctuation. *See* Fluency.

Purpose for reading. *See* Comprehension, Strategies, set purpose for reading.

Questions, answer. *See* Comprehension, Strategies.

Questions, ask. *See* Comprehension, Strategies.

Rate. *See* Fluency.

Reader response, *V1* 6, 9, 12, 14, 22, 25, 28, 30, 38, 41, 44, 46, 54, 57, 60, 62, 70, 73, 76, 78, 86, 89, 92, 94, 102, 105, 108, 110, 118, 121, 124, 126, 134, 137, 140, 142, 150, 153, 156, 158, 166, 169, 172, 174, 182, 185, 188, 190, 198, 201, 204, 206, 214, 217, 222, 220, 230, 233, 236, 238; *V2* 6, 9, 12, 14, 22, 25, 28, 30, 38, 41, 44, 46, 54, 57, 60, 62, 70, 73, 76, 78, 86, 89, 92, 94, 102, 105, 108, 110, 118, 121, 124, 126, 134, 137, 140, 142, 150, 153, 156, 158, 166, 169, 172, 174, 182, 185, 188, 190, 198, 201, 204, 206, 214, 217, 220, 222, 230, 233, 236, 238

Reading levels, *Welcome to My Sidewalks,* 14–15; *V1* xii–xiii; *V2* xii–xiii

Reading rate. *See* Fluency.

Realistic fiction. *See* Genres.

Recall and retell. *See* Comprehension, Strategies.

Recipe. *See* Genres.

Reference sources, *V1* 70, 190, 230

Repeated reading. *See* Fluency.

Research

bibliography, *Welcome to My Sidewalks,* 30

research base for My Sidewalks, *Welcome to My Sidewalks,* 6, 18–29, 30

Respond to literature. *See* Reader response.

Response to literature, *V1* 9, 15, 17, 25, 31, 33, 41, 47, 49, 57, 63, 65, 73, 79, 81, 89, 95, 97, 105, 111, 113, 121, 127, 129, 137, 143, 145, 153, 159, 161, 169, 175, 177, 185, 191, 193, 201, 207, 209, 217, 223, 225, 233, 239, 241; *V2* 9, 15, 17, 25, 31, 33, 41, 47, 49, 57, 63, 65, 73, 79, 81, 89, 95, 97, 105, 111, 113, 121, 127, 129, 137, 143, 145, 153, 159, 161, 169, 175, 177, 185, 191, 193, 201, 207, 209, 217, 223, 225, 233, 239, 241

Retelling. *See* Comprehension, Strategies, recall and retell.

Rhyme. *See* Genres.

Rhythm. *See* Sound devices and poetic elements.

Riddle. *See* Genres.

Routines. Instructional routines provide the framework for lessons. *See also* Routine Cards at the back of this Teacher's Guide.

Scaffolded instruction, *Welcome to My Sidewalks,* 9; *V1* 4, 5, 6, 7, 8, 9, 10, 12, 13, 20, 21, 22, 23, 24, 25, 26, 28, 29, 36, 37, 38, 39, 40, 41, 42, 44, 45, 52, 53, 54, 55, 56, 57, 58, 60, 61, 68, 69, 70, 71, 72, 73, 74, 76, 77, 84, 85, 86, 87, 88, 89, 90, 92, 93, 100, 101, 102, 103, 104, 105, 106, 108, 109, 116, 117, 118, 119, 120, 121, 122, 124, 125, 132, 133, 134, 135, 136, 137, 138, 140, 141, 148, 149, 150, 151, 152, 153, 154, 156, 157, 164, 165, 166, 167, 168, 169, 170, 172, 173, 180, 181 182, 183, 184, 185, 186, 188, 189, 196, 197, 198, 199, 200, 201, 202, 204, 205, 212, 213, 214, 215, 217, 218, 220, 221, 228, 229, 230, 231, 232, 233, 234, 235, 236, 237; *V2* 4, 5, 6, 7, 8, 9, 10, 12, 13, 20, 21, 22, 23, 24, 25, 26, 28, 29, 36, 37, 38, 39, 40, 41, 42, 44, 45, 52, 53, 54, 55, 57, 58, 60, 61, 68, 69, 70, 71, 72, 73, 74, 76, 77, 84, 85, 86, 87, 89, 90, 92, 93, 100, 101, 102, 103, 104, 105, 106, 108, 109, 116, 117, 118, 119, 120, 121, 122, 124, 125, 132, 133, 134, 135, 136, 137, 138, 140, 141, 148, 149, 150, 151, 152, 153, 154, 156, 157, 164, 165, 166, 167, 168, 169, 170, 172, 173, 180, 181 182, 183, 184, 185, 186, 188, 189, 196, 197, 198, 199, 200, 201, 202, 204, 205, 212, 213, 214, 215, 216, 217, 218, 220, 221, 228, 229, 230, 231, 232, 233, 234, 236, 237. *See also* Modeling.

School-home connection, *V1* 16, 32, 48, 64, 80, 96, 112, 128, 144, 160, 176, 186, 208, 224, 240; *V2* 16, 32, 48, 64, 80, 96, 112, 128, 144, 160, 176, 192, 208, 224, 240

Science. *See* Content-area texts.

Self-monitor. *See* Comprehension, Strategies.

Self-question. *See* Comprehension, Strategies, ask questions.

Self-selected reading, *V1* 260–263; *V2* 260–263

Sentence frames, *V1* 9, 25, 41, 57, 73, 89, 105, 121, 137, 153, 169, 185, 201, 217, 233; *V2* 9, 25, 41, 57, 73, 89, 105, 121, 137, 153, 169, 185, 201, 217, 233

Sentence stems. *See* Sentence frames.

Sequence. *See* Comprehension, Skills.

Set purpose for reading. *See* Comprehension, Strategies.

Setting. *See* Comprehension, Strategies, story structure.

Shared reading, *V1* 6, 9, 12, 22, 25, 28, 38, 41, 44, 54, 57, 60, 70, 73, 76, 86, 89, 92, 102, 105, 108, 118, 121, 124, 134, 137, 140, 150, 153, 156, 166, 169, 172, 182, 185, 188, 198, 201, 204, 214, 217, 220, 230, 233, 236; *V2* 6, 9, 12, 22, 25, 28, 38, 41, 44, 54, 57, 60, 70, 73, 76, 86, 89, 92, 102, 105, 108, 118, 121, 124, 134, 137, 140, 150, 153, 156, 166, 169, 172, 182, 185, 188, 198, 201, 204, 214, 217, 220, 230, 233, 236

Sight words. *See* High-frequency words.

Sign. *See* Graphic sources.

Sing with Me Big Book, *V1* 5, 21, 37, 53, 69, 85, 101, 117, 133, 149, 165, 181, 197, 213, 229; *V2* 5, 21, 37, 53, 69, 85, 101, 117, 133, 149, 165, 181, 197, 213, 229

Social studies. *See* Content-area texts.

Song. *See* Genres.

Sound devices and poetic elements

  alliteration, *V1* 280; *V2* 280

  rhyme, *V1* 206, 280; *V2* 78, 94, 110, 190, 280

  rhythm and cadence, *V1* 142, 206; *V2* 14, 78, 110, 190

Sound Pronunciation Guide, *Welcome to My Sidewalks,* 31–32

Sound-Spelling Cards, *V1* 4, 8, 20, 24, 36, 52, 68, 72, 84, 100, 116, 120, 132, 148, 164, 180, 196, 200, 212, 228, 232; *V2* 4, 20, 24, 36, 40, 52, 68, 84, 100, 116, 132, 148, 152, 164, 180, 196, 200, 212, 228

Spelling

  high-frequency words, *Welcome to My Sidewalks,* 20; *V1* 5, 8, 11, 21, 24, 27, 37, 40, 43, 53, 56, 59, 69, 72, 75, 85, 88, 91, 101, 104, 107, 117, 120, 123, 133, 136, 139, 149, 152, 155, 165, 168, 171, 181, 184, 187, 197, 200, 203, 213, 216, 219, 229, 232, 235; *V2* 5, 8, 11, 21, 24, 27, 37, 40, 43, 53, 56, 59, 69, 72, 75, 85, 88, 91, 101, 104, 107, 117, 120, 123, 133, 136, 139, 149, 152, 155, 165, 168, 171, 181, 184, 187, 197, 200, 203, 213, 216, 219, 229, 232, 235

  phonics, use to spell words, *V1* 4, 8, 20, 24, 36, 40, 52, 68, 72, 116, 132, 148, 164, 180, 196, 200; *V2* 132, 164, 200, 212

  Sound-Spelling Cards, *V1* 4, 8, 20, 24, 36, 52, 68, 72, 84, 100, 116, 120, 132, 148, 164, 180, 196, 200, 212, 228, 232; *V2* 4, 20, 24, 36, 40, 52, 68, 84, 100, 116, 132, 148, 152, 164, 180, 196, 200, 212, 228

Structural analysis. *See* Word structure.

Suffixes. *See* Word structure.

Summarize. *See* Comprehension, Strategies.

Syllables. *See* Word structure, syllable patterns.

Technology. *See* Content-area texts.

Tested Vocabulary Cards, *Welcome to My Sidewalks,* 20; *V1* 5, 8, 11, 21, 24, 27, 37, 40, 43, 53, 56, 59, 69, 72, 75, 85, 88, 91, 101, 104, 107, 117, 120, 123, 133, 136, 139, 149, 152, 155, 165, 168, 171, 181, 184, 187, 197, 200, 203, 213, 216, 219, 229, 232, 235; *V2* 5, 8, 11, 21, 24, 27, 37, 40, 43, 53, 56, 59, 69, 72, 75, 85, 88, 91, 101, 104, 107, 117, 120, 123, 133, 136, 139, 149, 152, 155, 165, 168, 171, 181, 184, 187, 197, 200, 203, 213, 216, 219, 229, 232, 235

Testing, formal and informal. *See* Assessment.

Text features. *See* Comprehension, Strategies.

Think alouds. *See* Comprehension, Strategies.

Tiers of Intervention, *Welcome to My Sidewalks,* 4

Time line. *See* Graphic sources.

Timed reading. *See* Fluency, assessment.

Tracking print, *V1* 15, 31, 47, 63, 79, 95, 111, 127, 143, 159, 175, 191, 207, 223, 239; *V2* 15, 31, 47, 63, 79, 95, 111, 127, 143, 159, 175, 191, 207, 223, 239

Trade books. *See* Self-selected reading.

Unfamiliar words. *See* Amazing Words.

Vocabulary

  Amazing Words. *See* Oral vocabulary.

  high-frequency words. *See* High-frequency words.

  oral vocabulary (Amazing Words). *See* Oral Vocabulary.

  Sing with Me Big Book, *V1* 5, 21, 37, 53, 69, 85, 101, 117, 133, 149, 165, 181, 197, 213, 229; *V2* 5, 21, 37, 53, 69, 85, 101, 117, 133, 149, 165, 181, 197, 213, 229

  structural analysis. *See* Word structure.

  Tested Vocabulary Cards. *See* Tested Vocabulary Cards.

  unfamiliar words. *See* Amazing Words.

Word Wall, *V1* 5, 21, 37, 53, 69, 85, 101, 117, 133, 149, 165, 181, 197, 213, 229; *V2* 5, 21, 37, 53, 69, 85, 101, 117, 133, 149, 165, 181, 197, 213, 229

Word reading. *See* Fluency.

Word structure

base words

without spelling changes, *V1* 56, 58, 88, 90, 100, 109; *V2* 45, 120, 141

with spelling changes, *V1* 104, 106, 109, 136, 138, 184, 189; *V2* 45, 120, 216, 218, 221, 232, 234

blending strategy, *V1* 56, 88, 100, 104, 136, 152, 168, 184, 212, 216, 228; *V2* 8, 36, 68, 72, 84, 88, 100, 120, 136, 168, 196, 216, 218, 221, 232

compound words, *V2* 8, 10, 84, 88, 90, 173

contractions, *V1* 168, 170, 228, 234; *V2* 13, 93, 196, 202

corrective feedback, *V1* 56, 88, 100, 104, 136, 152, 168, 184, 212, 228, 232; *V2* 8, 36, 68, 72, 84, 88, 100, 104, 120, 136, 168, 184, 196, 216, 232

cumulative review, *V1* 109, 189, 221; *V2* 13, 45, 77, 93, 109, 125, 141, 173, 221, 237

endings, comparative, superlative, *V2* 36, 42, 45, 125, 221

endings, inflected, *V1* 56, 58, 88, 90, 100, 104, 106, 109, 136, 138, 184, 186, 189; *V2* 45, 125, 141, 216, 221, 232

plurals, *V1* 56, 58, 184, 186

possessives, *V1* 152, 154, 221

prefixes, *V2* 136, 138, 141, 184, 186, 216, 218, 221, 232, 234

suffixes, *V2* 120, 122, 125, 141, 168, 170, 216, 218, 221, 232, 234

syllable -er, *V1* 232, 234

syllable patterns, *V2* 237

consonant + *le,* *V2* 100, 104, 106, 109, 237

syllable er, *V1* 232, 234

VC/CV, *V1* 212, 216, 218; *V2* 77, 109, 237

VC/V, *V2* 68, 72, 74, 77, 109, 237

V/CV, *V2* 68, 72, 74, 77, 109, 237

Word study. *See* Phonics; Word structure; Vocabulary.

Word Wall, *V1* 5, 21, 37, 53, 69, 85, 101, 117, 133, 149, 165, 181, 197, 213, 229; *V2* 5, 21, 37, 53, 69, 85, 101, 117, 133, 149, 165, 181, 197, 213, 229

Writing

independent writing, *V1* 15, 17, 31, 33, 47, 49, 63, 65, 79, 81, 95, 97, 111, 113, 127, 129, 143, 145, 159, 161, 175, 177, 191, 193, 207, 209, 223, 225, 239, 241; *V2* 15, 17, 31, 33, 47, 49, 63, 65, 79, 81, 95, 97, 111, 113, 127, 129, 143, 145, 159, 161, 175, 177, 191, 193, 207, 209, 223, 225, 239, 241

interactive writing, *V1* 15, 31, 47, 63, 79, 95, 111, 127, 143, 159, 175, 191, 207, 223, 239; *V2* 15, 31, 47, 63, 79, 95, 111, 127, 143, 159, 175, 191, 207, 223, 239

journal writing, *V1* 15, 31, 47, 63, 79, 95, 111, 127, 143, 159, 175, 191, 207, 223, 239; *V2* 15, 31, 47, 63, 79, 95, 111, 127, 143, 159, 175, 191, 207, 223, 239

response to literature, *V1* 9, 15, 17, 25, 31, 33, 41, 47, 49, 57, 63, 65, 73, 79, 81, 89, 95, 97, 105, 111, 113, 121, 127, 129, 137, 143, 145, 153, 159, 161, 169, 175, 177, 185, 191, 193, 201, 207, 209, 217, 223, 225, 233, 239, 241; *V2* 9, 15, 17, 25, 31, 33, 41, 47, 49, 57, 63, 65, 73, 79, 81, 89, 95, 97, 105, 111, 113, 121, 127, 129, 137, 143, 145, 153, 159, 161, 169, 175, 177, 185, 191, 193, 201, 207, 209, 217, 223, 225, 233, 239, 241

sentence frames, *V1* 9, 25, 41, 57, 73, 89, 105, 121, 137, 153, 169, 185, 201, 217, 233; *V2* 9, 25, 41, 57, 73, 89, 105, 121, 137, 153, 169, 185, 201, 217, 233

sentence stems. *See* Writing, sentence frames.

shared writing, *V1* 9, 25, 41, 57, 73, 89, 105, 121, 137, 153, 169, 185, 201, 217, 233; *V2* 9, 25, 41, 57, 73, 89, 105, 121, 137, 153, 169, 185, 201, 217, 233

Writing elements

conventions, *V1* 17, 33, 47, 49, 65, 81, 95, 97, 111, 113, 127, 129, 145, 161, 177, 193, 209, 223, 225, 241; *V2* 17, 33, 49, 65, 81, 97, 113, 127, 129, 145, 161, 177, 193, 209, 225, 241

focus, *V1* 33, 65, 81, 241; *V2* 65, 145, 225

organization, *V1* 97, 113, 193, 225; *V2* 33, 49, 65, 81, 97, 129, 209

support, *V1* 17, 49, 65, 81, 97, 113, 129, 145, 161, 177, 193, 209, 241; *V2* 17, 33, 49, 97, 113, 145, 177, 193, 209, 225, 241

Writing purpose

descriptive writing, *V1* 17, 161, 209; *V2* 17, 49, 113, 145, 177, 225

expository writing, *V1* 49, 65, 97, 129, 177, 193, 241; *V2* 33, 81, 97

narrative writing, *V1* 33, 81, 113, 145, 225; *V2* 65, 209

personal narrative, *V2* 129, 161, 193, 241

Teacher Notes

Teacher Notes

Teacher Notes

Blending Strategy

Teach children to blend words using this Routine.

1 Connect Relate the new sound-spelling to previously learned sound-spellings.

2 Use Sound-Spelling Card Display the card for the sound-spelling. Say the sound. Have children say it.

3 Listen and Write Have children write the letter(s) as they say the sound.

4 Model Demonstrate how to blend words with the sound-spelling. Have children blend a word with you.

5 Group and Individual Practice Have children work together to segment and blend several words with the sound-spelling. Then have each child blend two words individually. Provide corrective feedback.

Monitor Word and Story Reading

Use these approaches to monitor children's decoding and use of context as they read.

If... children come to a word they don't know, **then...** prompt them to blend the word.

1 Look at each letter and think of its sound.

2 Blend the sounds.

3 Read the new word.

4 Is the new word a word you know?

5 Does it make sense in the story?

Comprehension Strategy: Ask Questions

During reading, teach children to ask themselves these questions:

- **Nonfiction**

  Before   What do I think this is mostly about?
  What do I already know about this?

  During   What have I read so far?
  Do I understand what I've read?

  After   What did I find out that I didn't know before?

Fluency Practice

Use one of these Routines for fluency practice. Provide corrective feedback as you listen to each child read.

- **Oral Reading** Have children read a passage orally. To achieve optimal fluency, children should reread the text three or four times.

- **Paired Reading** Reader 1 begins. Children read, switching readers at the end of each page. Then Reader 2 begins, as the partners reread the passage. For optimal fluency, children should reread three or four times.

- **Audio-Assisted Reading** The child reads aloud while listening to the recording. On the first reading, children point to words while they listen. On subsequent readings, they read along with the recording.

Routine Card 1

Use immediate corrective feedback to help children blend words.

If... children pause between sounds,
then... model blending the word without pauses. Then have children blend it again.

If... children say the wrong sound,
then... keep your finger on the missed sound, model it correctly, and have children repeat the sound. Then have them blend the word again.

If... children say the wrong sound when they say the word quickly,
then... model the correct word and have children repeat it. Have children say the sounds again slowly and then quickly to make it sound like a real word.

Routine Card 2

• **Fiction**

Story Questions

Who is in this story?

Where/When does this story take place?

What happens in this story?

Making Connections

Have I ever read a story like this before?

Has anything like this happened to me before?

Do any of the characters remind me of someone I know?

Routine Card 3

If... children have difficulty reading a story,
then... read a sentence aloud as children point to each word. Then have the group reread the sentence as they continue pointing. Continue reading in this way before children read individually.

If... children cannot read a high-frequency word,
then... tell them the word and have them repeat it. Have children spell the word and tell what word they spelled. Have them practice in pairs with word cards,
or... mark the missed word on a high-frequency word list and send the list home for additional practice, or have children practice with a fluent reader.

If... children have trouble reading words with the letter-sound patterns taught this week,
then... reteach the blending strategy lessons for the week.

Routine Card 4

Use these strategies to help children develop fluency.

• **Model Fluency** Model reading "as if you were speaking," attending to punctuation and phrasing and reading with expression (prosody).

• **Provide Corrective Feedback** Provide feedback on oral reading.

If... children misread a word,
then... help them decode it and have them reread the sentence.

If... children read at an inappropriate or unsteady pace,
then... model an appropriate pace, having children echo.

If... children lack oral expression,
then... model how to read based on the meaning of the passage. Tell children that their expression should show their understanding.

• **Monitor Fluency** See pp. 244–245 for assessment options.

Oral Vocabulary Routines

Use this Routine to teach each Amazing Word and any other oral vocabulary you may wish to introduce.

1 Introduce the Word Relate the word to a song or story children are learning. Supply a child-friendly definition. Have children say the word.

2 Demonstrate Provide several familiar examples to demonstrate meaning. When possible, use gestures or sketches to help convey meaning.

3 Apply Have children demonstrate understanding with a simple activity.

4 Display the Word Write the word on a card and display it in the classroom. Have children identify familiar letter-sounds or word parts.

Picture Walk Routine

To build concepts and vocabulary, conduct a structured picture walk before reading.

1 Prepare Preview the selection and list key concepts and vocabulary you wish to develop.

2 Discuss As children look at the pages, discuss illustrations, have children point to pictured items, and/or ask questions that target key concepts and vocabulary.

3 Elaborate Elaborate on children's responses to reinforce correct use of the vocabulary and to provide additional exposure to key concepts.

4 Practice For more practice with key concepts, have each child turn to a partner and do the picture walk using the key concept vocabulary.

Comprehension Strategies

Before, During, and After Reading strategies should be reinforced daily. Use the Routine on the back of this card to teach

- **Previewing Text** What do the title and pictures tell about the text?

- **Setting a Purpose for Reading** What do I want to find out?

- **Using Prior Knowledge** Does the selection remind me of anything I already know?

- **Making, Modifying, and Confirming Predictions** What do I think will happen next? Did it happen as I predicted?

- **Recognizing Story Structure** Who is in the story? Where/When does it take place? What happens at the beginning? in the middle? at the end?

- **Summarizing Text** What are the main ideas?

Reading Long Words

Model these strategies to teach children to read long words.

Syllable Patterns

VC/CV as in *mit/ten, nap/kin*
V/CV (open) as in *pi/lot, o/pen*
VC/V (closed) as in *sev/en, fin/ish*
C+le as in *tum/ble, ca/ble*

1 Look for Chunks Divide the word into syllables, or chunks.

2 Blend Sound out each syllable, or chunk.

3 Say Chunks Slowly Slowly say each syllable from left to right.

4 Say It Fast Say the chunks fast to make a word.

Routine Card 5

Use this Routine to monitor understanding of concepts and vocabulary taught each week.

1 Display the week's background-building passage (*Let's Find Out*) in the Student Reader.

2 Remind the child of the concept that the class has been talking about that week.

3 Ask the child to tell you about the *Let's Find Out* passage and illustrations using some of the week's Amazing Words.

4 Ask questions about the passage and illustrations using the Amazing Words. Note which questions the child can respond to. Reteach unknown words using the Oral Vocabulary Routine.

Routine Card 6

Routine Card 7

1 Teach Describe each strategy explicitly, explaining when and how to use it.

2 Model Think aloud to model applying the strategy with different selections.

3 Practice Have children practice using the strategy, with support and prompting.

4 Apply Independently Expect children to begin using these strategies independently.

Routine Card 8

Base Words and Affixes

1 Look for Word Parts Figure out if the word has prefixes, endings, or suffixes.

2 Take Off Parts Take off the prefixes, endings, or suffixes.

3 Figure Out the Base Word Read the base word or sound it out.

4 Say Parts Slowly Slowly say each word part from left to right.

5 Say It Fast Say the word parts fast to make a word.